BETRAYAL
PART ONE

AGE OF BRONZE

Volume 3A

BETRAYAL

PART ONE

by Eric Shanower

Age of Bronze
Volume 3A
Betrayal Part One
Copyright © 2007 by Eric Shanower. All rights reserved.

978-1-58240-755-5 (Trade Paperback)

Published by Image Comics, Inc.
Office of Publication: 2001 Center St., Sixth Floor
Berkeley, CA, 94704
Image and its logos are ® and © 2013 by Image Comics, Inc. All rights reserved.

Robert Kirkman *Chief Operating Officer*
Erik Larsen *Chief Financial Officer*
Todd McFarlane *President*
Marc Silvestri *Chief Executive Officer*
Jim Valentino *Vice-President*
Eric Stephenson *Publisher*
Ron Richards *Director of Business Development*
Jennifer de Guzman *PR & Marketing Director*
Branwyn Bigglestone *Accounts Manager*
Emily Miller *Accounting Assistant*
Jamie Parreno *Marketing Assistant*
Jenna Savage *Administrative Assistant*
Kevin Yuen *Digital Rights Coordinator*
Jonathan Chan *Production Manager*
Drew Gill *Art Director*
Tyler Shainline *Print Manager*
Monica Garcia *Production Artist*
Vincent Kukua *Production Artist*
Jana Cook *Production Artist*

The story of *Betrayal Part One* was originally serialized in the comic book series
Age of Bronze, issues 20 through 26.

First printing January 2008
Second Printing April 2013

Visit the *Age of Bronze* website at
www.age-of-bronze.com

Age of Bronze is a trademark of Eric Shanower.

Friends of Troy is an organization for those interested in Troy and its legends.
It supports the ongoing activities of the International Troy Excavation Project.
All Friends of Troy receive the annual newsletter and updates on Troy-related news.
Friends are welcome at Troy and are given guided tours of the site and excavation.
If you would like to become a Friend of Troy, send your name and address to

Institute for Mediterranean Studies
7086 Aracoma Drive
Cincinatti, OH 45237
USA

Phone: 513/631-8049
Fax: 513/631-1715
E-mail: studies@usa.net
Website: www.studies.org
Or see: www.uni-tuebingen.de/troia/eng/freunde.html

For information on the TROIA FOUNDATION which supports
the International Troy Excavation Project, see the website
www.uni-tuebingen.de/troia/eng/troiastiftung.html

Printed in the U.S.A.
For information regarding the CPSIA on this printed material, call: 203-595-3636 and
provide reference # RICH - 477190.

For Foreign Licensing and International Rights, please contact: foreignlicensing@imagecomics.com

This one is for you,
Elizabeth.

Contents

Maps
8

Our Story So Far
12

Betrayal
Part One
19

Glossary of Names
164

Genealogical Charts
168

Bibliography
170

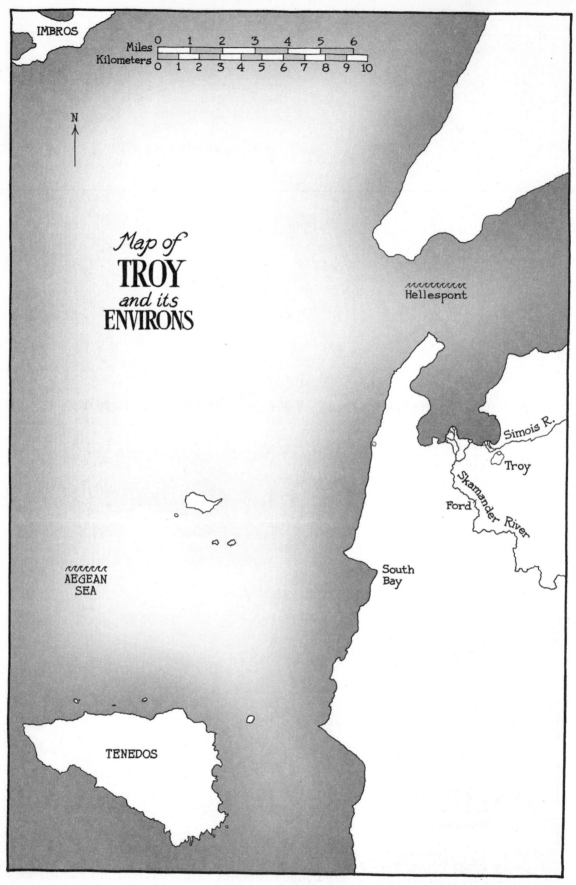

Map of
TROY
and its
ENVIRONS

IMBROS

Miles
Kilometers

N

Hellespont

Simois R.

Troy

Skamander River

Ford

South
Bay

AEGEAN
SEA

TENEDOS

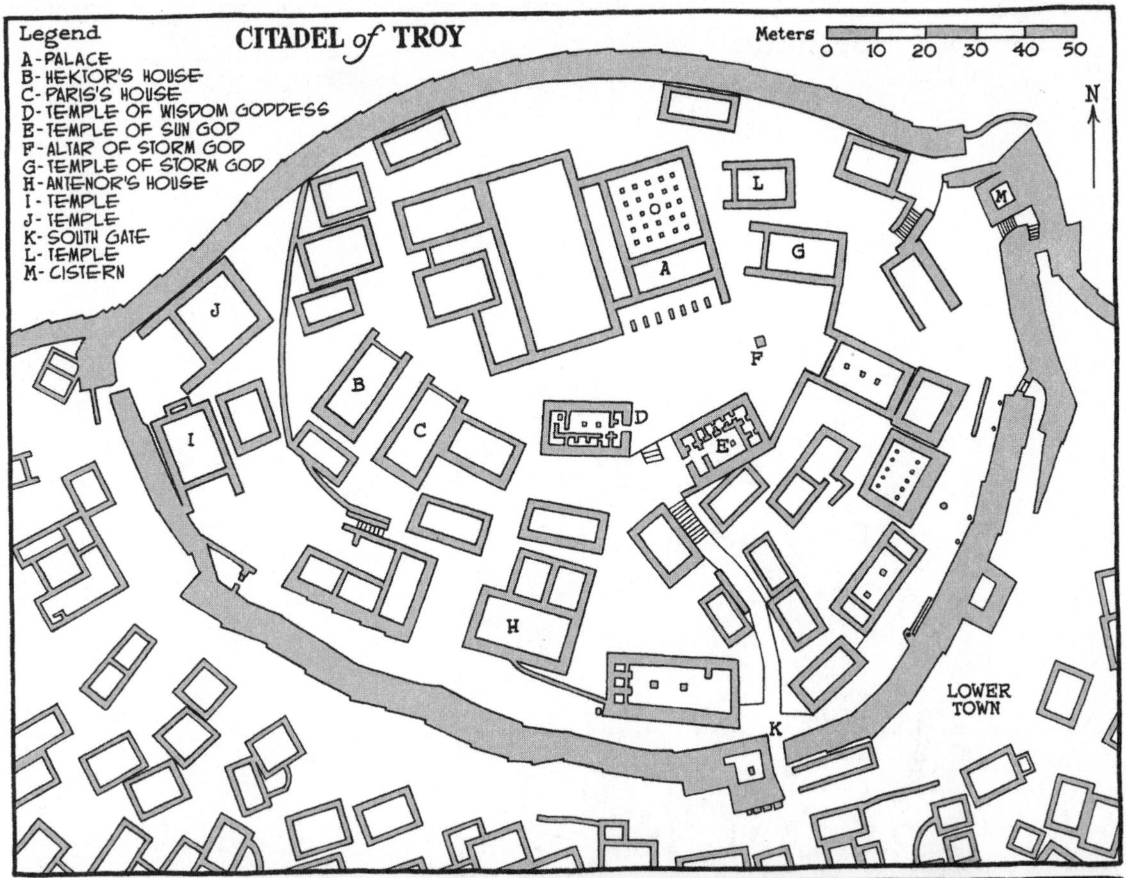
CITADEL of TROY
Legend
A-PALACE
B-HEKTOR'S HOUSE
C-PARIS'S HOUSE
D-TEMPLE OF WISDOM GODDESS
E-TEMPLE OF SUN GOD
F-ALTAR OF STORM GOD
G-TEMPLE OF STORM GOD
H-ANTENOR'S HOUSE
I-TEMPLE
J-TEMPLE
K-SOUTH GATE
L-TEMPLE
M-CISTERN
Meters 0 10 20 30 40 50
N
LOWER TOWN

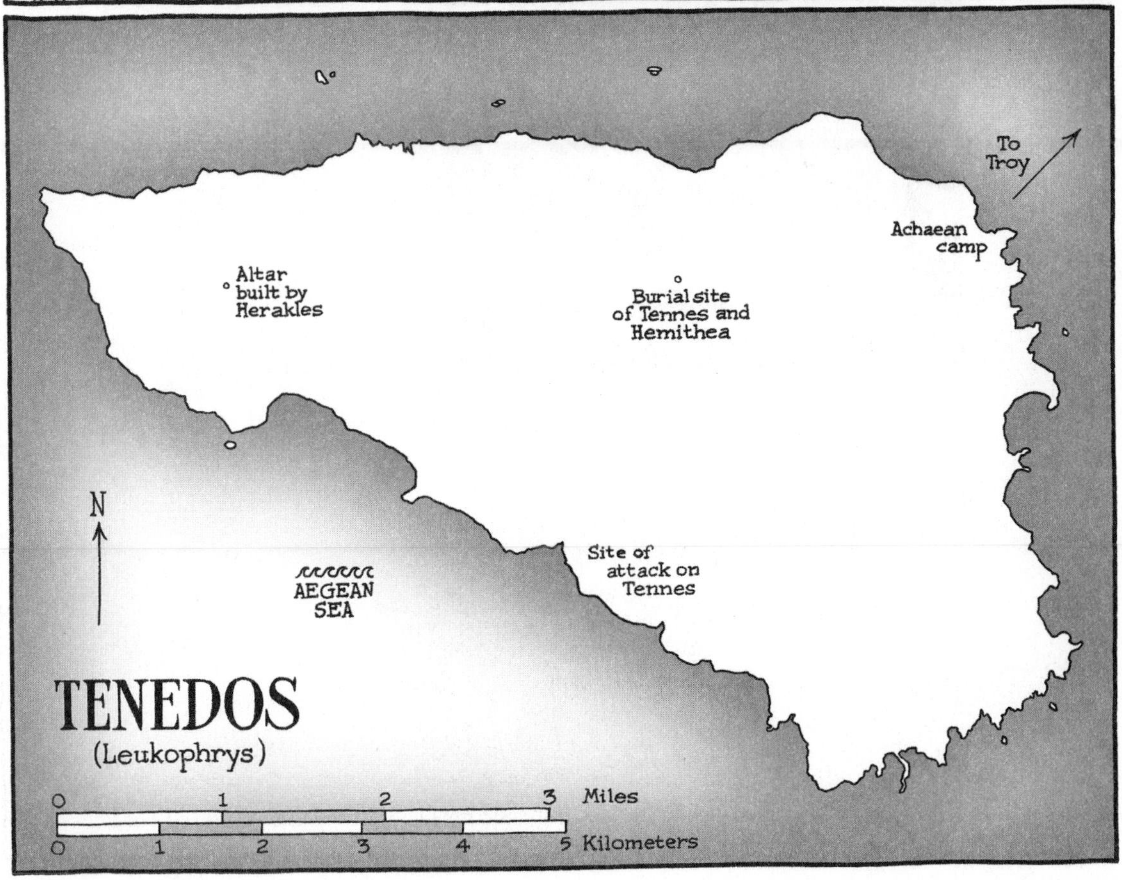
TENEDOS
(Leukophrys)
To Troy
Achaean camp
Altar built by Herakles
Burial site of Tennes and Hemithea
Site of attack on Tennes
AEGEAN SEA
N
0 1 2 3 Miles
0 1 2 3 4 5 Kilometers

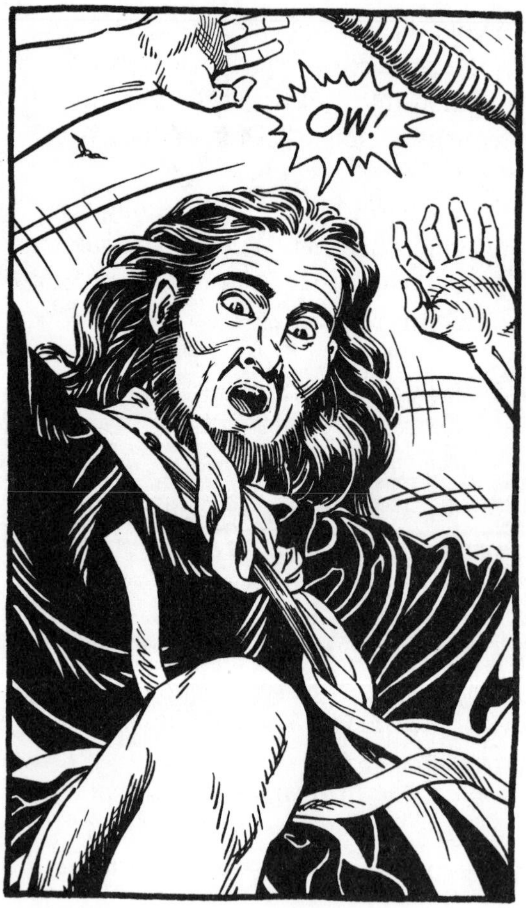
OW!

PHILOCTETES: . . . here I am before you, the man of whom you have perhaps heard as lord of the bow of Heracles, Philoctetes the
son of Poeas. I am he whom the two marshalls and the
Cephallenian king shamelessly hurled to this solitude which
you see,
when I was wasting with a fierce disease, stricken by the
savage bite of the murderous serpent. With that plague for
my sole companion, boy, those men put me out here alone
and left, after they landed here with their fleet from
sea-washed Chryse.
Delighted they were then, when they saw me asleep after
much tossing on the waves, in the shelter of a cave upon the
shore, and they abandoned me, first setting out a few rags,
as though for an unfortunate beggar, and a bit of food, too—
a small work of charity. But may they get what they gave
me!
Can you imagine, boy, what kind of awakening I had when
they had gone, and I rose from sleep that day?—what sting-
ing tears I wept, and what miseries I bewailed when I saw
that the ships with which I had sailed were all gone, and that
there was no man in the place,
not one to help me, not one to ease the sickness that
afflicted me, when looking all around me, I could find
nothing at hand, save agony—but of that a ready store?

Philoctetes
Sophocles, 409 BCE
Trans. Sir Richard C. Jebb, 1898

TROY.

OUR STORY SO FAR

PARIS

WE'RE *HERE*-- ITS *TRUE*! TROY.

I WANT TO FEEL ITS WARM STONES BENEATH MY OWN HANDS...

HELEN

MY GRANDSON.

HE MUST REMAIN IN TROY WHEN YOU LEAVE.

PRIAM

DURING THE LATE BRONZE AGE—about the 13th century BCE—the powerful city of Troy flourishes under the Great King Priam's rule. Years before, Priam's sister Hesione was captured by Achaean raiders during an assault on Troy. Now Priam commands Paris, a prince of Troy recently reunited with his father and his mother Hekuba, to bring Hesione back. Priam's daughter Kassandra and her twin brother Helenus predict calamity, but no one takes their warnings seriously.

Accompanied by his cousin Aeneas, Paris sails to the Achaean city of Sparta where Menelaus is king. Paris forgets his pregnant lover, the mountain nymph Oenone, and ignoring his brother

HEKTOR

Hektor's warning to follow their father Priam's instructions, he seduces Menelaus's wife Helen away from Sparta with her serving women and infant son Pleisthenes. They sail to Cyprus, then to Sidon.

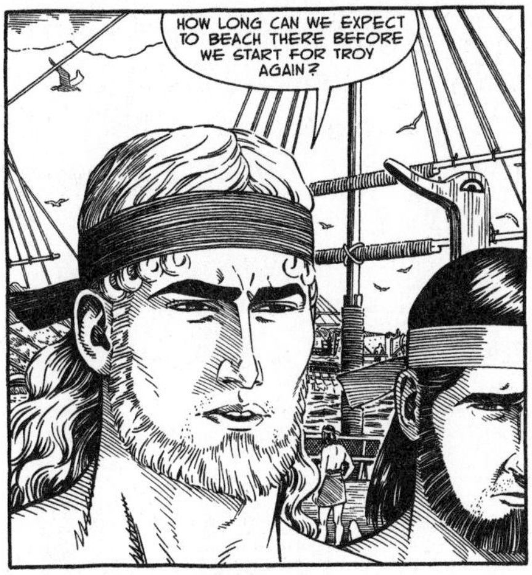
HOW LONG CAN WE EXPECT TO BEACH THERE BEFORE WE START FOR TROY AGAIN?

MENELAUS

Helen's brothers, Kastor and Polydeukes, pursue, but are lost in a storm at sea.

Menelaus is eager to recover his wife, while his brother Agamemnon, king of Mycenae and High King of the Achaeans, is eager to gain Troy's control of rich trade routes through the Hellespont. So they summon the many Achaean kings who once swore an oath to help Helen's husband for her sake. At the bay at Aulis a massive army with hundreds of ships and thousands of men assembles. The army pledges to follow High King Agamemnon as commander in an attack on Troy.

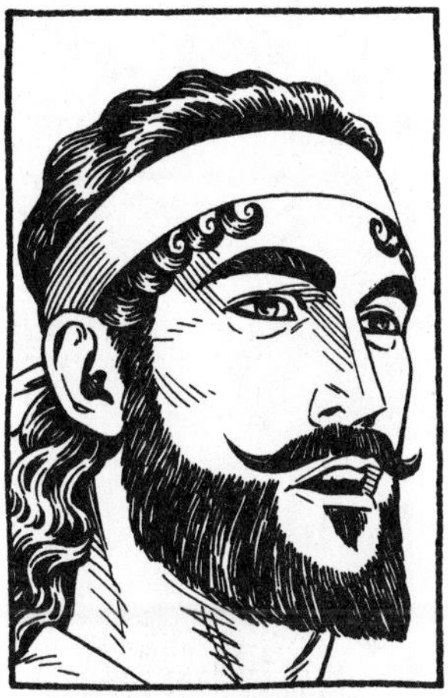

AGAMEMNON

The Achaean priestess Thetis foresees the death of her son, Achilles, at Troy. To circumvent this, she takes the boy from his teacher, the kentaur Cheiron, and hides him, disguised as a girl called Pyrrha, among the daughters of Lykomedes on the island of Skyros. There, Achilles rapes Lykomedes's eldest daughter Deidamia, who bears a son. Deidamia calls the child Pyrrhus; Achilles calls him Neoptolemus.

A prophecy foretells that if Odysseus, king of Ithaka, goes to Troy with the army, he'll return home to his wife Penelope and son Telemachus after twenty years, alone and unrecognized. To avoid this fate, Odysseus pretends to be mad. But Palamedes, prince of Nauplia, exposes Odysseus's ploy, thus earning his enmity.

Kalchas, Trojan priest of the sun god, has visions that show him Troy's fall. He joins the Achaeans, leaving his recently widowed daughter Cressida at Troy in the care of her uncle Pandarus. The Trojan prince Troilus falls in love with Cressida, but Pandarus discourages Troilus from pursuing her prematurely.

All signs point to eventual success for the Achaean army. The Delphic oracle predicts Achaean victory over Troy, contingent, however, upon conflict among Achaeans. And Kalchas foretells Achaean triumph in the tenth year, provided that Achilles joins the army.

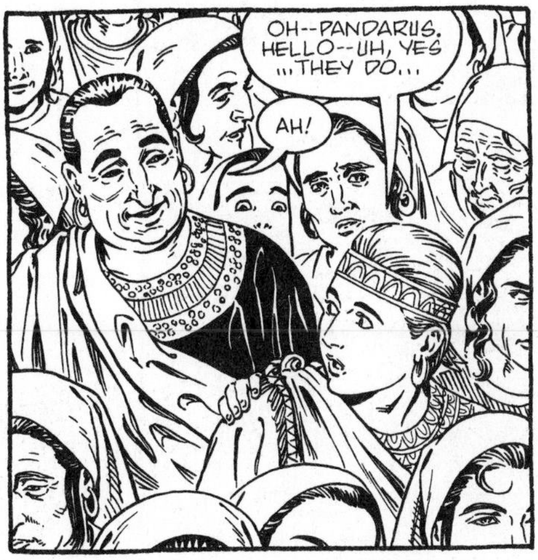
OH--PANDARUS, HELLO--UH, YES ...THEY DO...
AH!

PANDARUS AND TROILUS

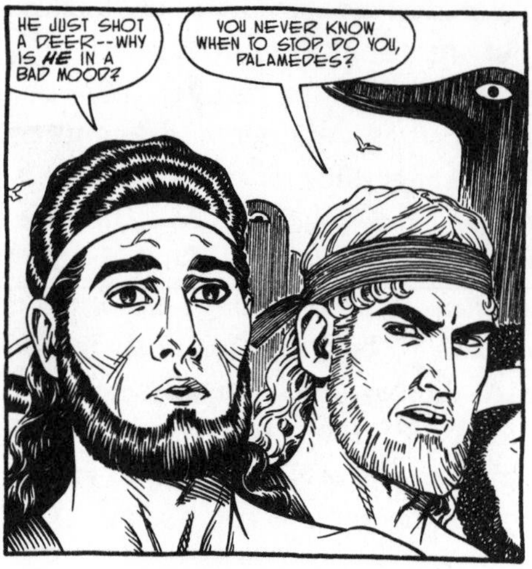
HE JUST SHOT A DEER--WHY IS HE IN A BAD MOOD?
YOU NEVER KNOW WHEN TO STOP, DO YOU, PALAMEDES?

PALAMEDES AND MENELAUS

Odysseus tricks Achilles into shedding his disguise and brings him to Aulis. Achilles assumes leadership of his father Peleus's Myrmidons from Phthia, choosing a short life fighting gloriously at Troy rather than a long life in obscurity.

After Palamedes remedies a food shortage by bringing supplies from Delos, the army at last sets sail for war with Troy.

Meanwhile, Paris and Helen finally reach Troy. Priam confronts them outside the city. Paris presents Helen as a substitute for Hesione. Priam resists. But when Paris reveals that Helen is pregnant with his child, Priam has no other choice but to welcome Helen to Troy.

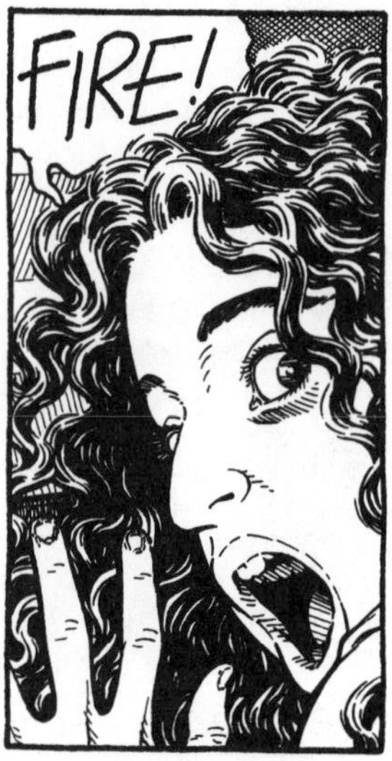
FIRE!

KASSANDRA

Kassandra grows so frantic at Helen's presence in Troy that Priam has her shut away.

Aeneas claims the hand of Kreusa, daughter of Priam, in marriage. Priam refuses to grant this, so Aeneas and Kreusa secretly leave Troy.

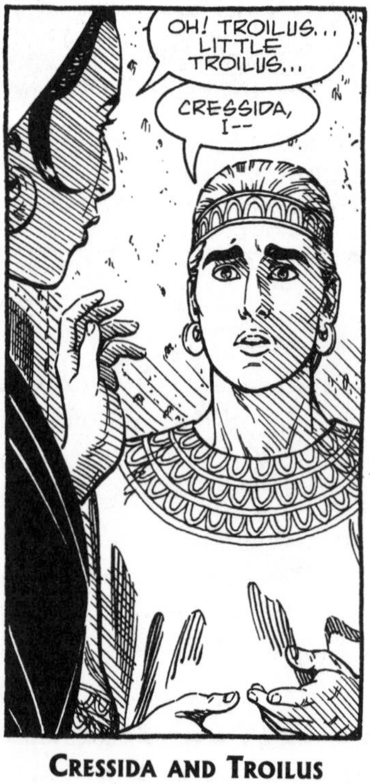
OH! TROILUS... LITTLE TROILUS...
CRESSIDA, I--

CRESSIDA AND TROILUS

Troilus tells Cressida that he loves her, but she laughs at him.

The Achaean fleet, having sailed from Aulis, mistakes the coast of Mysia for Troy. Achilles attacks the inhabitants, assuming they're Trojans. In response, Telephus, king of Mysia, assembles an army and marches against the Achaeans. Soon the Achaeans discover their mistake and make peace, but not before Achilles has wounded Telephus.

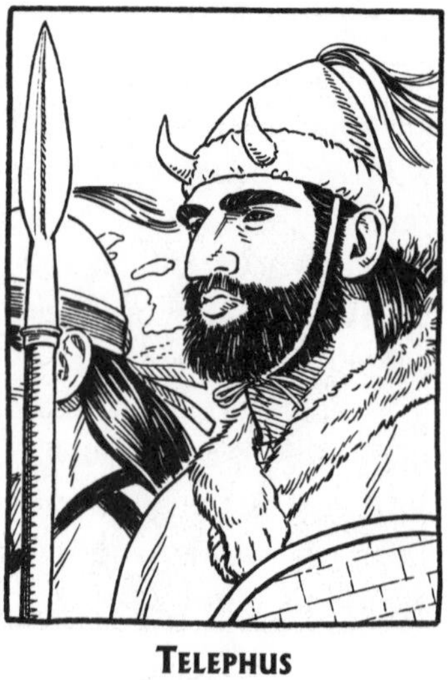

TELEPHUS

Upon departing Mysia, a massive storm scatters the Achaean fleet. The leaders and their armies return to their various homes. Odysseus accompanies Agamemnon to Mycenae where they nurse grudges against Palamedes and plot strategy for reattempting the attack on Troy. When Diomedes at last brings news that the Trojans are renewing their defences and gathering their own allies in preparation for war, Agamemnon re-summons the Achaeans to Aulis.

LET'S STAY CALM. I'LL BRING AGAMEMNON AND MENELAUS BACK WITH ME IF YOU'LL AGREE TO LET MACHAON AND PODALIRIUS TREAT YOUR WOUND.

Odysseus

Kalchas asks Agamemnon to save Cressida from the war, but the High King refuses, insulted by Kalchas's manipulative use of Agamemnon's daughters.

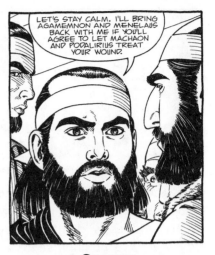

I MUST GO TO MOUNT PELION.
PELION!
THAT'S WHERE...

Thetis

On Skyros Achilles spurns Deidamia and declares his love for his companion, Patroklus. The two young men go to Phthia where Achilles receives summons to rejoin the Achaean army. Achilles's mother Thetis fails to prevent him from going, so she decides to go along, too.

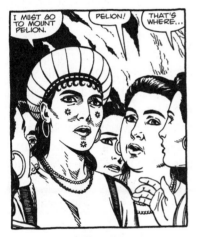

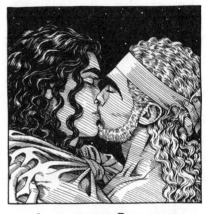

Achilles and Patroklus

NOW THE MOTHER BIRD!
SQUARR

Kalchas

Telephus appears unexpectedly in Mycenae, crazed with suffering from the now-infected wound Achilles inflicted. At Aulis, Achilles, with the help of the Achaean healers Machaon and Podalirius, heals Telephus's wound.

The army is finally at full strength again when a contrary wind springs up, preventing the fleet from sailing. Kalchas reveals to Agamemnon that the goddess Artemis requires the sacrifice of Agamemnon's first-born daughter, Iphigenia, in order to reverse the wind and release the fleet.

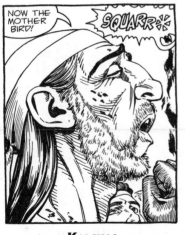

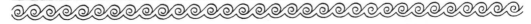

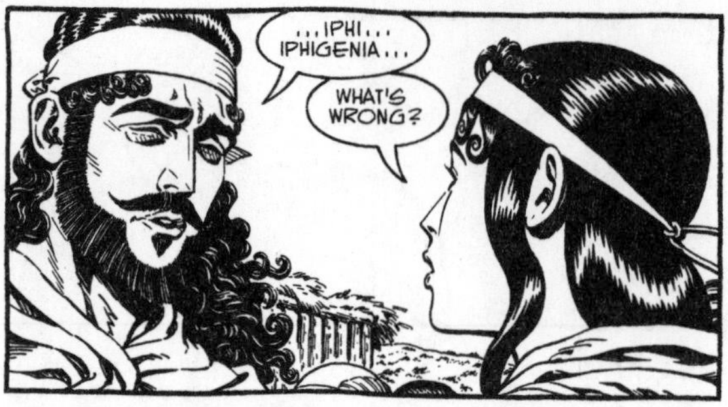
...IPHI... IPHIGENIA...
WHAT'S WRONG?

AGAMEMNON AND IPHIGENIA

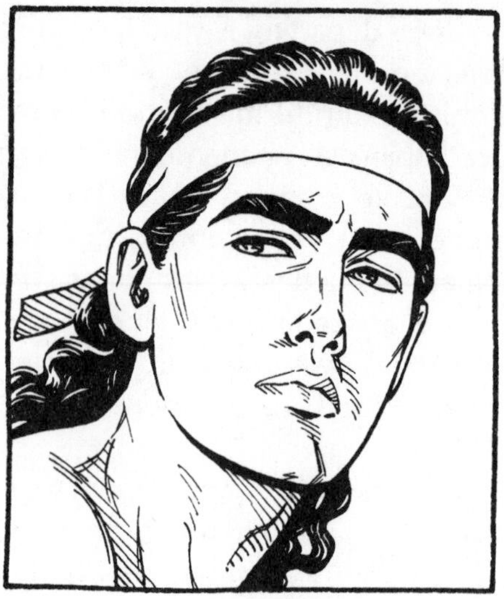

ACHILLES

Agamemnon is torn. Odysseus and Menelaus persuade him that he must submit to the goddess's demands. Prompted by Odysseus, Agamemnon sends a letter summoning Iphigenia to Aulis. The letter falsely explains that she will marry Achilles. Agamemnon secretly sends a second letter that countermands the first, but Menelaus intercepts it. Iphigenia arrives at Aulis with her mother, Klytemnestra.

Achilles and Klytemnestra uncover the truth. They hope to rescue Iphigenia, but the army, impatient to set sail, is against them. Iphigenia realizes that she can't escape, so she decides to accept death with grace. Achilles and his companions arm themselves in case Iphigenia calls on them to save her at the last moment.

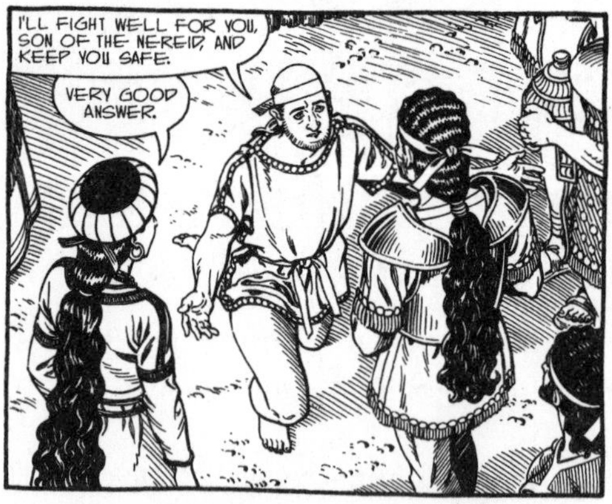
I'LL FIGHT WELL FOR YOU, SON OF THE NEREID, AND KEEP YOU SAFE.
VERY GOOD ANSWER.

THETIS, MNEMON, AND ACHILLES

Thetis knows that the sun god will kill Achilles in retaliation for Achilles killing one of the sun god's sons. She charges Mnemon to accompany Achilles and steer him clear of all sons of the god.

At the altar Iphigenia accepts the knife without flinching. The wind turns favorable. Devastated, Klytemnestra departs Aulis.

The Achaean army is ready to sail once more for Troy.

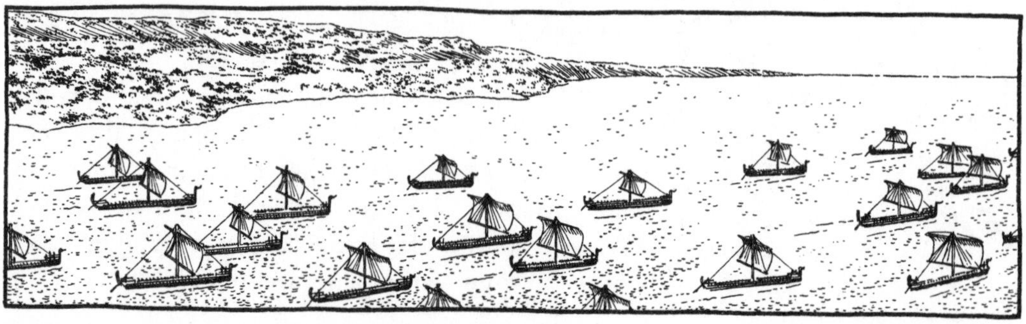

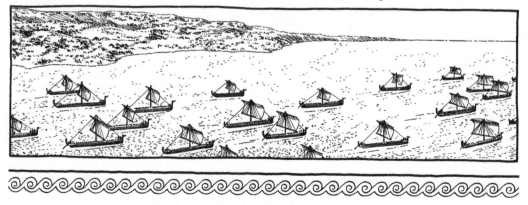

BETRAYAL
PART ONE

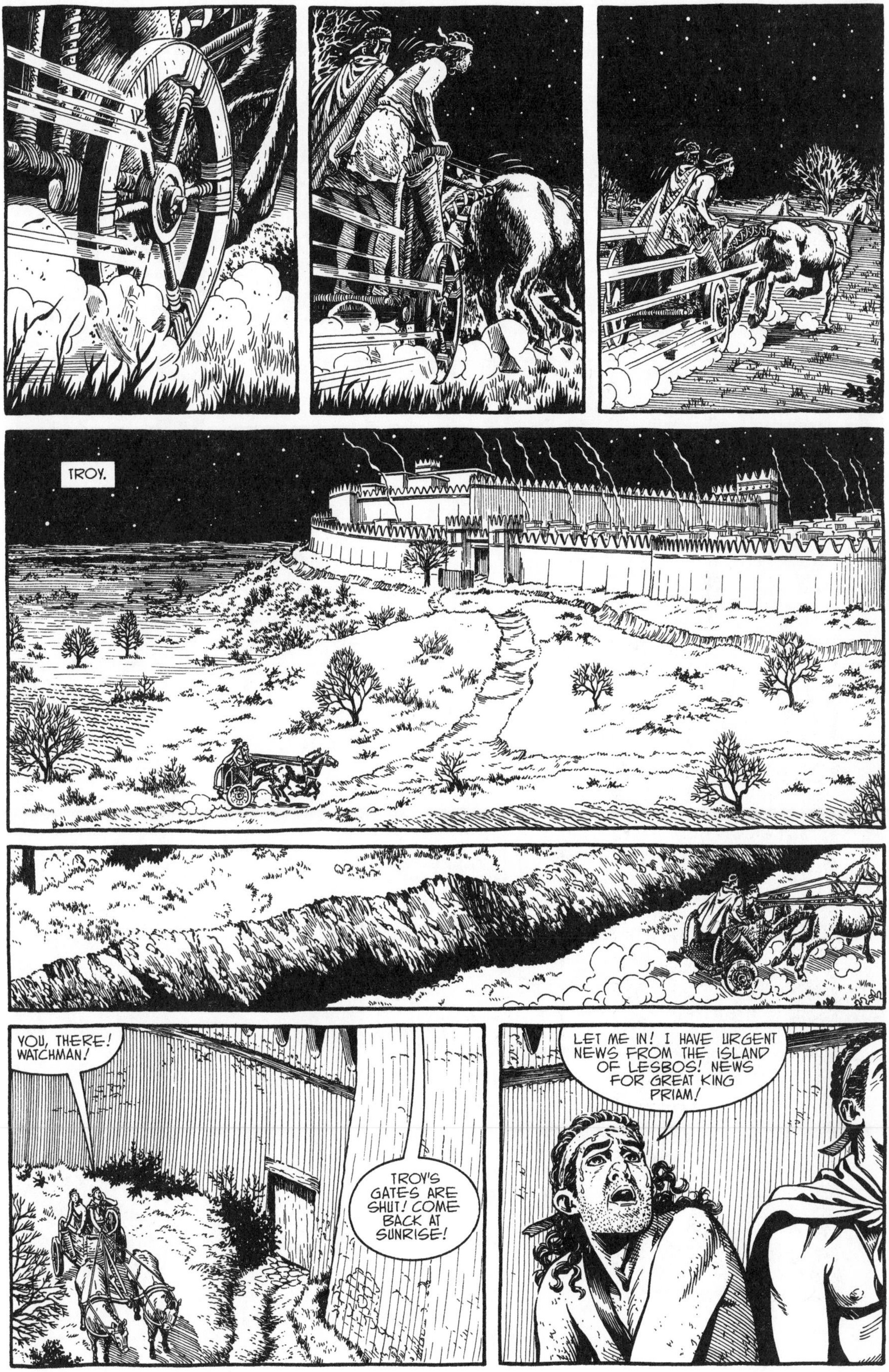
TROY.
YOU, THERE! WATCHMAN!
TROY'S GATES ARE SHUT! COME BACK AT SUNRISE!
LET ME IN! I HAVE URGENT NEWS FROM THE ISLAND OF LESBOS! NEWS FOR GREAT KING PRIAM!

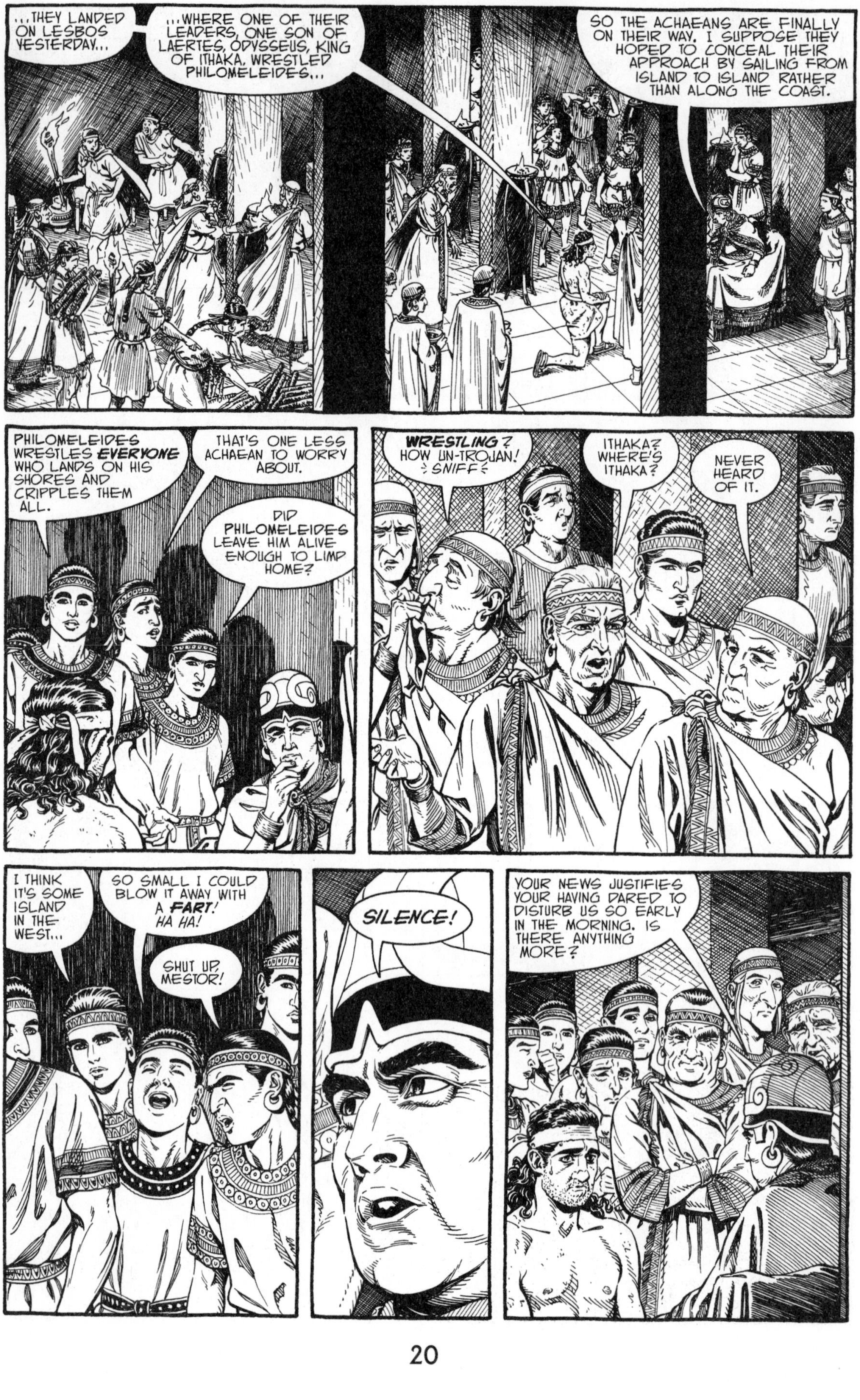
...THEY LANDED ON LESBOS YESTERDAY...
...WHERE ONE OF THEIR LEADERS, ONE SON OF LAERTES, ODYSSEUS, KING OF ITHAKA, WRESTLED PHILOMELEIDES...
SO THE ACHAEANS ARE FINALLY ON THEIR WAY. I SUPPOSE THEY HOPED TO CONCEAL THEIR APPROACH BY SAILING FROM ISLAND TO ISLAND RATHER THAN ALONG THE COAST.
PHILOMELEIDES WRESTLES EVERYONE WHO LANDS ON HIS SHORES AND CRIPPLES THEM ALL.
THAT'S ONE LESS ACHAEAN TO WORRY ABOUT.
DID PHILOMELEIDES LEAVE HIM ALIVE ENOUGH TO LIMP HOME?
WRESTLING? HOW UN-TROJAN! SNIFF
ITHAKA? WHERE'S ITHAKA?
NEVER HEARD OF IT.
I THINK IT'S SOME ISLAND IN THE WEST...
SO SMALL I COULD BLOW IT AWAY WITH A FART! HA HA!
SHUT UP, MESTOR!
SILENCE!
YOUR NEWS JUSTIFIES YOUR HAVING DARED TO DISTURB US SO EARLY IN THE MORNING. IS THERE ANYTHING MORE?

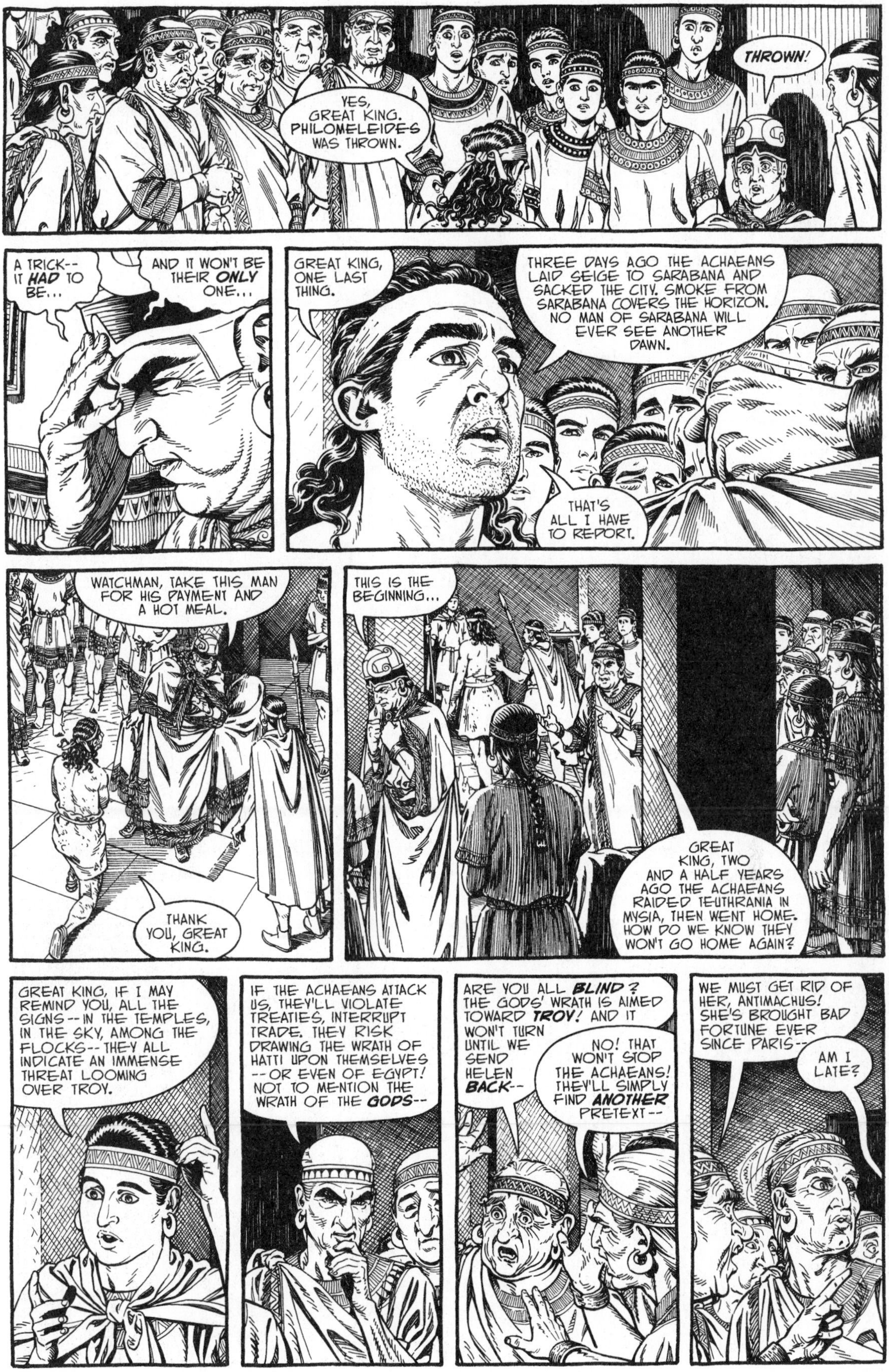
YES, GREAT KING. PHILOMELEIDES WAS THROWN.
THROWN!
A TRICK-- IT HAD TO BE...
AND IT WON'T BE THEIR ONLY ONE...
GREAT KING, ONE LAST THING.
THREE DAYS AGO THE ACHAEANS LAID SEIGE TO SARABANA AND SACKED THE CITY. SMOKE FROM SARABANA COVERS THE HORIZON. NO MAN OF SARABANA WILL EVER SEE ANOTHER DAWN.
THAT'S ALL I HAVE TO REPORT.
WATCHMAN, TAKE THIS MAN FOR HIS PAYMENT AND A HOT MEAL.
THANK YOU, GREAT KING.
THIS IS THE BEGINNING...
GREAT KING, TWO AND A HALF YEARS AGO THE ACHAEANS RAIDED TEUTHRANIA IN MYSIA, THEN WENT HOME. HOW DO WE KNOW THEY WON'T GO HOME AGAIN?
GREAT KING, IF I MAY REMIND YOU, ALL THE SIGNS--IN THE TEMPLES, IN THE SKY, AMONG THE FLOCKS--THEY ALL INDICATE AN IMMENSE THREAT LOOMING OVER TROY.
IF THE ACHAEANS ATTACK US, THEY'LL VIOLATE TREATIES, INTERRUPT TRADE. THEY RISK DRAWING THE WRATH OF HATTI UPON THEMSELVES --OR EVEN OF EGYPT! NOT TO MENTION THE WRATH OF THE GODS--
ARE YOU ALL BLIND? THE GODS' WRATH IS AIMED TOWARD TROY! AND IT WON'T TURN UNTIL WE SEND HELEN BACK--
NO! THAT WON'T STOP THE ACHAEANS! THEY'LL SIMPLY FIND ANOTHER PRETEXT--
WE MUST GET RID OF HER, ANTIMACHUS! SHE'S BROUGHT BAD FORTUNE EVER SINCE PARIS--
AM I LATE?

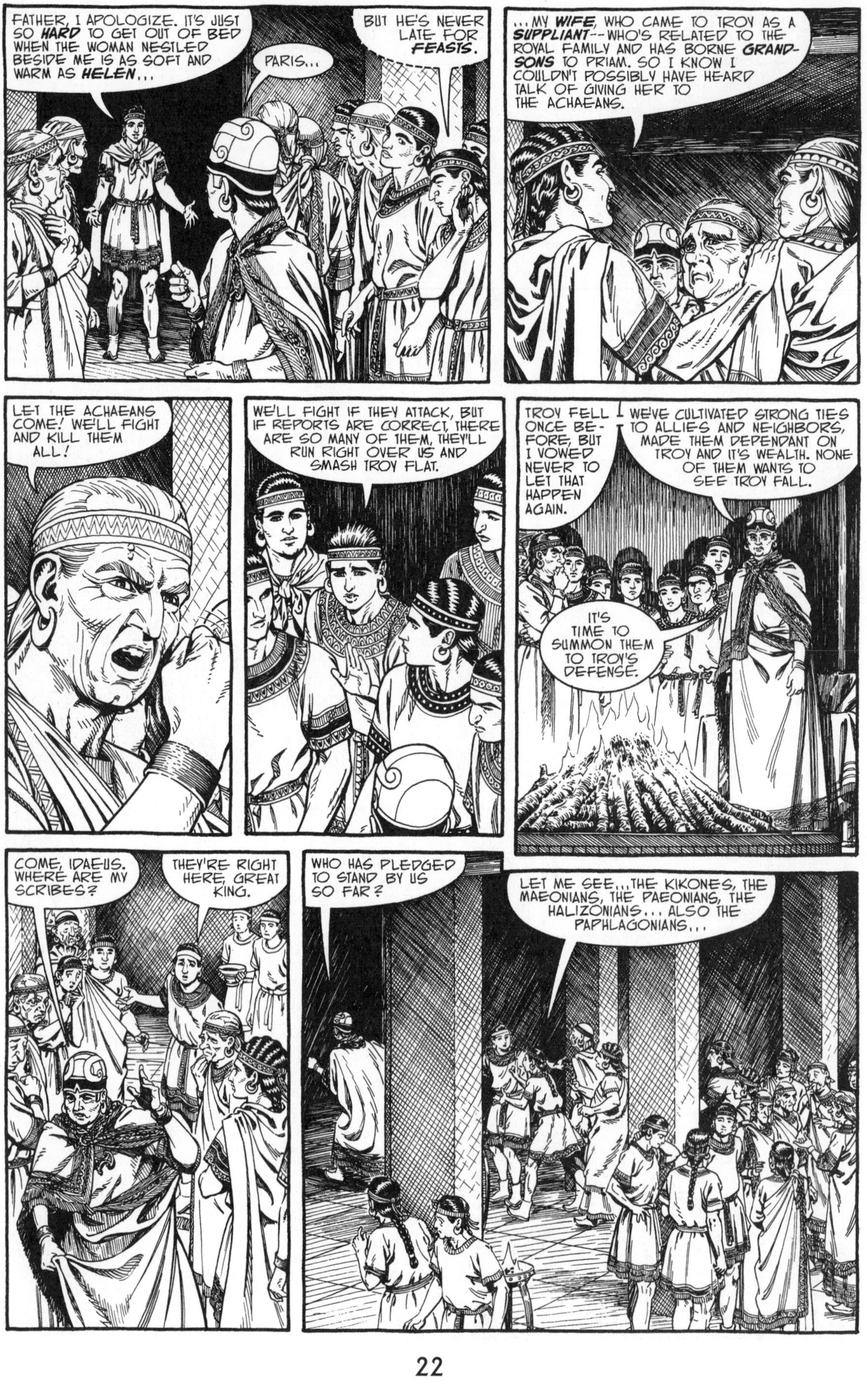

FATHER, I APOLOGIZE. IT'S JUST SO HARD TO GET OUT OF BED WHEN THE WOMAN NESTLED BESIDE ME IS AS SOFT AND WARM AS HELEN...
PARIS...
BUT HE'S NEVER LATE FOR FEASTS.
...MY WIFE, WHO CAME TO TROY AS A SUPPLIANT--WHO'S RELATED TO THE ROYAL FAMILY AND HAS BORNE GRANDSONS TO PRIAM. SO I KNOW I COULDN'T POSSIBLY HAVE HEARD TALK OF GIVING HER TO THE ACHAEANS.
LET THE ACHAEANS COME! WE'LL FIGHT AND KILL THEM ALL!
WE'LL FIGHT IF THEY ATTACK, BUT IF REPORTS ARE CORRECT, THERE ARE SO MANY OF THEM, THEY'LL RUN RIGHT OVER US AND SMASH TROY FLAT.
TROY FELL ONCE BEFORE, BUT I VOWED NEVER TO LET THAT HAPPEN AGAIN.
WE'VE CULTIVATED STRONG TIES TO ALLIES AND NEIGHBORS, MADE THEM DEPENDANT ON TROY AND IT'S WEALTH. NONE OF THEM WANTS TO SEE TROY FALL.
IT'S TIME TO SUMMON THEM TO TROY'S DEFENSE.
COME, IDAEUS. WHERE ARE MY SCRIBES?
THEY'RE RIGHT HERE, GREAT KING.
WHO HAS PLEDGED TO STAND BY US SO FAR?
LET ME SEE...THE KIKONES, THE MAEONIANS, THE PAEONIANS, THE HALIZONIANS... ALSO THE PAPHLAGONIANS...

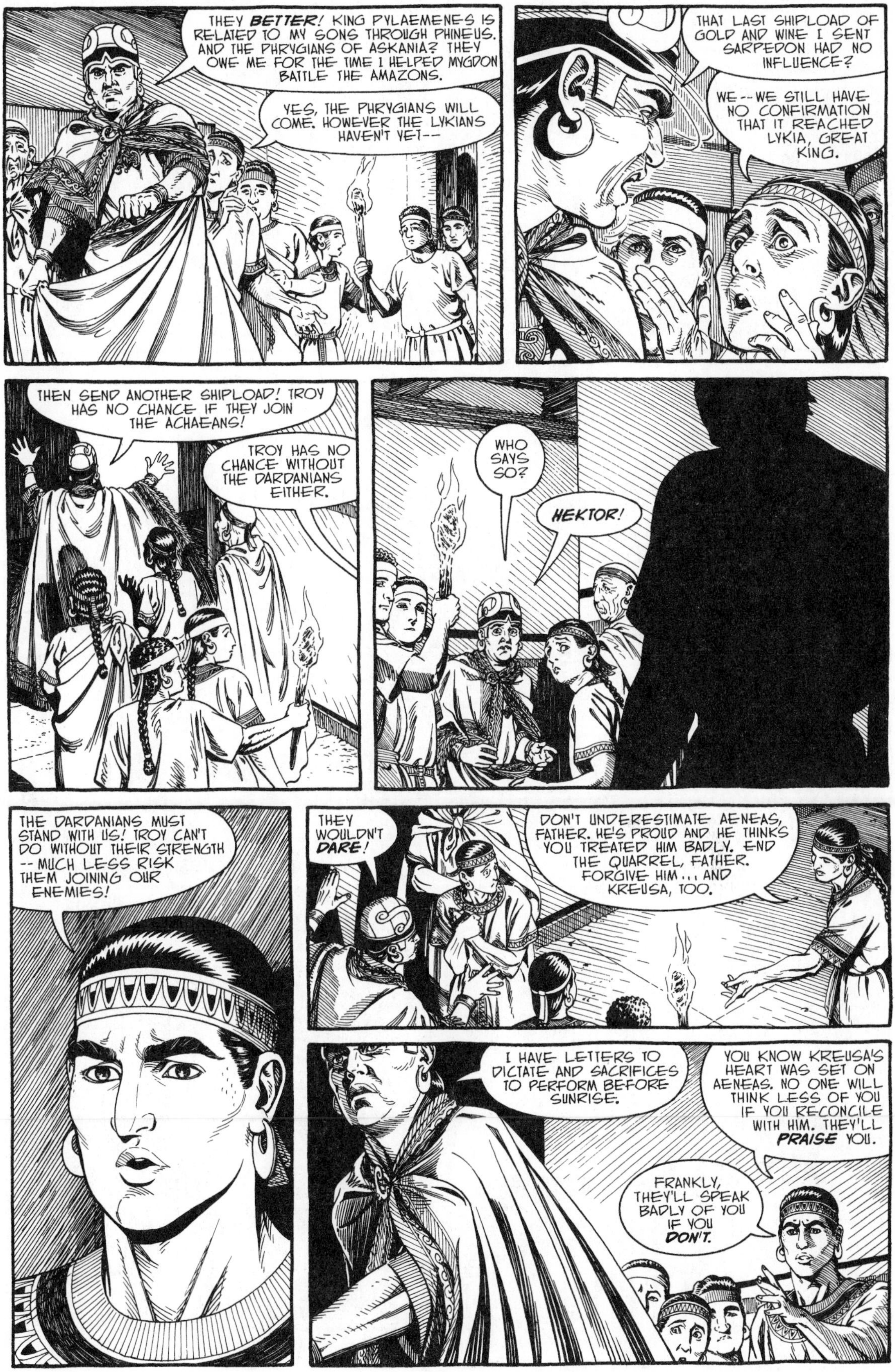
THEY **BETTER**! KING PYLAEMENES IS RELATED TO MY SONS THROUGH PHINEUS. AND THE PHRYGIANS OF ASKANIA? THEY OWE ME FOR THE TIME I HELPED MYGDON BATTLE THE AMAZONS.
YES, THE PHRYGIANS WILL COME. HOWEVER THE LYKIANS HAVEN'T YET--
THAT LAST SHIPLOAD OF GOLD AND WINE I SENT SARPEDON HAD NO INFLUENCE?
WE--WE STILL HAVE NO CONFIRMATION THAT IT REACHED LYKIA, GREAT KING.
THEN SEND ANOTHER SHIPLOAD! TROY HAS NO CHANCE IF THEY JOIN THE ACHAEANS!
TROY HAS NO CHANCE WITHOUT THE DARDANIANS EITHER.
WHO SAYS SO?
HEKTOR!
THE DARDANIANS MUST STAND WITH US! TROY CAN'T DO WITHOUT THEIR STRENGTH --MUCH LESS RISK THEM JOINING OUR ENEMIES!
THEY WOULDN'T **DARE**!
DON'T UNDERESTIMATE AENEAS, FATHER. HE'S PROUD AND HE THINKS YOU TREATED HIM BADLY. END THE QUARREL, FATHER. FORGIVE HIM... AND KREUSA, TOO.
I HAVE LETTERS TO DICTATE AND SACRIFICES TO PERFORM BEFORE SUNRISE.
YOU KNOW KREUSA'S HEART WAS SET ON AENEAS. NO ONE WILL THINK LESS OF YOU IF YOU RECONCILE WITH HIM. THEY'LL **PRAISE** YOU.
FRANKLY, THEY'LL SPEAK BADLY OF YOU IF YOU **DON'T**.

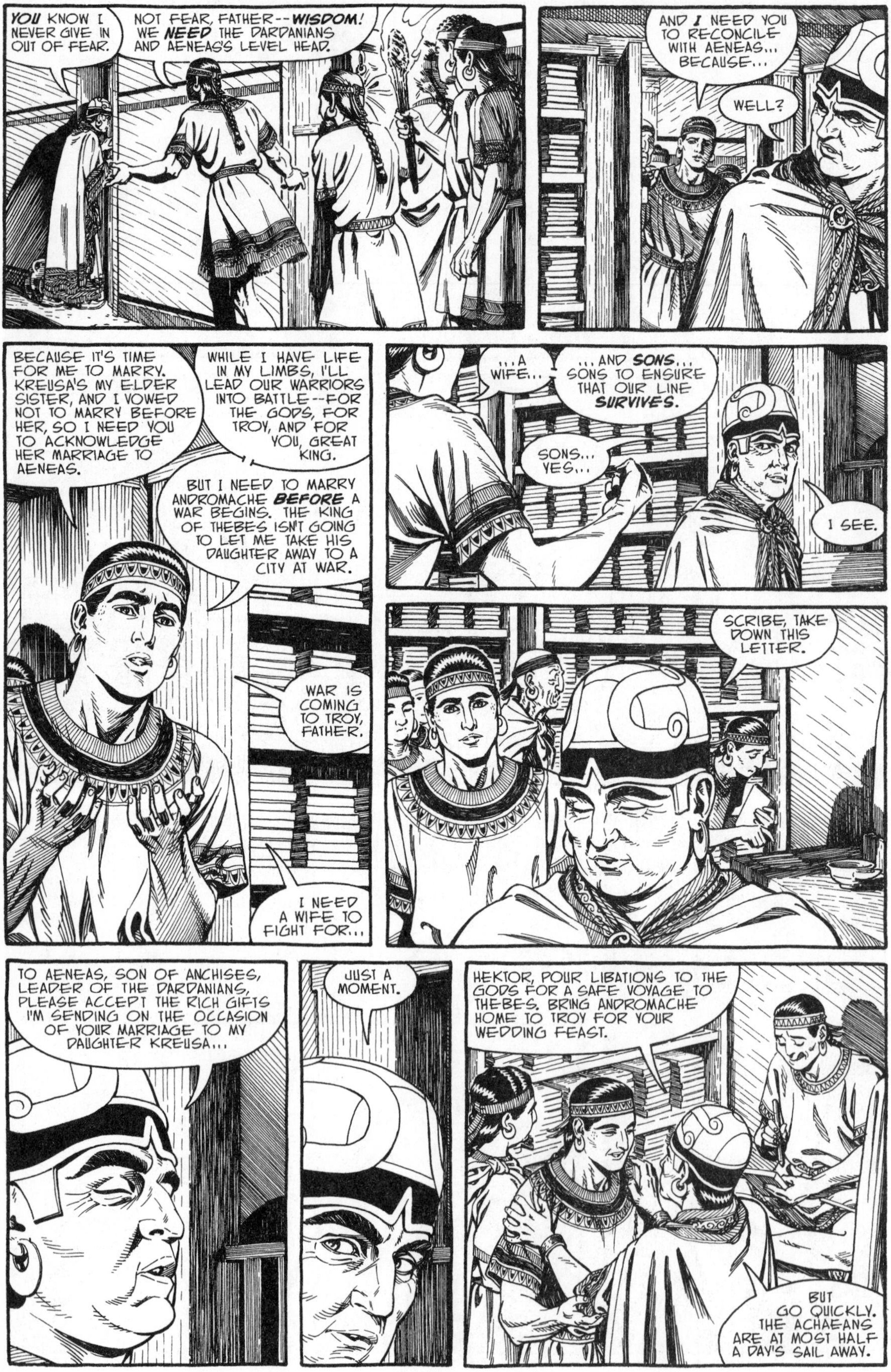
YOU KNOW I NEVER GIVE IN OUT OF FEAR.
NOT FEAR, FATHER--WISDOM! WE NEED THE DARDANIANS AND AENEAS'S LEVEL HEAD.
AND I NEED YOU TO RECONCILE WITH AENEAS... BECAUSE...
WELL?
BECAUSE IT'S TIME FOR ME TO MARRY. KREUSA'S MY ELDER SISTER, AND I VOWED NOT TO MARRY BEFORE HER, SO I NEED YOU TO ACKNOWLEDGE HER MARRIAGE TO AENEAS.
WHILE I HAVE LIFE IN MY LIMBS, I'LL LEAD OUR WARRIORS INTO BATTLE--FOR THE GODS, FOR TROY, AND FOR YOU, GREAT KING.
BUT I NEED TO MARRY ANDROMACHE BEFORE A WAR BEGINS. THE KING OF THEBES ISN'T GOING TO LET ME TAKE HIS DAUGHTER AWAY TO A CITY AT WAR.
WAR IS COMING TO TROY, FATHER.
I NEED A WIFE TO FIGHT FOR...
...A WIFE...
...AND SONS... SONS TO ENSURE THAT OUR LINE SURVIVES.
SONS... YES...
I SEE.
SCRIBE, TAKE DOWN THIS LETTER.
TO AENEAS, SON OF ANCHISES, LEADER OF THE DARDANIANS, PLEASE ACCEPT THE RICH GIFTS I'M SENDING ON THE OCCASION OF YOUR MARRIAGE TO MY DAUGHTER KREUSA...
JUST A MOMENT.
HEKTOR, POUR LIBATIONS TO THE GODS FOR A SAFE VOYAGE TO THEBES. BRING ANDROMACHE HOME TO TROY FOR YOUR WEDDING FEAST.
BUT GO QUICKLY. THE ACHAEANS ARE AT MOST HALF A DAY'S SAIL AWAY.

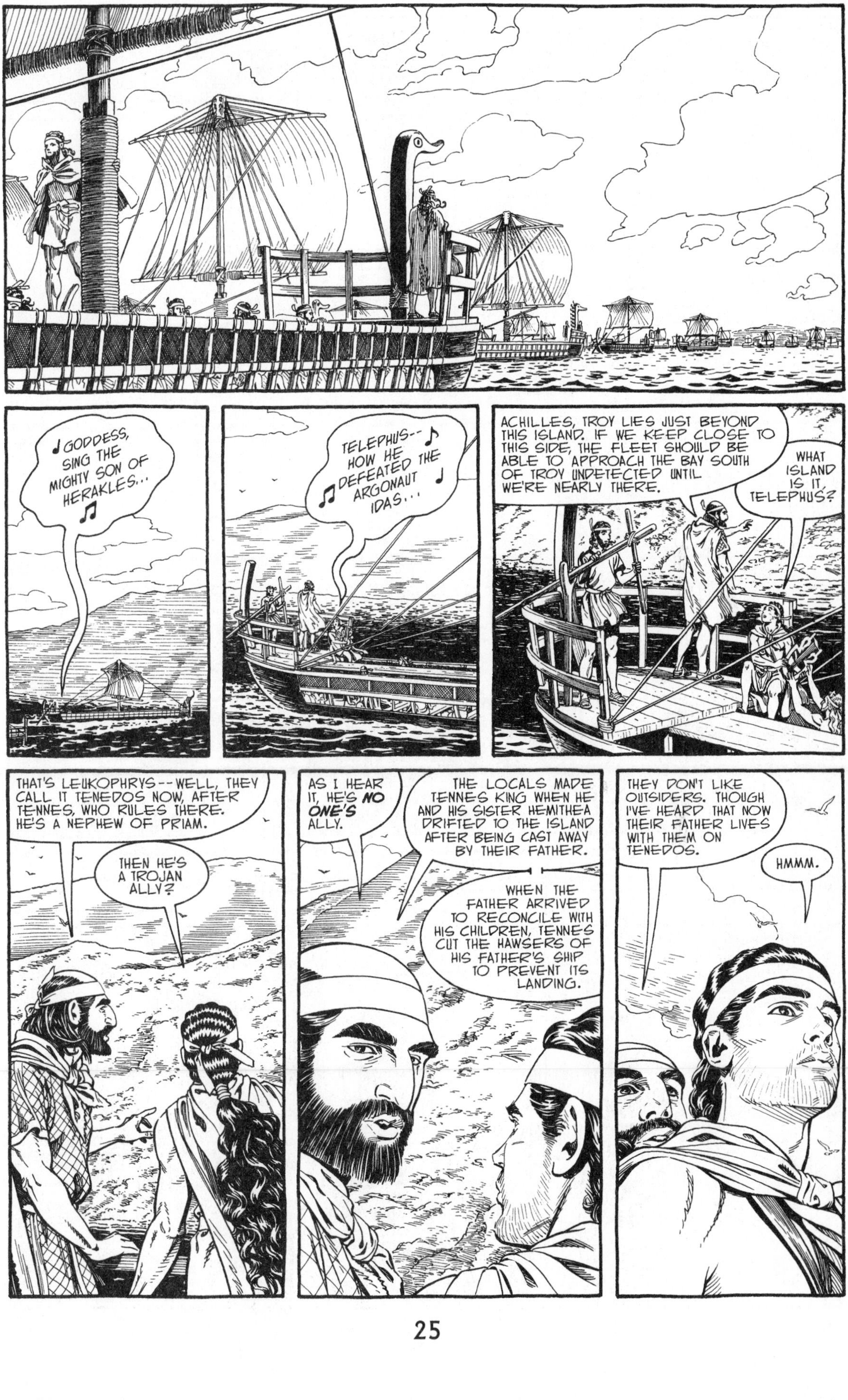
♩GODDESS, SING THE MIGHTY SON OF HERAKLES... ♫
TELEPHUS-- ♪ HOW HE DEFEATED THE ARGONAUT IDAS... ♩
ACHILLES, TROY LIES JUST BEYOND THIS ISLAND. IF WE KEEP CLOSE TO THIS SIDE, THE FLEET SHOULD BE ABLE TO APPROACH THE BAY SOUTH OF TROY UNDETECTED UNTIL WE'RE NEARLY THERE.
WHAT ISLAND IS IT, TELEPHUS?
THAT'S LEUKOPHRYS--WELL, THEY CALL IT TENEDOS NOW, AFTER TENNES, WHO RULES THERE. HE'S A NEPHEW OF PRIAM.
THEN HE'S A TROJAN ALLY?
AS I HEAR IT, HE'S NO ONE'S ALLY.
THE LOCALS MADE TENNES KING WHEN HE AND HIS SISTER HEMITHEA DRIFTED TO THE ISLAND AFTER BEING CAST AWAY BY THEIR FATHER.
WHEN THE FATHER ARRIVED TO RECONCILE WITH HIS CHILDREN, TENNES CUT THE HAWSERS OF HIS FATHER'S SHIP TO PREVENT ITS LANDING.
THEY DON'T LIKE OUTSIDERS. THOUGH I'VE HEARD THAT NOW THEIR FATHER LIVES WITH THEM ON TENEDOS.
HMMM.

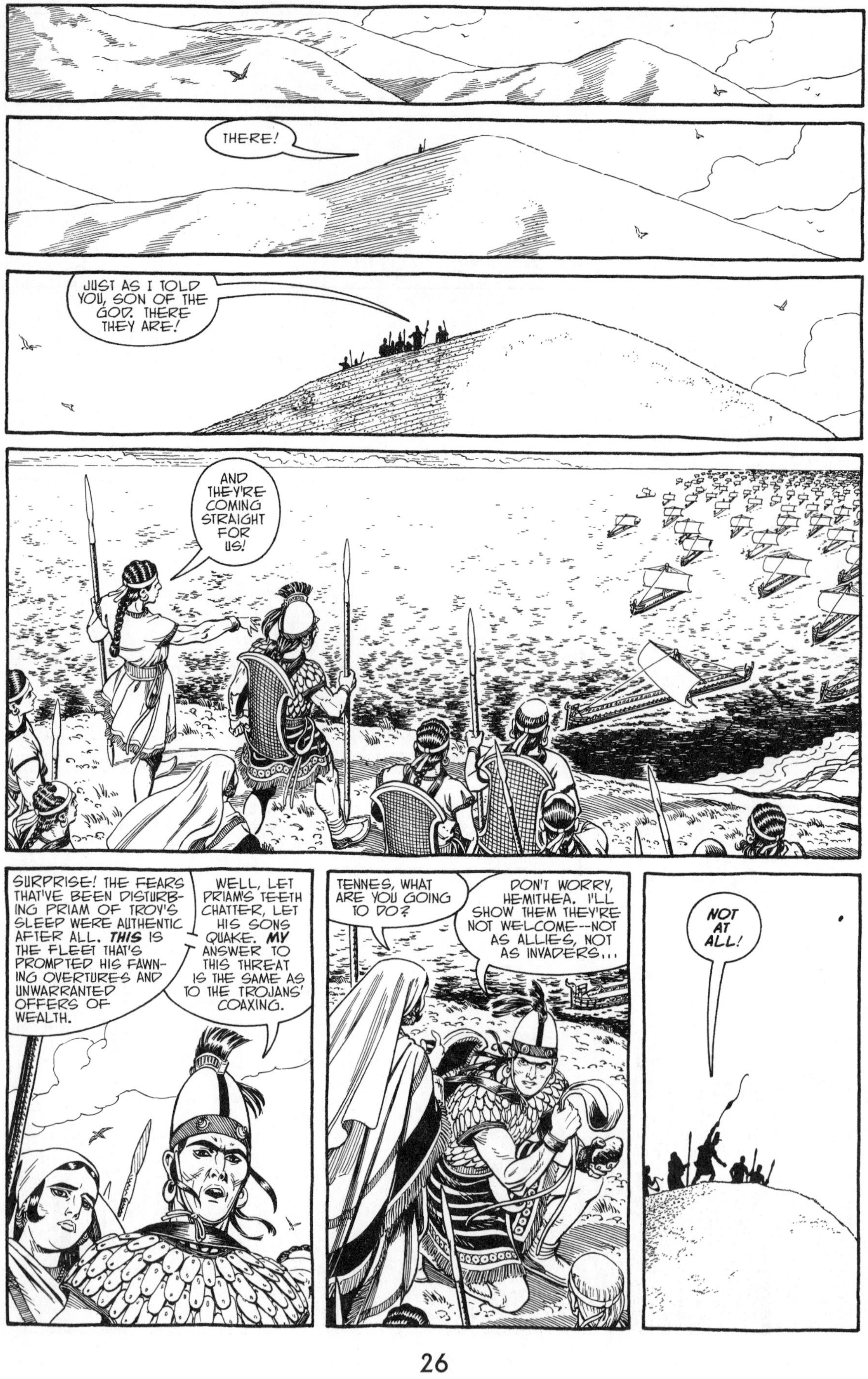
THERE!
JUST AS I TOLD YOU, SON OF THE GOD. THERE THEY ARE!
AND THEY'RE COMING STRAIGHT FOR US!
SURPRISE! THE FEARS THAT'VE BEEN DISTURBING PRIAM OF TROY'S SLEEP WERE AUTHENTIC AFTER ALL. THIS IS THE FLEET THAT'S PROMPTED HIS FAWNING OVERTURES AND UNWARRANTED OFFERS OF WEALTH.
WELL, LET PRIAM'S TEETH CHATTER, LET HIS SONS QUAKE. MY ANSWER TO THIS THREAT IS THE SAME AS TO THE TROJANS' COAXING.
TENNES, WHAT ARE YOU GOING TO DO?
DON'T WORRY, HEMITHEA. I'LL SHOW THEM THEY'RE NOT WELCOME--NOT AS ALLIES, NOT AS INVADERS...
NOT AT ALL!

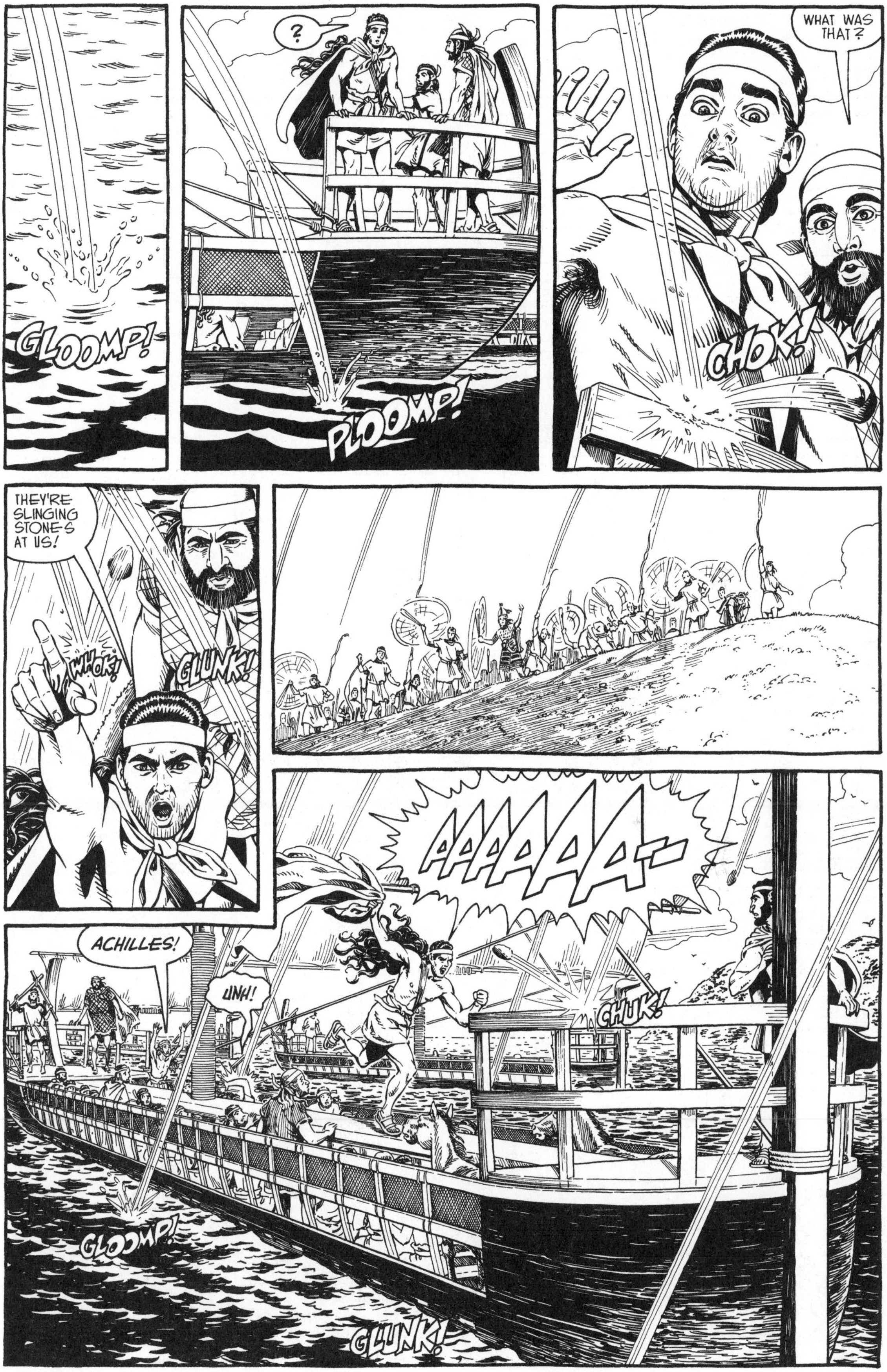
GLOOMP!
?
PLOOMP!
WHAT WAS THAT?
CHOK!
THEY'RE SLINGING STONES AT US!
WHOK!
GLUNK!
AAAAAA-
ACHILLES!
UNH!
CHUK!
GLOOMP!
GLUNK!

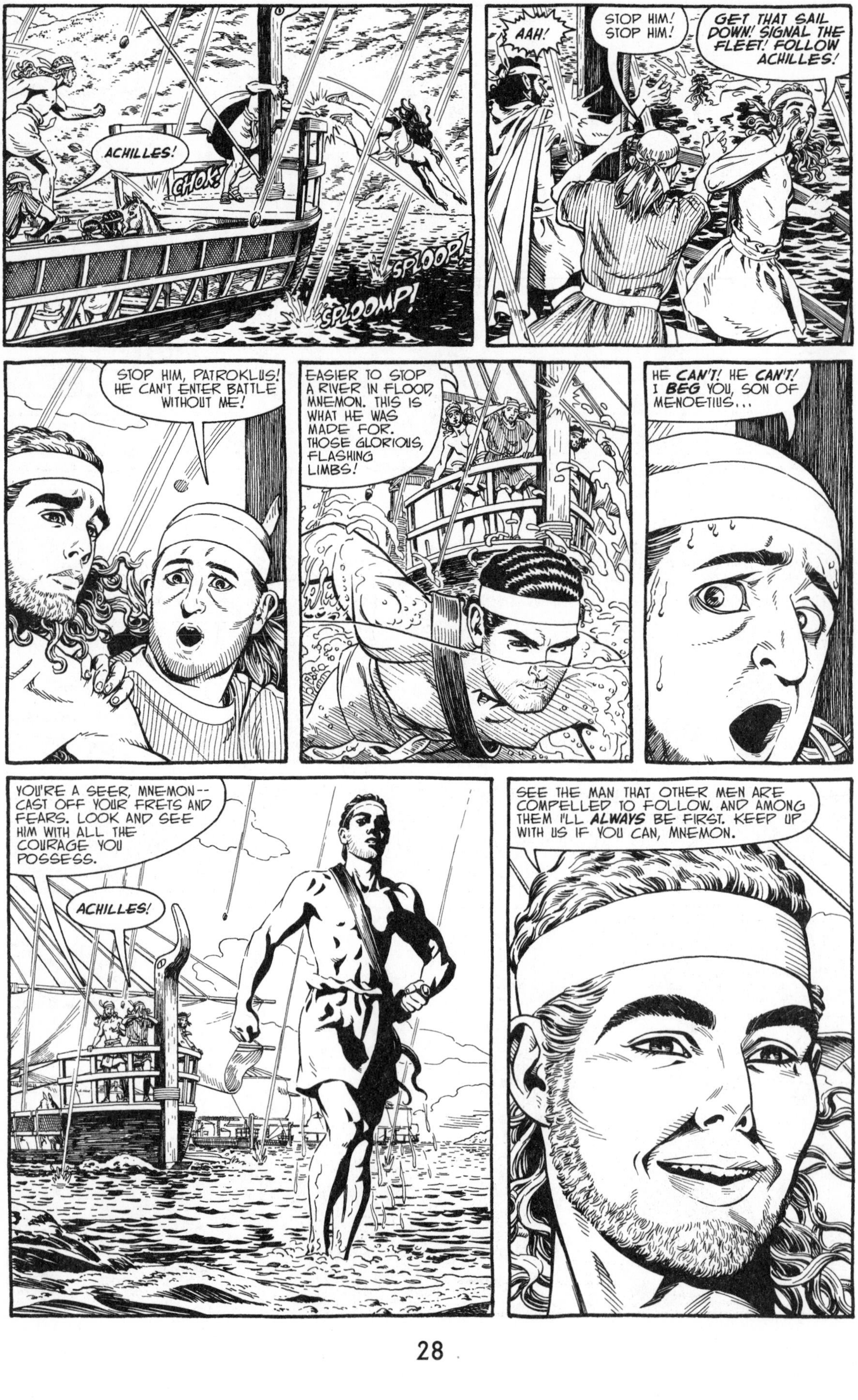
ACHILLES!
CHOK!
SPLOOP!
SPLOOMP!
AAH!
STOP HIM! STOP HIM!
GET THAT SAIL DOWN! SIGNAL THE FLEET! FOLLOW ACHILLES!
STOP HIM, PATROKLUS! HE CAN'T ENTER BATTLE WITHOUT ME!
EASIER TO STOP A RIVER IN FLOOD, MNEMON. THIS IS WHAT HE WAS MADE FOR. THOSE GLORIOUS, FLASHING LIMBS!
HE CAN'T! HE CAN'T! I BEG YOU, SON OF MENOETIUS...
YOU'RE A SEER, MNEMON-- CAST OFF YOUR FRETS AND FEARS. LOOK AND SEE HIM WITH ALL THE COURAGE YOU POSSESS.
ACHILLES!
SEE THE MAN THAT OTHER MEN ARE COMPELLED TO FOLLOW. AND AMONG THEM I'LL ALWAYS BE FIRST. KEEP UP WITH US IF YOU CAN, MNEMON.

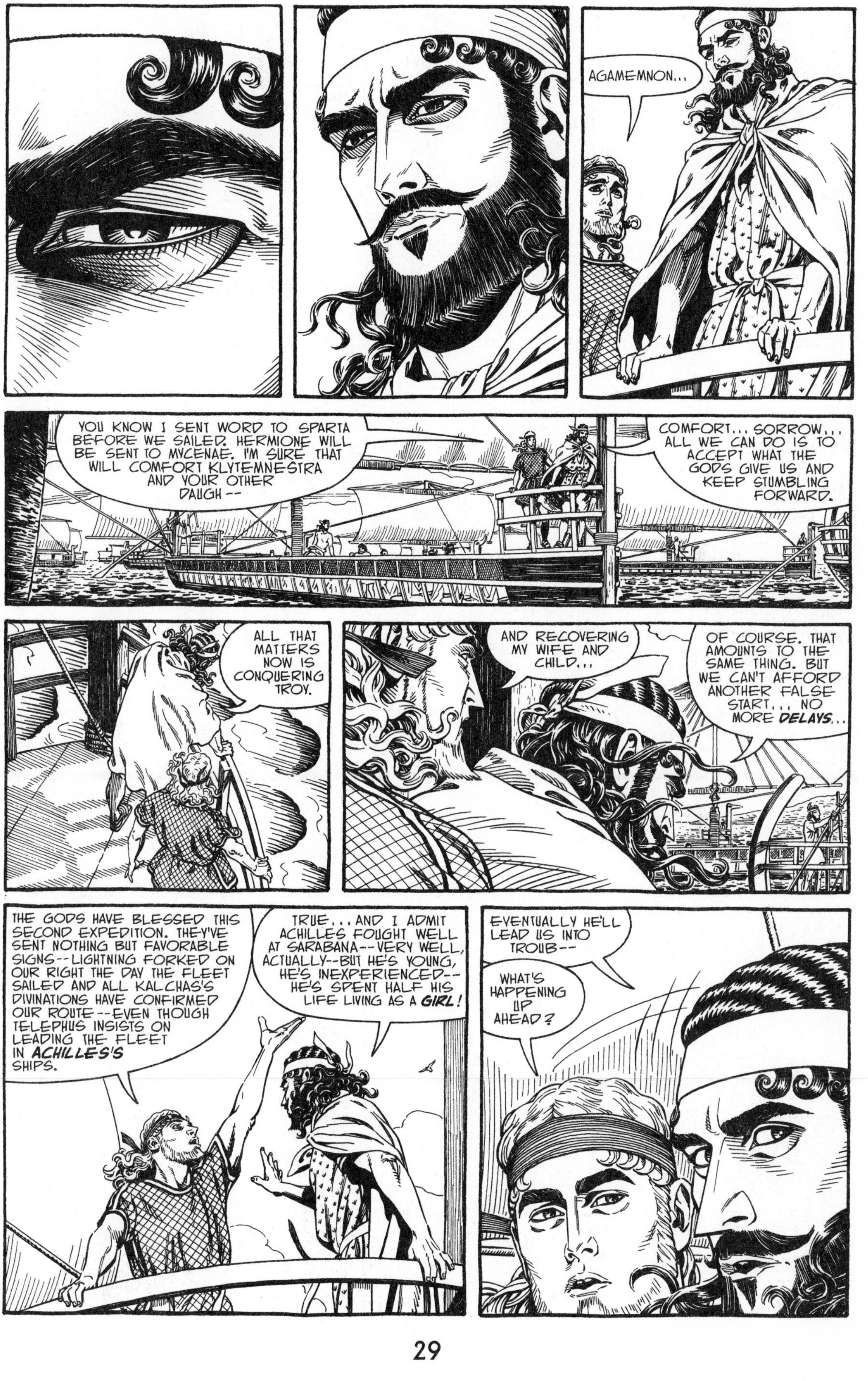
AGAMEMNON...
YOU KNOW I SENT WORD TO SPARTA BEFORE WE SAILED. HERMIONE WILL BE SENT TO MYCENAE. I'M SURE THAT WILL COMFORT KLYTEMNESTRA AND YOUR OTHER DAUGH--
COMFORT... SORROW... ALL WE CAN DO IS TO ACCEPT WHAT THE GODS GIVE US AND KEEP STUMBLING FORWARD.
ALL THAT MATTERS NOW IS CONQUERING TROY.
AND RECOVERING MY WIFE AND CHILD...
OF COURSE. THAT AMOUNTS TO THE SAME THING. BUT WE CAN'T AFFORD ANOTHER FALSE START... NO MORE DELAYS...
THE GODS HAVE BLESSED THIS SECOND EXPEDITION. THEY'VE SENT NOTHING BUT FAVORABLE SIGNS--LIGHTNING FORKED ON OUR RIGHT THE DAY THE FLEET SAILED AND ALL KALCHAS'S DIVINATIONS HAVE CONFIRMED OUR ROUTE--EVEN THOUGH TELEPHUS INSISTS ON LEADING THE FLEET IN ACHILLES'S SHIPS.
TRUE... AND I ADMIT ACHILLES FOUGHT WELL AT SARABANA--VERY WELL, ACTUALLY--BUT HE'S YOUNG, HE'S INEXPERIENCED--HE'S SPENT HALF HIS LIFE LIVING AS A GIRL!
EVENTUALLY HE'LL LEAD US INTO TROUB--
WHAT'S HAPPENING UP AHEAD?

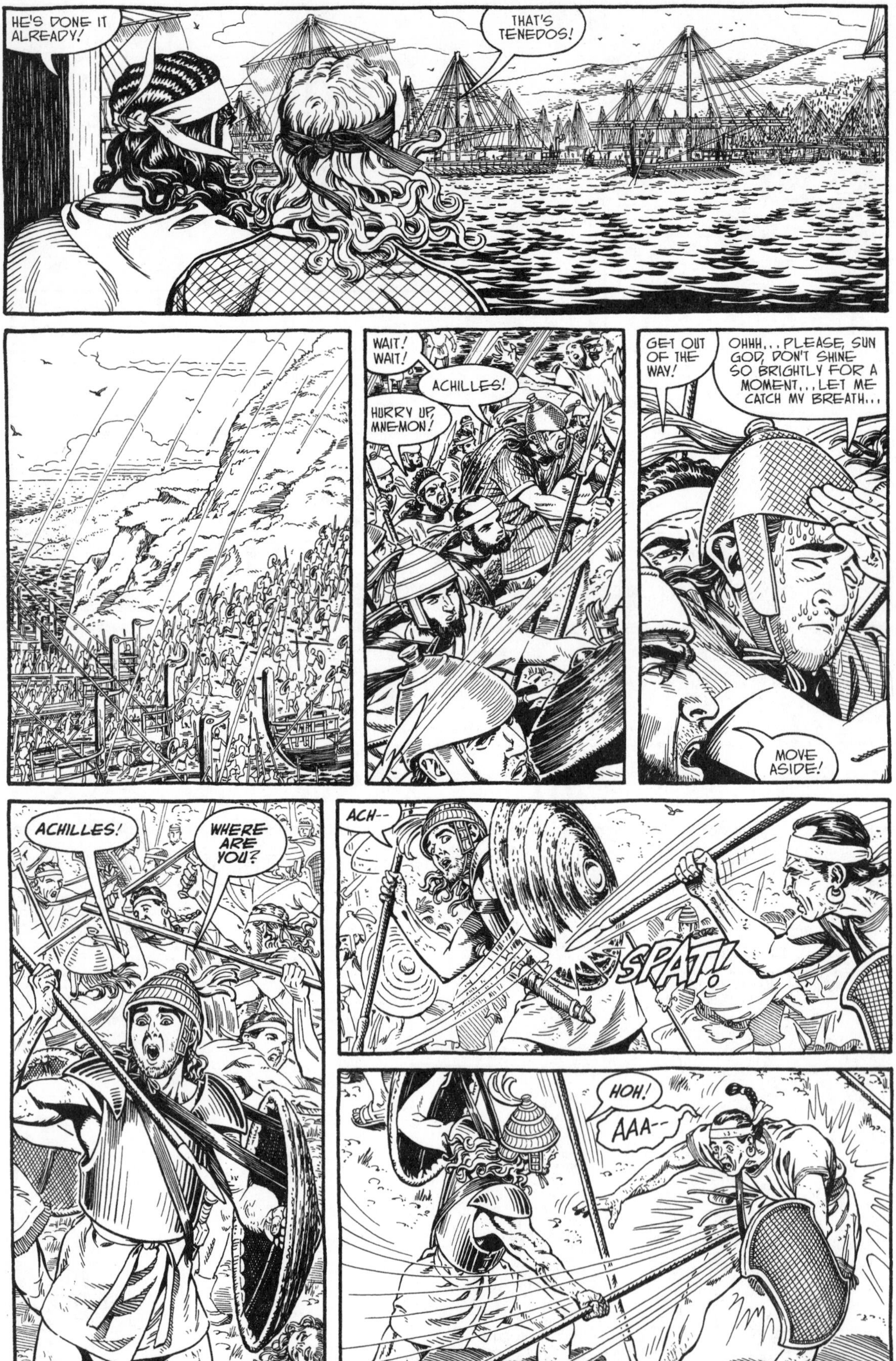
HE'S DONE IT ALREADY!
THAT'S TENEDOS!
WAIT! WAIT!
ACHILLES!
HURRY UP, MNE-MON!
GET OUT OF THE WAY!
OHHH... PLEASE, SUN GOD, DON'T SHINE SO BRIGHTLY FOR A MOMENT... LET ME CATCH MY BREATH...
MOVE ASIDE!
ACHILLES!
WHERE ARE YOU?
ACH--
SPAT!
HOH!
AAA--

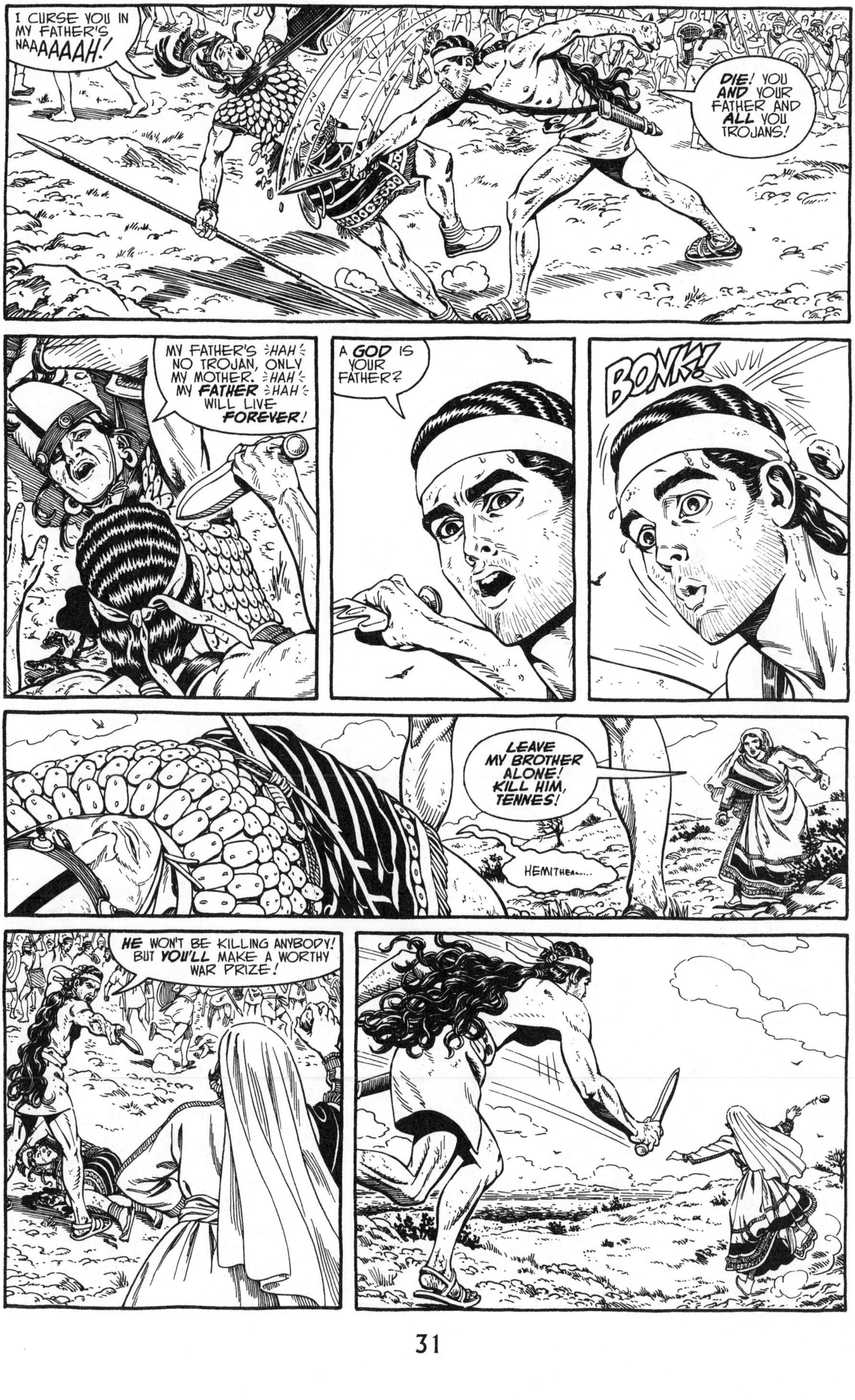
I CURSE YOU IN MY FATHER'S NAAAAAAH!
DIE! YOU AND YOUR FATHER AND ALL YOU TROJANS!
MY FATHER'S HAH NO TROJAN, ONLY MY MOTHER. HAH MY FATHER HAH WILL LIVE FOREVER!
A GOD IS YOUR FATHER?
BONK!
LEAVE MY BROTHER ALONE! KILL HIM, TENNES!
HEMITHEA....
HE WON'T BE KILLING ANYBODY! BUT YOU'LL MAKE A WORTHY WAR PRIZE!

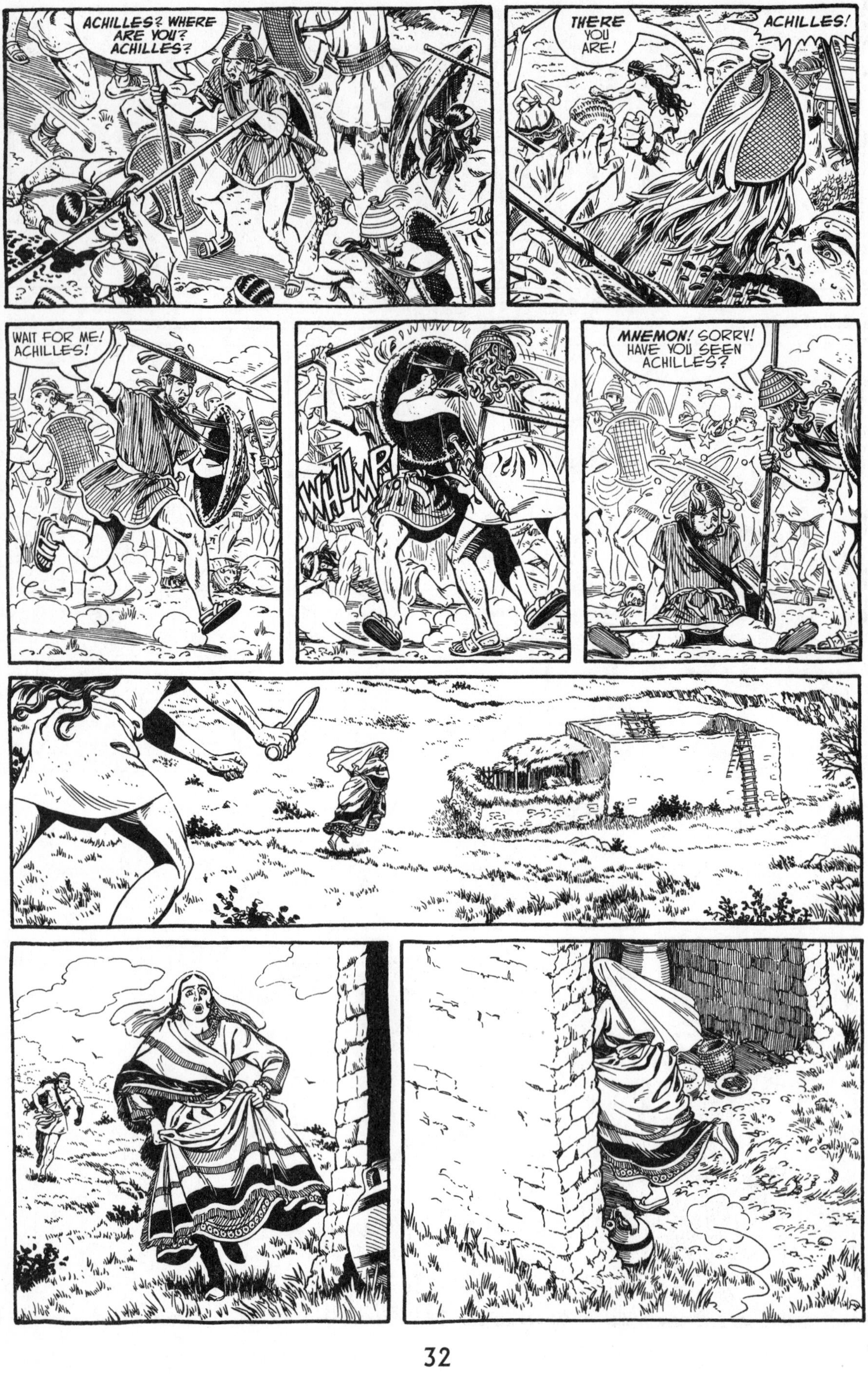
ACHILLES? WHERE ARE YOU!? ACHILLES?
THERE YOU ARE!
ACHILLES!
WAIT FOR ME! ACHILLES!
WHUMP!
MNEMON! SORRY! HAVE YOU SEEN ACHILLES?

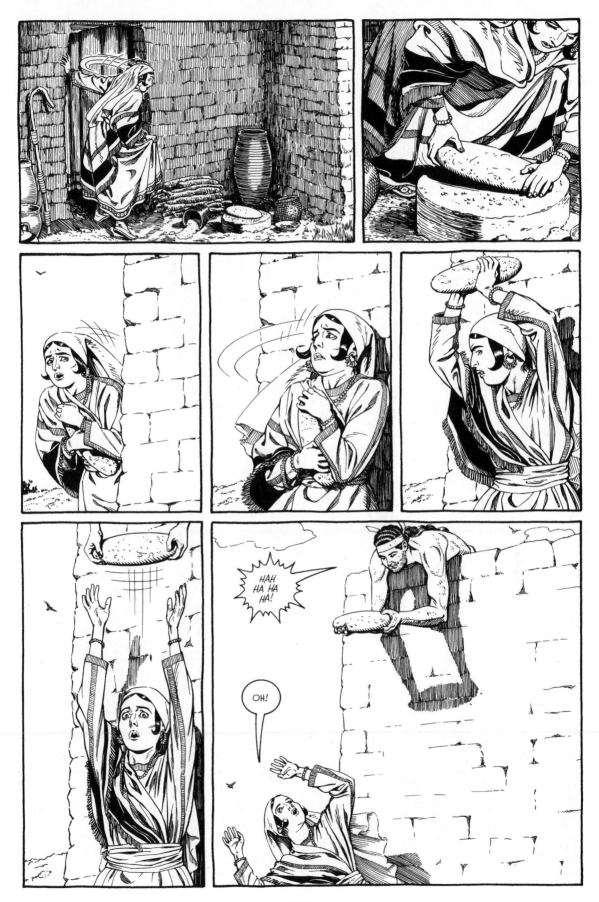

HAH HA HA HA!

OH!

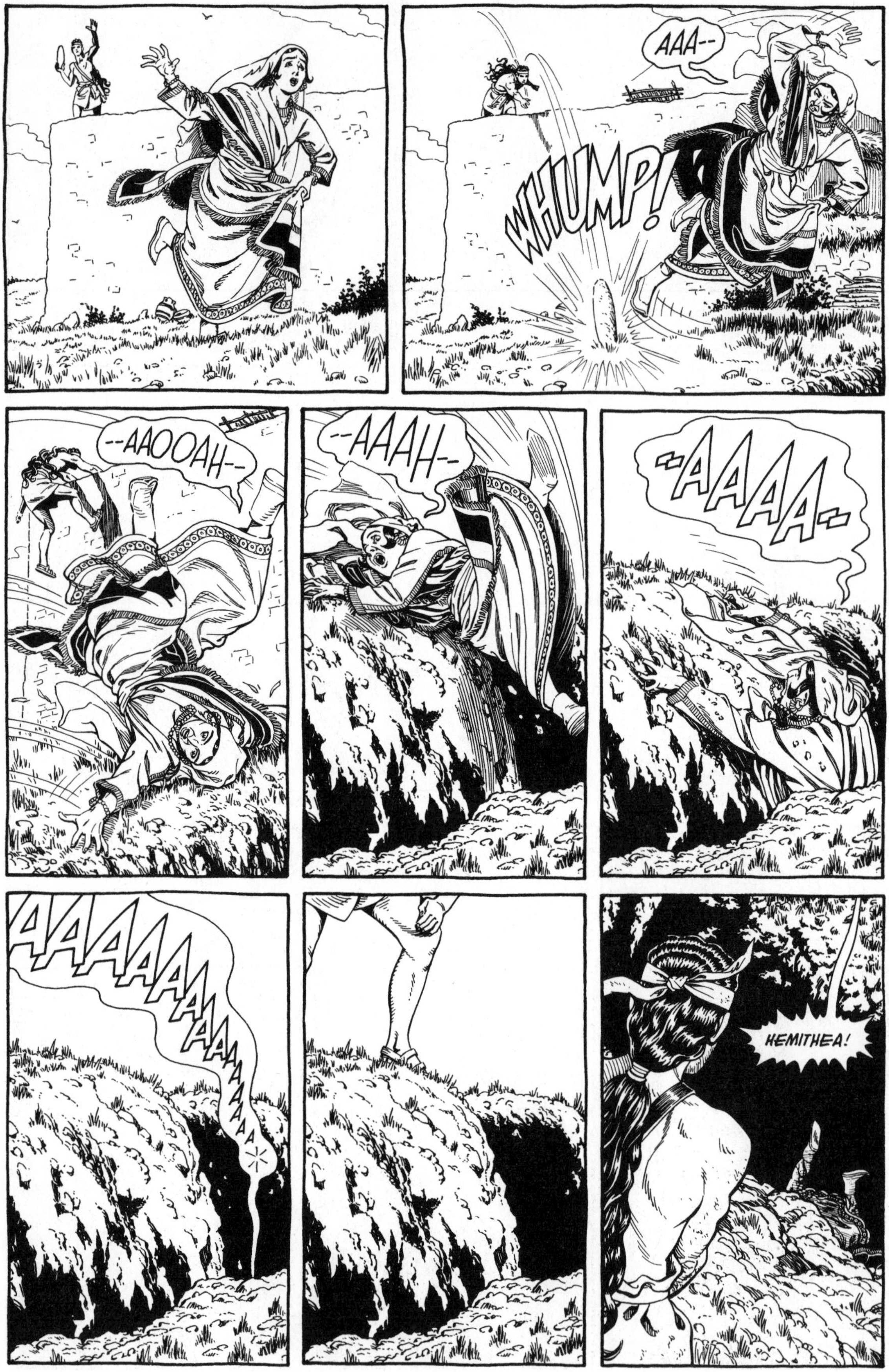
AAA--
WHUMP!
--AAOOAH--
--AAAH--
-AAAA-
AAAAAAAAAAAAAA
HEMITHEA!

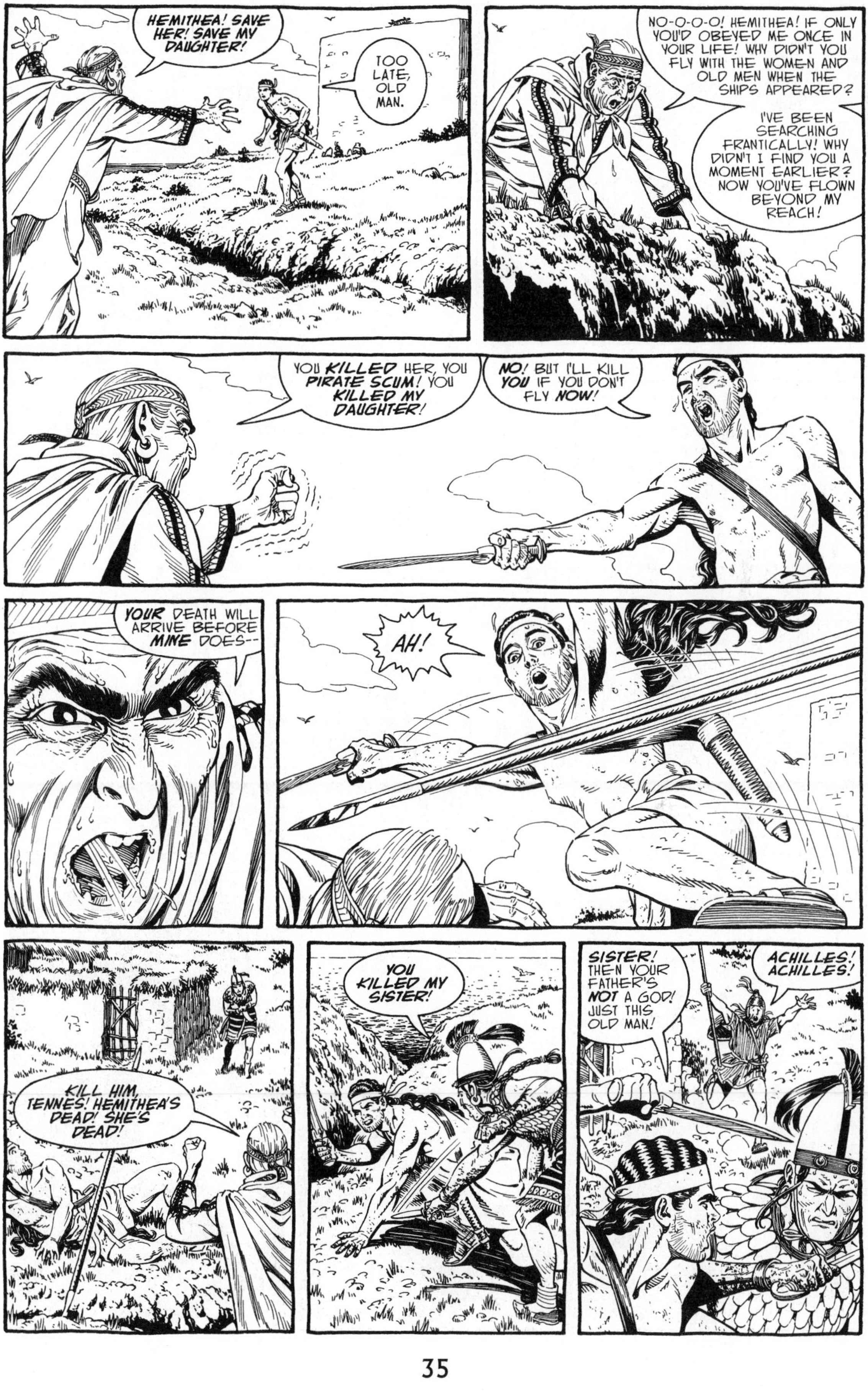
HEMITHEA! SAVE HER! SAVE MY DAUGHTER!
TOO LATE, OLD MAN.
NO-O-O-O! HEMITHEA! IF ONLY YOU'D OBEYED ME ONCE IN YOUR LIFE! WHY DIDN'T YOU FLY WITH THE WOMEN AND OLD MEN WHEN THE SHIPS APPEARED?
I'VE BEEN SEARCHING FRANTICALLY! WHY DIDN'T I FIND YOU A MOMENT EARLIER? NOW YOU'VE FLOWN BEYOND MY REACH!
YOU KILLED HER, YOU PIRATE SCUM! YOU KILLED MY DAUGHTER!
NO! BUT I'LL KILL YOU IF YOU DON'T FLY NOW!
YOUR DEATH WILL ARRIVE BEFORE MINE DOES--
AH!
KILL HIM, TENNES! HEMITHEA'S DEAD! SHE'S DEAD!
YOU KILLED MY SISTER!
SISTER! THEN YOUR FATHER'S NOT A GOD! JUST THIS OLD MAN!
ACHILLES! ACHILLES!

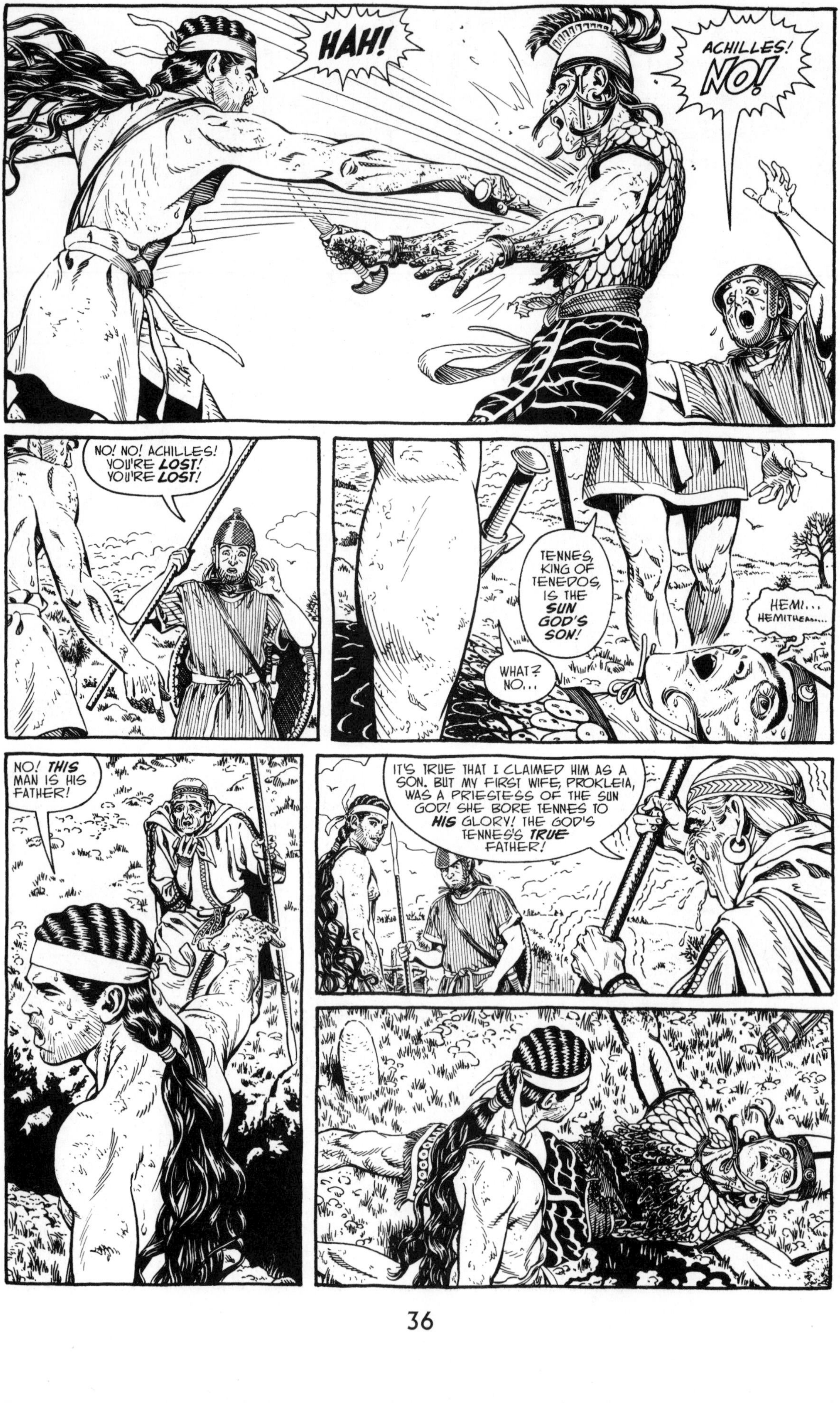
HAH!
ACHILLES! NO!
NO! NO! ACHILLES! YOU'RE LOST! YOU'RE LOST!
TENNES, KING OF TENEDOS, IS THE SUN GOD'S SON!
WHAT? NO...
HEMI... HEMITHEA....
NO! THIS MAN IS HIS FATHER!
IT'S TRUE THAT I CLAIMED HIM AS A SON. BUT MY FIRST WIFE, PROKLEIA, WAS A PRIESTESS OF THE SUN GOD! SHE BORE TENNES TO HIS GLORY! THE GOD'S TENNES'S TRUE FATHER!

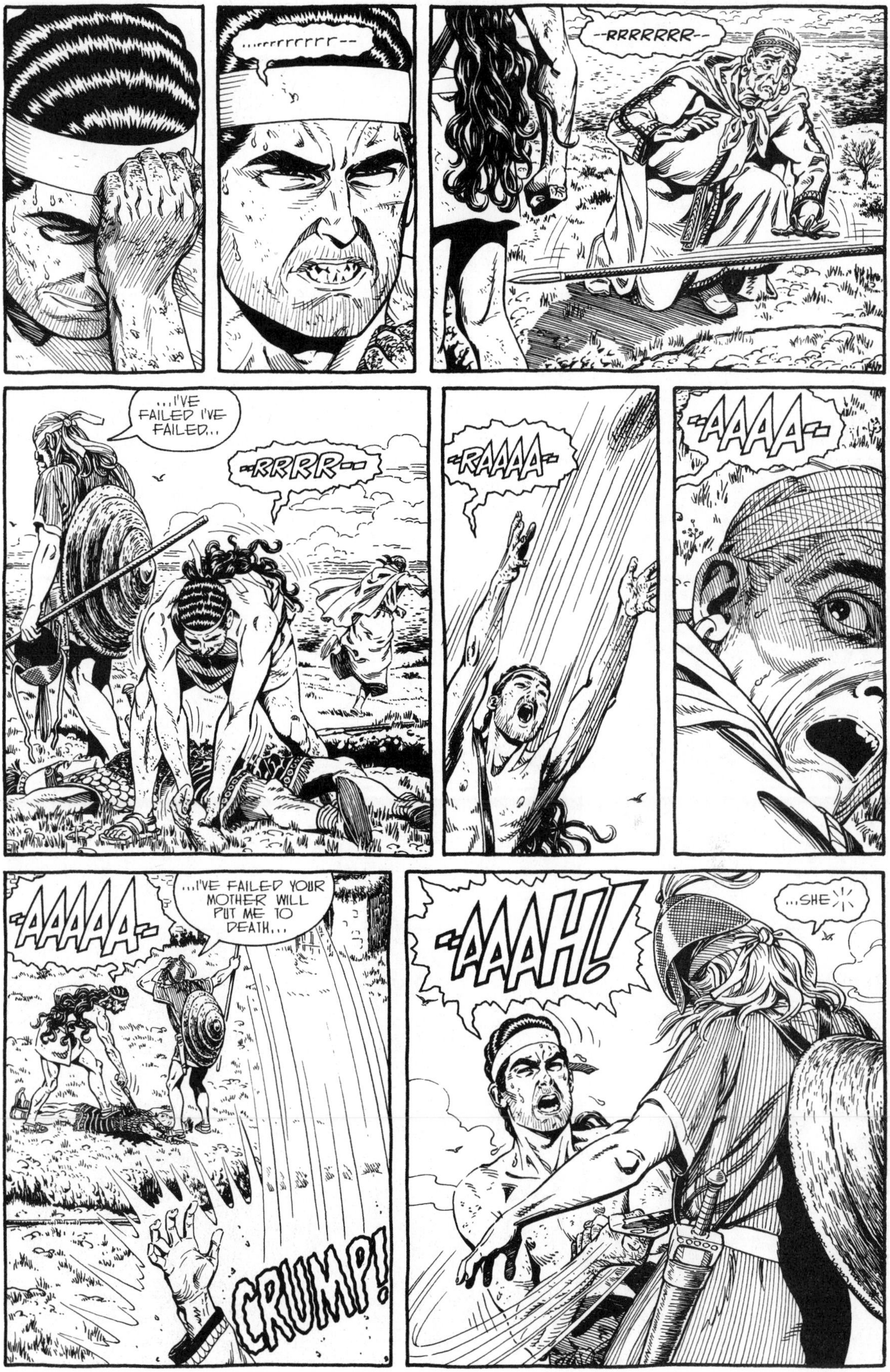
...rrrrrrrr--
--RRRRRRR--
...I'VE FAILED I'VE FAILED...
--RRRR--
--RAAAA--
--AAAA--
--AAAAA--
...I'VE FAILED YOUR MOTHER WILL PUT ME TO DEATH...
CRUMP!
--AAAH!
...SHE

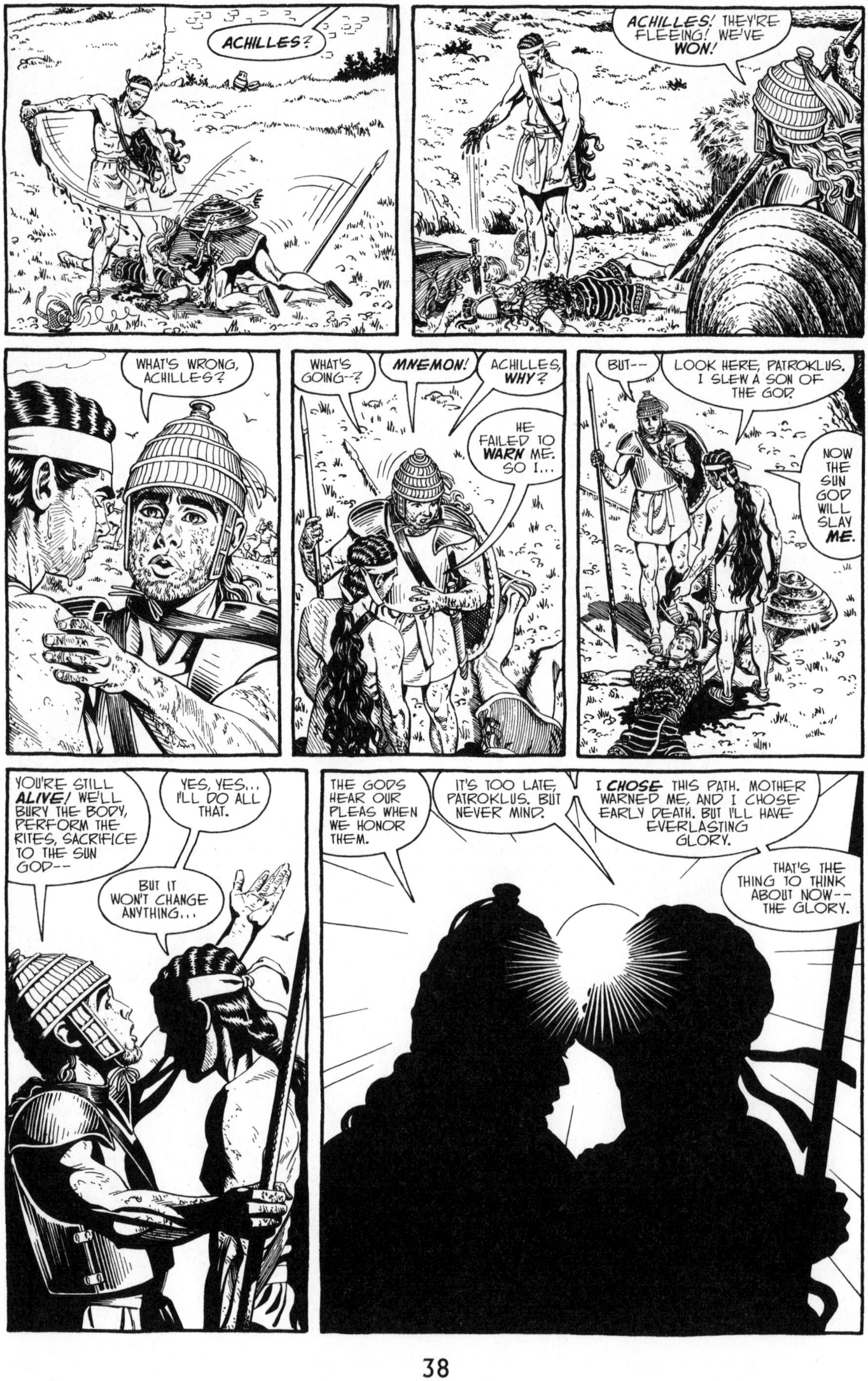
ACHILLES?
ACHILLES! THEY'RE FLEEING! WE'VE WON!
WHAT'S WRONG, ACHILLES?
WHAT'S GOING--?
MNEMON!
ACHILLES, WHY?
HE FAILED TO WARN ME. SO I...
BUT--
LOOK HERE, PATROKLUS. I SLEW A SON OF THE GOD.
NOW THE SUN GOD WILL SLAY ME.
YOU'RE STILL ALIVE! WE'LL BURY THE BODY, PERFORM THE RITES, SACRIFICE TO THE SUN GOD--
YES, YES... I'LL DO ALL THAT.
BUT IT WON'T CHANGE ANYTHING...
THE GODS HEAR OUR PLEAS WHEN WE HONOR THEM.
IT'S TOO LATE, PATROKLUS. BUT NEVER MIND.
I CHOSE THIS PATH. MOTHER WARNED ME, AND I CHOSE EARLY DEATH. BUT I'LL HAVE EVERLASTING GLORY.
THAT'S THE THING TO THINK ABOUT NOW-- THE GLORY.

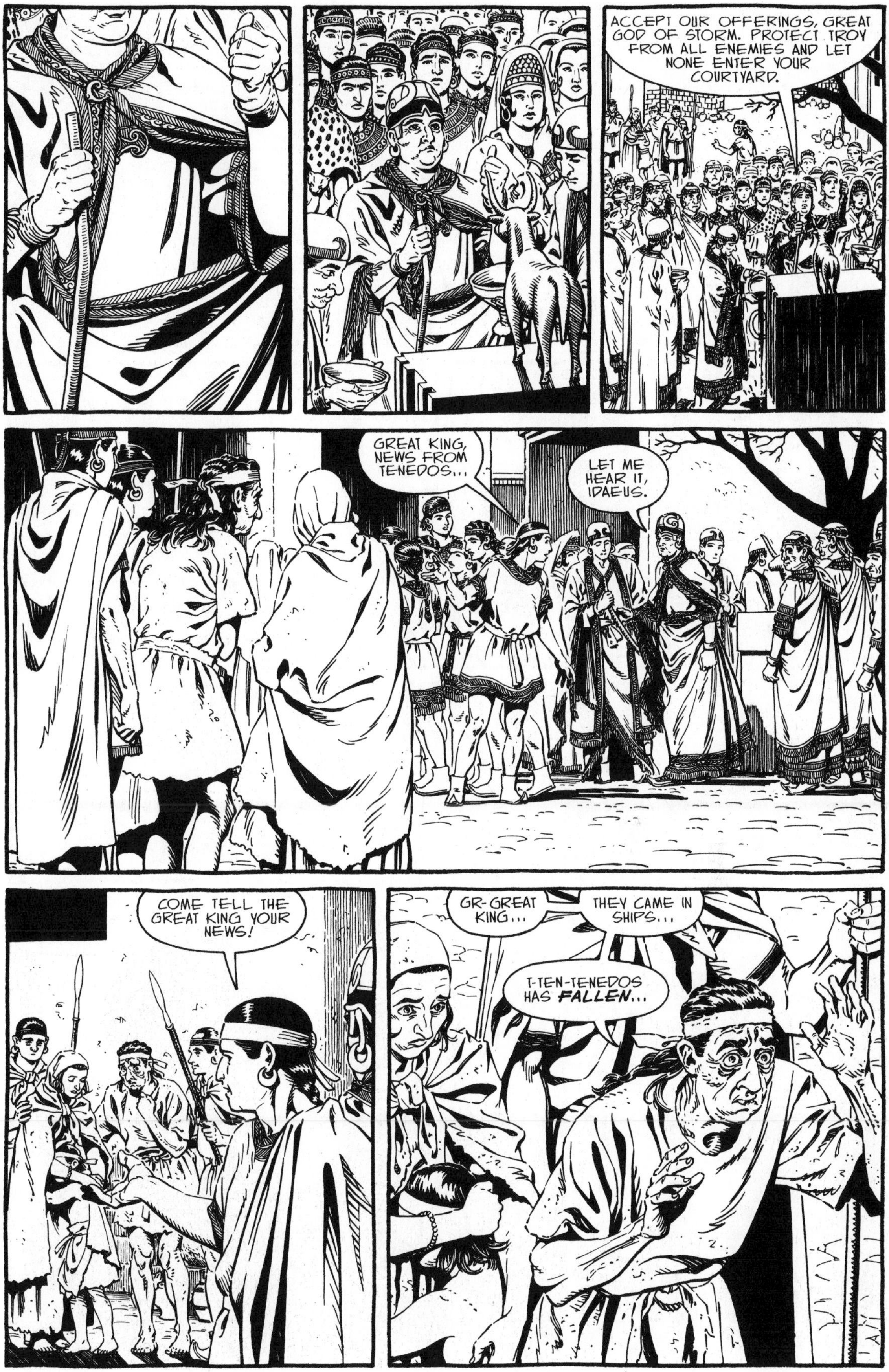
ACCEPT OUR OFFERINGS, GREAT GOD OF STORM. PROTECT TROY FROM ALL ENEMIES AND LET NONE ENTER YOUR COURTYARD.
GREAT KING, NEWS FROM TENEDOS...
LET ME HEAR IT, IDAEUS.
COME TELL THE GREAT KING YOUR NEWS!
GR-GREAT KING...
THEY CAME IN SHIPS...
T-TEN-TENEDOS HAS FALLEN...

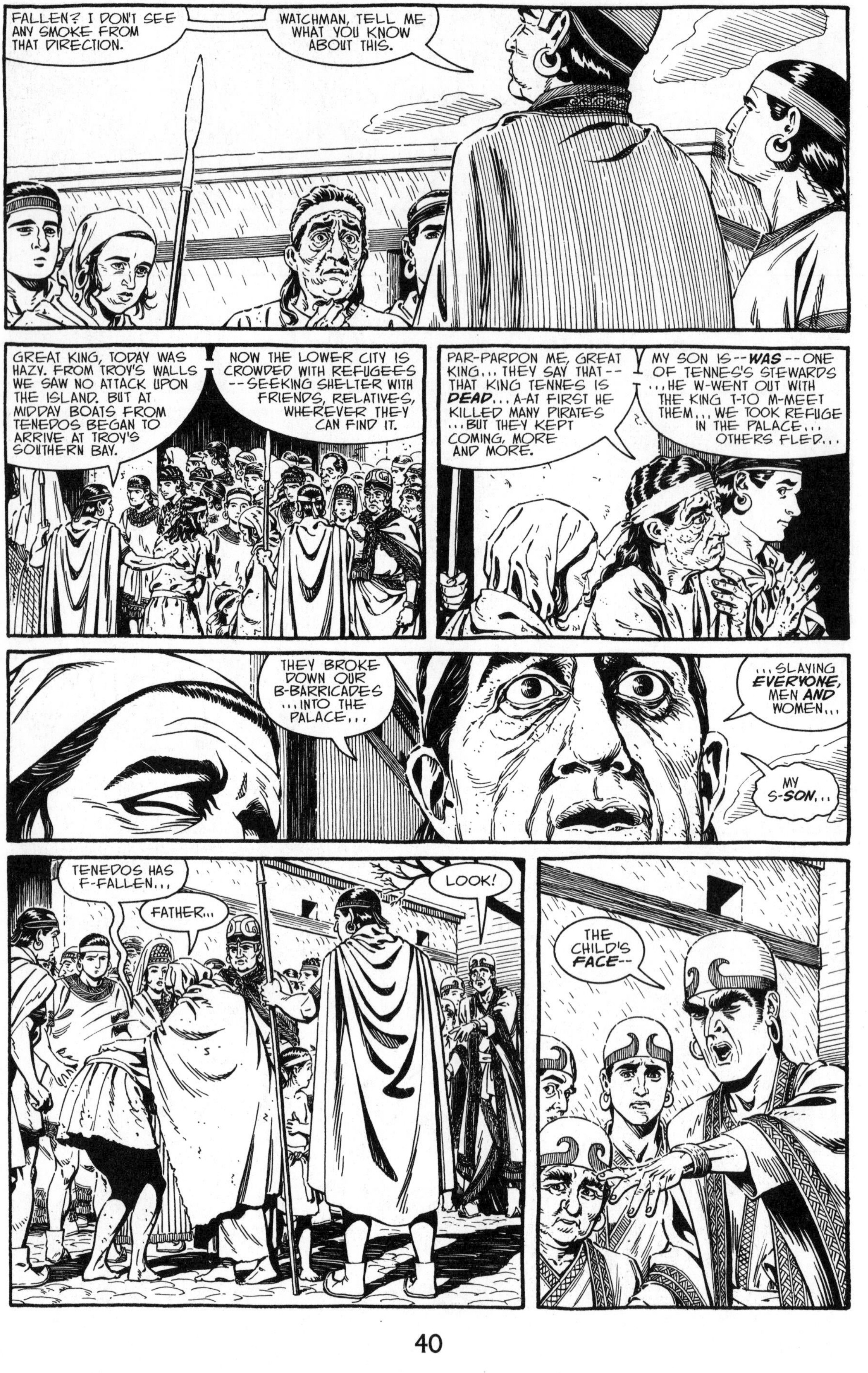
FALLEN? I DON'T SEE ANY SMOKE FROM THAT DIRECTION.
WATCHMAN, TELL ME WHAT YOU KNOW ABOUT THIS.
GREAT KING, TODAY WAS HAZY. FROM TROY'S WALLS WE SAW NO ATTACK UPON THE ISLAND. BUT AT MIDDAY BOATS FROM TENEDOS BEGAN TO ARRIVE AT TROY'S SOUTHERN BAY.
NOW THE LOWER CITY IS CROWDED WITH REFUGEES --SEEKING SHELTER WITH FRIENDS, RELATIVES, WHEREVER THEY CAN FIND IT.
PAR-PARDON ME, GREAT KING... THEY SAY THAT-- THAT KING TENNES IS DEAD... A-AT FIRST HE KILLED MANY PIRATES ...BUT THEY KEPT COMING, MORE AND MORE.
MY SON IS--WAS--ONE OF TENNES'S STEWARDS ...HE W-WENT OUT WITH THE KING T-TO M-MEET THEM... WE TOOK REFUGE IN THE PALACE... OTHERS FLED...
THEY BROKE DOWN OUR B-BARRICADES ...INTO THE PALACE...
...SLAYING EVERYONE, MEN AND WOMEN...
MY S-SON...
TENEDOS HAS F-FALLEN...
FATHER...
LOOK!
THE CHILD'S FACE--

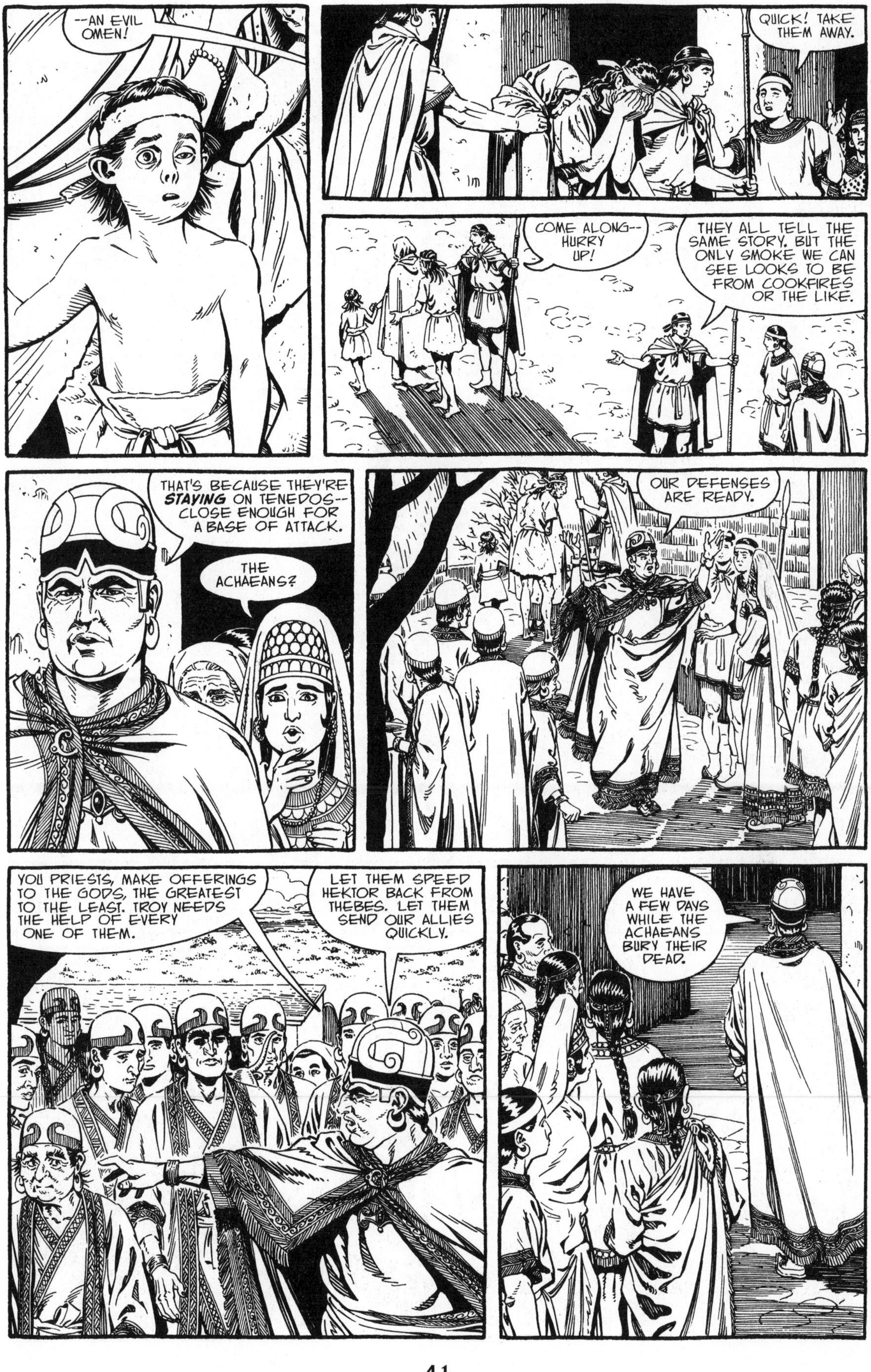
--AN EVIL OMEN!
QUICK! TAKE THEM AWAY.
COME ALONG-- HURRY UP!
THEY ALL TELL THE SAME STORY. BUT THE ONLY SMOKE WE CAN SEE LOOKS TO BE FROM COOKFIRES OR THE LIKE.
THAT'S BECAUSE THEY'RE STAYING ON TENEDOS-- CLOSE ENOUGH FOR A BASE OF ATTACK.
THE ACHAEANS?
OUR DEFENSES ARE READY.
YOU PRIESTS, MAKE OFFERINGS TO THE GODS, THE GREATEST TO THE LEAST. TROY NEEDS THE HELP OF EVERY ONE OF THEM.
LET THEM SPEED HEKTOR BACK FROM THEBES. LET THEM SEND OUR ALLIES QUICKLY.
WE HAVE A FEW DAYS WHILE THE ACHAEANS BURY THEIR DEAD.

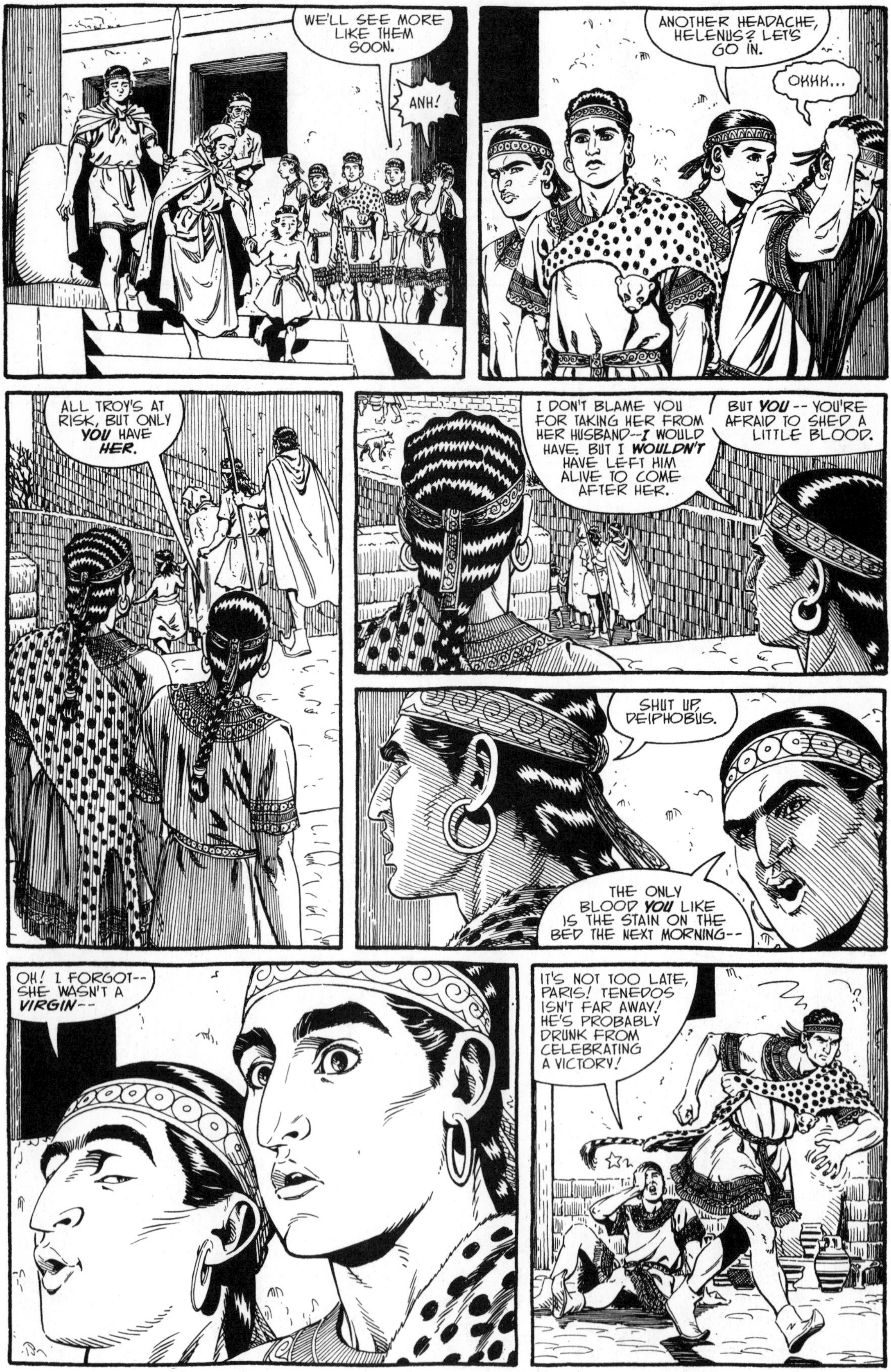
WE'LL SEE MORE LIKE THEM SOON.
ANH!
ANOTHER HEADACHE, HELENUS? LET'S GO IN.
OHHH...
ALL TROY'S AT RISK, BUT ONLY **YOU** HAVE **HER**.
I DON'T BLAME YOU FOR TAKING HER FROM HER HUSBAND--**I** WOULD HAVE. BUT I **WOULDN'T** HAVE LEFT HIM ALIVE TO COME AFTER HER.
BUT **YOU** -- YOU'RE AFRAID TO SHED A LITTLE BLOOD.
SHUT UP, DEIPHOBUS.
THE ONLY BLOOD **YOU** LIKE IS THE STAIN ON THE BED THE NEXT MORNING--
OH! I FORGOT-- SHE WASN'T A **VIRGIN**--
IT'S NOT TOO LATE, PARIS! TENEDOS ISN'T FAR AWAY! HE'S PROBABLY DRUNK FROM CELEBRATING A VICTORY!

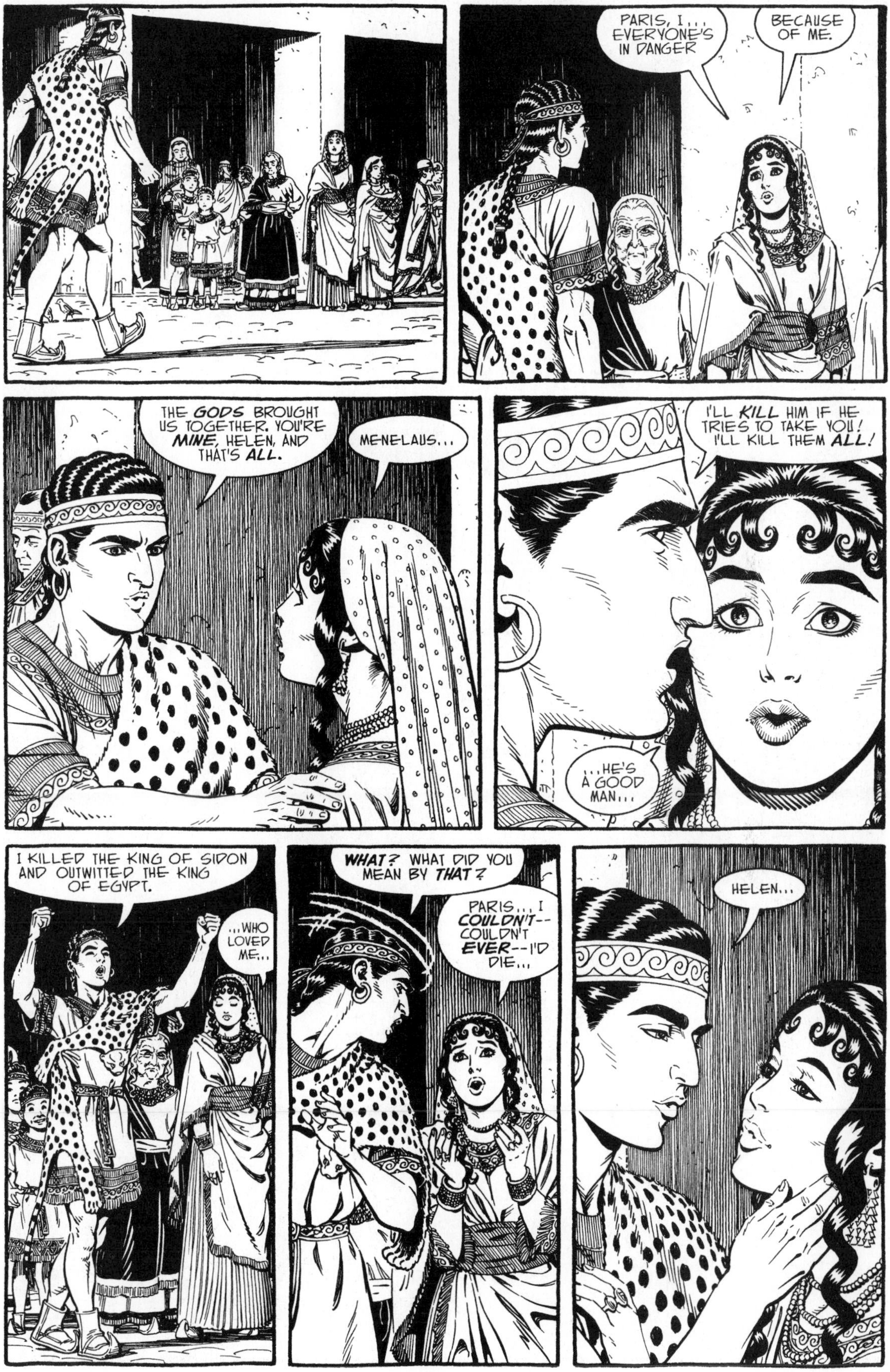
PARIS, I... EVERYONE'S IN DANGER
BECAUSE OF ME.
THE GODS BROUGHT US TOGETHER. YOU'RE MINE, HELEN, AND THAT'S ALL.
MENELAUS...
I'LL KILL HIM IF HE TRIES TO TAKE YOU! I'LL KILL THEM ALL!
...HE'S A GOOD MAN...
I KILLED THE KING OF SIDON AND OUTWITTED THE KING OF EGYPT.
...WHO LOVED ME...
WHAT? WHAT DID YOU MEAN BY THAT?
PARIS... I COULDN'T-- COULDN'T EVER--I'D DIE...
HELEN...

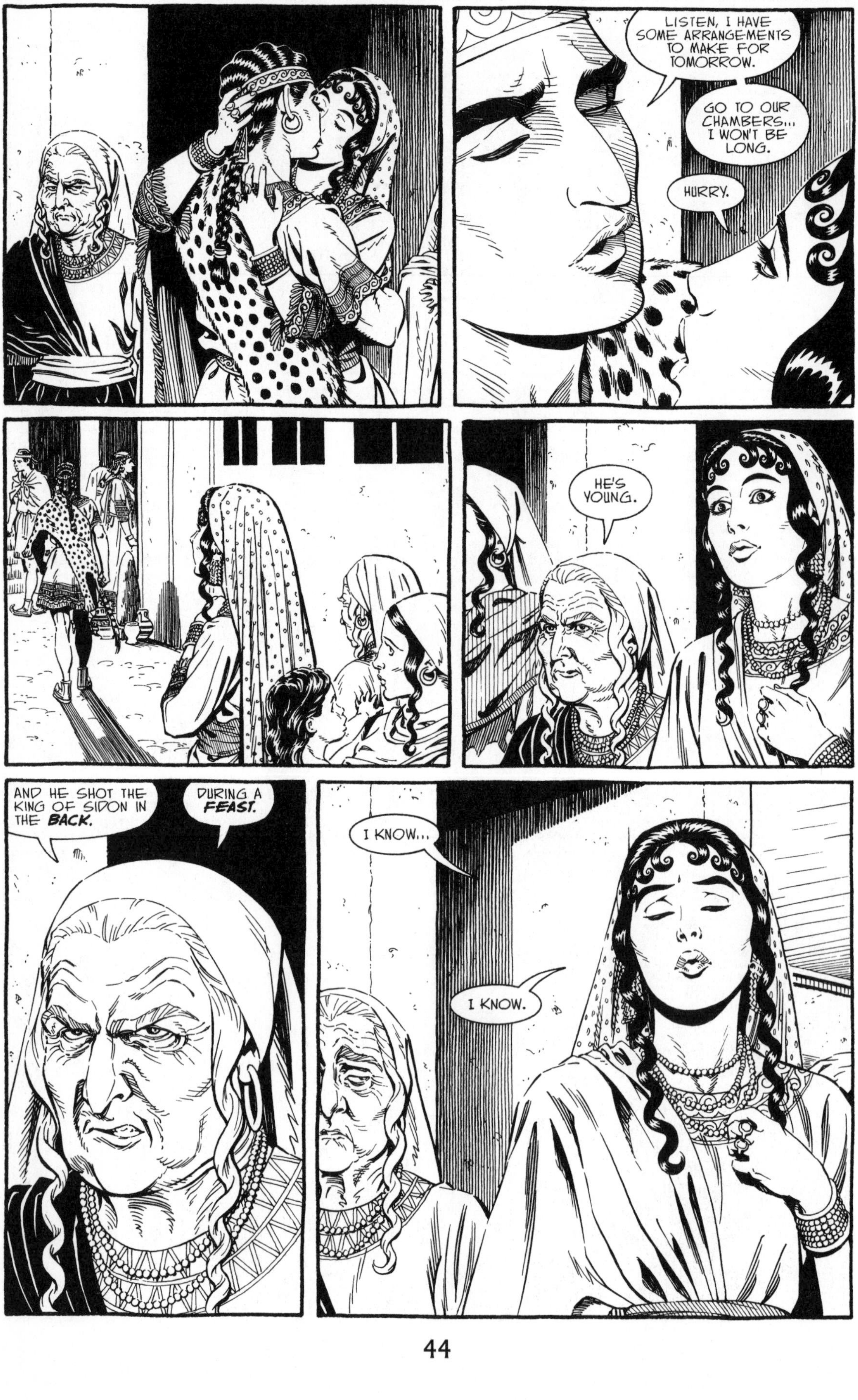

LISTEN, I HAVE SOME ARRANGEMENTS TO MAKE FOR TOMORROW.
GO TO OUR CHAMBERS... I WON'T BE LONG.
HURRY.
HE'S YOUNG.
AND HE SHOT THE KING OF SIDON IN THE **BACK.**
DURING A **FEAST.**
I KNOW...
I KNOW.

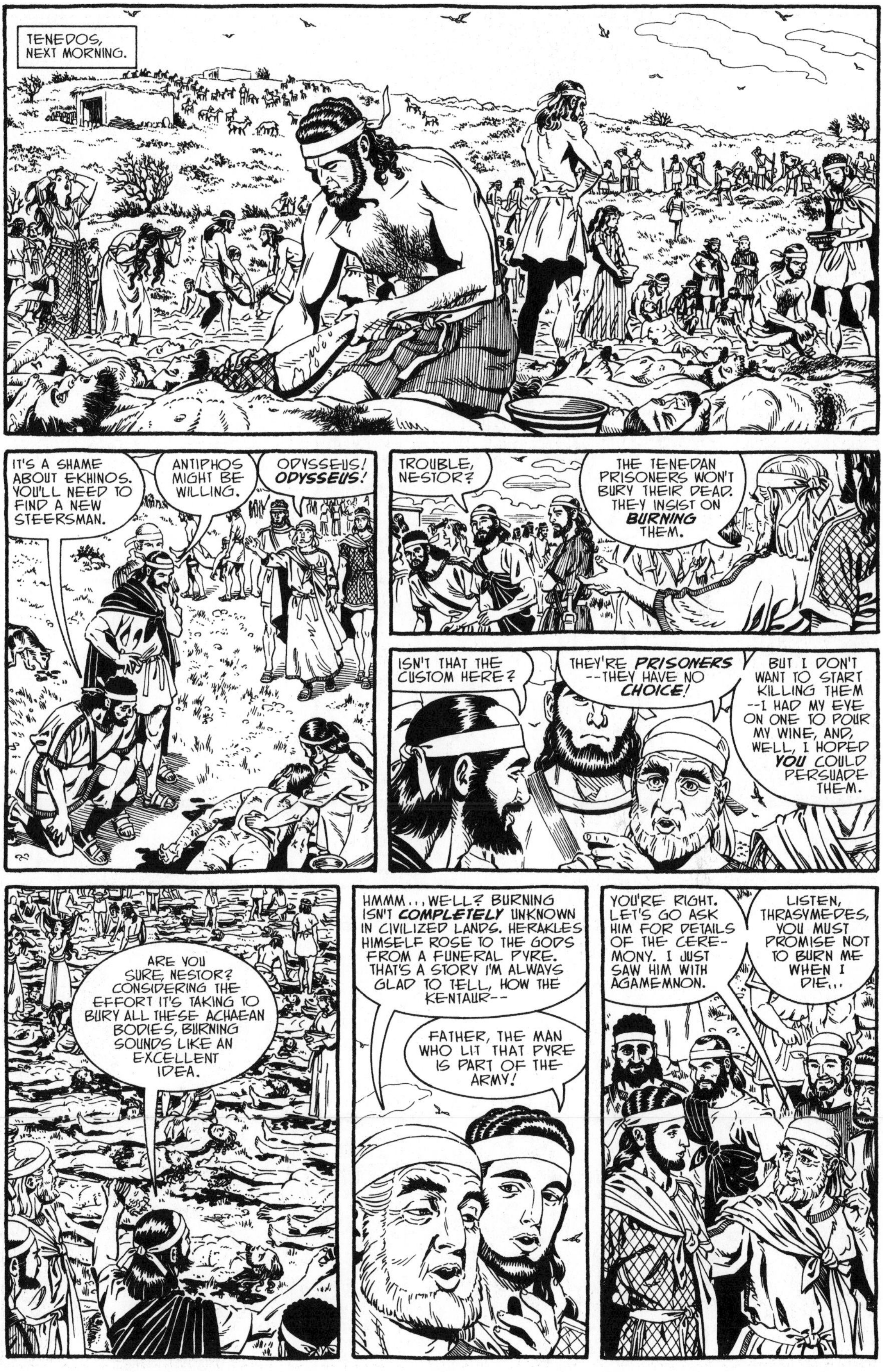
TENEDOS,
NEXT MORNING.
IT'S A SHAME ABOUT EKHINOS. YOU'LL NEED TO FIND A NEW STEERSMAN.
ANTIPHOS MIGHT BE WILLING.
ODYSSEUS! ODYSSEUS!
TROUBLE, NESTOR?
THE TENEDAN PRISONERS WON'T BURY THEIR DEAD. THEY INSIST ON BURNING THEM.
ISN'T THAT THE CUSTOM HERE?
THEY'RE PRISONERS --THEY HAVE NO CHOICE!
BUT I DON'T WANT TO START KILLING THEM --I HAD MY EYE ON ONE TO POUR MY WINE, AND, WELL, I HOPED YOU COULD PERSUADE THEM.
ARE YOU SURE, NESTOR? CONSIDERING THE EFFORT IT'S TAKING TO BURY ALL THESE ACHAEAN BODIES, BURNING SOUNDS LIKE AN EXCELLENT IDEA.
HMMM... WELL? BURNING ISN'T COMPLETELY UNKNOWN IN CIVILIZED LANDS. HERAKLES HIMSELF ROSE TO THE GODS FROM A FUNERAL PYRE. THAT'S A STORY I'M ALWAYS GLAD TO TELL, HOW THE KENTAUR--
FATHER, THE MAN WHO LIT THAT PYRE IS PART OF THE ARMY!
YOU'RE RIGHT. LET'S GO ASK HIM FOR DETAILS OF THE CEREMONY. I JUST SAW HIM WITH AGAMEMNON.
LISTEN, THRASYMEDES, YOU MUST PROMISE NOT TO BURN ME WHEN I DIE...

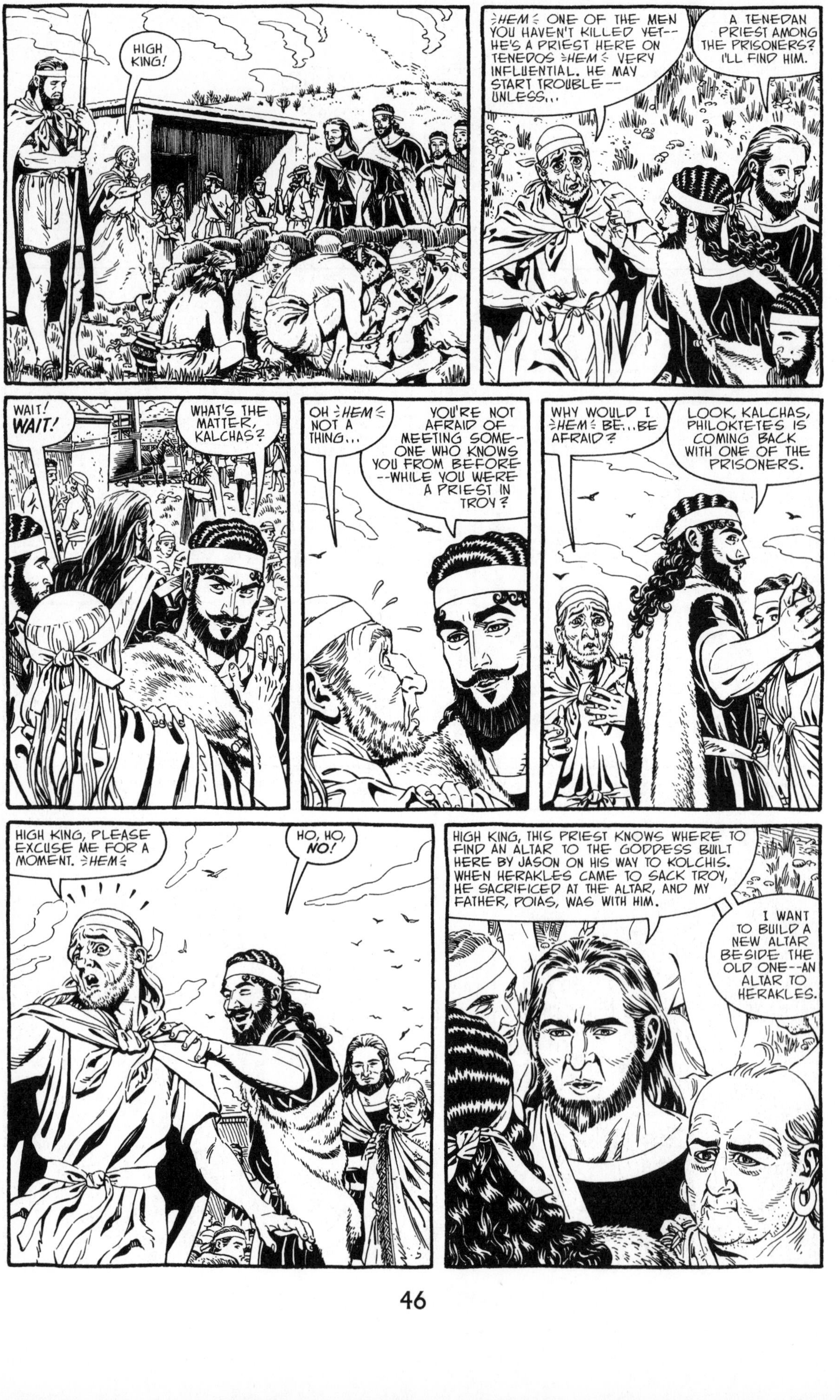
HIGH KING!
≶HEM≷ ONE OF THE MEN YOU HAVEN'T KILLED YET--HE'S A PRIEST HERE ON TENEDOS ≶HEM≷ VERY INFLUENTIAL. HE MAY START TROUBLE--UNLESS...
A TENEDAN PRIEST AMONG THE PRISONERS? I'LL FIND HIM.
WAIT! WAIT!
WHAT'S THE MATTER, KALCHAS?
OH ≶HEM≷ NOT A THING...
YOU'RE NOT AFRAID OF MEETING SOMEONE WHO KNOWS YOU FROM BEFORE--WHILE YOU WERE A PRIEST IN TROY?
WHY WOULD I ≶HEM≷ BE...BE AFRAID?
LOOK, KALCHAS, PHILOKTETES IS COMING BACK WITH ONE OF THE PRISONERS.
HIGH KING, PLEASE EXCUSE ME FOR A MOMENT. ≶HEM≷
HO, HO, NO!
HIGH KING, THIS PRIEST KNOWS WHERE TO FIND AN ALTAR TO THE GODDESS BUILT HERE BY JASON ON HIS WAY TO KOLCHIS. WHEN HERAKLES CAME TO SACK TROY, HE SACRIFICED AT THE ALTAR, AND MY FATHER, POIAS, WAS WITH HIM.
I WANT TO BUILD A NEW ALTAR BESIDE THE OLD ONE--AN ALTAR TO HERAKLES.

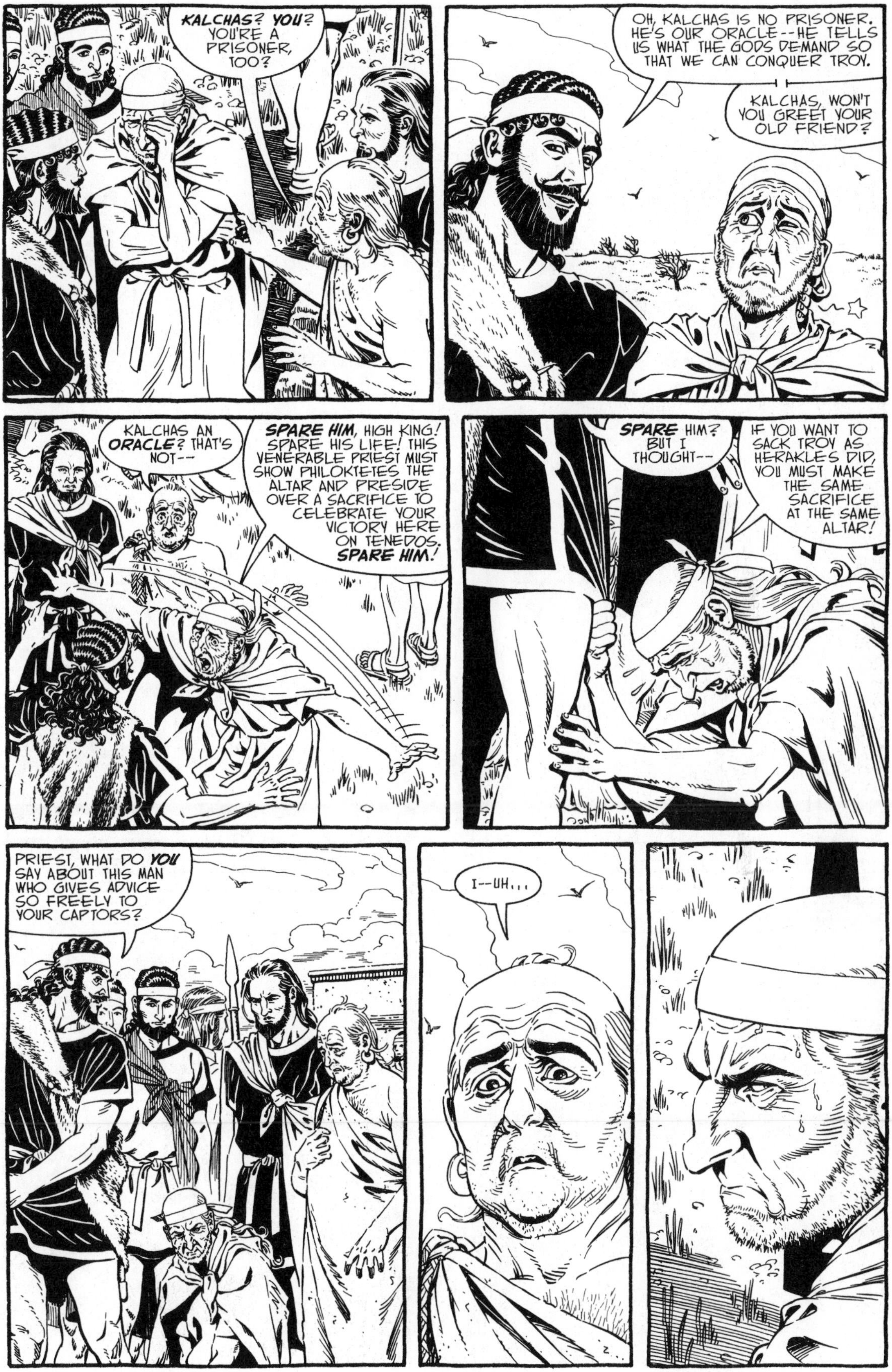
KALCHAS? YOU? YOU'RE A PRISONER, TOO?
OH, KALCHAS IS NO PRISONER. HE'S OUR ORACLE--HE TELLS US WHAT THE GODS DEMAND SO THAT WE CAN CONQUER TROY.
KALCHAS, WON'T YOU GREET YOUR OLD FRIEND?
KALCHAS AN ORACLE? THAT'S NOT--
SPARE HIM, HIGH KING! SPARE HIS LIFE! THIS VENERABLE PRIEST MUST SHOW PHILOKTETES THE ALTAR AND PRESIDE OVER A SACRIFICE TO CELEBRATE YOUR VICTORY HERE ON TENEDOS. SPARE HIM!
SPARE HIM? BUT I THOUGHT--
IF YOU WANT TO SACK TROY AS HERAKLES DID, YOU MUST MAKE THE SAME SACRIFICE AT THE SAME ALTAR!
PRIEST, WHAT DO YOU SAY ABOUT THIS MAN WHO GIVES ADVICE SO FREELY TO YOUR CAPTORS?
I--UH...

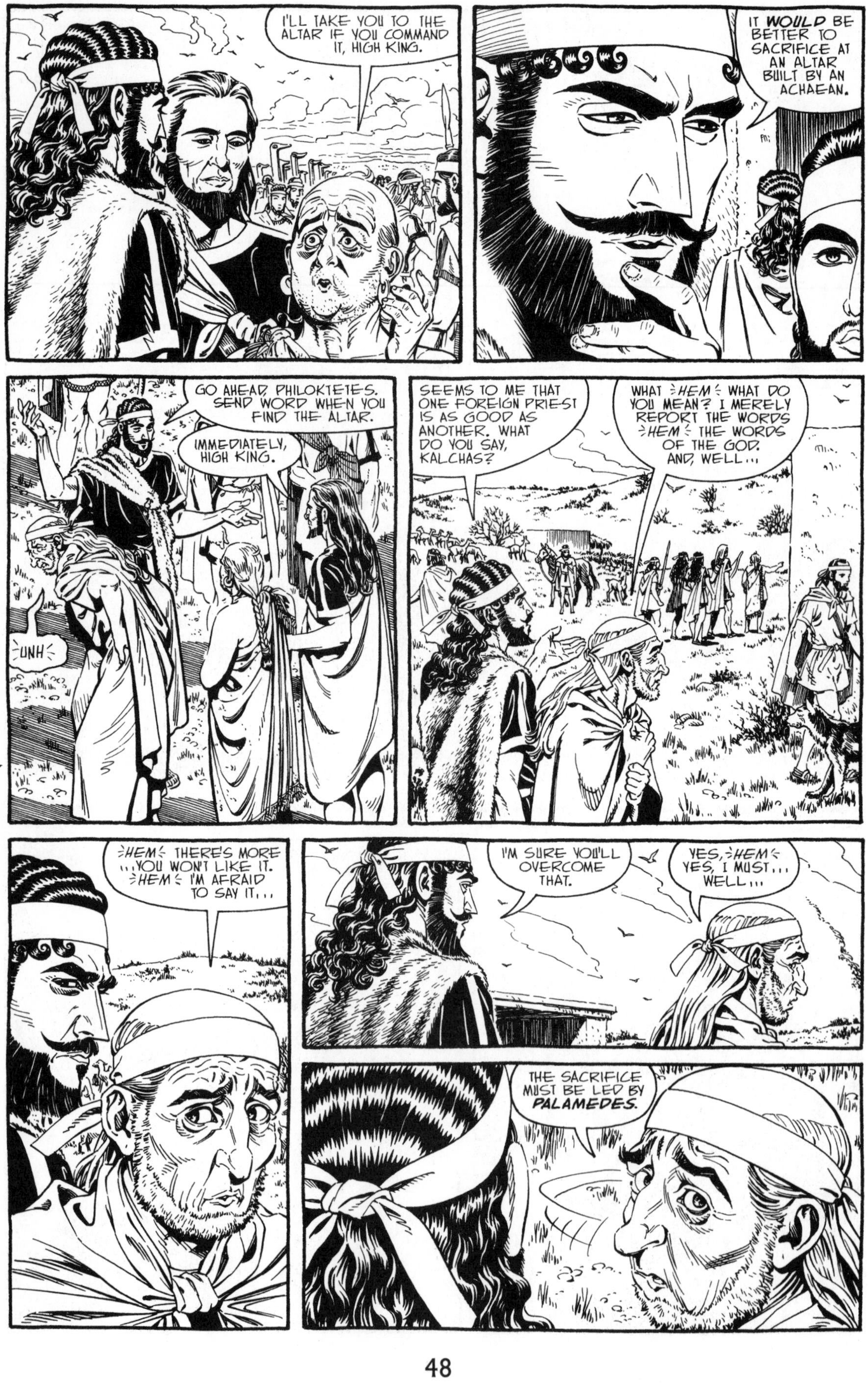
I'LL TAKE YOU TO THE ALTAR IF YOU COMMAND IT, HIGH KING.
IT WOULD BE BETTER TO SACRIFICE AT AN ALTAR BUILT BY AN ACHAEAN.
GO AHEAD, PHILOKTETES. SEND WORD WHEN YOU FIND THE ALTAR.
IMMEDIATELY, HIGH KING.
UNH
SEEMS TO ME THAT ONE FOREIGN PRIEST IS AS GOOD AS ANOTHER. WHAT DO YOU SAY, KALCHAS?
WHAT HEM WHAT DO YOU MEAN? I MERELY REPORT THE WORDS HEM THE WORDS OF THE GOD. AND, WELL...
HEM THERE'S MORE ...YOU WON'T LIKE IT. HEM I'M AFRAID TO SAY IT...
I'M SURE YOU'LL OVERCOME THAT.
YES, HEM YES, I MUST... WELL...
THE SACRIFICE MUST BE LED BY PALAMEDES.

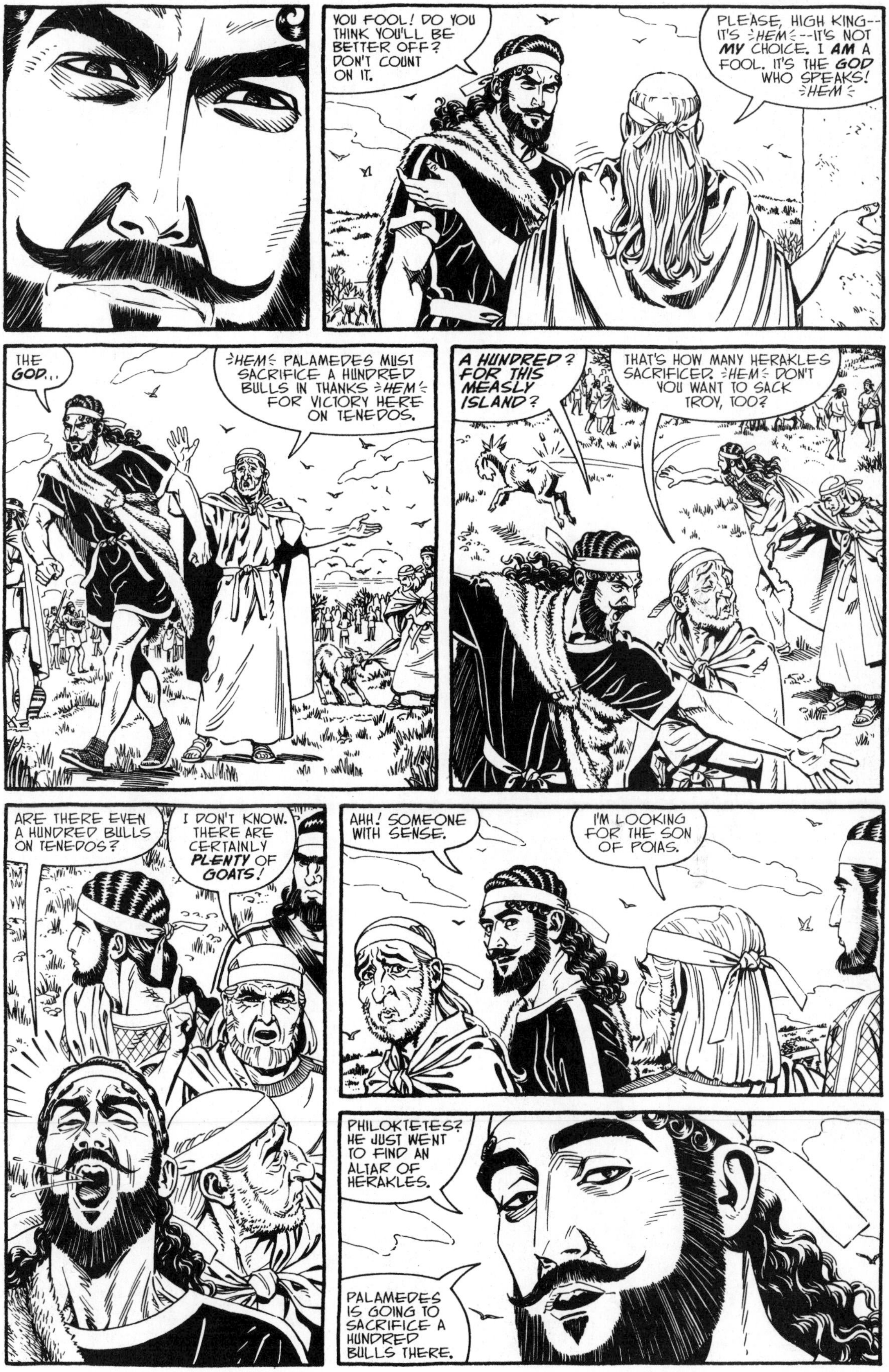

YOU FOOL! DO YOU THINK YOU'LL BE BETTER OFF? DON'T COUNT ON IT.
PLEASE, HIGH KING-- IT'S *HEM* --IT'S NOT **MY** CHOICE. I **AM** A FOOL. IT'S THE **GOD** WHO SPEAKS! *HEM*
THE **GOD**...
HEM PALAMEDES MUST SACRIFICE A HUNDRED BULLS IN THANKS *HEM* FOR VICTORY HERE ON TENEDOS.
A HUNDRED? FOR THIS MEASLY ISLAND?
THAT'S HOW MANY HERAKLES SACRIFICED. *HEM* DON'T YOU WANT TO SACK TROY, TOO?
ARE THERE EVEN A HUNDRED BULLS ON TENEDOS?
I DON'T KNOW. THERE ARE CERTAINLY **PLENTY** OF **GOATS**!
AHH! SOMEONE WITH SENSE.
I'M LOOKING FOR THE SON OF POIAS.
PHILOKTETES? HE JUST WENT TO FIND AN ALTAR OF HERAKLES.
PALAMEDES IS GOING TO SACRIFICE A HUNDRED BULLS THERE.

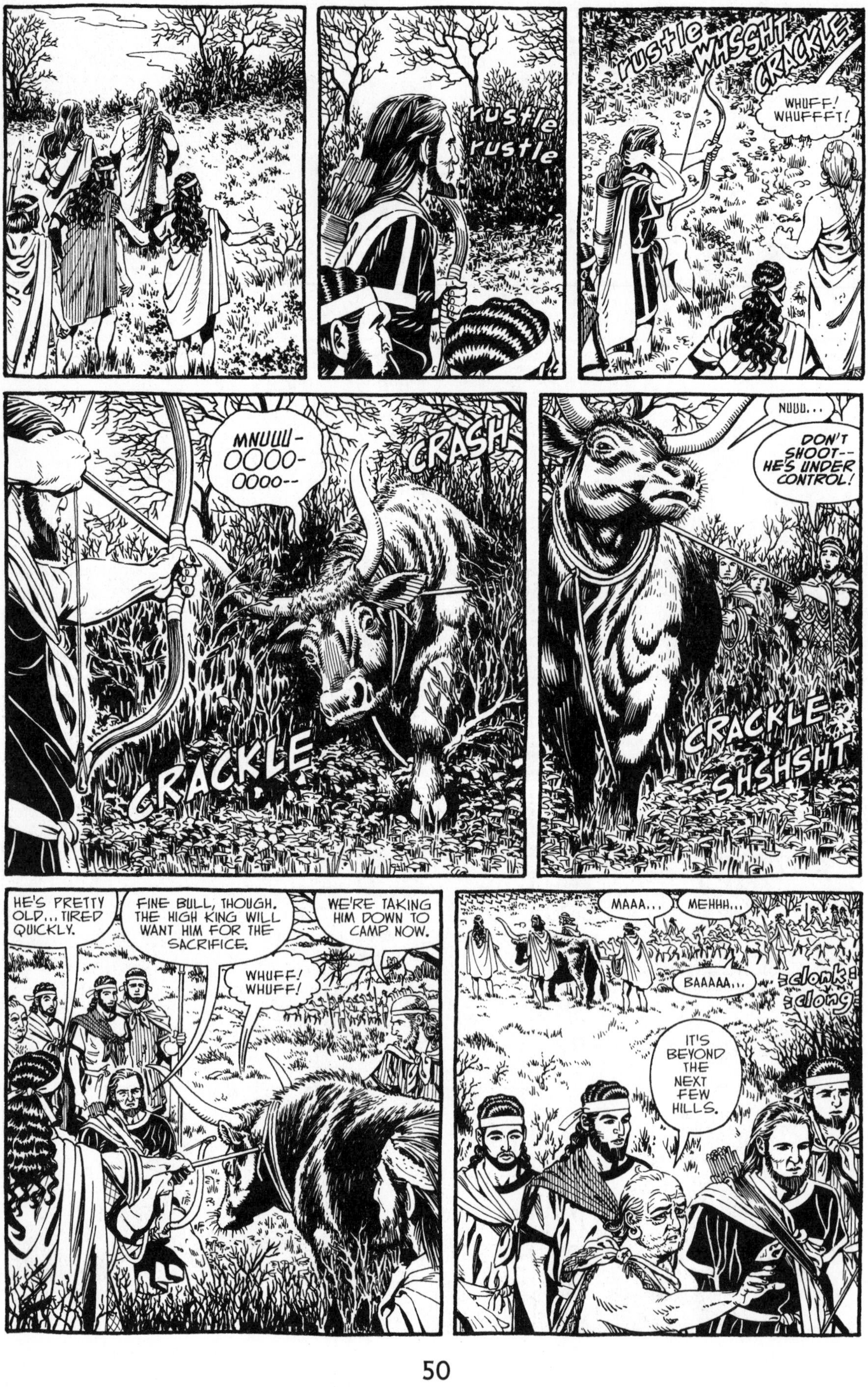
rustle rustle
rustle
WHSSHT
CRACKLE
WHUFF! WHUFFFT!
MNUUU-OOOO-OOOO--
CRASH
CRACKLE
NUUU...
DON'T SHOOT-- HE'S UNDER CONTROL!
CRACKLE
SHSHSHT
HE'S PRETTY OLD... TIRED QUICKLY.
FINE BULL, THOUGH. THE HIGH KING WILL WANT HIM FOR THE SACRIFICE.
WE'RE TAKING HIM DOWN TO CAMP NOW.
WHUFF! WHUFF!
MAAA...
MEHHH...
BAAAAA...
clonk
clong
IT'S BEYOND THE NEXT FEW HILLS.

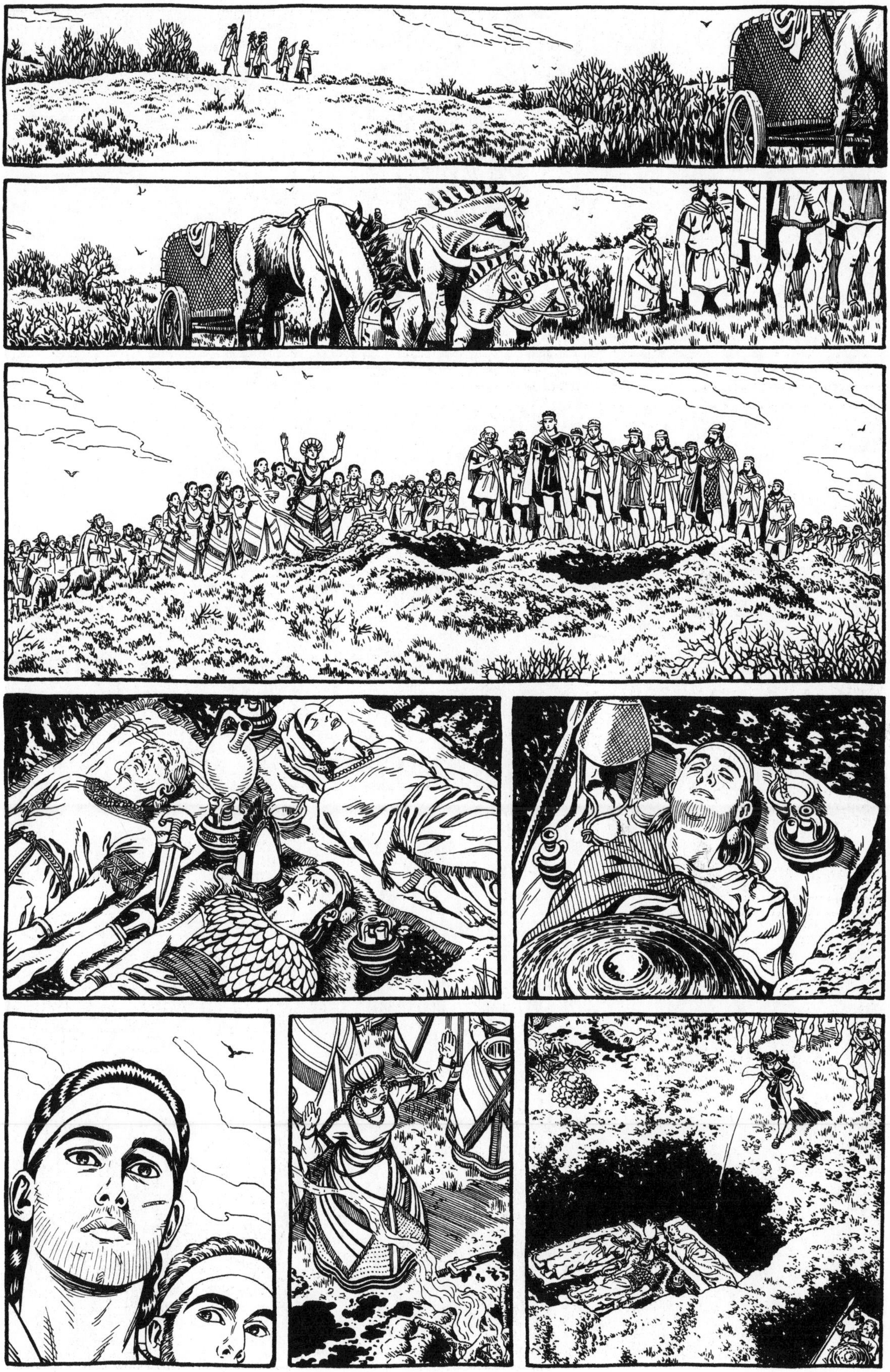

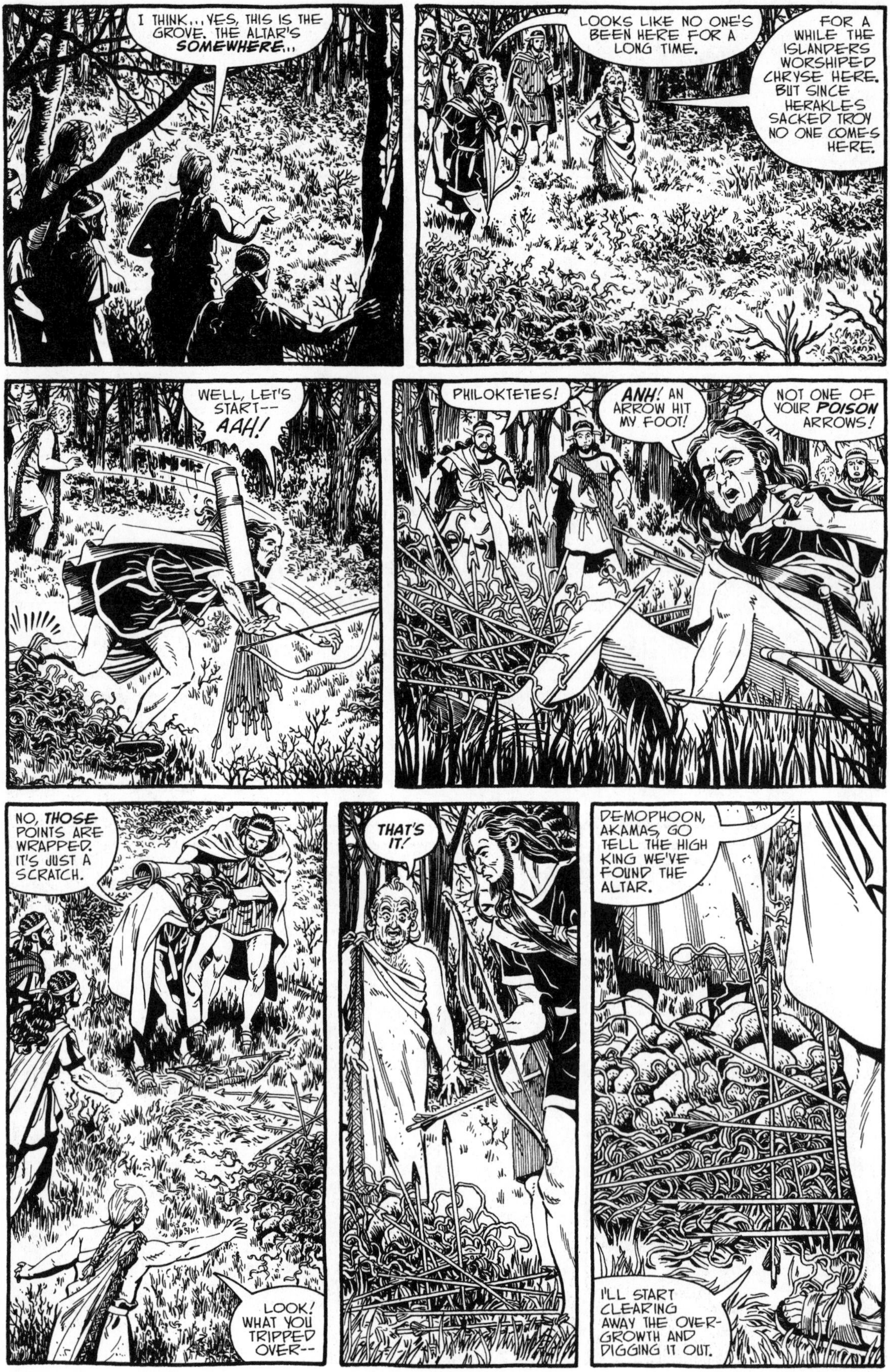
I THINK... YES, THIS IS THE GROVE. THE ALTAR'S **SOMEWHERE**...
LOOKS LIKE NO ONE'S BEEN HERE FOR A LONG TIME.
FOR A WHILE THE ISLANDERS WORSHIPED CHRYSE HERE. BUT SINCE HERAKLES SACKED TROY NO ONE COMES HERE.
WELL, LET'S START-- **AAH!**
PHILOKTETES!
ANH! AN ARROW HIT MY FOOT!
NOT ONE OF YOUR **POISON** ARROWS!
NO, **THOSE** POINTS ARE WRAPPED. IT'S JUST A SCRATCH.
LOOK! WHAT YOU TRIPPED OVER--
THAT'S IT!
DEMOPHOON, AKAMAS, GO TELL THE HIGH KING WE'VE FOUND THE ALTAR.
I'LL START CLEARING AWAY THE OVER-GROWTH AND DIGGING IT OUT.

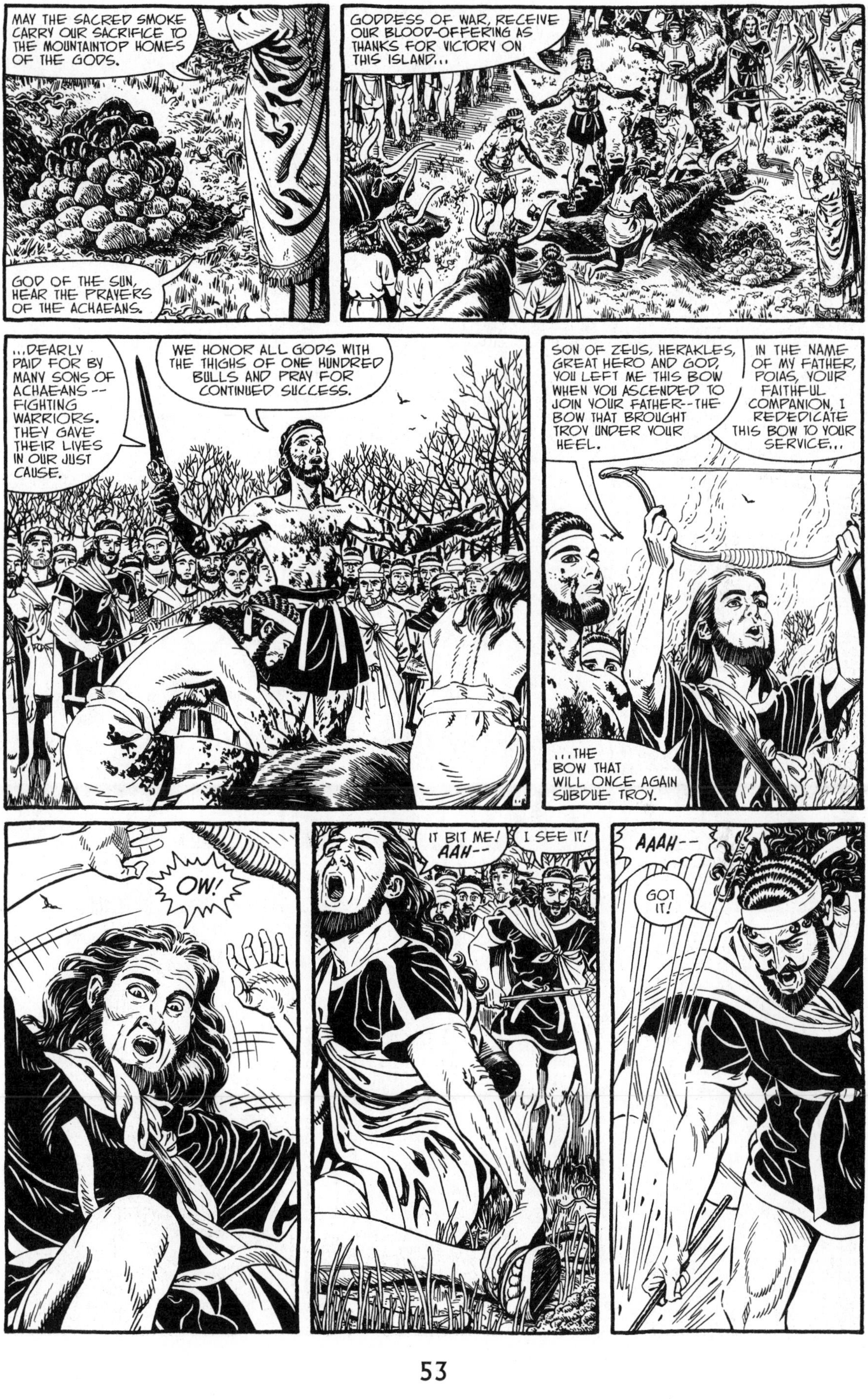

MAY THE SACRED SMOKE CARRY OUR SACRIFICE TO THE MOUNTAINTOP HOMES OF THE GODS.
GOD OF THE SUN, HEAR THE PRAYERS OF THE ACHAEANS.
GODDESS OF WAR, RECEIVE OUR BLOOD-OFFERING AS THANKS FOR VICTORY ON THIS ISLAND...
...DEARLY PAID FOR BY MANY SONS OF ACHAEANS -- FIGHTING WARRIORS. THEY GAVE THEIR LIVES IN OUR JUST CAUSE.
WE HONOR ALL GODS WITH THE THIGHS OF ONE HUNDRED BULLS AND PRAY FOR CONTINUED SUCCESS.
SON OF ZEUS, HERAKLES, GREAT HERO AND GOD, YOU LEFT ME THIS BOW WHEN YOU ASCENDED TO JOIN YOUR FATHER--THE BOW THAT BROUGHT TROY UNDER YOUR HEEL.
IN THE NAME OF MY FATHER, POIAS, YOUR FAITHFUL COMPANION, I REDEDICATE THIS BOW TO YOUR SERVICE...
...THE BOW THAT WILL ONCE AGAIN SUBDUE TROY.
OW!
IT BIT ME! AAH--
I SEE IT!
AAAH--
GOT IT!

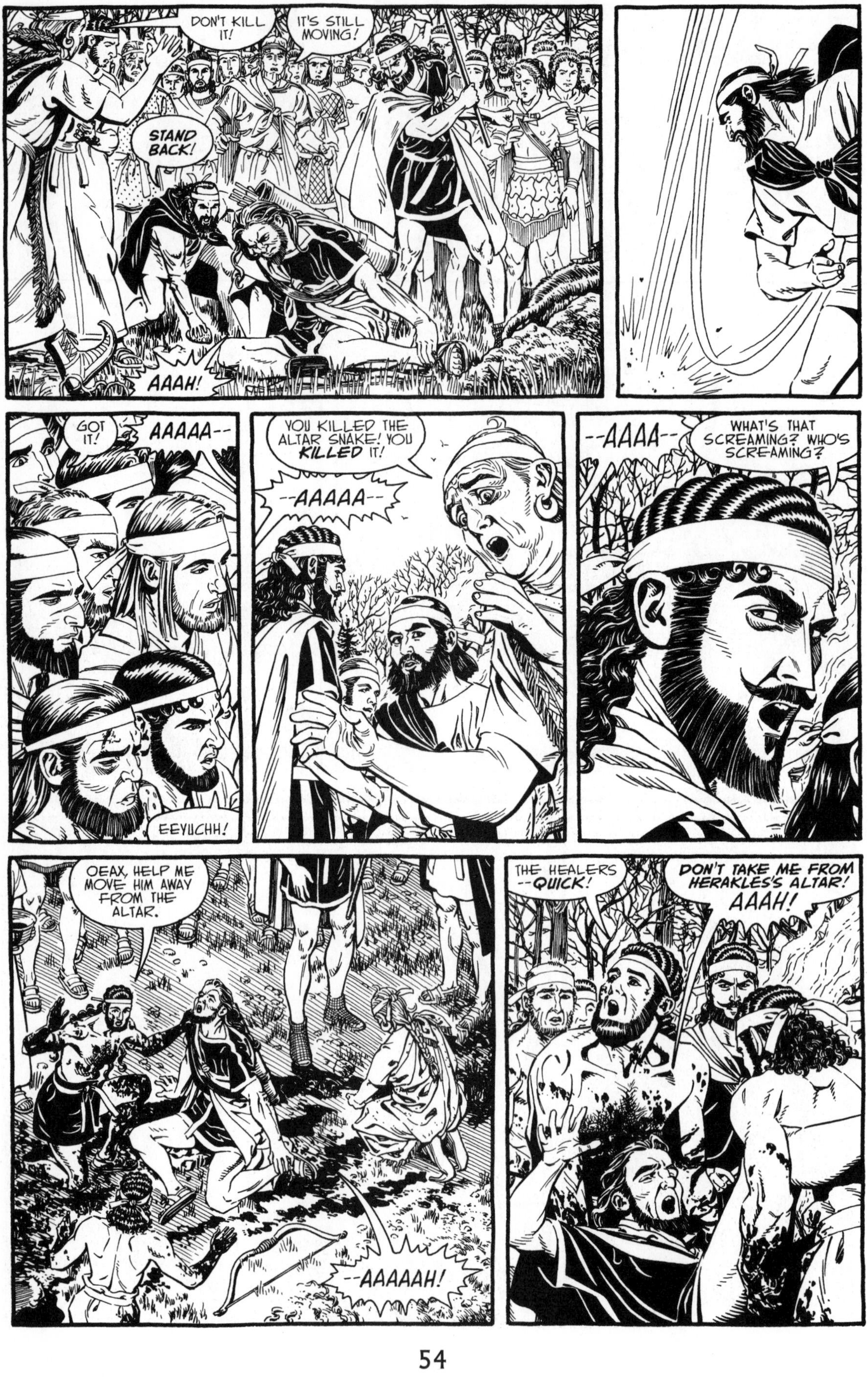
DON'T KILL IT!
IT'S STILL MOVING!
STAND BACK!
AAAH!
GOT IT!
AAAAA--
EEYUCHH!
YOU KILLED THE ALTAR SNAKE! YOU KILLED IT!
--AAAAA--
--AAAA--
WHAT'S THAT SCREAMING? WHO'S SCREAMING?
OEAX, HELP ME MOVE HIM AWAY FROM THE ALTAR.
--AAAAAH!
THE HEALERS --QUICK!
DON'T TAKE ME FROM HERAKLES'S ALTAR! AAAH!

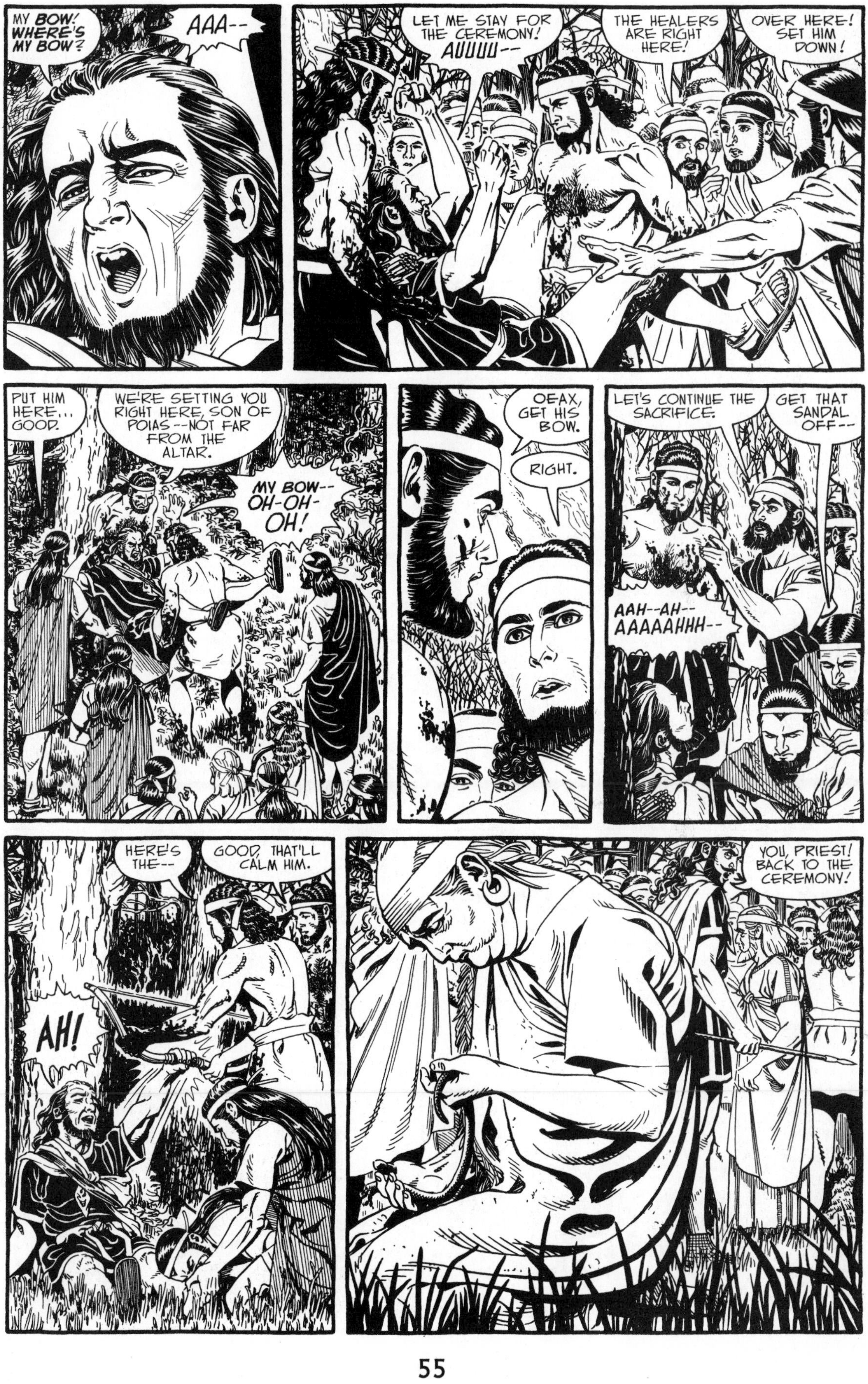
MY BOW! WHERE'S MY BOW?
AAA--
LET ME STAY FOR THE CEREMONY! AUUUU--
THE HEALERS ARE RIGHT HERE!
OVER HERE! SET HIM DOWN!
PUT HIM HERE... GOOD.
WE'RE SETTING YOU RIGHT HERE, SON OF POIAS--NOT FAR FROM THE ALTAR.
MY BOW-- OH-OH-OH!
OEAX, GET HIS BOW.
RIGHT.
LET'S CONTINUE THE SACRIFICE.
GET THAT SANDAL OFF--
AAH--AH-- AAAAAHHH--
HERE'S THE--
GOOD, THAT'LL CALM HIM.
AH!
YOU, PRIEST! BACK TO THE CEREMONY!

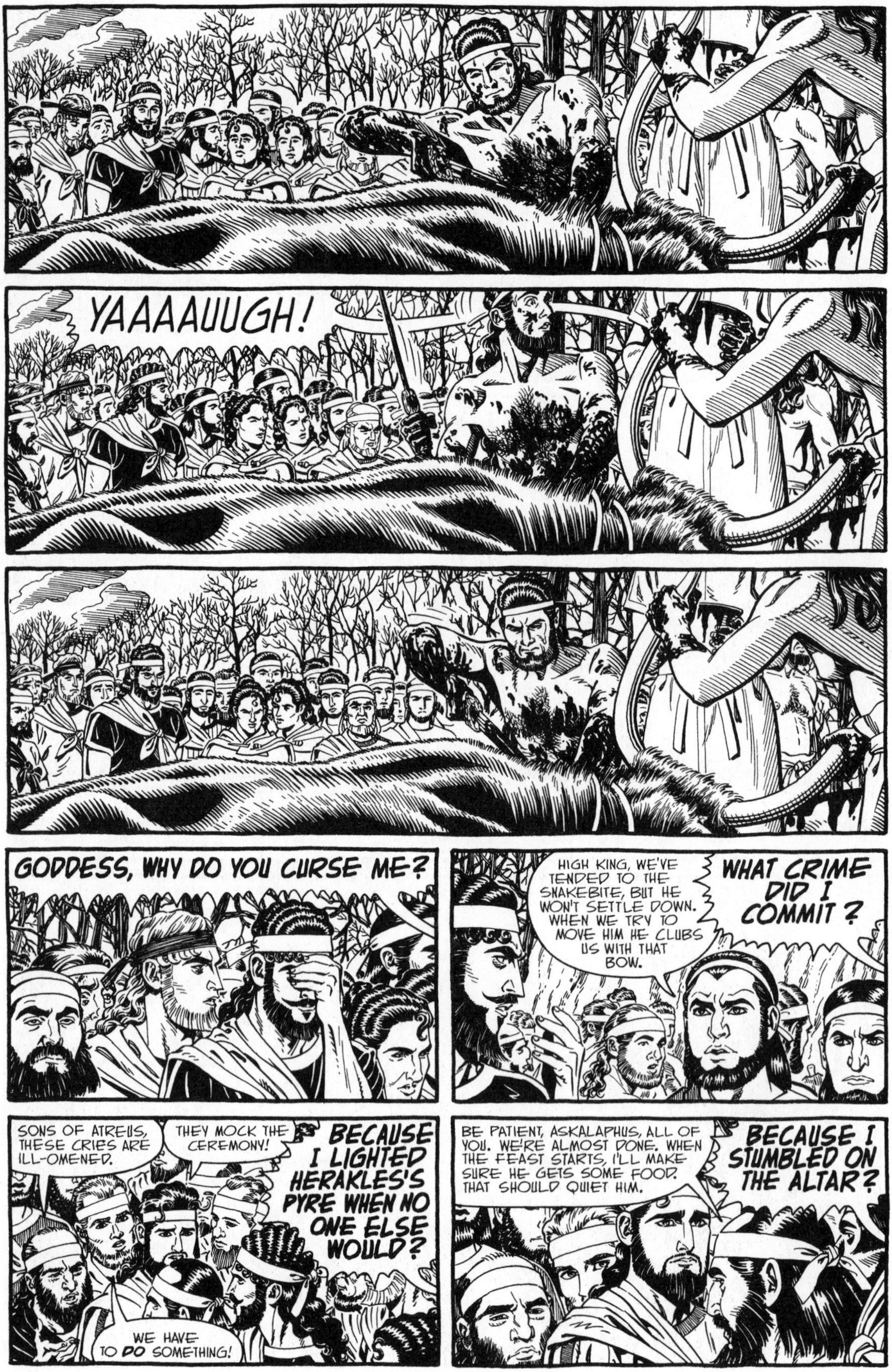
YAAAAUUGH!
GODDESS, WHY DO YOU CURSE ME?
HIGH KING, WE'VE TENDED TO THE SNAKEBITE, BUT HE WON'T SETTLE DOWN. WHEN WE TRY TO MOVE HIM HE CLUBS US WITH THAT BOW.
WHAT CRIME DID I COMMIT?
SONS OF ATREUS, THESE CRIES ARE ILL-OMENED.
THEY MOCK THE CEREMONY!
BECAUSE I LIGHTED HERAKLES'S PYRE WHEN NO ONE ELSE WOULD?
WE HAVE TO DO SOMETHING!
BE PATIENT, ASKALAPHUS, ALL OF YOU. WE'RE ALMOST DONE. WHEN THE FEAST STARTS, I'LL MAKE SURE HE GETS SOME FOOD. THAT SHOULD QUIET HIM.
BECAUSE I STUMBLED ON THE ALTAR?

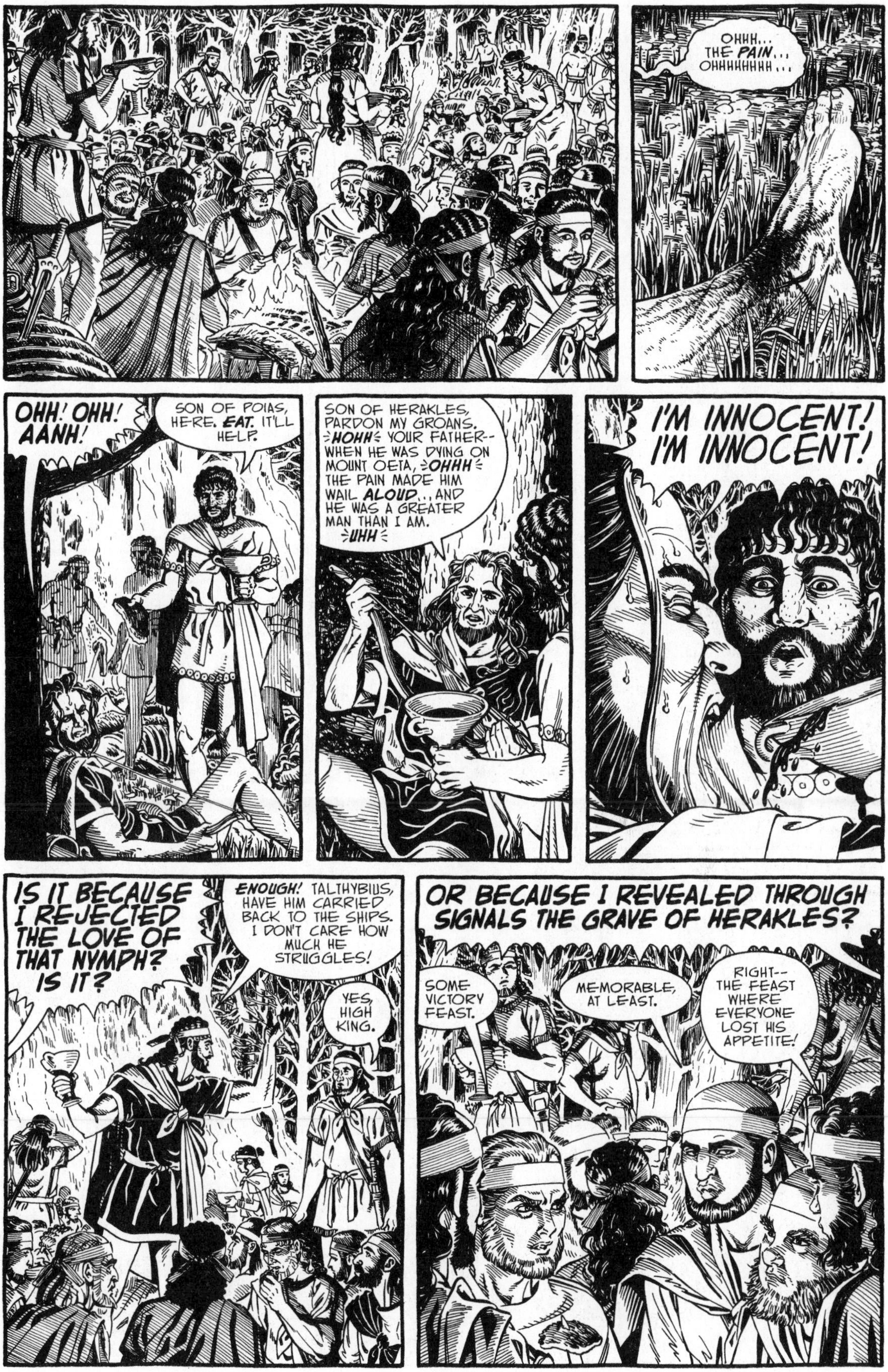
OHHH... THE PAIN... OHHHHHHHH...
OHH! OHH! AANH!
SON OF POIAS, HERE. EAT. IT'LL HELP.
SON OF HERAKLES, PARDON MY GROANS. HOHH YOUR FATHER-- WHEN HE WAS DYING ON MOUNT OETA, OHHH THE PAIN MADE HIM WAIL ALOUD... AND HE WAS A GREATER MAN THAN I AM. UHH
I'M INNOCENT! I'M INNOCENT!
IS IT BECAUSE I REJECTED THE LOVE OF THAT NYMPH? IS IT?
ENOUGH! TALTHYBIUS, HAVE HIM CARRIED BACK TO THE SHIPS. I DON'T CARE HOW MUCH HE STRUGGLES!
YES, HIGH KING.
OR BECAUSE I REVEALED THROUGH SIGNALS THE GRAVE OF HERAKLES?
SOME VICTORY FEAST.
MEMORABLE, AT LEAST.
RIGHT-- THE FEAST WHERE EVERYONE LOST HIS APPETITE!

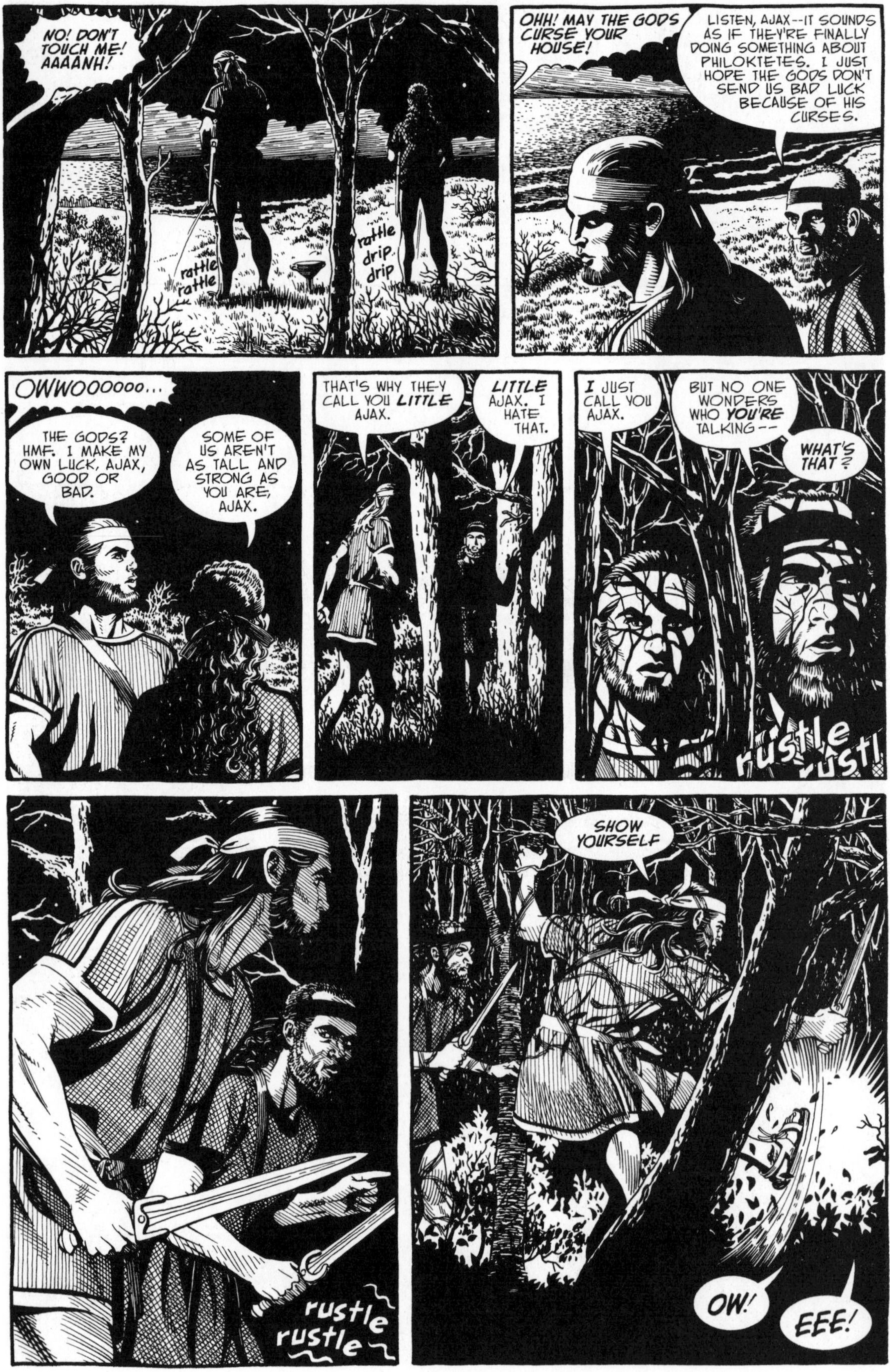

NO! DON'T TOUCH ME! AAAANH!
rattle rattle
rattle drip drip
OHH! MAY THE GODS CURSE YOUR HOUSE!
LISTEN, AJAX--IT SOUNDS AS IF THEY'RE FINALLY DOING SOMETHING ABOUT PHILOKTETES. I JUST HOPE THE GODS DON'T SEND US BAD LUCK BECAUSE OF HIS CURSES.
OWWOOOOOO...
THE GODS? HMF. I MAKE MY OWN LUCK, AJAX, GOOD OR BAD.
SOME OF US AREN'T AS TALL AND STRONG AS YOU ARE, AJAX.
THAT'S WHY THEY CALL YOU LITTLE AJAX.
LITTLE AJAX. I HATE THAT.
I JUST CALL YOU AJAX.
BUT NO ONE WONDERS WHO YOU'RE TALKING--
WHAT'S THAT?
rustle rustl
rustle rustle
SHOW YOURSELF
OW!
EEE!

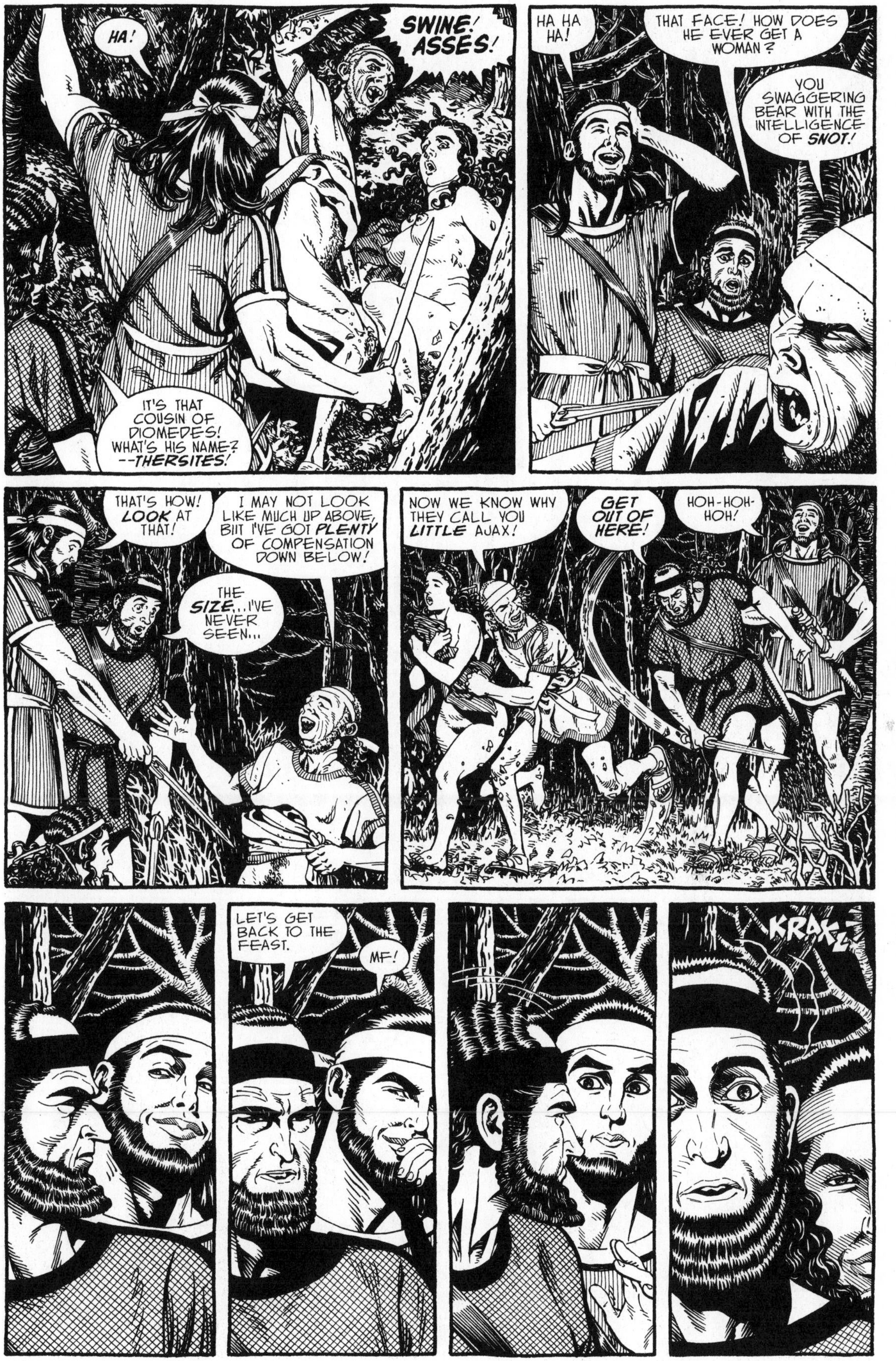
HA!
SWINE! ASSES!
IT'S THAT COUSIN OF DIOMEDES! WHAT'S HIS NAME? --THERSITES!
HA HA HA!
THAT FACE! HOW DOES HE EVER GET A WOMAN?
YOU SWAGGERING BEAR WITH THE INTELLIGENCE OF SNOT!
THAT'S HOW! LOOK AT THAT!
I MAY NOT LOOK LIKE MUCH UP ABOVE, BUT I'VE GOT PLENTY OF COMPENSATION DOWN BELOW!
THE SIZE... I'VE NEVER SEEN...
NOW WE KNOW WHY THEY CALL YOU LITTLE AJAX!
GET OUT OF HERE!
HOH-HOH-HOH!
LET'S GET BACK TO THE FEAST.
MF!
KRAK

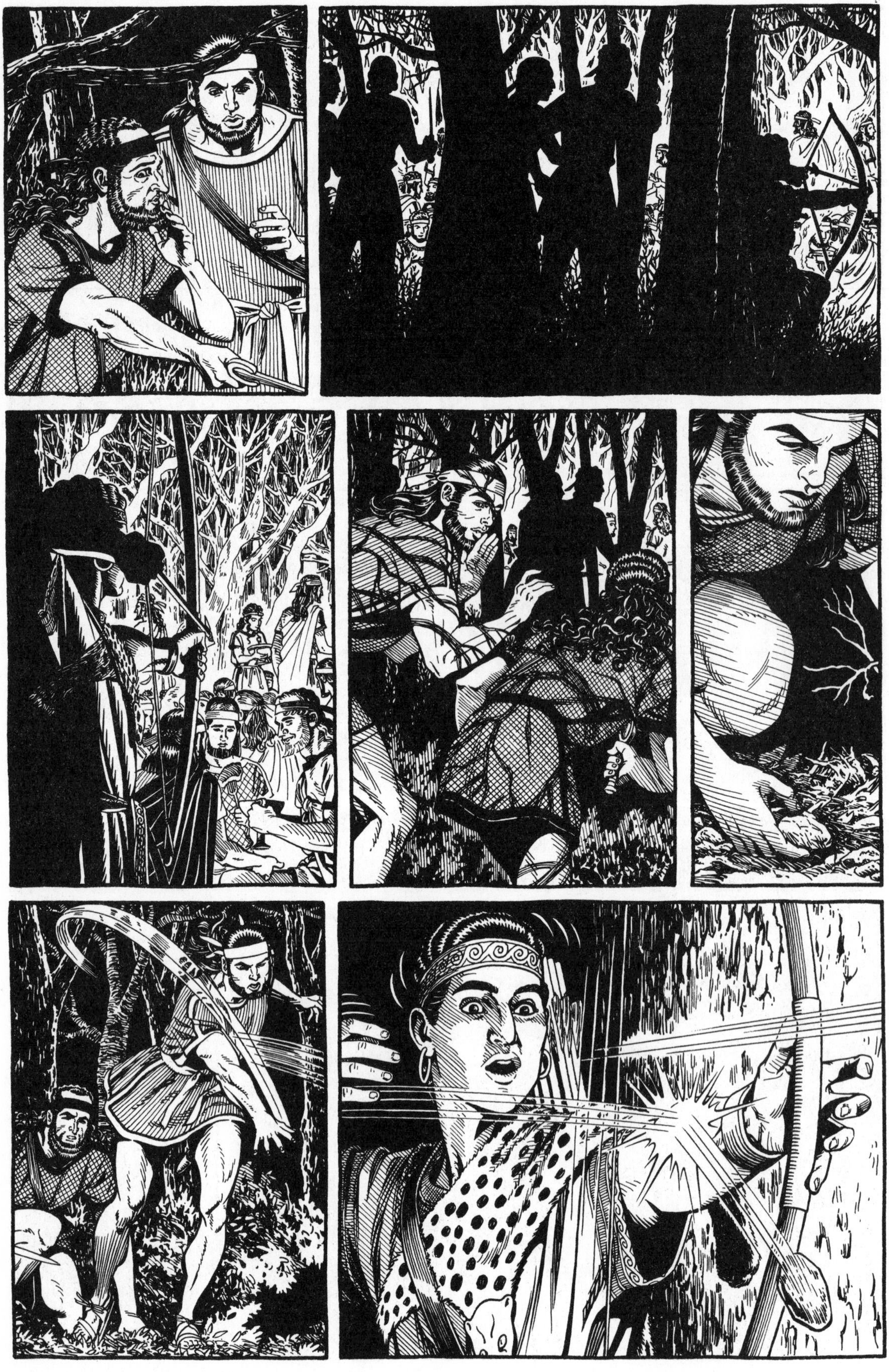

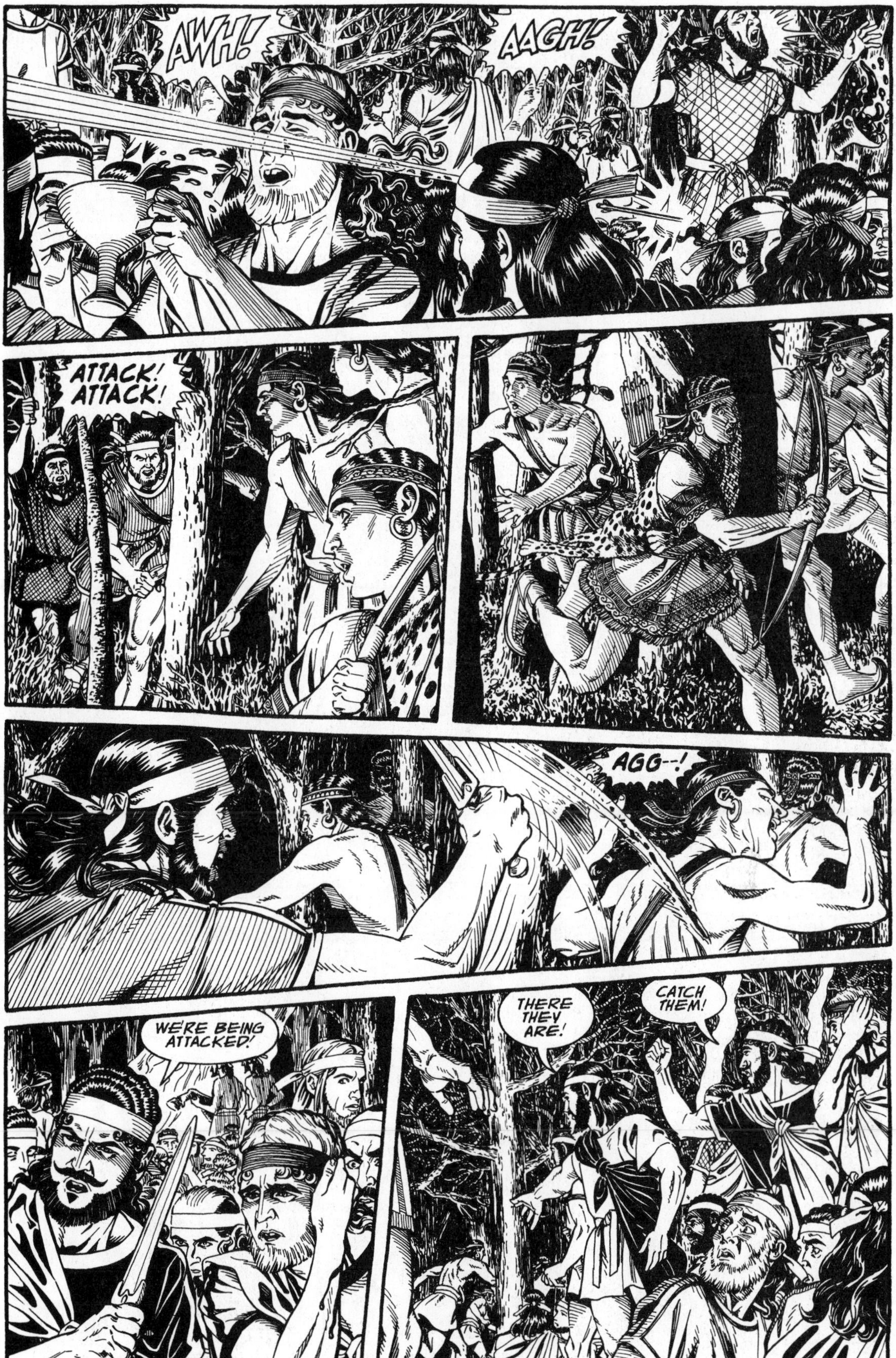
AWH!
AAGH!
ATTACK! ATTACK!
AGG--!
WE'RE BEING ATTACKED!
THERE THEY ARE!
CATCH THEM!

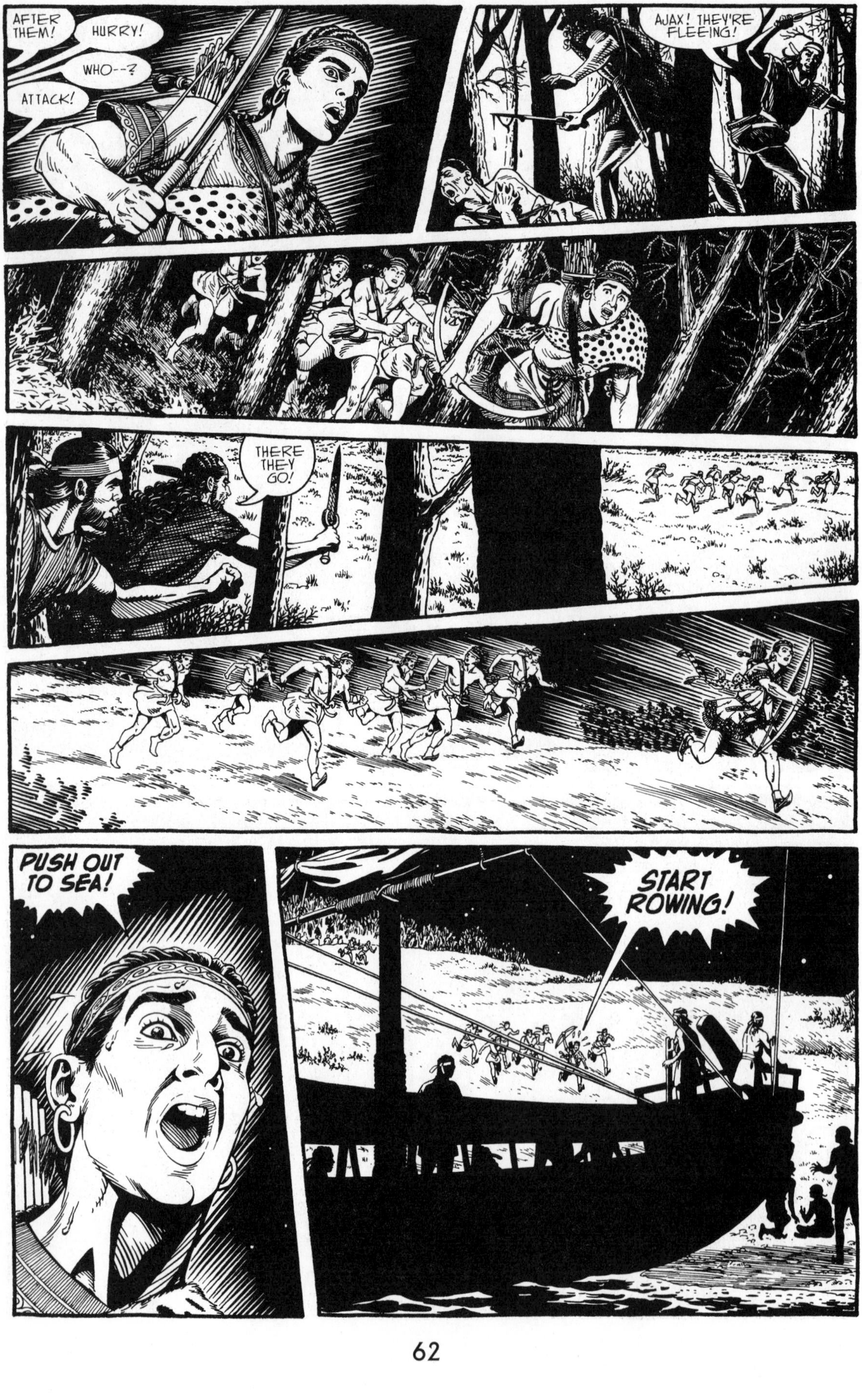
AFTER THEM!
HURRY!
WHO--?
ATTACK!
AJAX! THEY'RE FLEEING!
THERE THEY GO!
PUSH OUT TO SEA!
START ROWING!

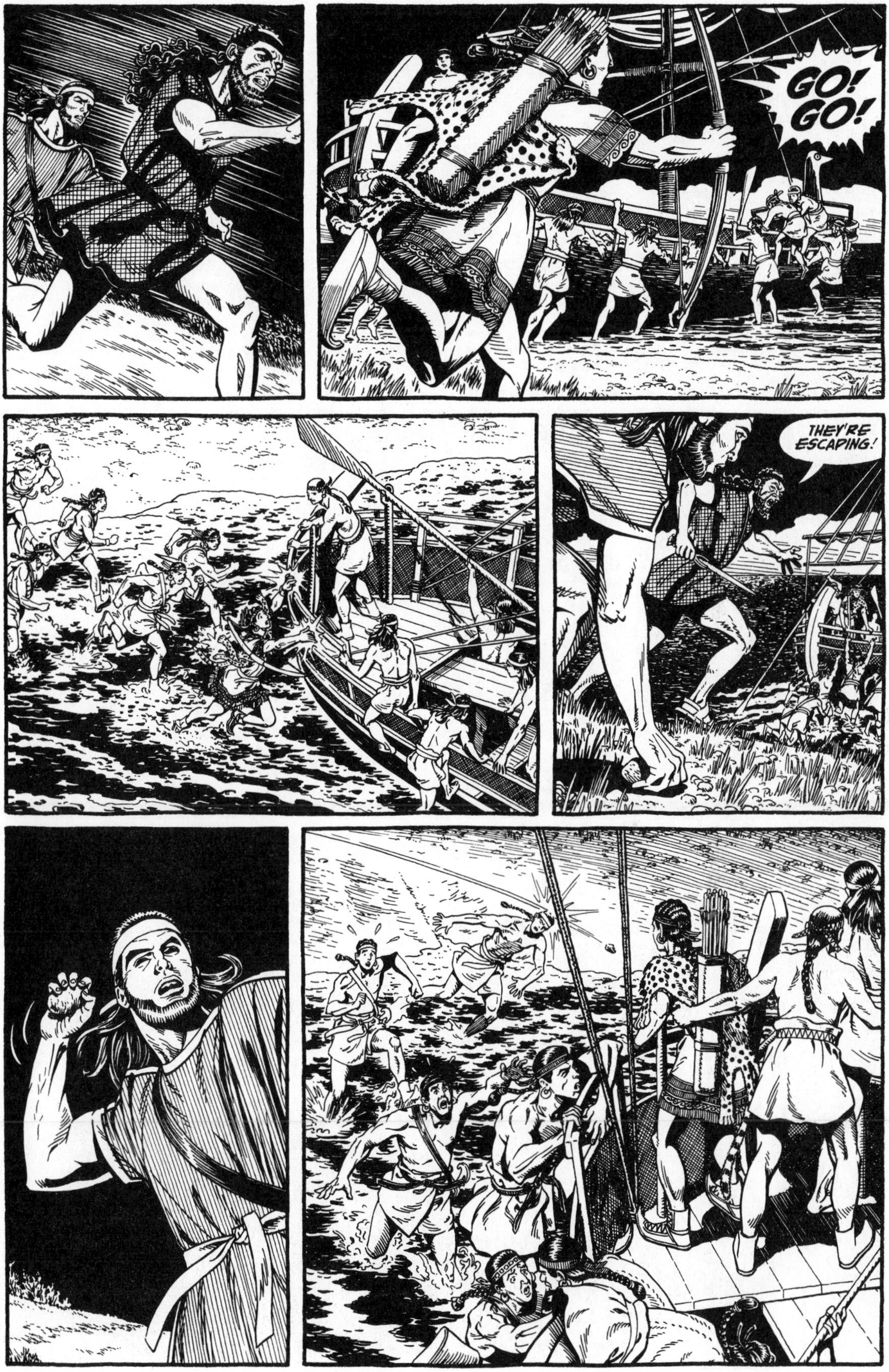
GO! GO!
THEY'RE ESCAPING!

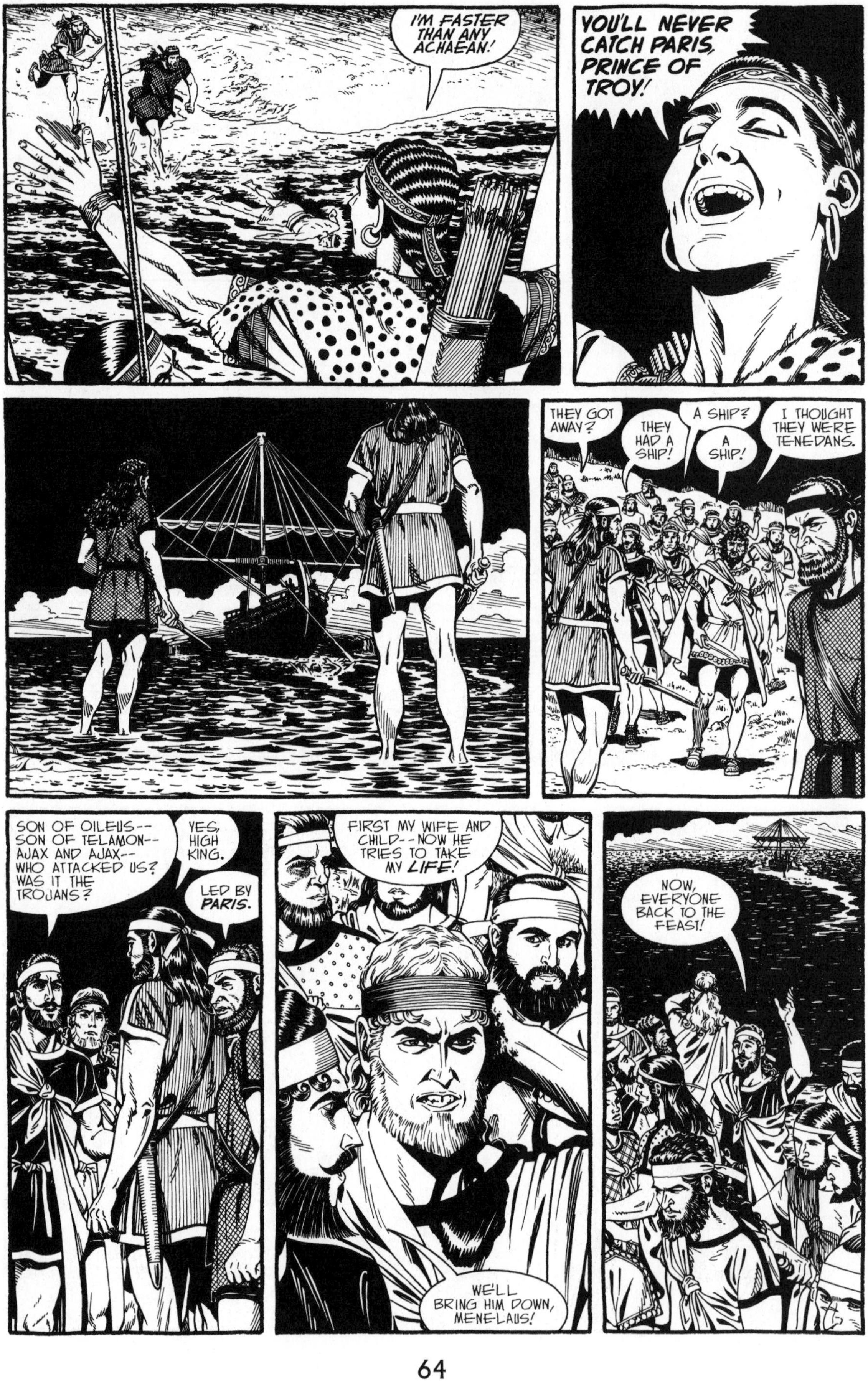
I'M FASTER THAN ANY ACHAEAN!
YOU'LL NEVER CATCH PARIS, PRINCE OF TROY!
THEY GOT AWAY?
THEY HAD A SHIP!
A SHIP?
A SHIP!
I THOUGHT THEY WERE TENEDANS.
SON OF OILEUS-- SON OF TELAMON-- AJAX AND AJAX-- WHO ATTACKED US? WAS IT THE TROJANS?
YES, HIGH KING.
LED BY PARIS.
FIRST MY WIFE AND CHILD--NOW HE TRIES TO TAKE MY LIFE!
WE'LL BRING HIM DOWN, MENELAUS!
NOW, EVERYONE BACK TO THE FEAST!

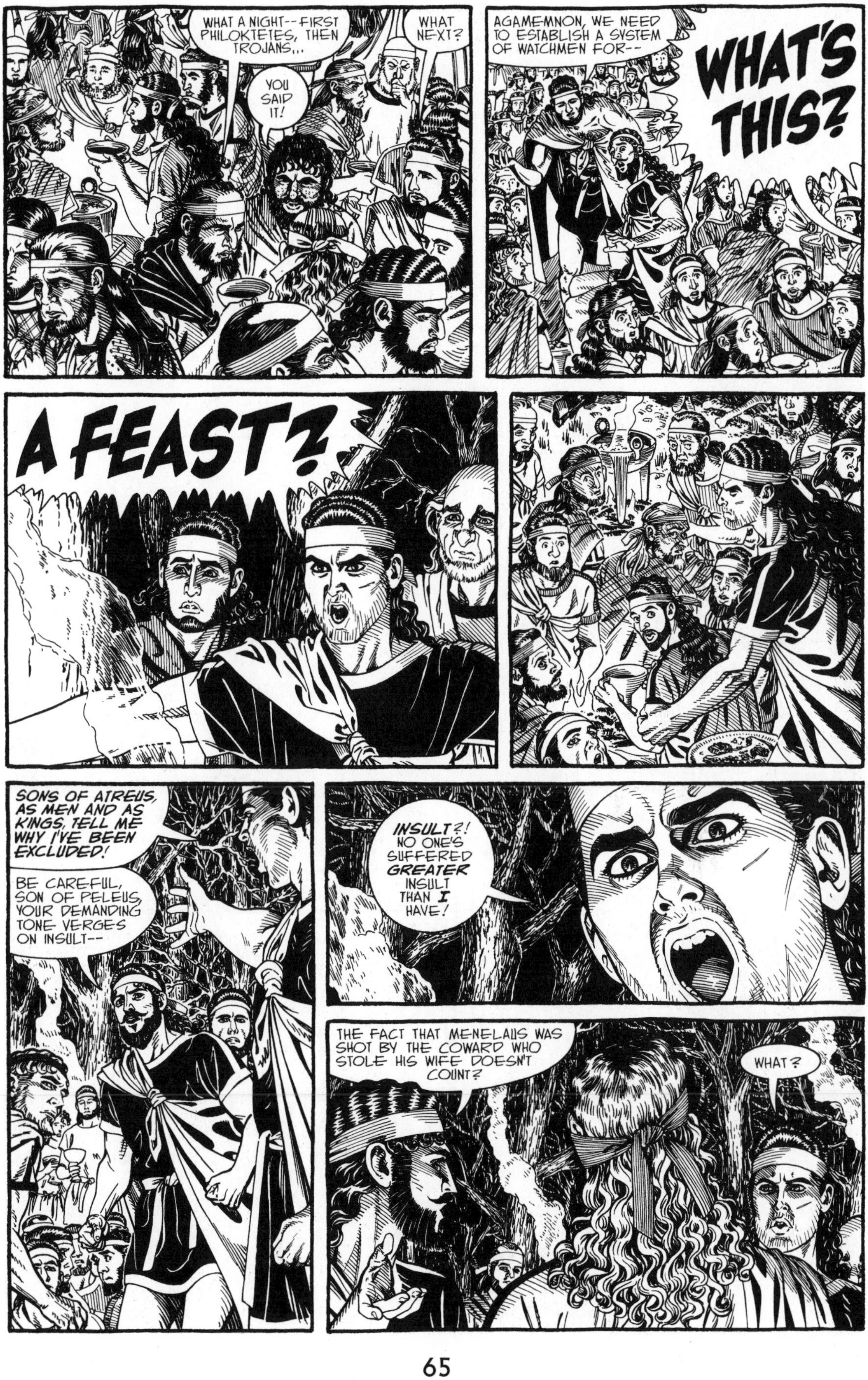
WHAT A NIGHT--FIRST PHILOKTETES, THEN TROJANS...
WHAT NEXT?
YOU SAID IT!
AGAMEMNON, WE NEED TO ESTABLISH A SYSTEM OF WATCHMEN FOR--
WHAT'S THIS?
A FEAST?
SONS OF ATREUS, AS MEN AND AS KINGS, TELL ME WHY I'VE BEEN EXCLUDED!
BE CAREFUL, SON OF PELEUS, YOUR DEMANDING TONE VERGES ON INSULT--
INSULT?! NO ONE'S SUFFERED GREATER INSULT THAN I HAVE!
THE FACT THAT MENELAUS WAS SHOT BY THE COWARD WHO STOLE HIS WIFE DOESN'T COUNT?
WHAT?

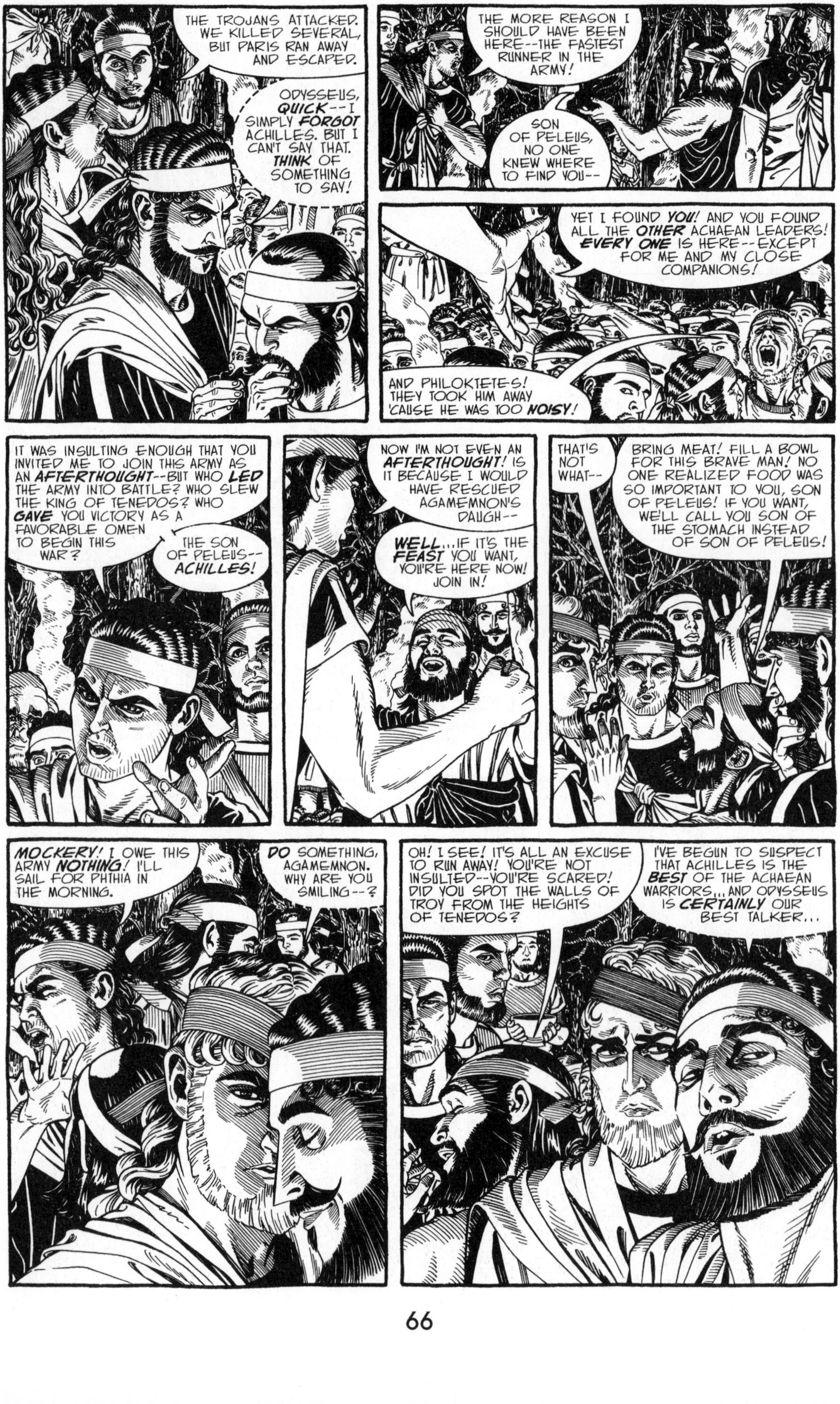
THE TROJANS ATTACKED. WE KILLED SEVERAL, BUT PARIS RAN AWAY AND ESCAPED.
ODYSSEUS, **QUICK**--I SIMPLY **FORGOT** ACHILLES. BUT I CAN'T SAY THAT. **THINK** OF SOMETHING TO SAY!
THE MORE REASON I SHOULD HAVE BEEN HERE--THE FASTEST RUNNER IN THE ARMY!
SON OF PELEUS, NO ONE KNEW WHERE TO FIND YOU--
YET I FOUND **YOU**! AND YOU FOUND ALL THE **OTHER** ACHAEAN LEADERS! **EVERY ONE** IS HERE--EXCEPT FOR ME AND MY CLOSE COMPANIONS!
AND PHILOKTETES! THEY TOOK HIM AWAY 'CAUSE HE WAS TOO **NOISY**!
IT WAS INSULTING ENOUGH THAT YOU INVITED ME TO JOIN THIS ARMY AS AN **AFTERTHOUGHT**--BUT WHO **LED** THE ARMY INTO BATTLE? WHO SLEW THE KING OF TENEDOS? WHO **GAVE** YOU VICTORY AS A FAVORABLE OMEN TO BEGIN THIS WAR?
THE SON OF PELEUS--**ACHILLES**!
NOW I'M NOT EVEN AN **AFTERTHOUGHT**! IS IT BECAUSE I WOULD HAVE RESCUED AGAMEMNON'S DAUGH--
WELL...IF IT'S THE **FEAST** YOU WANT, YOU'RE HERE NOW! JOIN IN!
THAT'S NOT WHAT--
BRING MEAT! FILL A BOWL FOR THIS BRAVE MAN! NO ONE REALIZED FOOD WAS SO IMPORTANT TO YOU, SON OF PELEUS! IF YOU WANT, WE'LL CALL YOU SON OF THE STOMACH INSTEAD OF SON OF PELEUS!
MOCKERY! I OWE THIS ARMY **NOTHING**! I'LL SAIL FOR PHTHIA IN THE MORNING.
DO SOMETHING, AGAMEMNON. WHY ARE YOU SMILING--?
OH! I SEE! IT'S ALL AN EXCUSE TO RUN AWAY! YOU'RE NOT INSULTED--YOU'RE SCARED! DID YOU SPOT THE WALLS OF TROY FROM THE HEIGHTS OF TENEDOS?
I'VE BEGUN TO SUSPECT THAT ACHILLES IS THE **BEST** OF THE ACHAEAN WARRIORS... AND ODYSSEUS IS **CERTAINLY** OUR BEST TALKER...

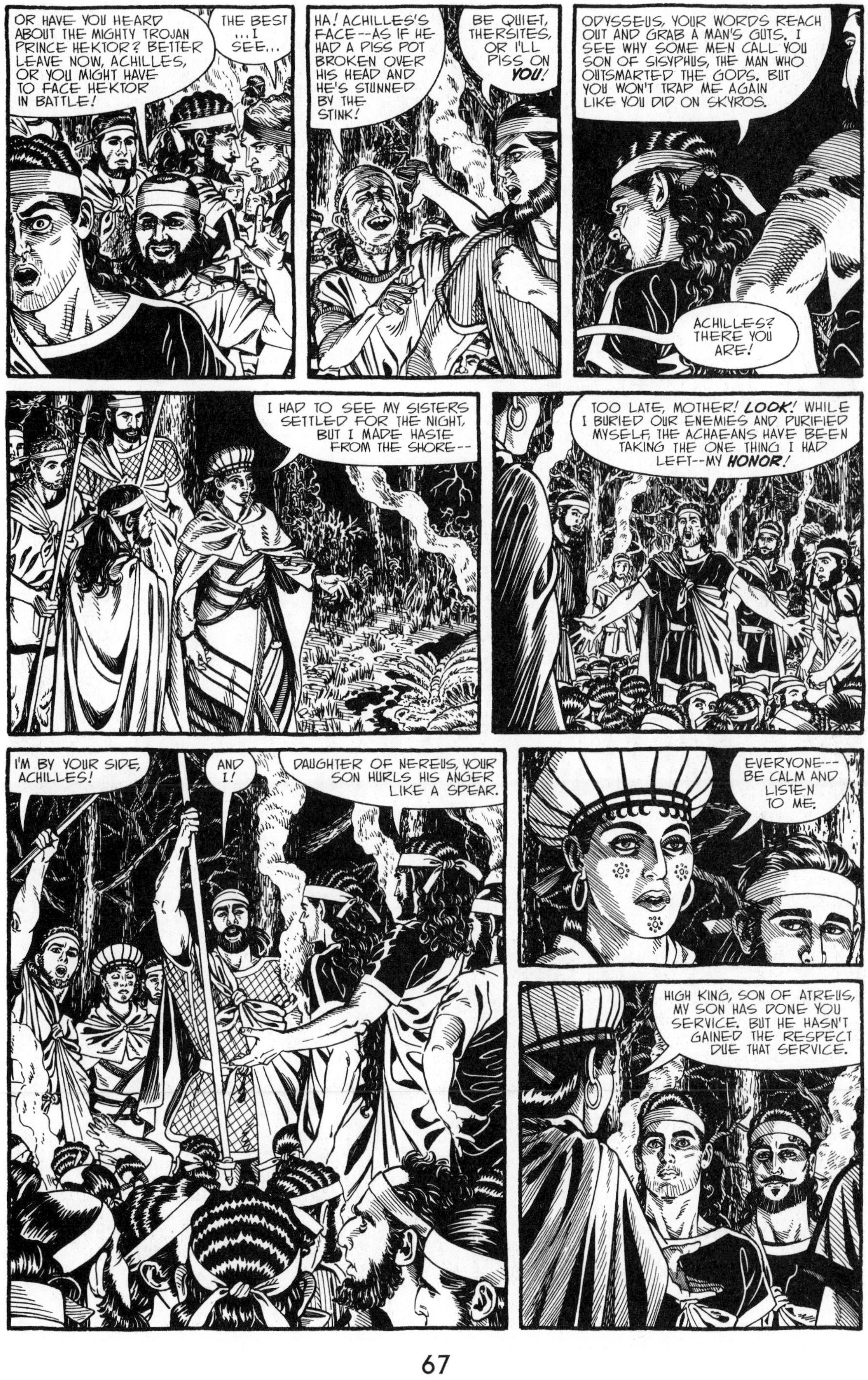
OR HAVE YOU HEARD ABOUT THE MIGHTY TROJAN PRINCE HEKTOR? BETTER LEAVE NOW, ACHILLES, OR YOU MIGHT HAVE TO FACE HEKTOR IN BATTLE!
THE BEST ...I SEE...
HA! ACHILLES'S FACE--AS IF HE HAD A PISS POT BROKEN OVER HIS HEAD AND HE'S STUNNED BY THE STINK!
BE QUIET, THERSITES, OR I'LL PISS ON YOU!
ODYSSEUS, YOUR WORDS REACH OUT AND GRAB A MAN'S GUTS. I SEE WHY SOME MEN CALL YOU SON OF SISYPHUS, THE MAN WHO OUTSMARTED THE GODS. BUT YOU WON'T TRAP ME AGAIN LIKE YOU DID ON SKYROS.
ACHILLES? THERE YOU ARE!
I HAD TO SEE MY SISTERS SETTLED FOR THE NIGHT, BUT I MADE HASTE FROM THE SHORE--
TOO LATE, MOTHER! LOOK! WHILE I BURIED OUR ENEMIES AND PURIFIED MYSELF, THE ACHAEANS HAVE BEEN TAKING THE ONE THING I HAD LEFT--MY HONOR!
I'M BY YOUR SIDE, ACHILLES!
AND I!
DAUGHTER OF NEREUS, YOUR SON HURLS HIS ANGER LIKE A SPEAR.
EVERYONE-- BE CALM AND LISTEN TO ME.
HIGH KING, SON OF ATREUS, MY SON HAS DONE YOU SERVICE. BUT HE HASN'T GAINED THE RESPECT DUE THAT SERVICE.

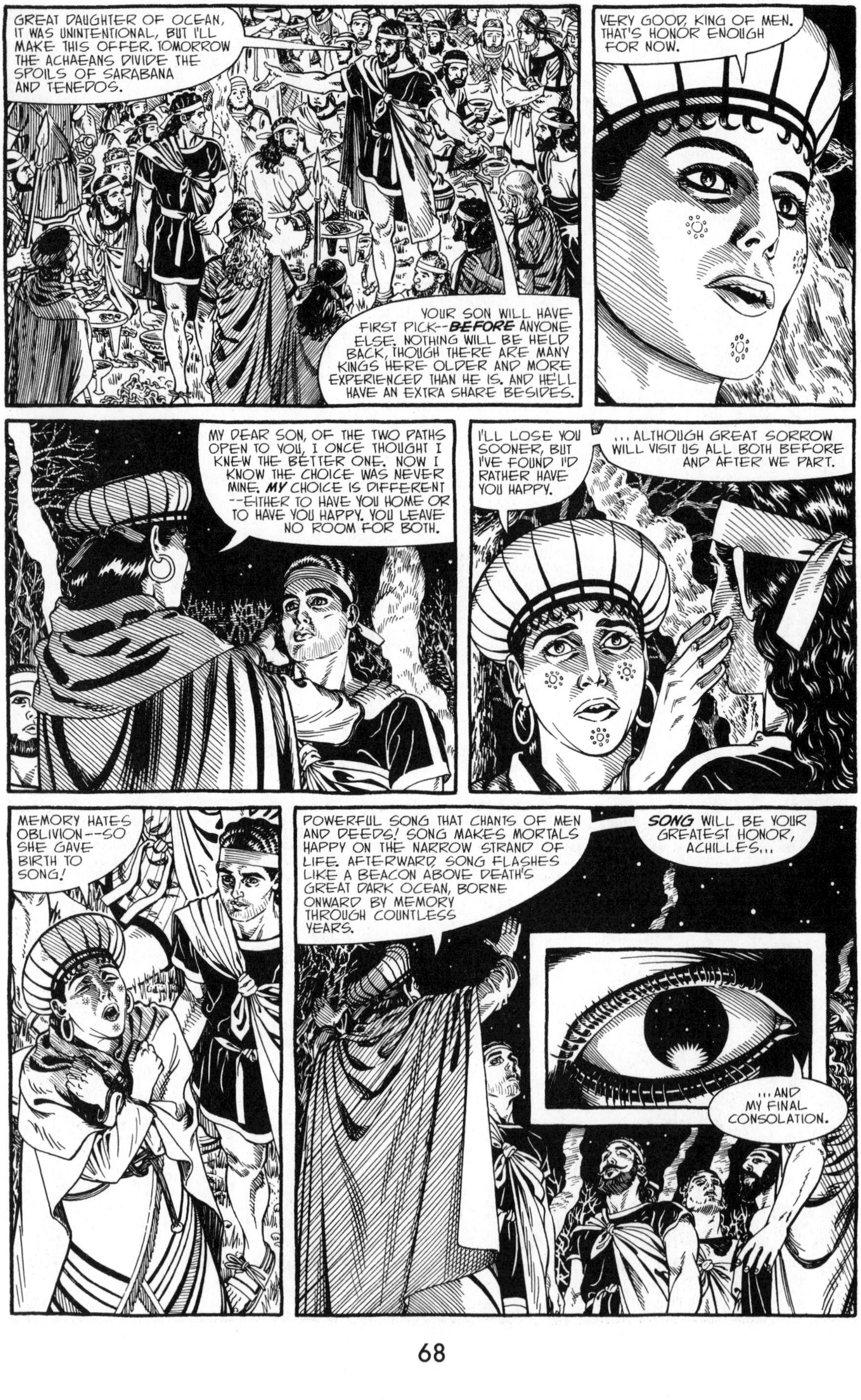
GREAT DAUGHTER OF OCEAN, IT WAS UNINTENTIONAL, BUT I'LL MAKE THIS OFFER. TOMORROW THE ACHAEANS DIVIDE THE SPOILS OF SARABANA AND TENEDOS.
YOUR SON WILL HAVE FIRST PICK--**BEFORE** ANYONE ELSE. NOTHING WILL BE HELD BACK, THOUGH THERE ARE MANY KINGS HERE OLDER AND MORE EXPERIENCED THAN HE IS. AND HE'LL HAVE AN EXTRA SHARE BESIDES.
VERY GOOD, KING OF MEN. THAT'S HONOR ENOUGH FOR NOW.
MY DEAR SON, OF THE TWO PATHS OPEN TO YOU, I ONCE THOUGHT I KNEW THE BETTER ONE. NOW I KNOW THE CHOICE WAS NEVER MINE. ***MY*** CHOICE IS DIFFERENT --EITHER TO HAVE YOU HOME OR TO HAVE YOU HAPPY. YOU LEAVE NO ROOM FOR BOTH.
I'LL LOSE YOU SOONER, BUT I'VE FOUND I'D RATHER HAVE YOU HAPPY.
...ALTHOUGH GREAT SORROW WILL VISIT US ALL BOTH BEFORE AND AFTER WE PART.
MEMORY HATES OBLIVION--SO SHE GAVE BIRTH TO SONG!
POWERFUL SONG THAT CHANTS OF MEN AND DEEDS! SONG MAKES MORTALS HAPPY ON THE NARROW STRAND OF LIFE. AFTERWARD, SONG FLASHES LIKE A BEACON ABOVE DEATH'S GREAT DARK OCEAN, BORNE ONWARD BY MEMORY THROUGH COUNTLESS YEARS.
SONG WILL BE YOUR GREATEST HONOR, ACHILLES...
...AND MY FINAL CONSOLATION.

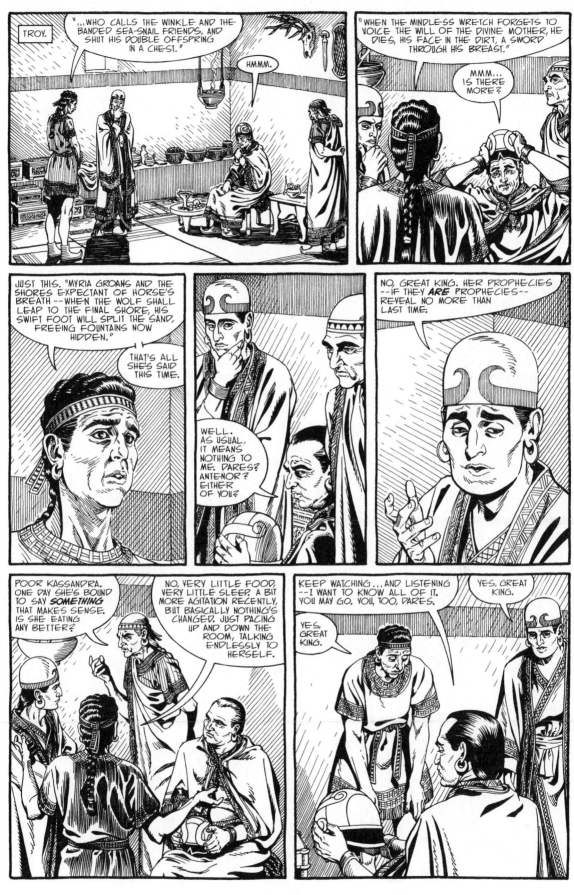

TROY.

"...WHO CALLS THE WINKLE AND THE BANDED SEA-SNAIL FRIENDS, AND SHUT HIS DOUBLE OFFSPRING IN A CHEST."

HMMM.

"WHEN THE MINDLESS WRETCH FORGETS TO VOICE THE WILL OF THE DIVINE MOTHER, HE DIES, HIS FACE IN THE DIRT, A SWORD THROUGH HIS BREAST."

MMM... IS THERE MORE?

JUST THIS. "MYRIA GROANS AND THE SHORES EXPECTANT OF HORSE'S BREATH -- WHEN THE WOLF SHALL LEAP TO THE FINAL SHORE, HIS SWIFT FOOT WILL SPLIT THE SAND, FREEING FOUNTAINS NOW HIDDEN."

THAT'S ALL SHE'S SAID THIS TIME.

WELL. AS USUAL, IT MEANS NOTHING TO ME. DARES? ANTENOR? EITHER OF YOU?

NO, GREAT KING. HER PROPHECIES --IF THEY ARE PROPHECIES-- REVEAL NO MORE THAN LAST TIME.

POOR KASSANDRA. ONE DAY SHE'S BOUND TO SAY SOMETHING THAT MAKES SENSE. IS SHE EATING ANY BETTER?

NO, VERY LITTLE FOOD, VERY LITTLE SLEEP. A BIT MORE AGITATION RECENTLY, BUT BASICALLY NOTHING'S CHANGED. JUST PACING UP AND DOWN THE ROOM, TALKING ENDLESSLY TO HERSELF.

KEEP WATCHING...AND LISTENING --I WANT TO KNOW ALL OF IT. YOU MAY GO. YOU, TOO, DARES.

YES, GREAT KING.

YES, GREAT KING.

69

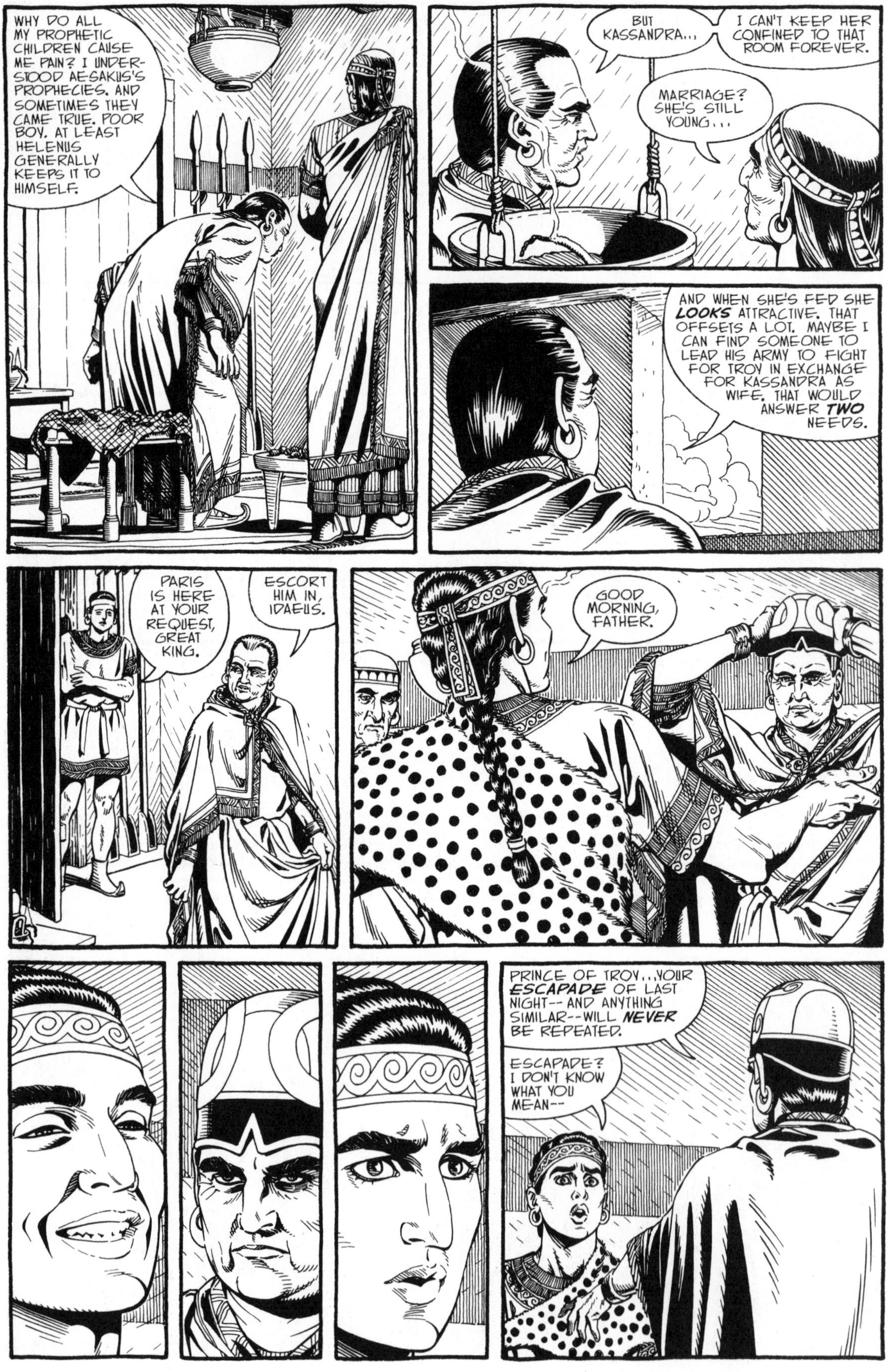
WHY DO ALL MY PROPHETIC CHILDREN CAUSE ME PAIN? I UNDERSTOOD AESAKUS'S PROPHECIES. AND SOMETIMES THEY CAME TRUE. POOR BOY. AT LEAST HELENUS GENERALLY KEEPS IT TO HIMSELF.
BUT KASSANDRA...
I CAN'T KEEP HER CONFINED TO THAT ROOM FOREVER.
MARRIAGE? SHE'S STILL YOUNG...
AND WHEN SHE'S FED SHE LOOKS ATTRACTIVE. THAT OFFSETS A LOT. MAYBE I CAN FIND SOMEONE TO LEAD HIS ARMY TO FIGHT FOR TROY IN EXCHANGE FOR KASSANDRA AS WIFE. THAT WOULD ANSWER TWO NEEDS.
PARIS IS HERE AT YOUR REQUEST, GREAT KING.
ESCORT HIM IN, IDAEUS.
GOOD MORNING, FATHER.
PRINCE OF TROY...YOUR ESCAPADE OF LAST NIGHT--AND ANYTHING SIMILAR--WILL NEVER BE REPEATED.
ESCAPADE? I DON'T KNOW WHAT YOU MEAN--

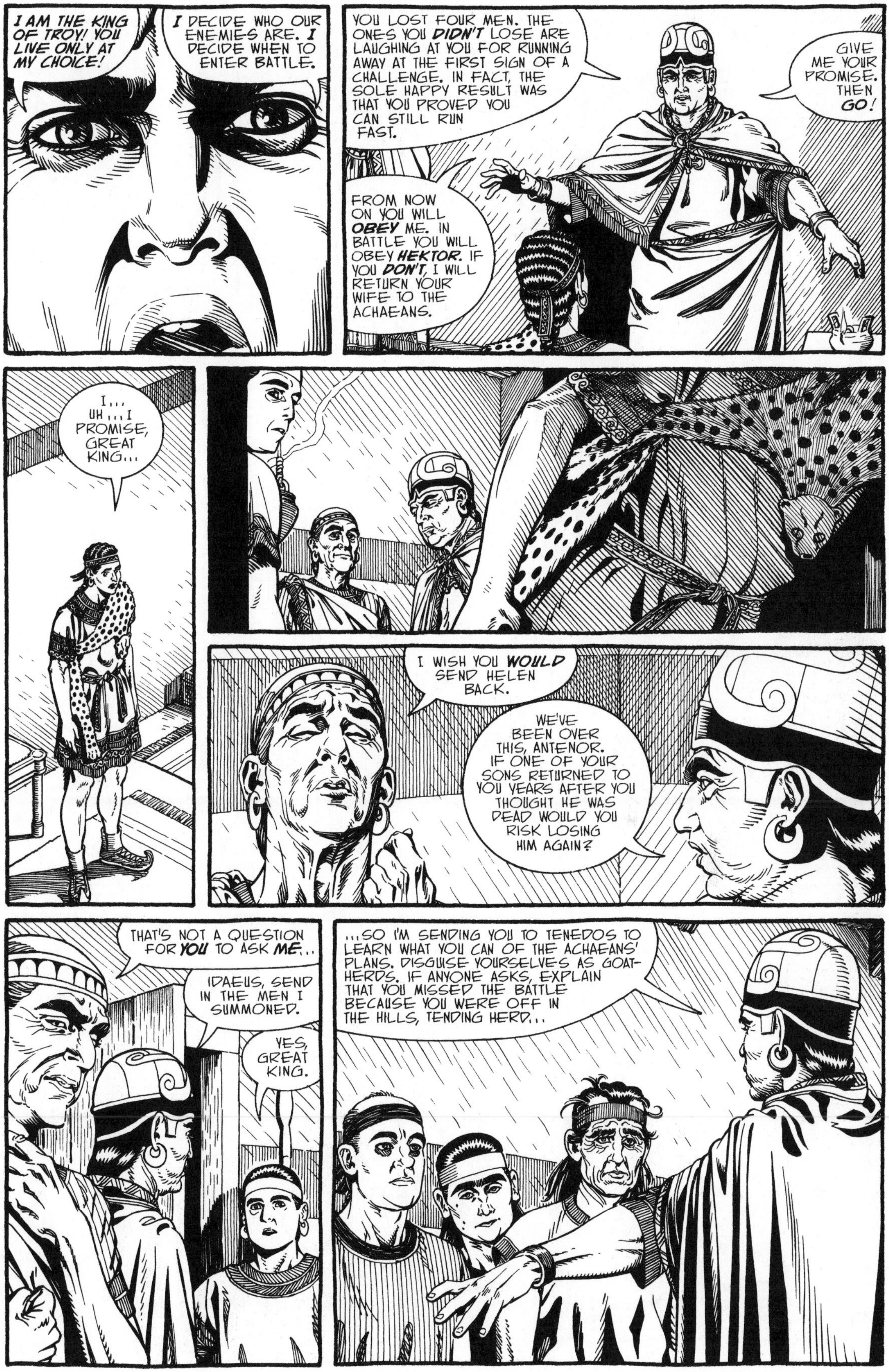
I AM THE KING OF TROY! YOU LIVE ONLY AT MY CHOICE!
I DECIDE WHO OUR ENEMIES ARE. I DECIDE WHEN TO ENTER BATTLE.
YOU LOST FOUR MEN. THE ONES YOU DIDN'T LOSE ARE LAUGHING AT YOU FOR RUNNING AWAY AT THE FIRST SIGN OF A CHALLENGE. IN FACT, THE SOLE HAPPY RESULT WAS THAT YOU PROVED YOU CAN STILL RUN FAST.
FROM NOW ON YOU WILL OBEY ME. IN BATTLE YOU WILL OBEY HEKTOR. IF YOU DON'T, I WILL RETURN YOUR WIFE TO THE ACHAEANS.
GIVE ME YOUR PROMISE. THEN GO!
I... UH...I PROMISE, GREAT KING...
I WISH YOU WOULD SEND HELEN BACK.
WE'VE BEEN OVER THIS, ANTENOR. IF ONE OF YOUR SONS RETURNED TO YOU YEARS AFTER YOU THOUGHT HE WAS DEAD WOULD YOU RISK LOSING HIM AGAIN?
THAT'S NOT A QUESTION FOR YOU TO ASK ME...
IDAEUS, SEND IN THE MEN I SUMMONED.
YES, GREAT KING.
...SO I'M SENDING YOU TO TENEDOS TO LEARN WHAT YOU CAN OF THE ACHAEANS' PLANS. DISGUISE YOURSELVES AS GOAT-HERDS. IF ANYONE ASKS, EXPLAIN THAT YOU MISSED THE BATTLE BECAUSE YOU WERE OFF IN THE HILLS, TENDING HERD...

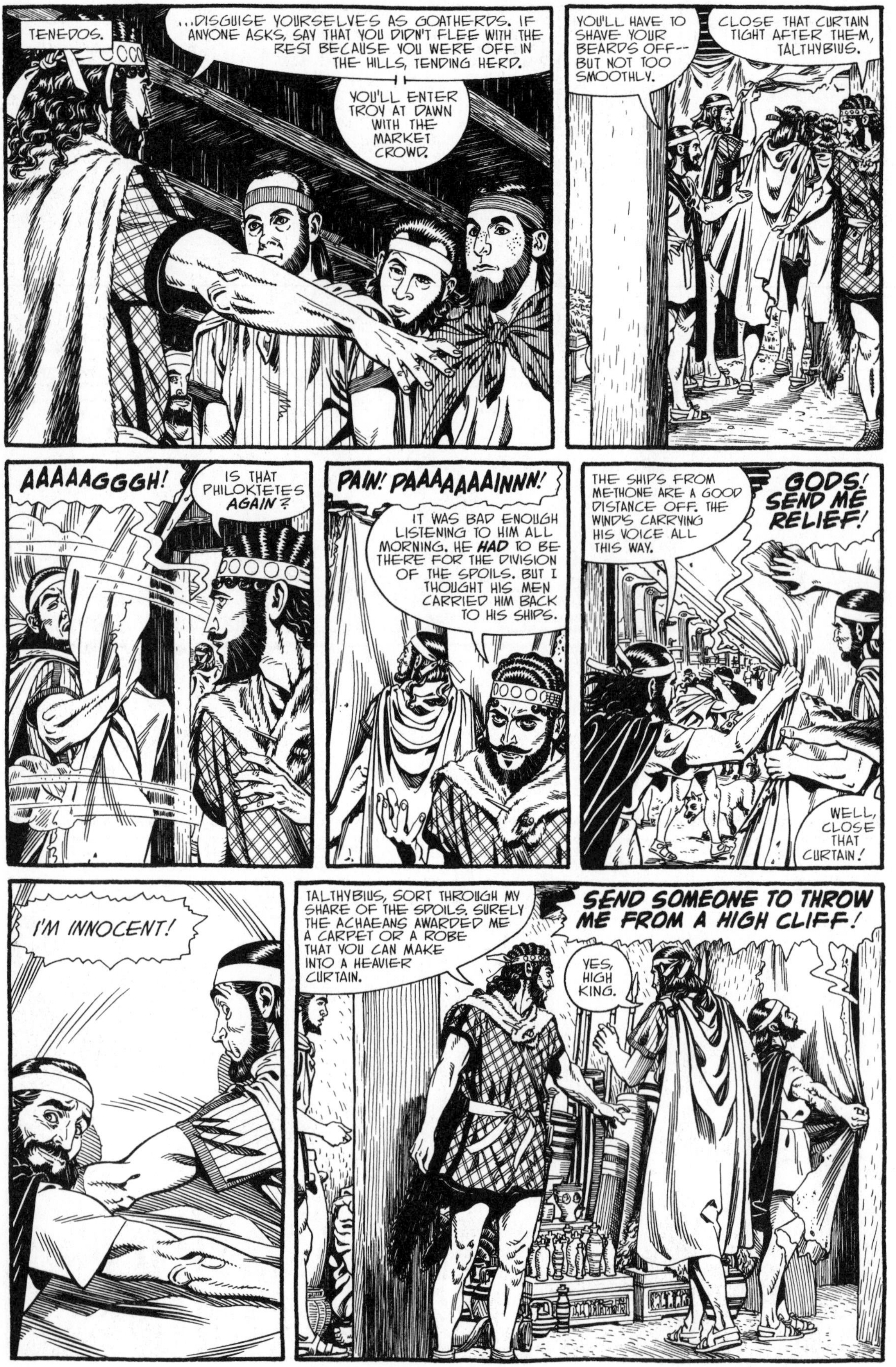
TENEDOS.
...DISGUISE YOURSELVES AS GOATHERDS. IF ANYONE ASKS, SAY THAT YOU DIDN'T FLEE WITH THE REST BECAUSE YOU WERE OFF IN THE HILLS, TENDING HERD.
YOU'LL ENTER TROY AT DAWN WITH THE MARKET CROWD.
YOU'LL HAVE TO SHAVE YOUR BEARDS OFF-- BUT NOT TOO SMOOTHLY.
CLOSE THAT CURTAIN TIGHT AFTER THEM, TALTHYBIUS.
AAAAAGGGH!
IS THAT PHILOKTETES AGAIN?
PAIN! PAAAAAAAAINNN!
IT WAS BAD ENOUGH LISTENING TO HIM ALL MORNING. HE HAD TO BE THERE FOR THE DIVISION OF THE SPOILS. BUT I THOUGHT HIS MEN CARRIED HIM BACK TO HIS SHIPS.
THE SHIPS FROM METHONE ARE A GOOD DISTANCE OFF. THE WIND'S CARRYING HIS VOICE ALL THIS WAY.
GODS! SEND ME RELIEF!
WELL, CLOSE THAT CURTAIN!
I'M INNOCENT!
TALTHYBIUS, SORT THROUGH MY SHARE OF THE SPOILS. SURELY THE ACHAEANS AWARDED ME A CARPET OR A ROBE THAT YOU CAN MAKE INTO A HEAVIER CURTAIN.
SEND SOMEONE TO THROW ME FROM A HIGH CLIFF!
YES, HIGH KING.

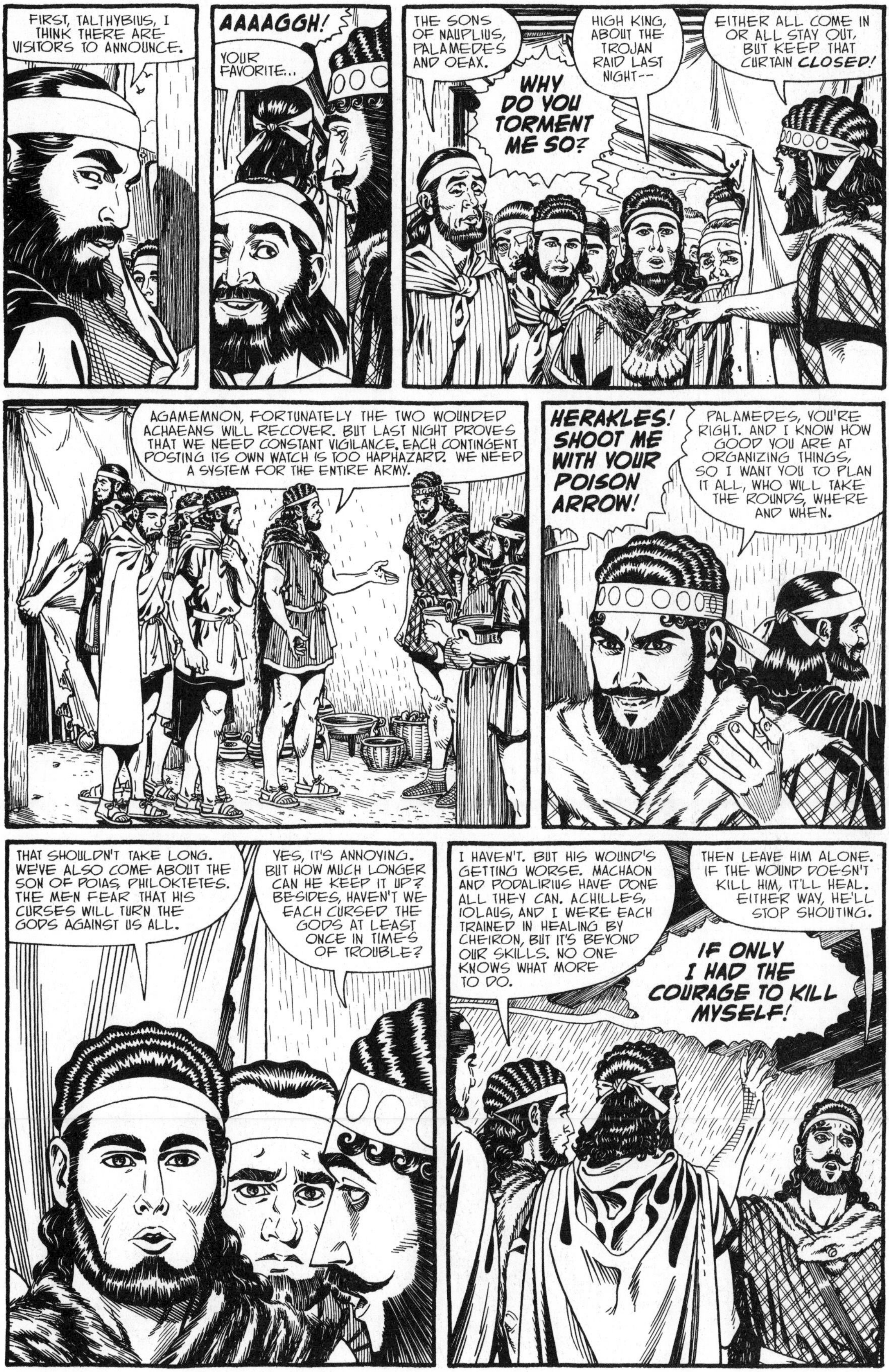
FIRST, TALTHYBIUS, I THINK THERE ARE VISITORS TO ANNOUNCE.
AAAAGGH!
YOUR FAVORITE...
THE SONS OF NAUPLIUS, PALAMEDES AND OEAX.
HIGH KING, ABOUT THE TROJAN RAID LAST NIGHT--
WHY DO YOU TORMENT ME SO?
EITHER ALL COME IN OR ALL STAY OUT, BUT KEEP THAT CURTAIN **CLOSED!**
AGAMEMNON, FORTUNATELY THE TWO WOUNDED ACHAEANS WILL RECOVER. BUT LAST NIGHT PROVES THAT WE NEED CONSTANT VIGILANCE. EACH CONTINGENT POSTING ITS OWN WATCH IS TOO HAPHAZARD. WE NEED A SYSTEM FOR THE ENTIRE ARMY.
HERAKLES! SHOOT ME WITH YOUR POISON ARROW!
PALAMEDES, YOU'RE RIGHT. AND I KNOW HOW GOOD YOU ARE AT ORGANIZING THINGS, SO I WANT YOU TO PLAN IT ALL, WHO WILL TAKE THE ROUNDS, WHERE AND WHEN.
THAT SHOULDN'T TAKE LONG. WE'VE ALSO COME ABOUT THE SON OF POIAS, PHILOKTETES. THE MEN FEAR THAT HIS CURSES WILL TURN THE GODS AGAINST US ALL.
YES, IT'S ANNOYING. BUT HOW MUCH LONGER CAN HE KEEP IT UP? BESIDES, HAVEN'T WE EACH CURSED THE GODS AT LEAST ONCE IN TIMES OF TROUBLE?
I HAVEN'T. BUT HIS WOUND'S GETTING WORSE. MACHAON AND PODALIRIUS HAVE DONE ALL THEY CAN. ACHILLES, IOLAUS, AND I WERE EACH TRAINED IN HEALING BY CHEIRON, BUT IT'S BEYOND OUR SKILLS. NO ONE KNOWS WHAT MORE TO DO.
THEN LEAVE HIM ALONE. IF THE WOUND DOESN'T KILL HIM, IT'LL HEAL. EITHER WAY, HE'LL STOP SHOUTING.
IF ONLY I HAD THE COURAGE TO KILL MYSELF!

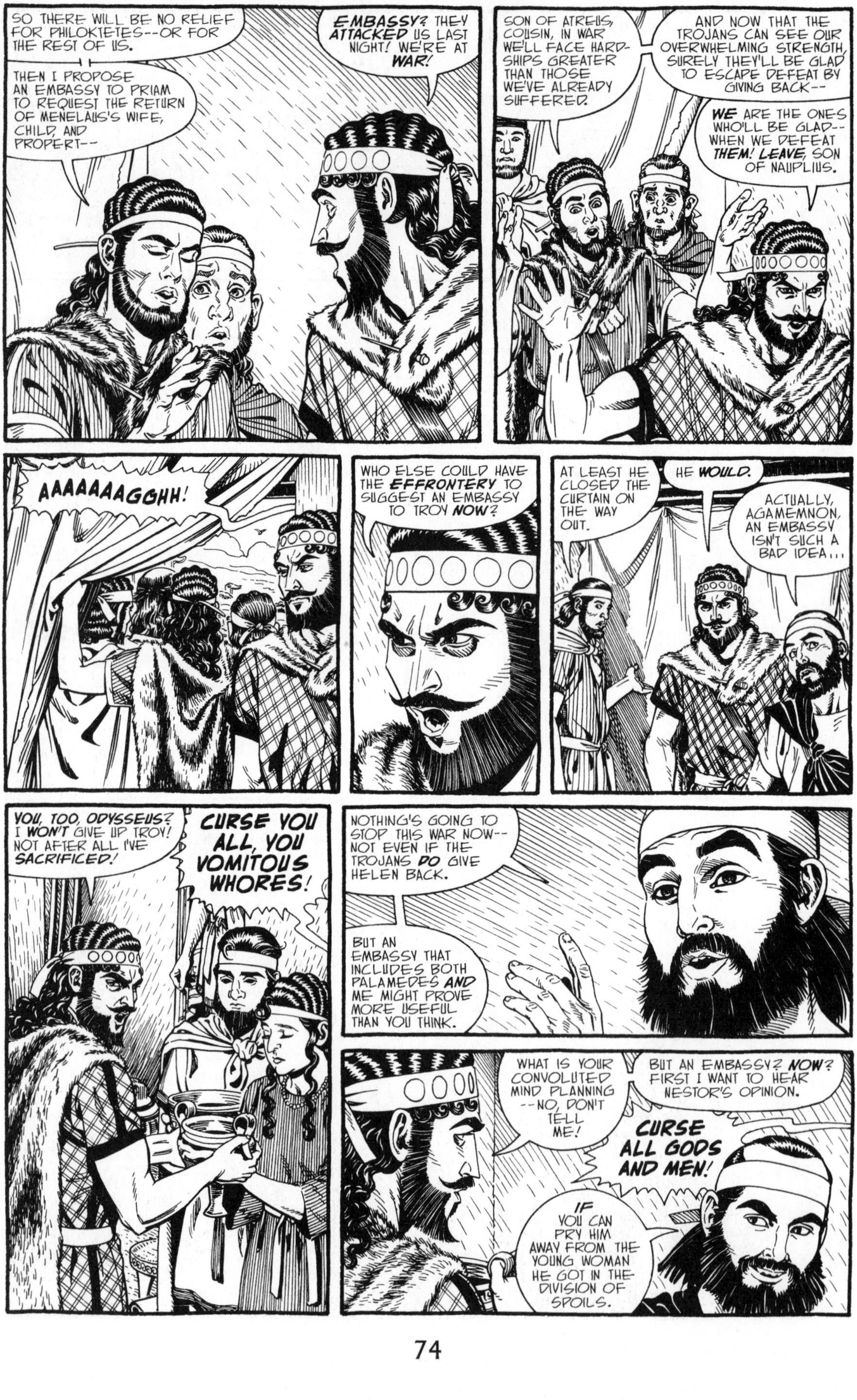
SO THERE WILL BE NO RELIEF FOR PHILOKTETES--OR FOR THE REST OF US.
THEN I PROPOSE AN EMBASSY TO PRIAM TO REQUEST THE RETURN OF MENELAUS'S WIFE, CHILD, AND PROPERT--
EMBASSY? THEY ATTACKED US LAST NIGHT! WE'RE AT WAR!
SON OF ATREUS, COUSIN, IN WAR WE'LL FACE HARDSHIPS GREATER THAN THOSE WE'VE ALREADY SUFFERED.
AND NOW THAT THE TROJANS CAN SEE OUR OVERWHELMING STRENGTH, SURELY THEY'LL BE GLAD TO ESCAPE DEFEAT BY GIVING BACK--
WE ARE THE ONES WHO'LL BE GLAD--WHEN WE DEFEAT THEM! LEAVE, SON OF NAUPLIUS.
AAAAAAAGGHH!
WHO ELSE COULD HAVE THE EFFRONTERY TO SUGGEST AN EMBASSY TO TROY NOW?
AT LEAST HE CLOSED THE CURTAIN ON THE WAY OUT.
HE WOULD.
ACTUALLY, AGAMEMNON, AN EMBASSY ISN'T SUCH A BAD IDEA...
YOU, TOO, ODYSSEUS? I WON'T GIVE UP TROY! NOT AFTER ALL I'VE SACRIFICED!
CURSE YOU ALL, YOU VOMITOUS WHORES!
NOTHING'S GOING TO STOP THIS WAR NOW--NOT EVEN IF THE TROJANS DO GIVE HELEN BACK.
BUT AN EMBASSY THAT INCLUDES BOTH PALAMEDES AND ME MIGHT PROVE MORE USEFUL THAN YOU THINK.
WHAT IS YOUR CONVOLUTED MIND PLANNING--NO, DON'T TELL ME!
BUT AN EMBASSY? NOW? FIRST I WANT TO HEAR NESTOR'S OPINION.
CURSE ALL GODS AND MEN!
IF YOU CAN PRY HIM AWAY FROM THE YOUNG WOMAN HE GOT IN THE DIVISION OF SPOILS.

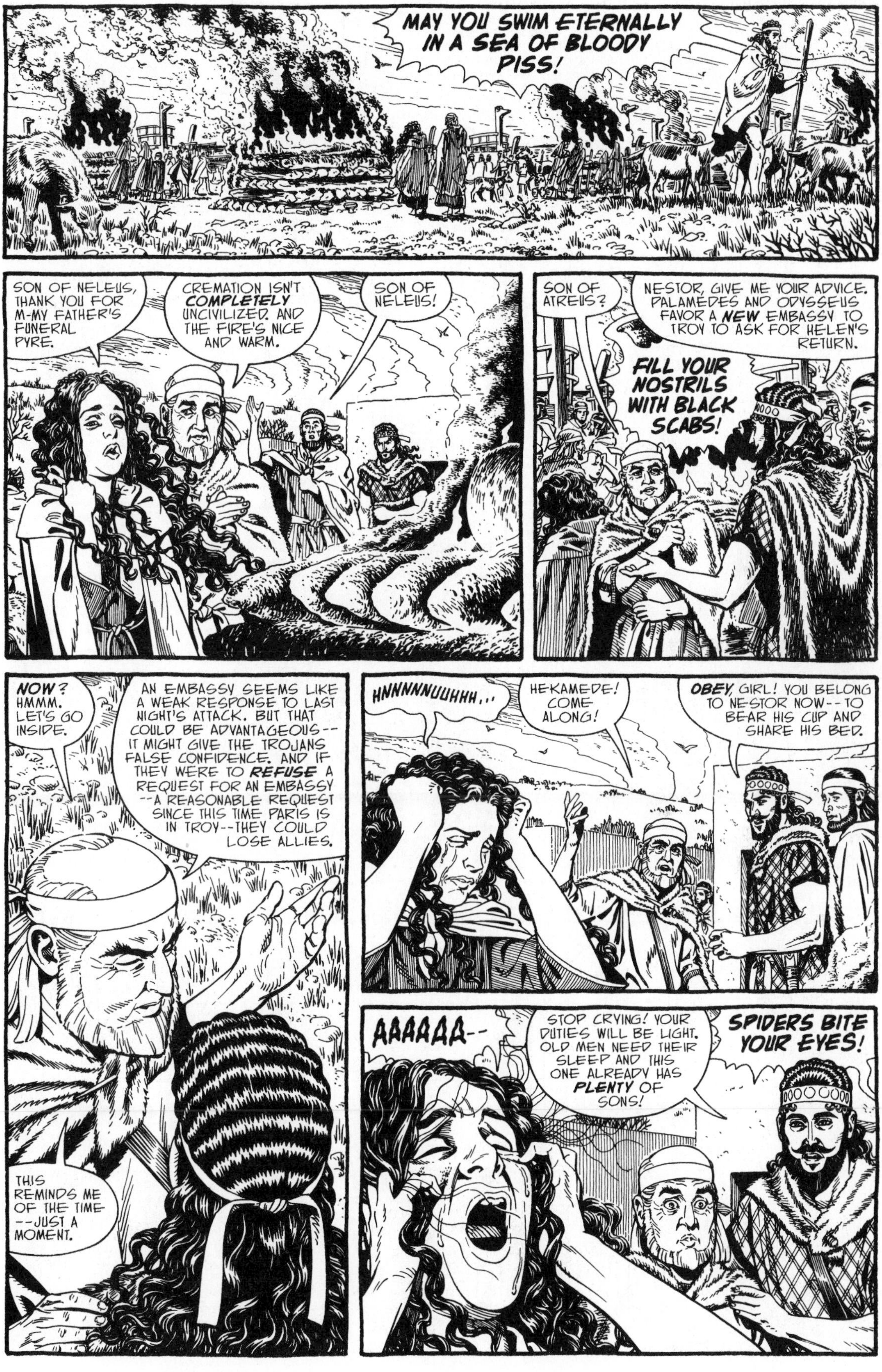
MAY YOU SWIM ETERNALLY IN A SEA OF BLOODY PISS!
SON OF NELEUS, THANK YOU FOR M-MY FATHER'S FUNERAL PYRE.
CREMATION ISN'T COMPLETELY UNCIVILIZED. AND THE FIRE'S NICE AND WARM.
SON OF NELEUS!
SON OF ATREUS?
NESTOR, GIVE ME YOUR ADVICE. PALAMEDES AND ODYSSEUS FAVOR A NEW EMBASSY TO TROY TO ASK FOR HELEN'S RETURN.
FILL YOUR NOSTRILS WITH BLACK SCABS!
NOW? HMMM. LET'S GO INSIDE.
AN EMBASSY SEEMS LIKE A WEAK RESPONSE TO LAST NIGHT'S ATTACK. BUT THAT COULD BE ADVANTAGEOUS-- IT MIGHT GIVE THE TROJANS FALSE CONFIDENCE. AND IF THEY WERE TO REFUSE A REQUEST FOR AN EMBASSY --A REASONABLE REQUEST SINCE THIS TIME PARIS IS IN TROY--THEY COULD LOSE ALLIES.
THIS REMINDS ME OF THE TIME --JUST A MOMENT.
HNNNNNUHHH...
HEKAMEDE! COME ALONG!
OBEY, GIRL! YOU BELONG TO NESTOR NOW--TO BEAR HIS CUP AND SHARE HIS BED.
AAAAAA--
STOP CRYING! YOUR DUTIES WILL BE LIGHT. OLD MEN NEED THEIR SLEEP AND THIS ONE ALREADY HAS PLENTY OF SONS!
SPIDERS BITE YOUR EYES!

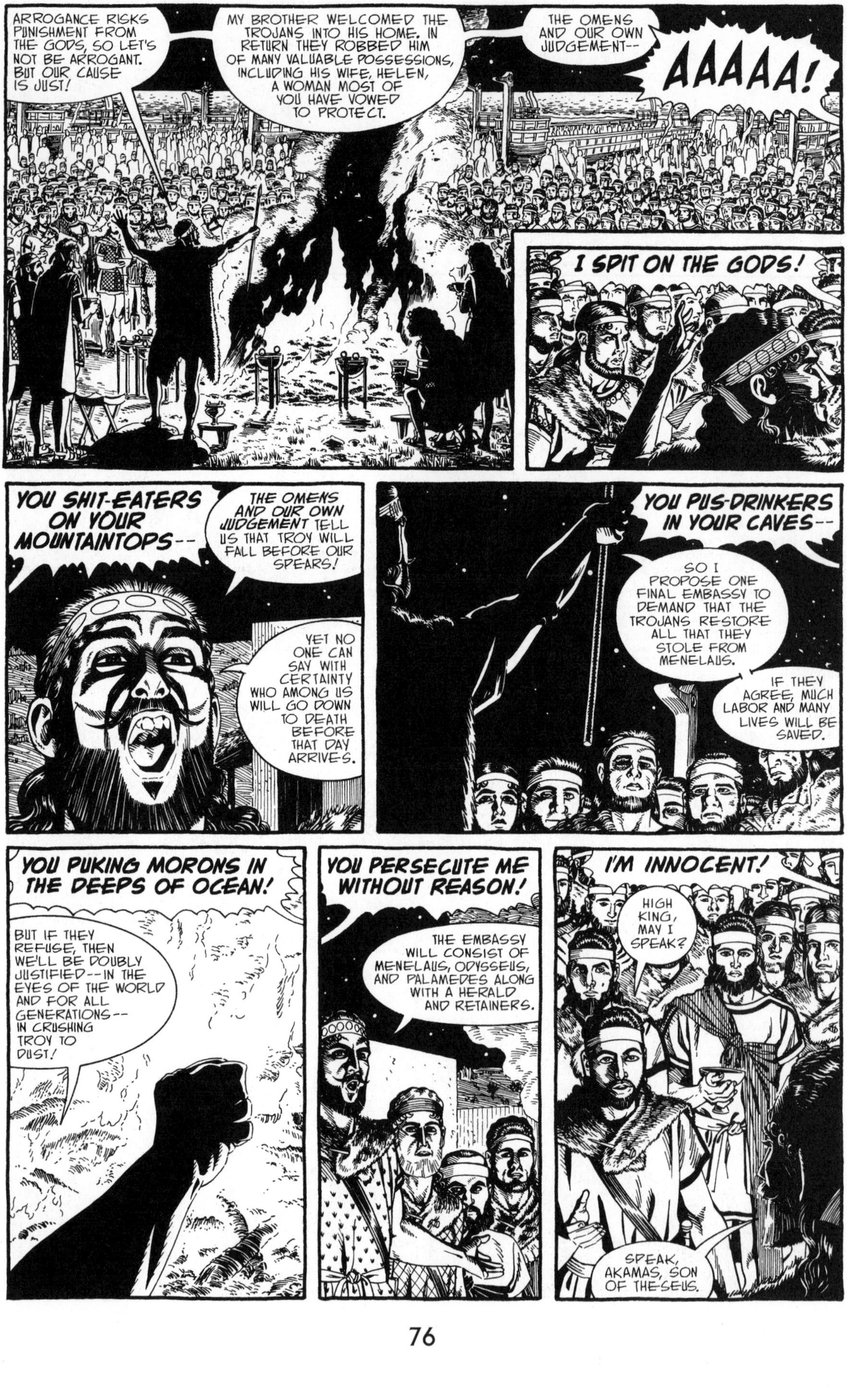
ARROGANCE RISKS PUNISHMENT FROM THE GODS, SO LET'S NOT BE ARROGANT. BUT OUR CAUSE IS JUST!
MY BROTHER WELCOMED THE TROJANS INTO HIS HOME. IN RETURN THEY ROBBED HIM OF MANY VALUABLE POSSESSIONS, INCLUDING HIS WIFE, HELEN, A WOMAN MOST OF YOU HAVE VOWED TO PROTECT.
THE OMENS AND OUR OWN JUDGEMENT--
AAAAA!
I SPIT ON THE GODS!
YOU SHIT-EATERS ON YOUR MOUNTAINTOPS--
THE OMENS AND OUR OWN JUDGEMENT TELL US THAT TROY WILL FALL BEFORE OUR SPEARS!
YET NO ONE CAN SAY WITH CERTAINTY WHO AMONG US WILL GO DOWN TO DEATH BEFORE THAT DAY ARRIVES.
YOU PUS-DRINKERS IN YOUR CAVES--
SO I PROPOSE ONE FINAL EMBASSY TO DEMAND THAT THE TROJANS RESTORE ALL THAT THEY STOLE FROM MENELAUS.
IF THEY AGREE, MUCH LABOR AND MANY LIVES WILL BE SAVED.
YOU PUKING MORONS IN THE DEEPS OF OCEAN!
BUT IF THEY REFUSE, THEN WE'LL BE DOUBLY JUSTIFIED--IN THE EYES OF THE WORLD AND FOR ALL GENERATIONS--IN CRUSHING TROY TO DUST!
YOU PERSECUTE ME WITHOUT REASON!
THE EMBASSY WILL CONSIST OF MENELAUS, ODYSSEUS, AND PALAMEDES ALONG WITH A HERALD AND RETAINERS.
I'M INNOCENT!
HIGH KING, MAY I SPEAK?
SPEAK, AKAMAS, SON OF THESEUS.

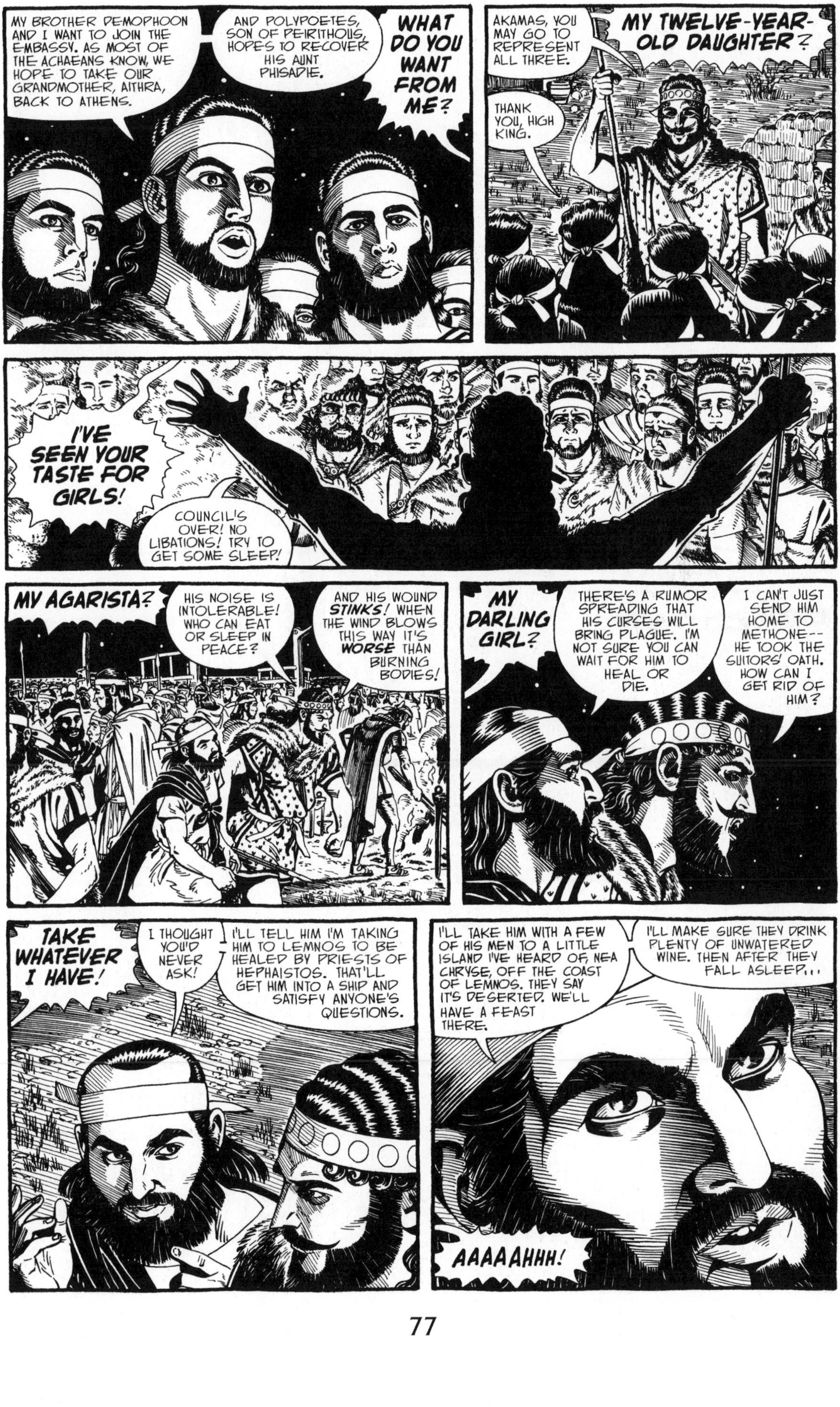
MY BROTHER DEMOPHOON AND I WANT TO JOIN THE EMBASSY. AS MOST OF THE ACHAEANS KNOW, WE HOPE TO TAKE OUR GRANDMOTHER, AITHRA, BACK TO ATHENS.
AND POLYPOETES, SON OF PEIRITHOUS, HOPES TO RECOVER HIS AUNT PHISADIE.
WHAT DO YOU WANT FROM ME?
AKAMAS, YOU MAY GO TO REPRESENT ALL THREE.
MY TWELVE-YEAR-OLD DAUGHTER?
THANK YOU, HIGH KING.
I'VE SEEN YOUR TASTE FOR GIRLS!
COUNCIL'S OVER! NO LIBATIONS! TRY TO GET SOME SLEEP!
MY AGARISTA?
HIS NOISE IS INTOLERABLE! WHO CAN EAT OR SLEEP IN PEACE?
AND HIS WOUND STINKS! WHEN THE WIND BLOWS THIS WAY IT'S WORSE THAN BURNING BODIES!
MY DARLING GIRL?
THERE'S A RUMOR SPREADING THAT HIS CURSES WILL BRING PLAGUE. I'M NOT SURE YOU CAN WAIT FOR HIM TO HEAL OR DIE.
I CAN'T JUST SEND HIM HOME TO METHONE-- HE TOOK THE SUITORS' OATH. HOW CAN I GET RID OF HIM?
TAKE WHATEVER I HAVE!
I THOUGHT YOU'D NEVER ASK!
I'LL TELL HIM I'M TAKING HIM TO LEMNOS TO BE HEALED BY PRIESTS OF HEPHAISTOS. THAT'LL GET HIM INTO A SHIP AND SATISFY ANYONE'S QUESTIONS.
I'LL TAKE HIM WITH A FEW OF HIS MEN TO A LITTLE ISLAND I'VE HEARD OF, NEA CHRYSE, OFF THE COAST OF LEMNOS. THEY SAY IT'S DESERTED. WE'LL HAVE A FEAST THERE.
I'LL MAKE SURE THEY DRINK PLENTY OF UNWATERED WINE. THEN AFTER THEY FALL ASLEEP...
AAAAAHHH!

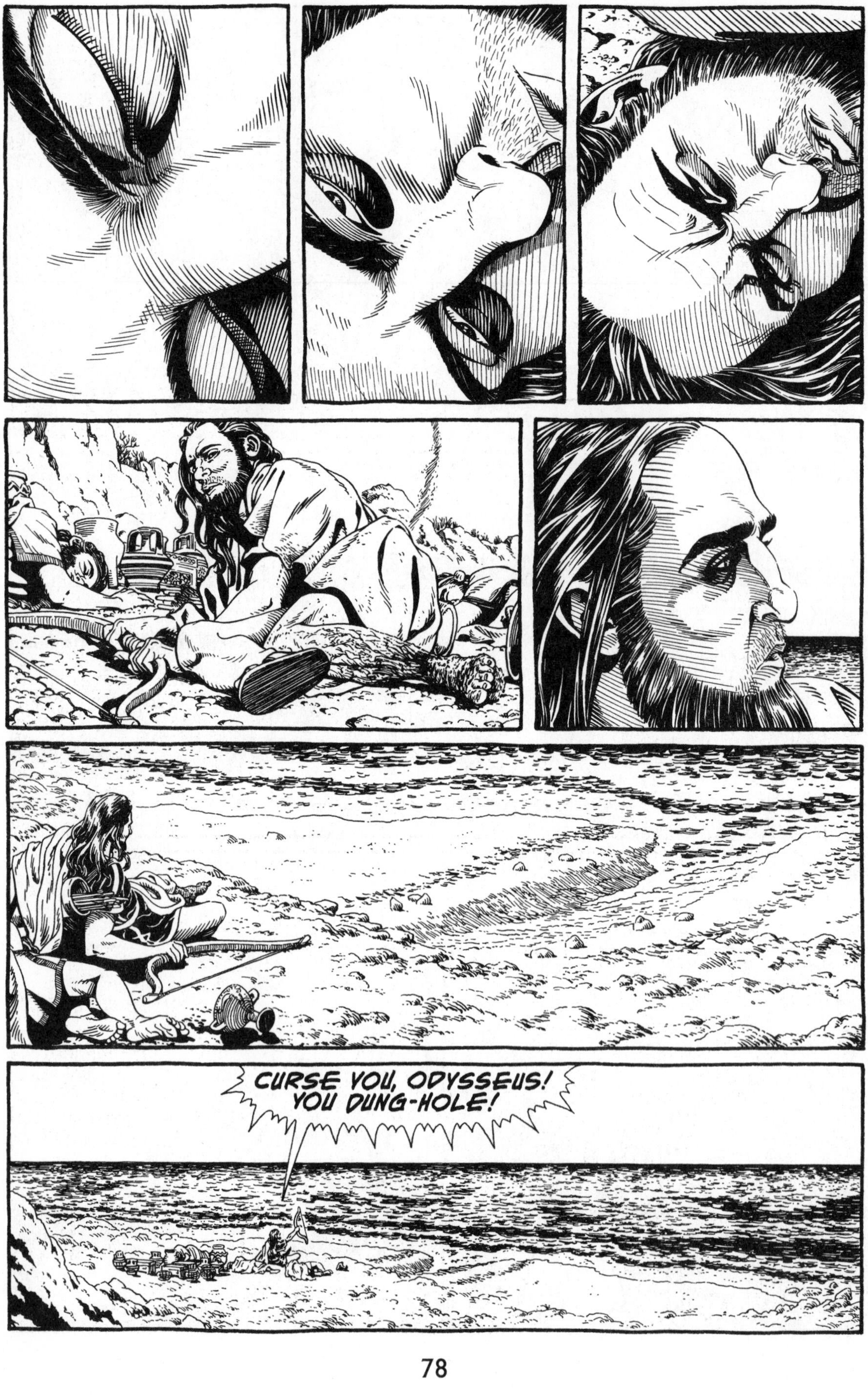
CURSE YOU, ODYSSEUS! YOU DUNG-HOLE!

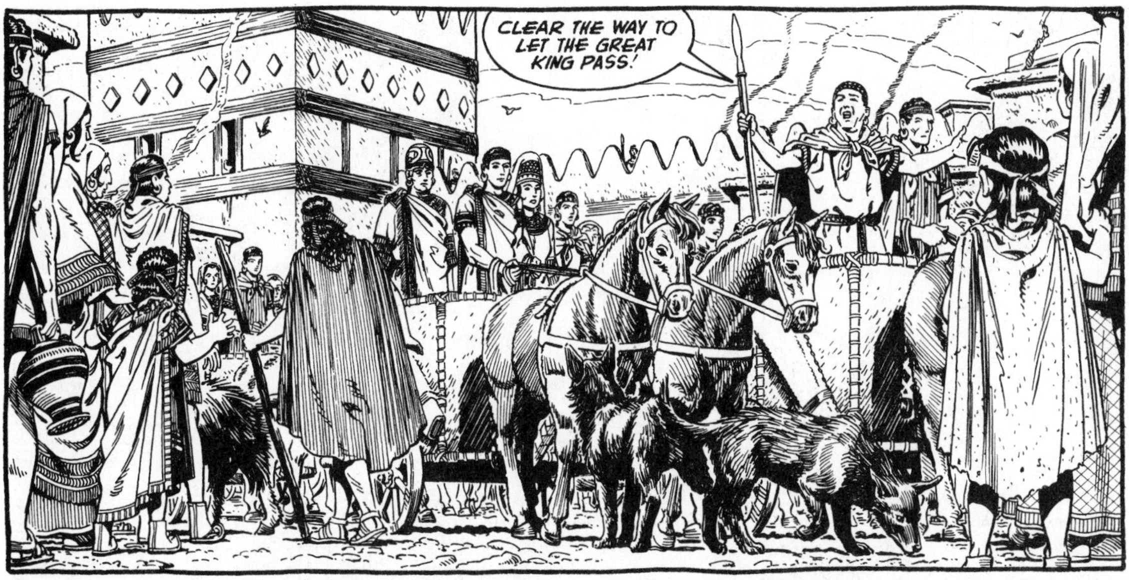
CLEAR THE WAY TO LET THE GREAT KING PASS!

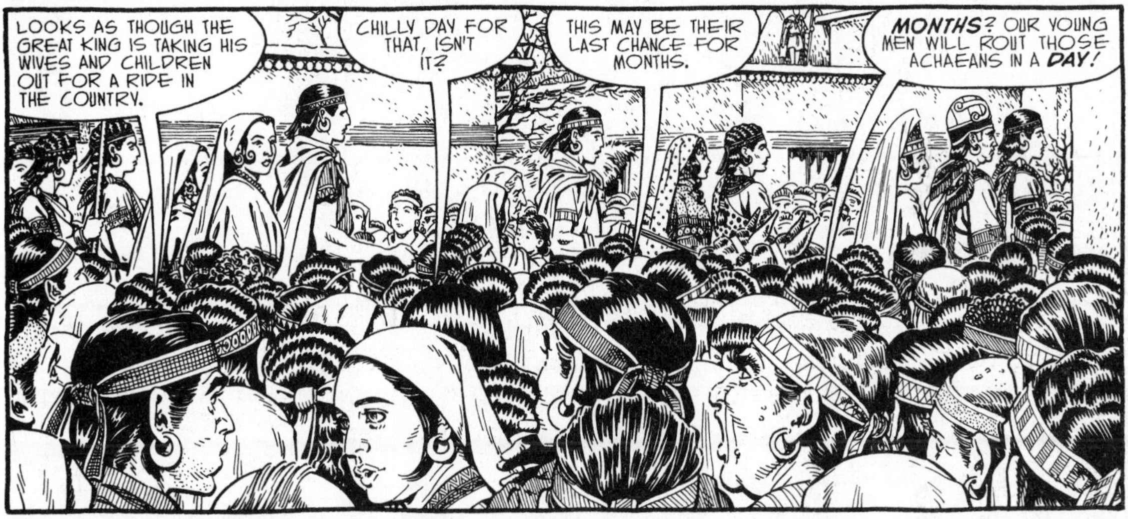
LOOKS AS THOUGH THE GREAT KING IS TAKING HIS WIVES AND CHILDREN OUT FOR A RIDE IN THE COUNTRY.
CHILLY DAY FOR THAT, ISN'T IT?
THIS MAY BE THEIR LAST CHANCE FOR MONTHS.
MONTHS? OUR YOUNG MEN WILL ROUT THOSE ACHAEANS IN A DAY!

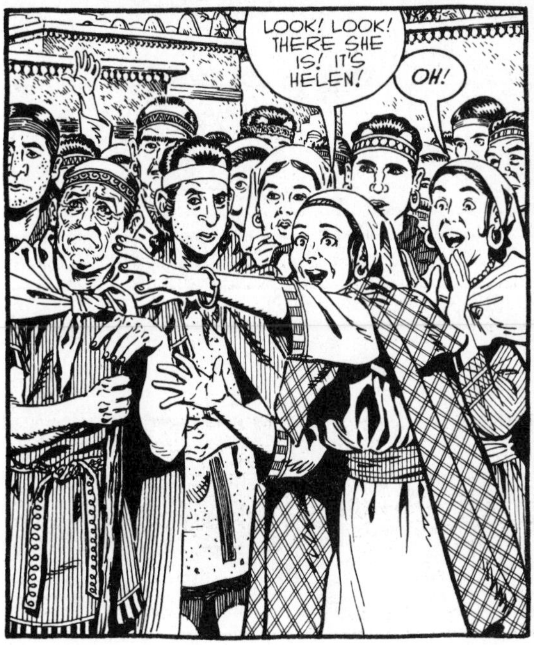
LOOK! LOOK! THERE SHE IS! IT'S HELEN!
OH!

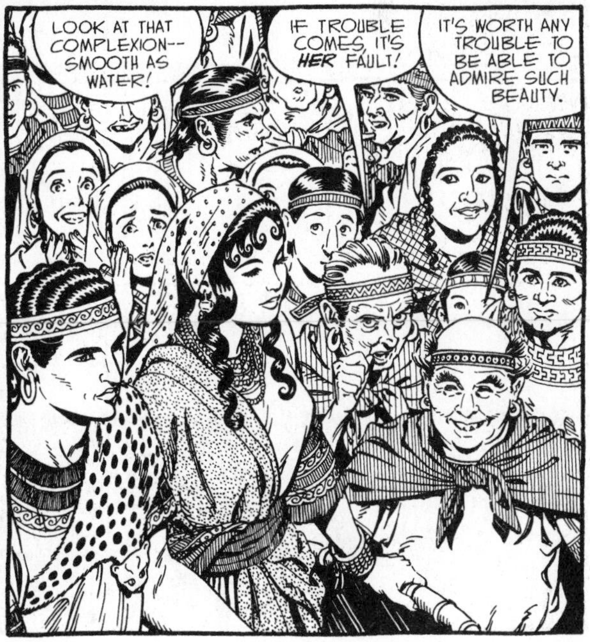
LOOK AT THAT COMPLEXION-- SMOOTH AS WATER!
IF TROUBLE COMES, IT'S HER FAULT!
IT'S WORTH ANY TROUBLE TO BE ABLE TO ADMIRE SUCH BEAUTY.

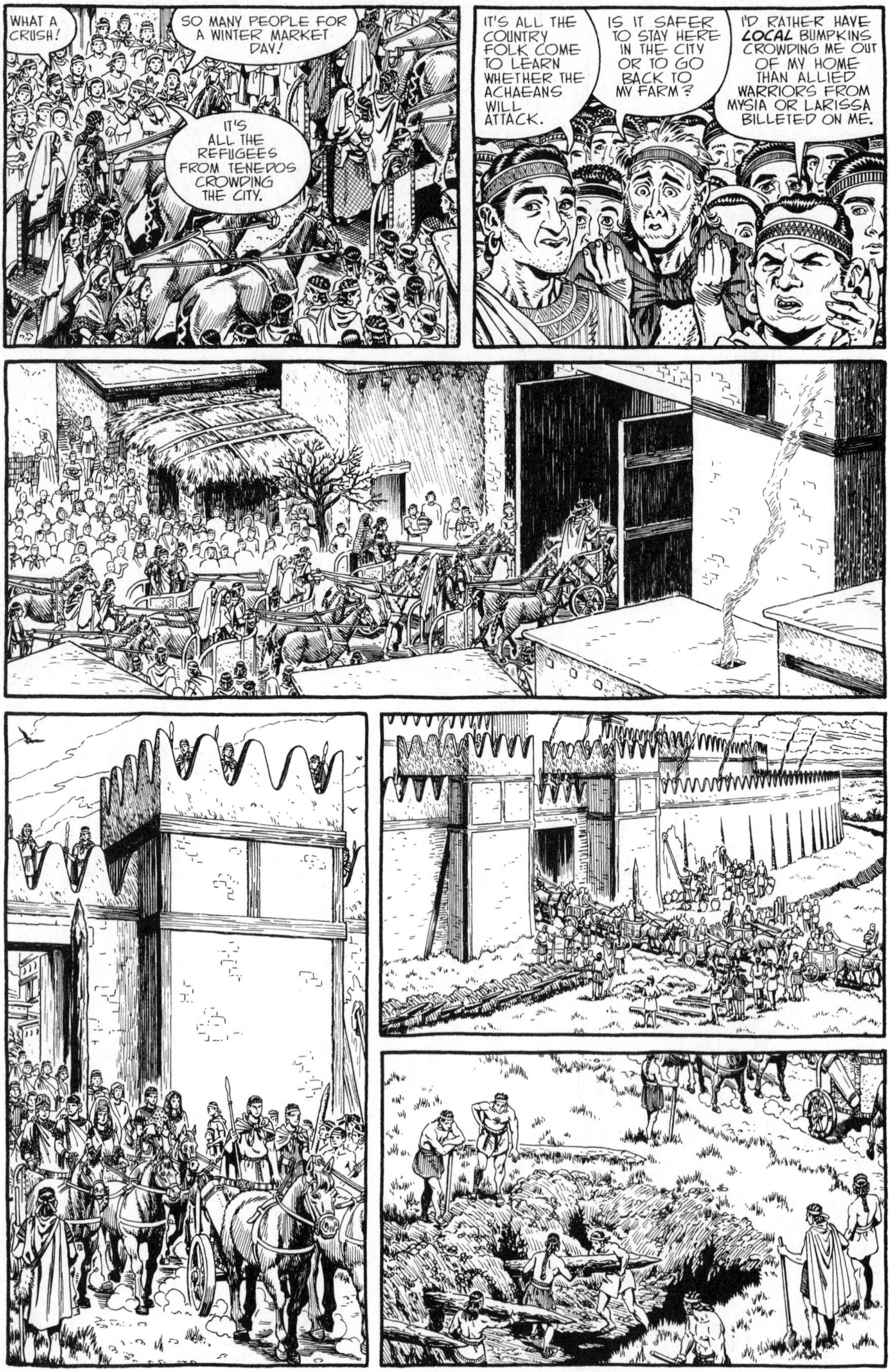
WHAT A CRUSH!
SO MANY PEOPLE FOR A WINTER MARKET DAY!
IT'S ALL THE REFUGEES FROM TENEDOS CROWDING THE CITY.
IT'S ALL THE COUNTRY FOLK COME TO LEARN WHETHER THE ACHAEANS WILL ATTACK.
IS IT SAFER TO STAY HERE IN THE CITY OR TO GO BACK TO MY FARM?
I'D RATHER HAVE LOCAL BUMPKINS CROWDING ME OUT OF MY HOME THAN ALLIED WARRIORS FROM MYSIA OR LARISSA BILLETED ON ME.

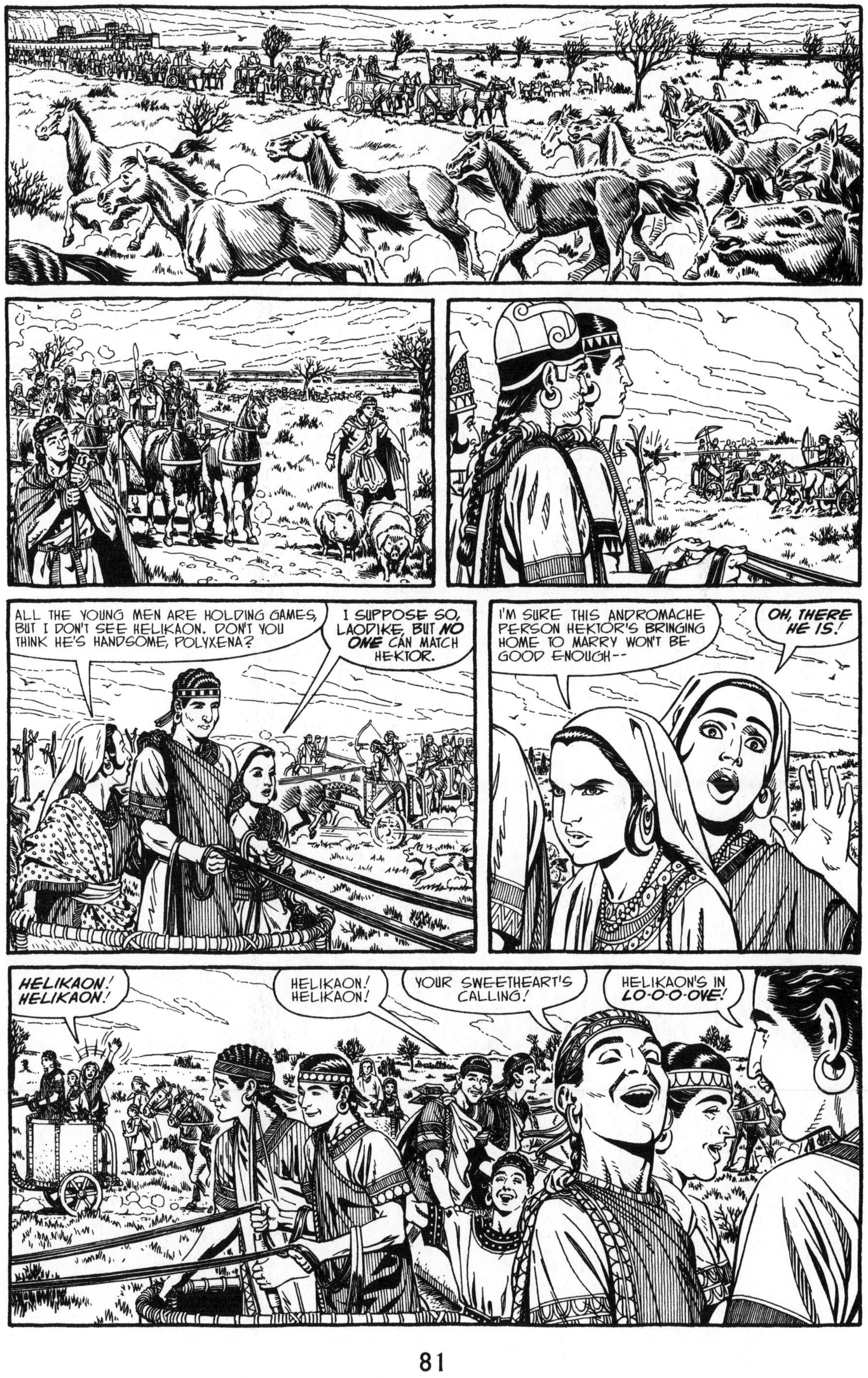
ALL THE YOUNG MEN ARE HOLDING GAMES, BUT I DON'T SEE HELIKAON. DON'T YOU THINK HE'S HANDSOME, POLYXENA?
I SUPPOSE SO, LAODIKE, BUT NO ONE CAN MATCH HEKTOR.
I'M SURE THIS ANDROMACHE PERSON HEKTOR'S BRINGING HOME TO MARRY WON'T BE GOOD ENOUGH--
OH, THERE HE IS!
HELIKAON! HELIKAON!
HELIKAON! HELIKAON!
YOUR SWEETHEART'S CALLING!
HELIKAON'S IN LO-O-O-OVE!

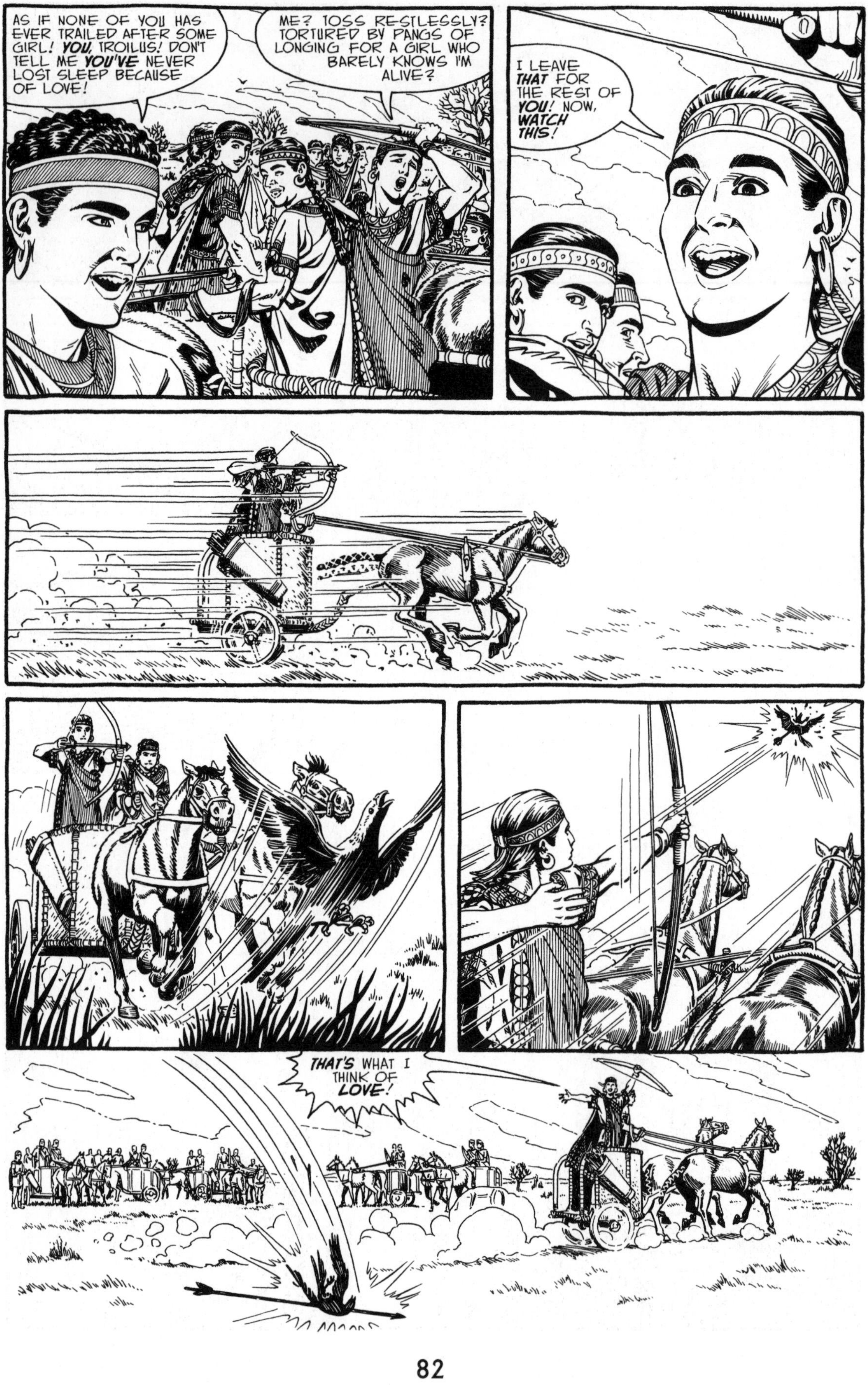
AS IF NONE OF YOU HAS EVER TRAILED AFTER SOME GIRL! YOU, TROILUS! DON'T TELL ME YOU'VE NEVER LOST SLEEP BECAUSE OF LOVE!
ME? TOSS RESTLESSLY? TORTURED BY PANGS OF LONGING FOR A GIRL WHO BARELY KNOWS I'M ALIVE?
I LEAVE THAT FOR THE REST OF YOU! NOW, WATCH THIS!
THAT'S WHAT I THINK OF LOVE!

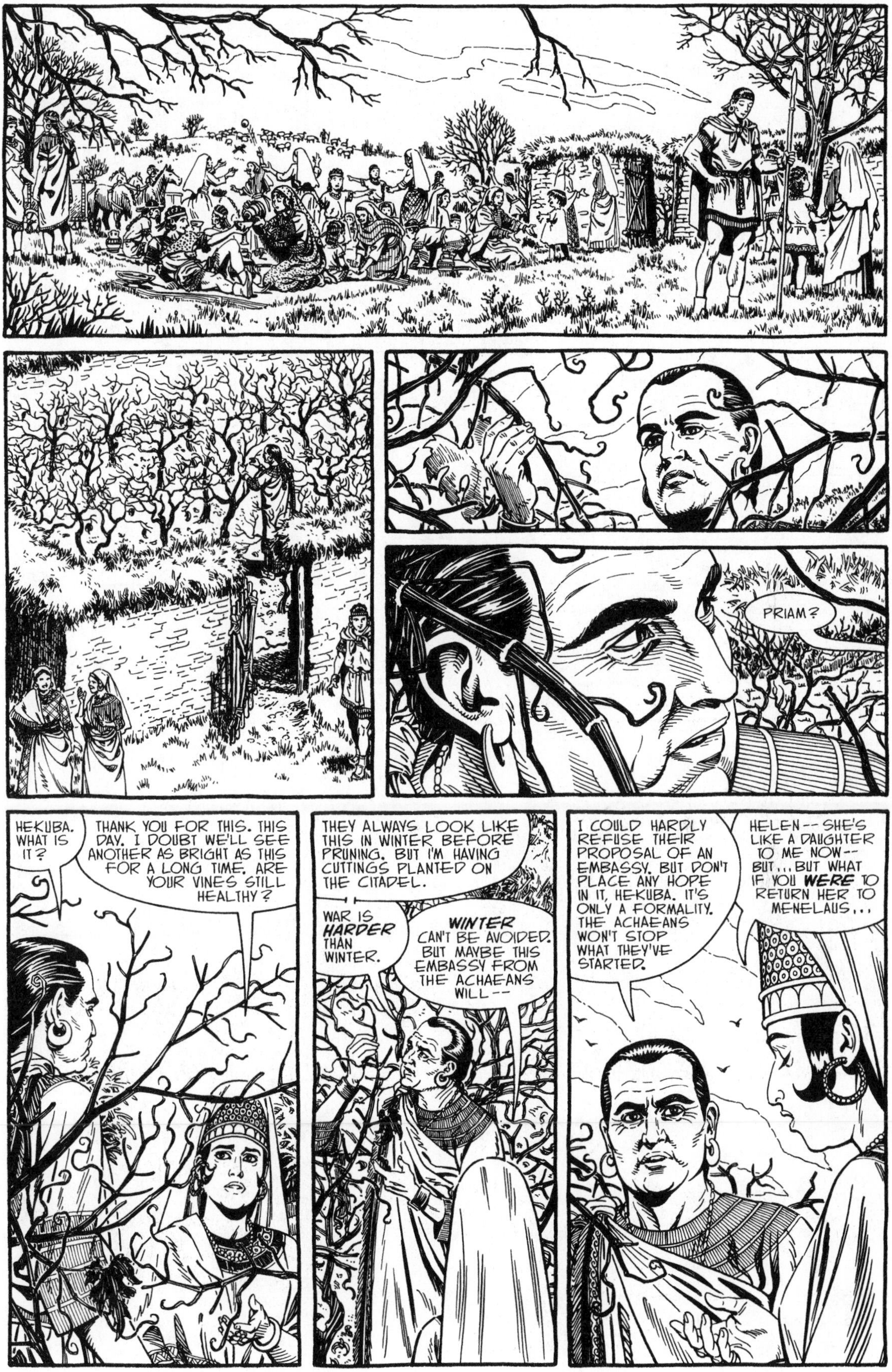
PRIAM?
HEKUBA. WHAT IS IT?
THANK YOU FOR THIS. THIS DAY. I DOUBT WE'LL SEE ANOTHER AS BRIGHT AS THIS FOR A LONG TIME. ARE YOUR VINES STILL HEALTHY?
THEY ALWAYS LOOK LIKE THIS IN WINTER BEFORE PRUNING. BUT I'M HAVING CUTTINGS PLANTED ON THE CITADEL.
WAR IS HARDER THAN WINTER.
WINTER CAN'T BE AVOIDED. BUT MAYBE THIS EMBASSY FROM THE ACHAEANS WILL--
I COULD HARDLY REFUSE THEIR PROPOSAL OF AN EMBASSY. BUT DON'T PLACE ANY HOPE IN IT, HEKUBA. IT'S ONLY A FORMALITY. THE ACHAEANS WON'T STOP WHAT THEY'VE STARTED.
HELEN--SHE'S LIKE A DAUGHTER TO ME NOW--BUT...BUT WHAT IF YOU WERE TO RETURN HER TO MENELAUS...

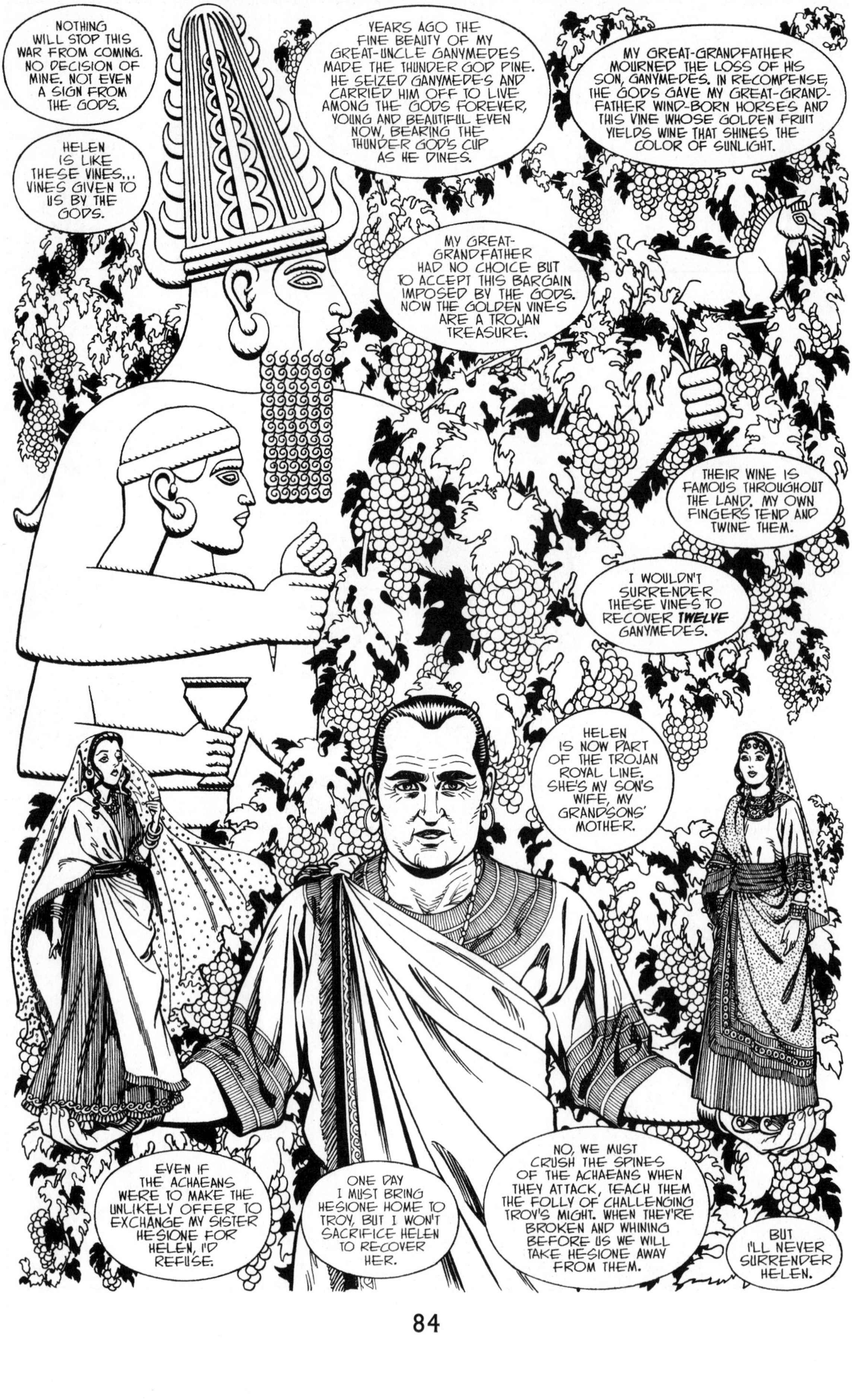
NOTHING WILL STOP THIS WAR FROM COMING. NO DECISION OF MINE. NOT EVEN A SIGN FROM THE GODS.
HELEN IS LIKE THESE VINES... VINES GIVEN TO US BY THE GODS.
YEARS AGO THE FINE BEAUTY OF MY GREAT-UNCLE GANYMEDES MADE THE THUNDER GOD PINE. HE SEIZED GANYMEDES AND CARRIED HIM OFF TO LIVE AMONG THE GODS FOREVER, YOUNG AND BEAUTIFUL EVEN NOW, BEARING THE THUNDER GOD'S CUP AS HE DINES.
MY GREAT-GRANDFATHER MOURNED THE LOSS OF HIS SON, GANYMEDES. IN RECOMPENSE, THE GODS GAVE MY GREAT-GRANDFATHER WIND-BORN HORSES AND THIS VINE WHOSE GOLDEN FRUIT YIELDS WINE THAT SHINES THE COLOR OF SUNLIGHT.
MY GREAT-GRANDFATHER HAD NO CHOICE BUT TO ACCEPT THIS BARGAIN IMPOSED BY THE GODS. NOW THE GOLDEN VINES ARE A TROJAN TREASURE.
THEIR WINE IS FAMOUS THROUGHOUT THE LAND. MY OWN FINGERS TEND AND TWINE THEM.
I WOULDN'T SURRENDER THESE VINES TO RECOVER **TWELVE** GANYMEDES.
HELEN IS NOW PART OF THE TROJAN ROYAL LINE. SHE'S MY SON'S WIFE, MY GRANDSONS' MOTHER.
EVEN IF THE ACHAEANS WERE TO MAKE THE UNLIKELY OFFER TO EXCHANGE MY SISTER HESIONE FOR HELEN, I'D REFUSE.
ONE DAY I MUST BRING HESIONE HOME TO TROY, BUT I WON'T SACRIFICE HELEN TO RECOVER HER.
NO, WE MUST CRUSH THE SPINES OF THE ACHAEANS WHEN THEY ATTACK, TEACH THEM THE FOLLY OF CHALLENGING TROY'S MIGHT. WHEN THEY'RE BROKEN AND WHINING BEFORE US WE WILL TAKE HESIONE AWAY FROM THEM.
BUT I'LL NEVER SURRENDER HELEN.

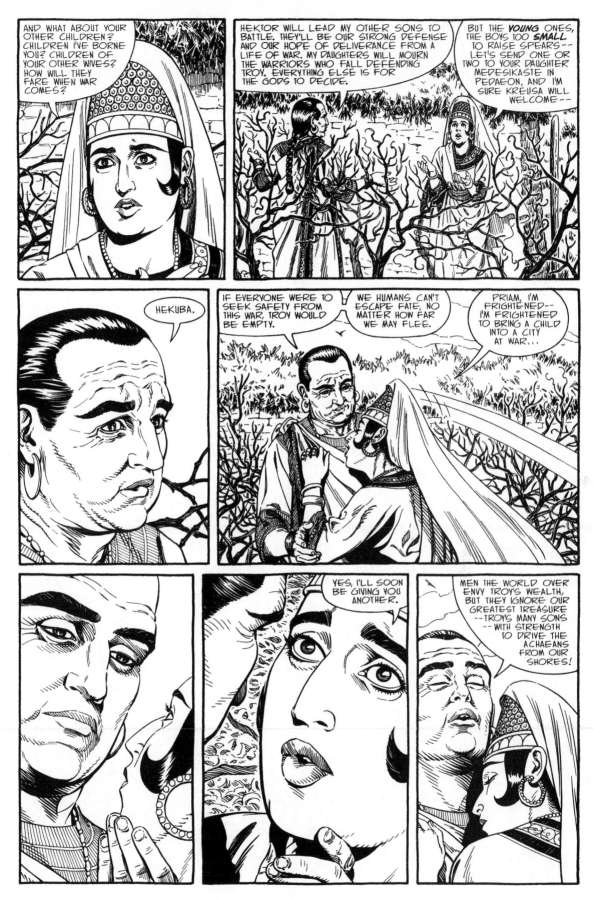

AND WHAT ABOUT YOUR OTHER CHILDREN? CHILDREN I'VE BORNE YOU? CHILDREN OF YOUR OTHER WIVES? HOW WILL THEY FARE WHEN WAR COMES?

HEKTOR WILL LEAD MY OTHER SONS TO BATTLE. THEY'LL BE OUR STRONG DEFENSE AND OUR HOPE OF DELIVERANCE FROM A LIFE OF WAR. MY DAUGHTERS WILL MOURN THE WARRIORS WHO FALL DEFENDING TROY. EVERYTHING ELSE IS FOR THE GODS TO DECIDE.

BUT THE *YOUNG* ONES, THE BOYS TOO *SMALL* TO RAISE SPEARS-- LET'S SEND ONE OR TWO TO YOUR DAUGHTER MEDESIKASTE IN PEDAEON, AND I'M SURE KREUSA WILL WELCOME--

HEKUBA.

IF EVERYONE WERE TO SEEK SAFETY FROM THIS WAR, TROY WOULD BE EMPTY.

WE HUMANS CAN'T ESCAPE FATE, NO MATTER HOW FAR WE MAY FLEE.

PRIAM, I'M FRIGHTENED-- I'M FRIGHTENED TO BRING A CHILD INTO A CITY AT WAR...

YES, I'LL SOON BE GIVING YOU ANOTHER.

MEN THE WORLD OVER ENVY TROY'S WEALTH, BUT THEY IGNORE OUR GREATEST TREASURE --TROY'S MANY SONS --WITH STRENGTH TO DRIVE THE ACHAEANS FROM OUR SHORES!

85

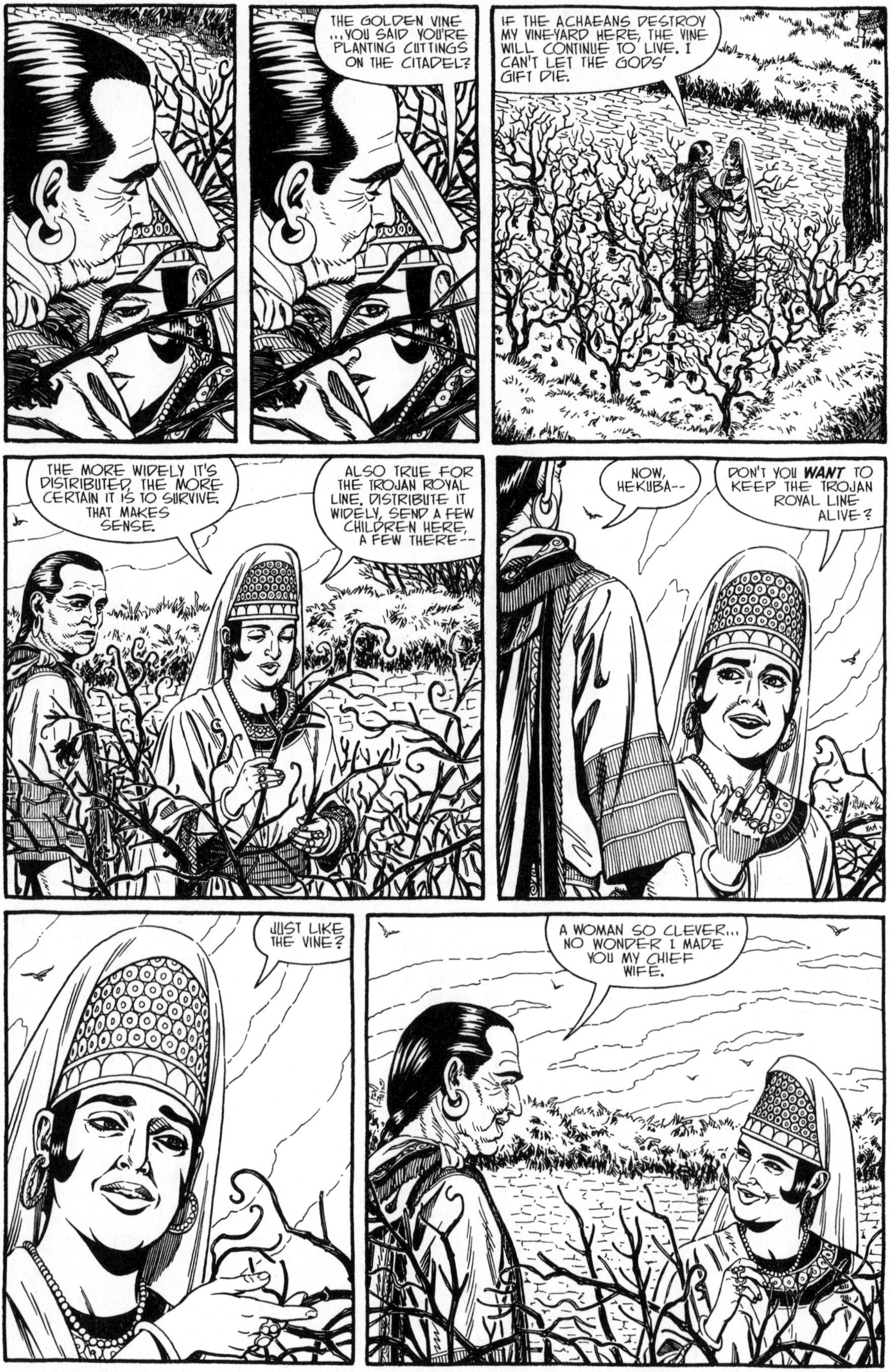
THE GOLDEN VINE ...YOU SAID YOU'RE PLANTING CUTTINGS ON THE CITADEL?
IF THE ACHAEANS DESTROY MY VINEYARD HERE, THE VINE WILL CONTINUE TO LIVE. I CAN'T LET THE GODS' GIFT DIE.
THE MORE WIDELY IT'S DISTRIBUTED, THE MORE CERTAIN IT IS TO SURVIVE. THAT MAKES SENSE.
ALSO TRUE FOR THE TROJAN ROYAL LINE. DISTRIBUTE IT WIDELY, SEND A FEW CHILDREN HERE, A FEW THERE--
NOW, HEKUBA--
DON'T YOU WANT TO KEEP THE TROJAN ROYAL LINE ALIVE?
JUST LIKE THE VINE?
A WOMAN SO CLEVER... NO WONDER I MADE YOU MY CHIEF WIFE.

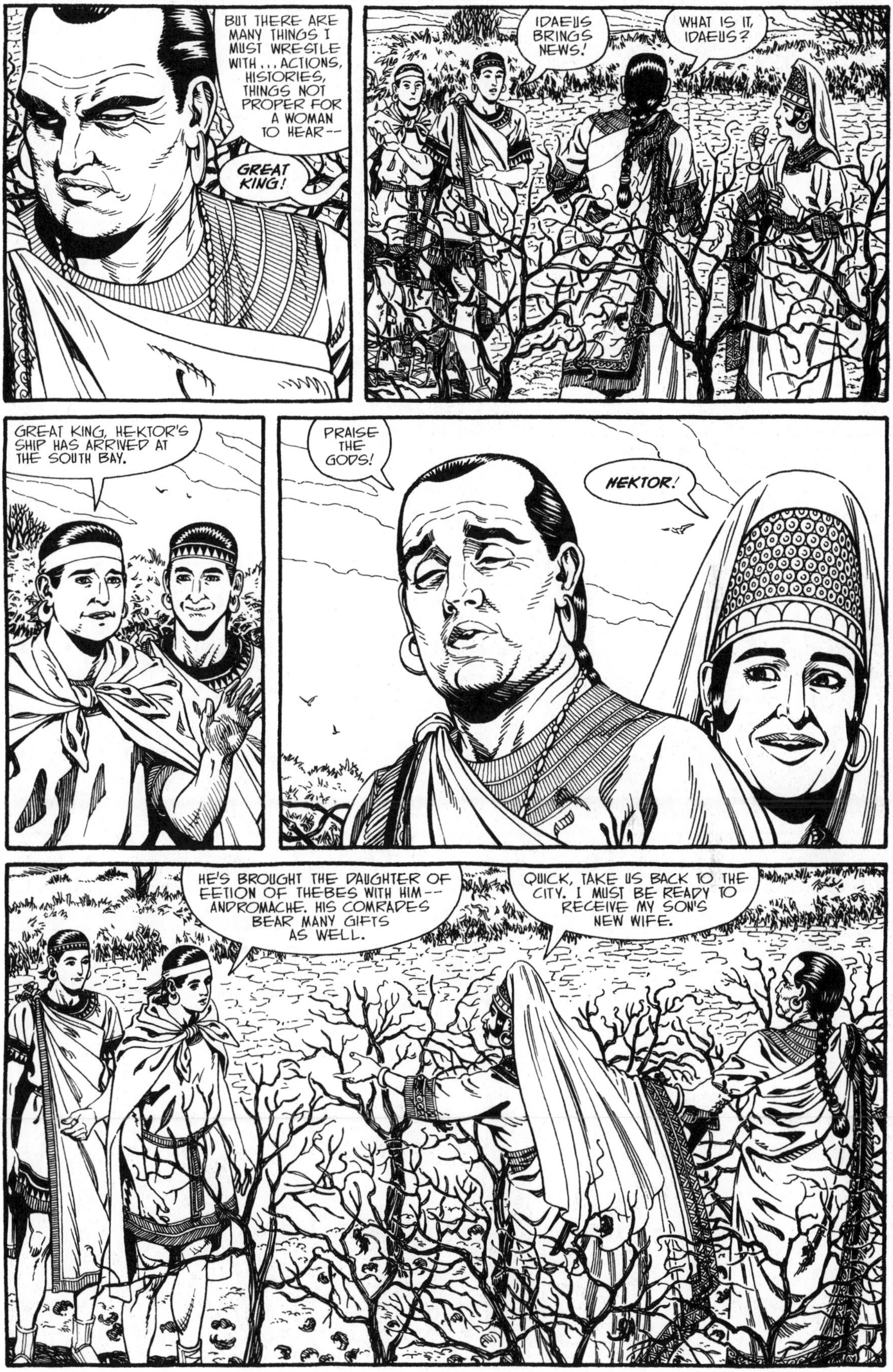
BUT THERE ARE MANY THINGS I MUST WRESTLE WITH... ACTIONS, HISTORIES, THINGS NOT PROPER FOR A WOMAN TO HEAR--
GREAT KING!
IDAEUS BRINGS NEWS!
WHAT IS IT, IDAEUS?
GREAT KING, HEKTOR'S SHIP HAS ARRIVED AT THE SOUTH BAY.
PRAISE THE GODS!
HEKTOR!
HE'S BROUGHT THE DAUGHTER OF EETION OF THEBES WITH HIM-- ANDROMACHE. HIS COMRADES BEAR MANY GIFTS AS WELL.
QUICK, TAKE US BACK TO THE CITY. I MUST BE READY TO RECEIVE MY SON'S NEW WIFE.

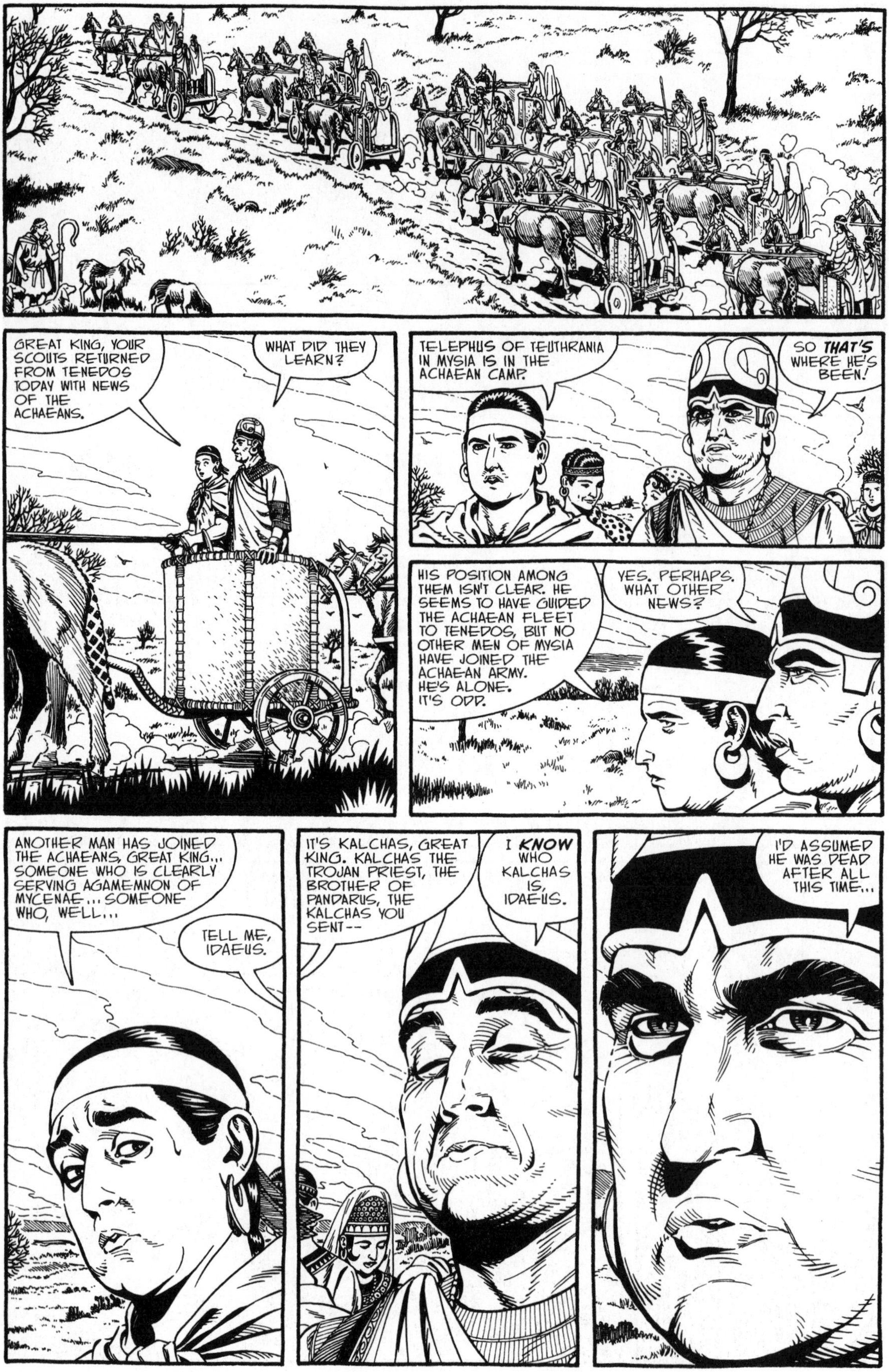
GREAT KING, YOUR SCOUTS RETURNED FROM TENEDOS TODAY WITH NEWS OF THE ACHAEANS.
WHAT DID THEY LEARN?
TELEPHUS OF TEUTHRANIA IN MYSIA IS IN THE ACHAEAN CAMP.
SO THAT'S WHERE HE'S BEEN!
HIS POSITION AMONG THEM ISN'T CLEAR. HE SEEMS TO HAVE GUIDED THE ACHAEAN FLEET TO TENEDOS, BUT NO OTHER MEN OF MYSIA HAVE JOINED THE ACHAEAN ARMY. HE'S ALONE. IT'S ODD.
YES. PERHAPS. WHAT OTHER NEWS?
ANOTHER MAN HAS JOINED THE ACHAEANS, GREAT KING... SOMEONE WHO IS CLEARLY SERVING AGAMEMNON OF MYCENAE... SOMEONE WHO, WELL...
TELL ME, IDAEUS.
IT'S KALCHAS, GREAT KING. KALCHAS THE TROJAN PRIEST, THE BROTHER OF PANDARUS, THE KALCHAS YOU SENT--
I KNOW WHO KALCHAS IS, IDAEUS.
I'D ASSUMED HE WAS DEAD AFTER ALL THIS TIME...

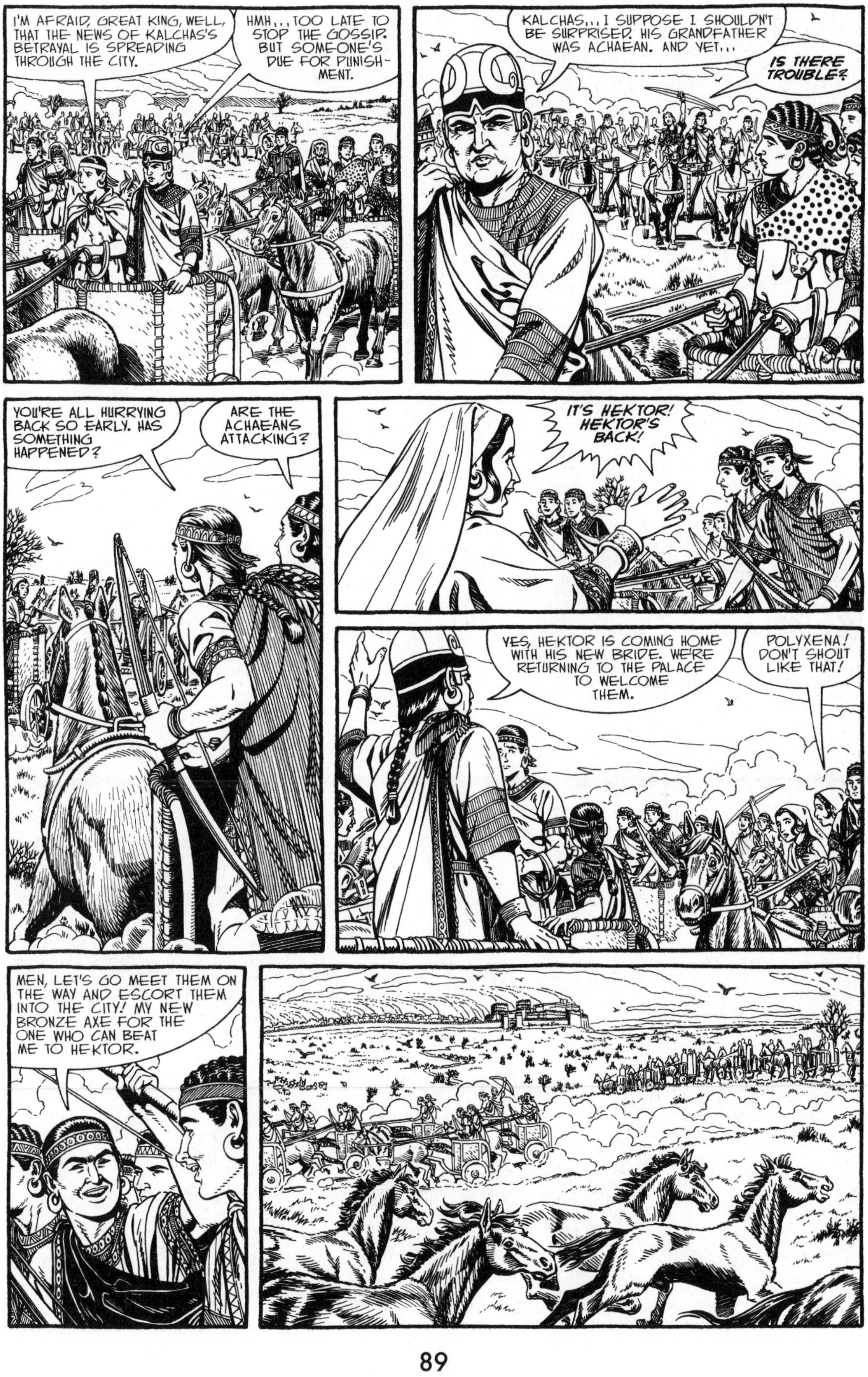
I'M AFRAID, GREAT KING, WELL, THAT THE NEWS OF KALCHAS'S BETRAYAL IS SPREADING THROUGH THE CITY.
HMH... TOO LATE TO STOP THE GOSSIP. BUT SOMEONE'S DUE FOR PUNISHMENT.
KALCHAS... I SUPPOSE I SHOULDN'T BE SURPRISED. HIS GRANDFATHER WAS ACHAEAN. AND YET...
IS THERE TROUBLE?
YOU'RE ALL HURRYING BACK SO EARLY. HAS SOMETHING HAPPENED?
ARE THE ACHAEANS ATTACKING?
IT'S HEKTOR! HEKTOR'S BACK!
YES, HEKTOR IS COMING HOME WITH HIS NEW BRIDE. WE'RE RETURNING TO THE PALACE TO WELCOME THEM.
POLYXENA! DON'T SHOUT LIKE THAT!
MEN, LET'S GO MEET THEM ON THE WAY AND ESCORT THEM INTO THE CITY! MY NEW BRONZE AXE FOR THE ONE WHO CAN BEAT ME TO HEKTOR.

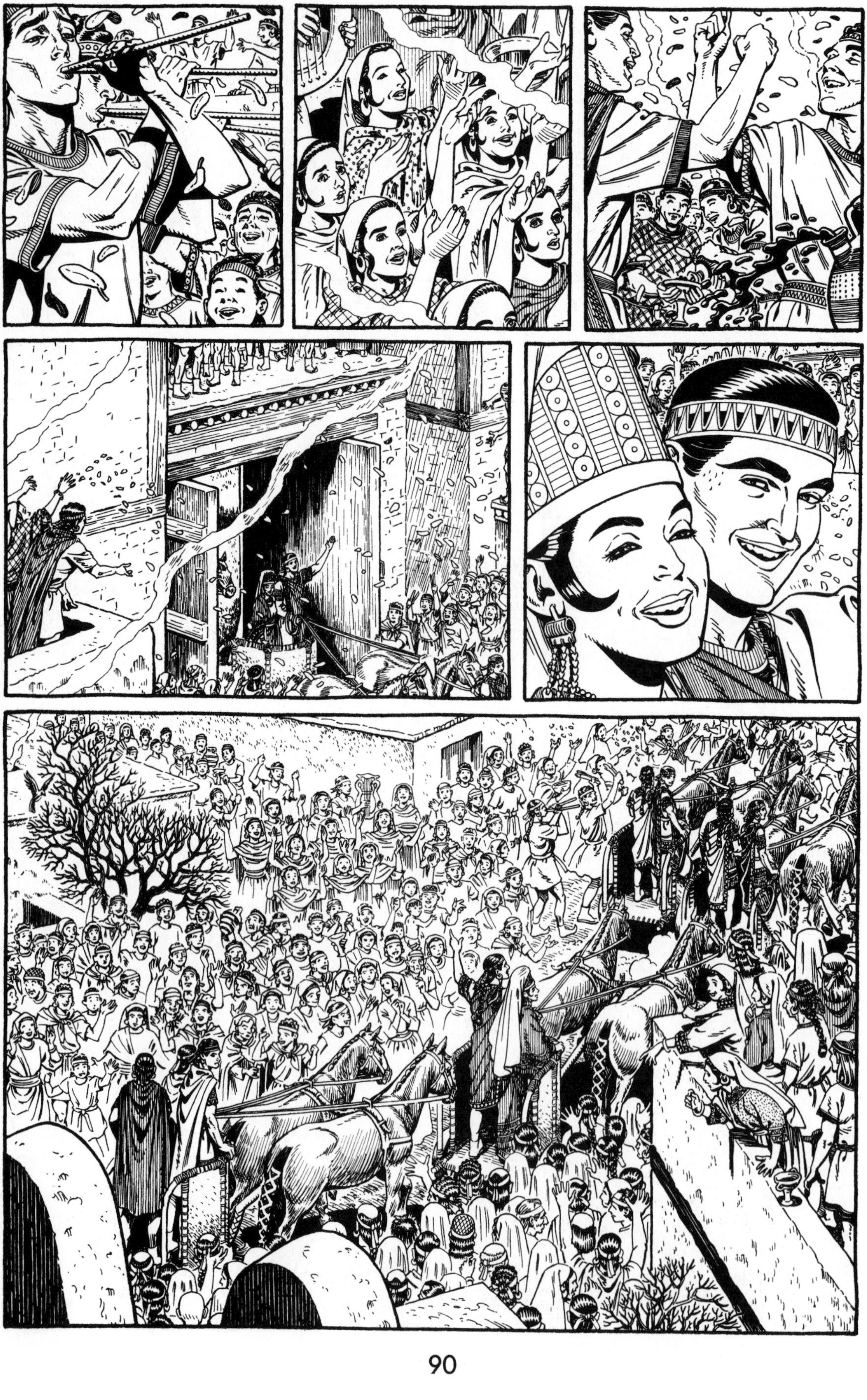

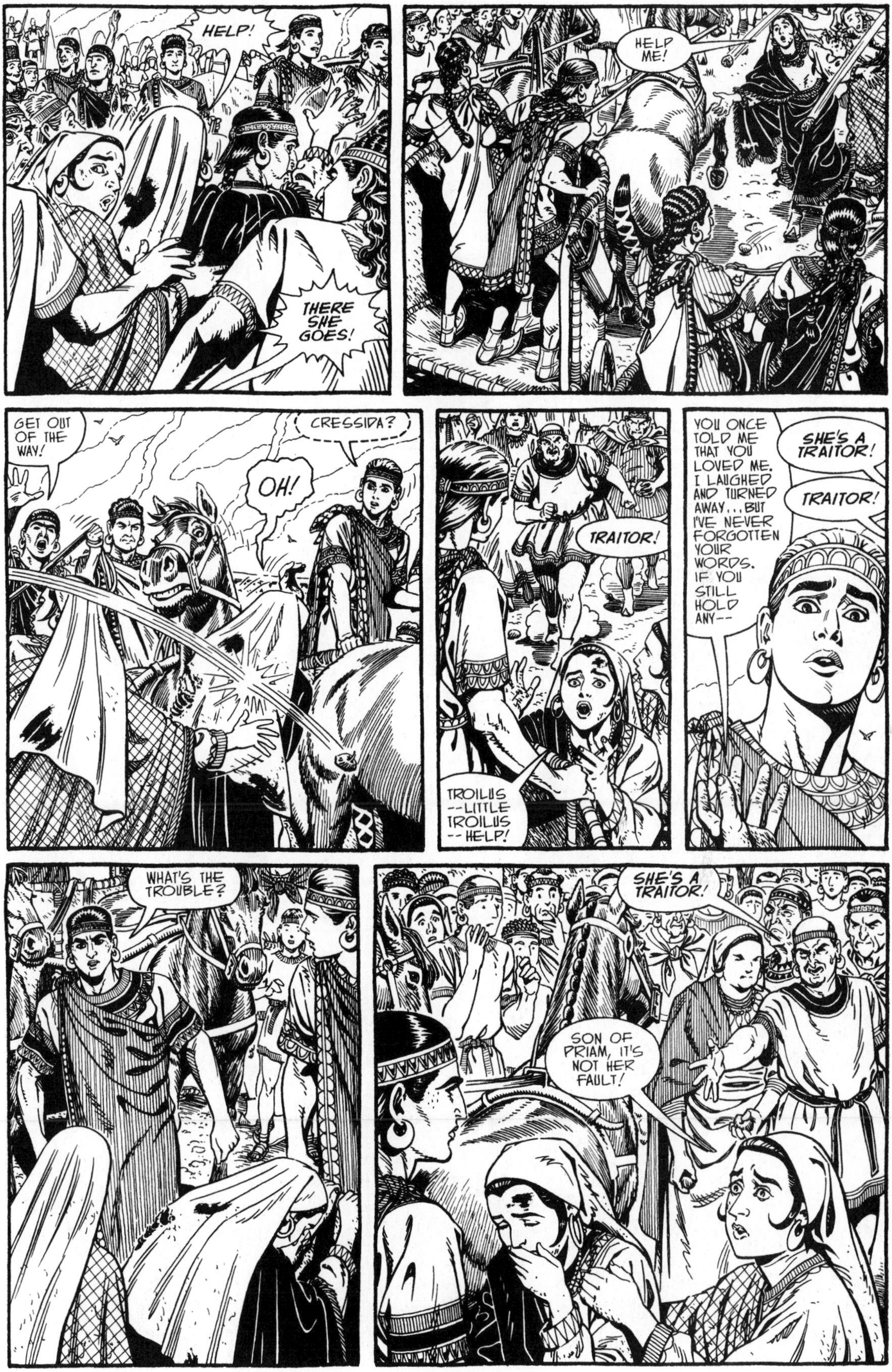
HELP!
THERE SHE GOES!
HELP ME!
GET OUT OF THE WAY!
CRESSIDA?
OH!
TRAITOR!
TROILUS --LITTLE TROILUS --HELP!
YOU ONCE TOLD ME THAT YOU LOVED ME. I LAUGHED AND TURNED AWAY... BUT I'VE NEVER FORGOTTEN YOUR WORDS. IF YOU STILL HOLD ANY--
SHE'S A TRAITOR!
TRAITOR!
WHAT'S THE TROUBLE?
SHE'S A TRAITOR!
SON OF PRIAM, IT'S NOT HER FAULT!

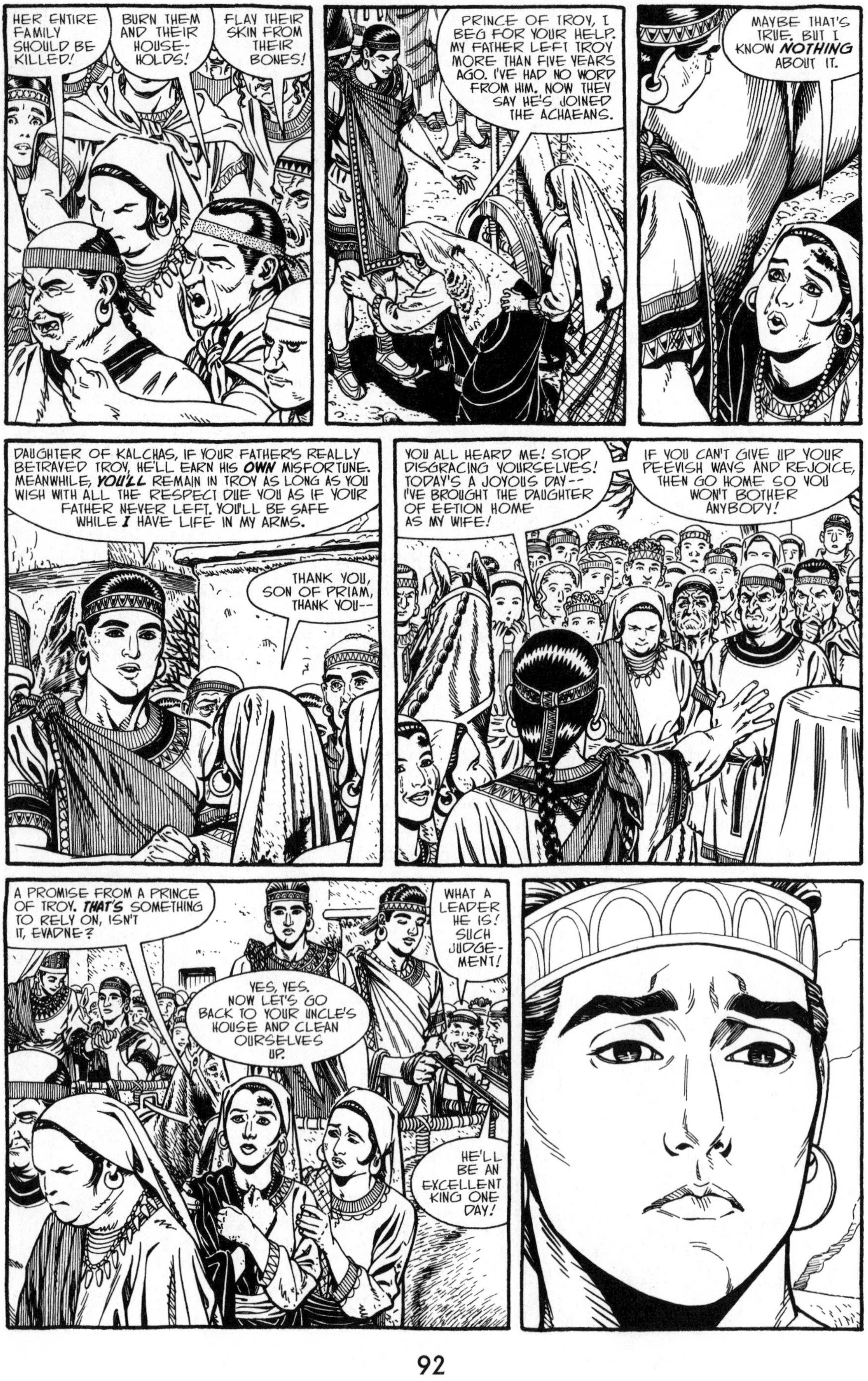
HER ENTIRE FAMILY SHOULD BE KILLED!
BURN THEM AND THEIR HOUSE-HOLDS!
FLAY THEIR SKIN FROM THEIR BONES!
PRINCE OF TROY, I BEG FOR YOUR HELP. MY FATHER LEFT TROY MORE THAN FIVE YEARS AGO. I'VE HAD NO WORD FROM HIM. NOW THEY SAY HE'S JOINED THE ACHAEANS.
MAYBE THAT'S TRUE. BUT I KNOW NOTHING ABOUT IT.
DAUGHTER OF KALCHAS, IF YOUR FATHER'S REALLY BETRAYED TROY, HE'LL EARN HIS OWN MISFORTUNE. MEANWHILE, YOU'LL REMAIN IN TROY AS LONG AS YOU WISH WITH ALL THE RESPECT DUE YOU AS IF YOUR FATHER NEVER LEFT. YOU'LL BE SAFE WHILE I HAVE LIFE IN MY ARMS.
THANK YOU, SON OF PRIAM, THANK YOU--
YOU ALL HEARD ME! STOP DISGRACING YOURSELVES! TODAY'S A JOYOUS DAY-- I'VE BROUGHT THE DAUGHTER OF EETION HOME AS MY WIFE!
IF YOU CAN'T GIVE UP YOUR PEEVISH WAYS AND REJOICE, THEN GO HOME SO YOU WON'T BOTHER ANYBODY!
A PROMISE FROM A PRINCE OF TROY. THAT'S SOMETHING TO RELY ON, ISN'T IT, EVADNE?
YES, YES. NOW LET'S GO BACK TO YOUR UNCLE'S HOUSE AND CLEAN OURSELVES UP.
WHAT A LEADER HE IS! SUCH JUDGEMENT!
HE'LL BE AN EXCELLENT KING ONE DAY!

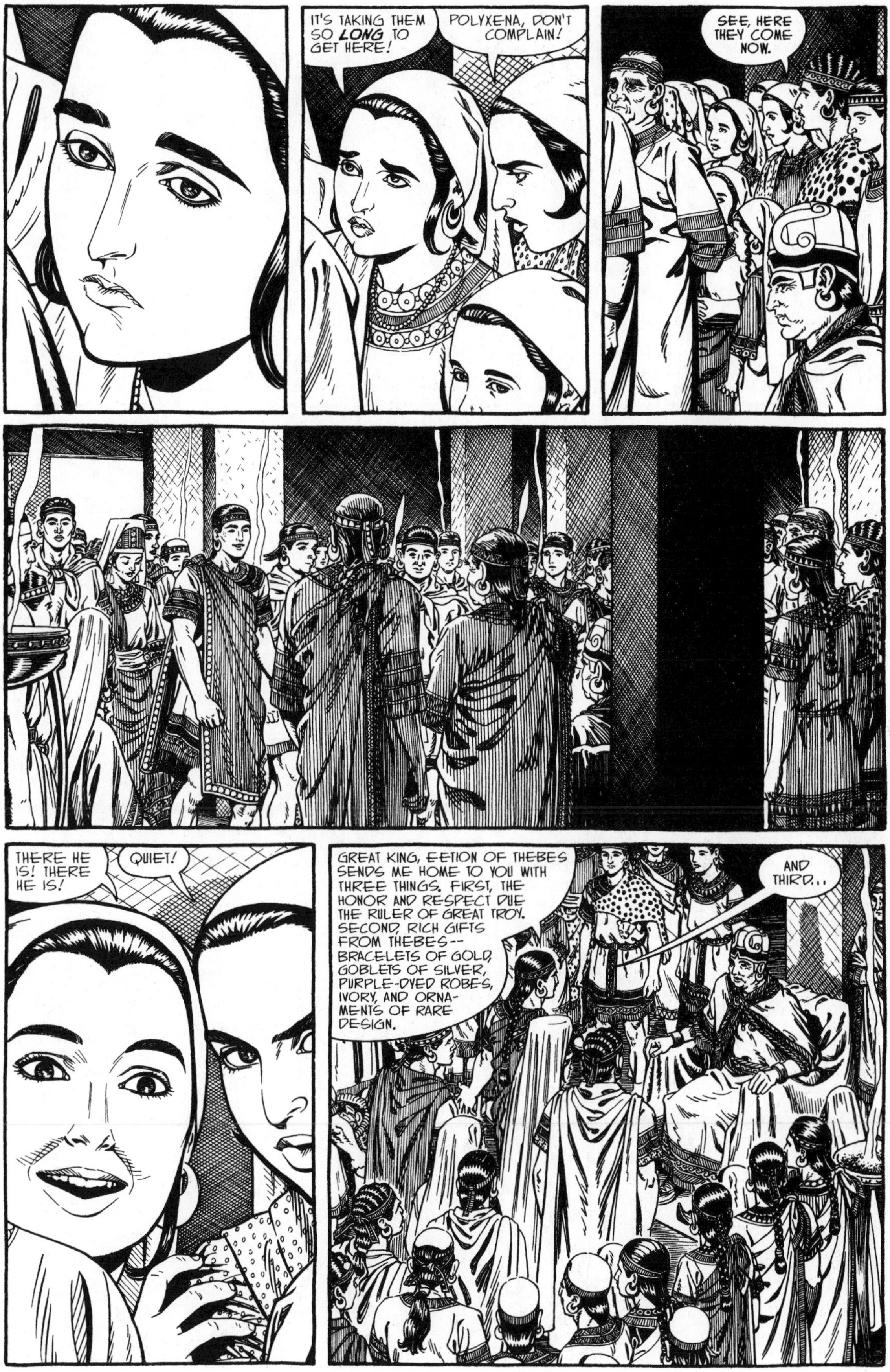
IT'S TAKING THEM SO LONG TO GET HERE!
POLYXENA, DON'T COMPLAIN!
SEE, HERE THEY COME NOW.
THERE HE IS! THERE HE IS!
QUIET!
GREAT KING, EETION OF THEBES SENDS ME HOME TO YOU WITH THREE THINGS. FIRST, THE HONOR AND RESPECT DUE THE RULER OF GREAT TROY. SECOND, RICH GIFTS FROM THEBES-- BRACELETS OF GOLD, GOBLETS OF SILVER, PURPLE-DYED ROBES, IVORY, AND ORNAMENTS OF RARE DESIGN.
AND THIRD...

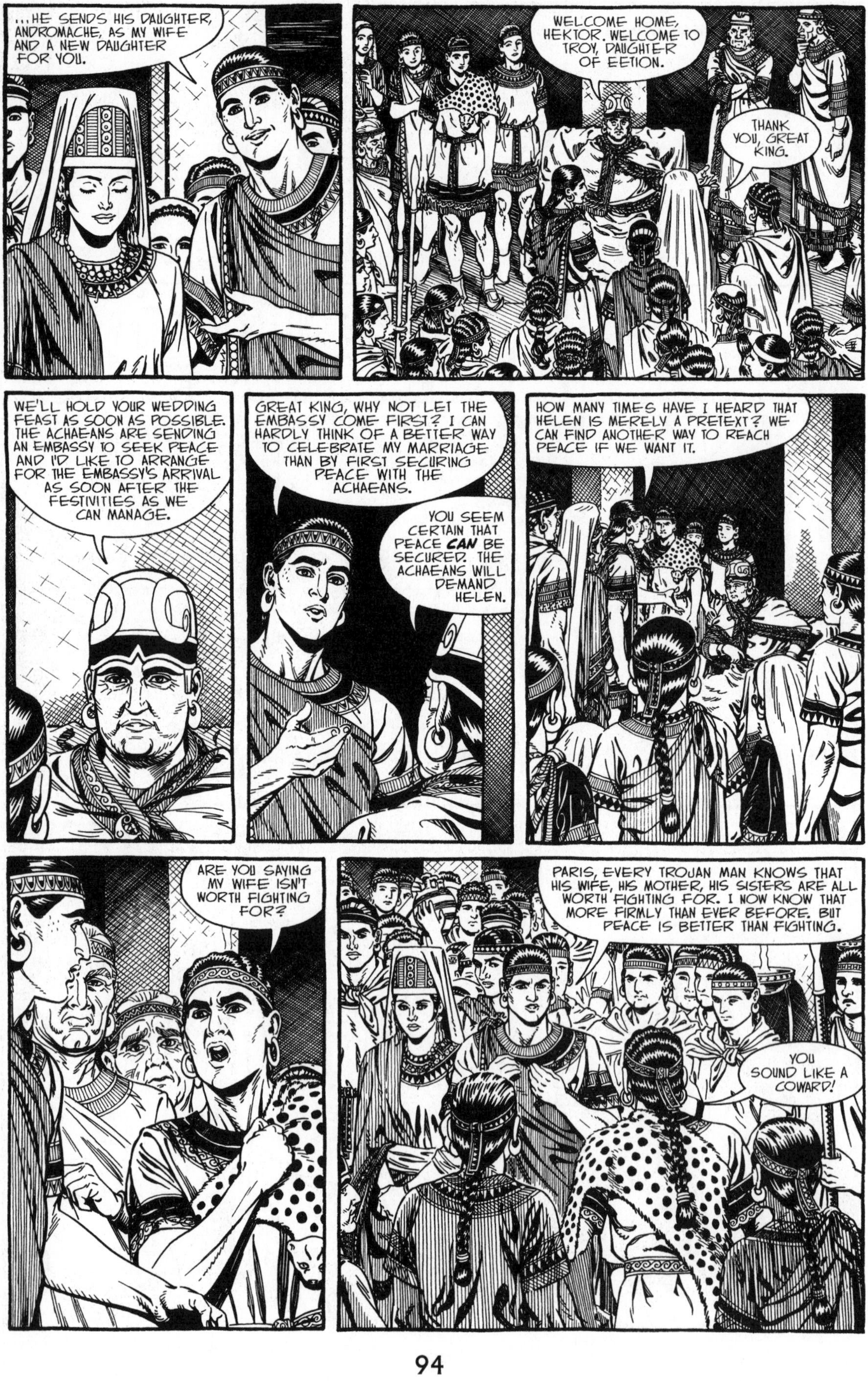
...HE SENDS HIS DAUGHTER, ANDROMACHE, AS MY WIFE AND A NEW DAUGHTER FOR YOU.
WELCOME HOME, HEKTOR. WELCOME TO TROY, DAUGHTER OF EETION.
THANK YOU, GREAT KING.
WE'LL HOLD YOUR WEDDING FEAST AS SOON AS POSSIBLE. THE ACHAEANS ARE SENDING AN EMBASSY TO SEEK PEACE AND I'D LIKE TO ARRANGE FOR THE EMBASSY'S ARRIVAL AS SOON AFTER THE FESTIVITIES AS WE CAN MANAGE.
GREAT KING, WHY NOT LET THE EMBASSY COME FIRST? I CAN HARDLY THINK OF A BETTER WAY TO CELEBRATE MY MARRIAGE THAN BY FIRST SECURING PEACE WITH THE ACHAEANS.
YOU SEEM CERTAIN THAT PEACE CAN BE SECURED. THE ACHAEANS WILL DEMAND HELEN.
HOW MANY TIMES HAVE I HEARD THAT HELEN IS MERELY A PRETEXT? WE CAN FIND ANOTHER WAY TO REACH PEACE IF WE WANT IT.
ARE YOU SAYING MY WIFE ISN'T WORTH FIGHTING FOR?
PARIS, EVERY TROJAN MAN KNOWS THAT HIS WIFE, HIS MOTHER, HIS SISTERS ARE ALL WORTH FIGHTING FOR. I NOW KNOW THAT MORE FIRMLY THAN EVER BEFORE. BUT PEACE IS BETTER THAN FIGHTING.
YOU SOUND LIKE A COWARD!

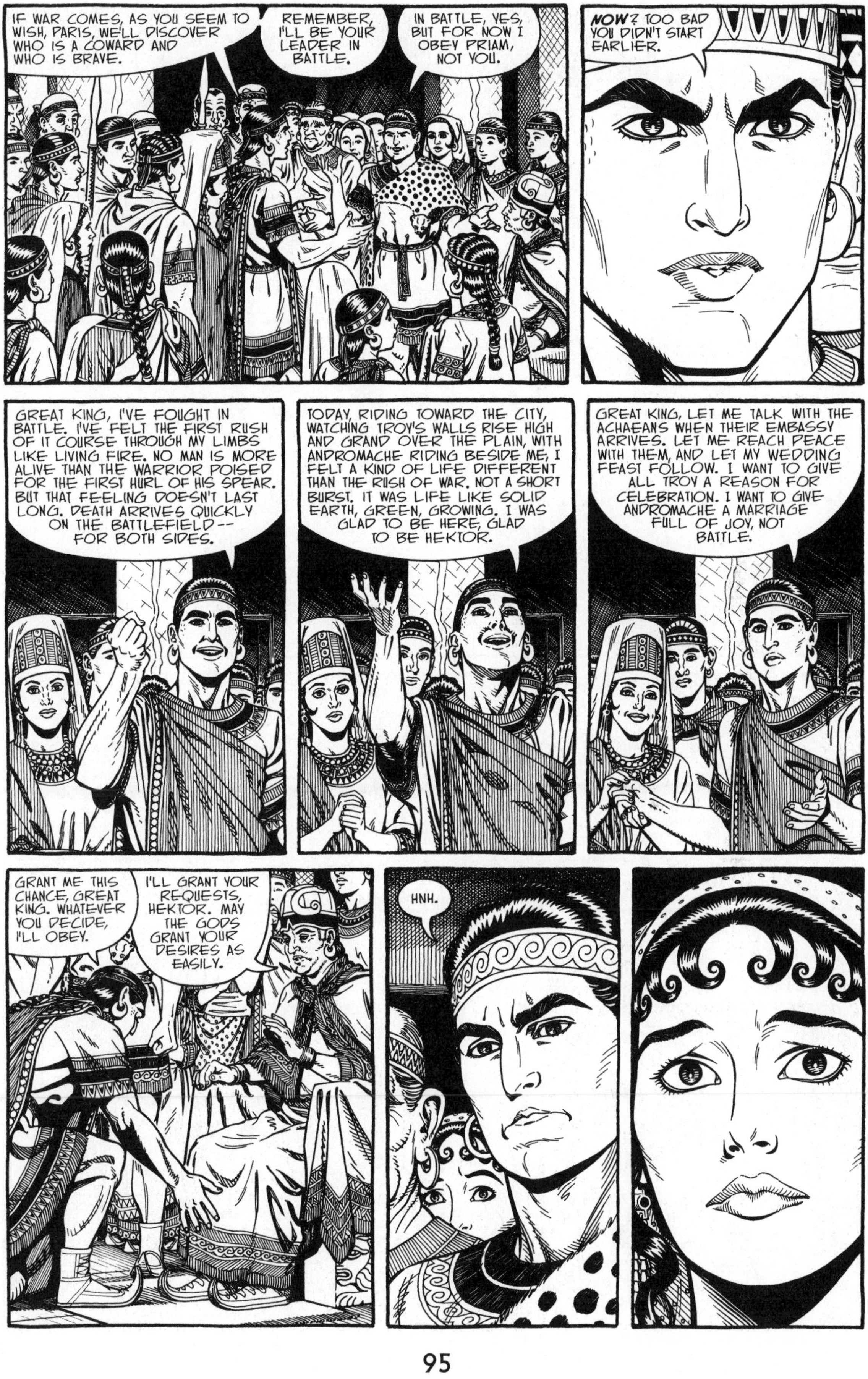

IF WAR COMES, AS YOU SEEM TO WISH, PARIS, WE'LL DISCOVER WHO IS A COWARD AND WHO IS BRAVE.
REMEMBER, I'LL BE YOUR LEADER IN BATTLE.
IN BATTLE, YES, BUT FOR NOW I OBEY PRIAM, NOT YOU.
NOW? TOO BAD YOU DIDN'T START EARLIER.
GREAT KING, I'VE FOUGHT IN BATTLE. I'VE FELT THE FIRST RUSH OF IT COURSE THROUGH MY LIMBS LIKE LIVING FIRE. NO MAN IS MORE ALIVE THAN THE WARRIOR POISED FOR THE FIRST HURL OF HIS SPEAR. BUT THAT FEELING DOESN'T LAST LONG. DEATH ARRIVES QUICKLY ON THE BATTLEFIELD-- FOR BOTH SIDES.
TODAY, RIDING TOWARD THE CITY, WATCHING TROY'S WALLS RISE HIGH AND GRAND OVER THE PLAIN, WITH ANDROMACHE RIDING BESIDE ME, I FELT A KIND OF LIFE DIFFERENT THAN THE RUSH OF WAR. NOT A SHORT BURST. IT WAS LIFE LIKE SOLID EARTH, GREEN, GROWING. I WAS GLAD TO BE HERE, GLAD TO BE HEKTOR.
GREAT KING, LET ME TALK WITH THE ACHAEANS WHEN THEIR EMBASSY ARRIVES. LET ME REACH PEACE WITH THEM, AND LET MY WEDDING FEAST FOLLOW. I WANT TO GIVE ALL TROY A REASON FOR CELEBRATION. I WANT TO GIVE ANDROMACHE A MARRIAGE FULL OF JOY, NOT BATTLE.
GRANT ME THIS CHANCE, GREAT KING. WHATEVER YOU DECIDE, I'LL OBEY.
I'LL GRANT YOUR REQUESTS, HEKTOR. MAY THE GODS GRANT YOUR DESIRES AS EASILY.
HNH.

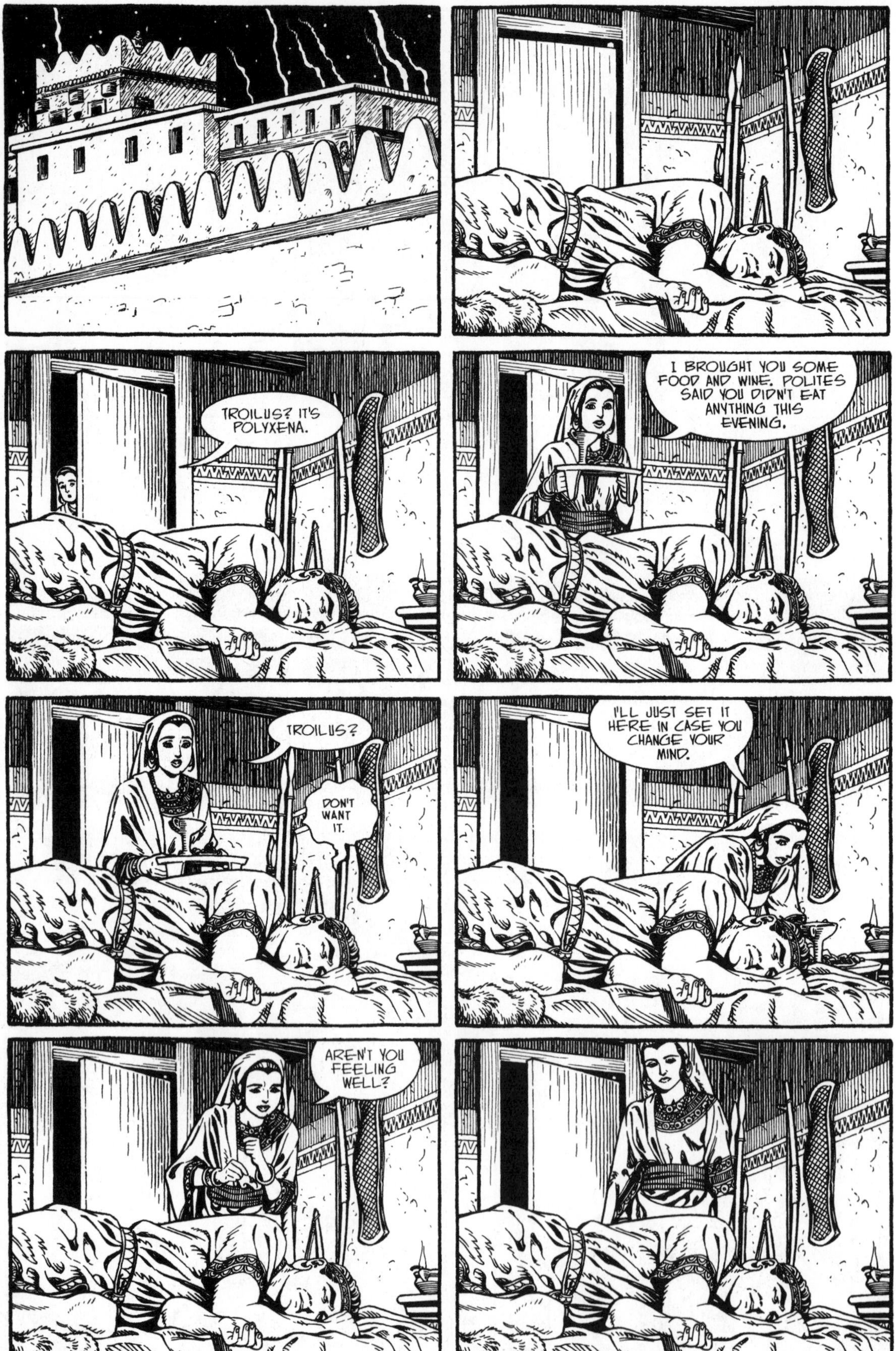
TROILUS? IT'S POLYXENA.
I BROUGHT YOU SOME FOOD AND WINE. POLITES SAID YOU DIDN'T EAT ANYTHING THIS EVENING.
TROILUS?
DON'T WANT IT.
I'LL JUST SET IT HERE IN CASE YOU CHANGE YOUR MIND.
AREN'T YOU FEELING WELL?

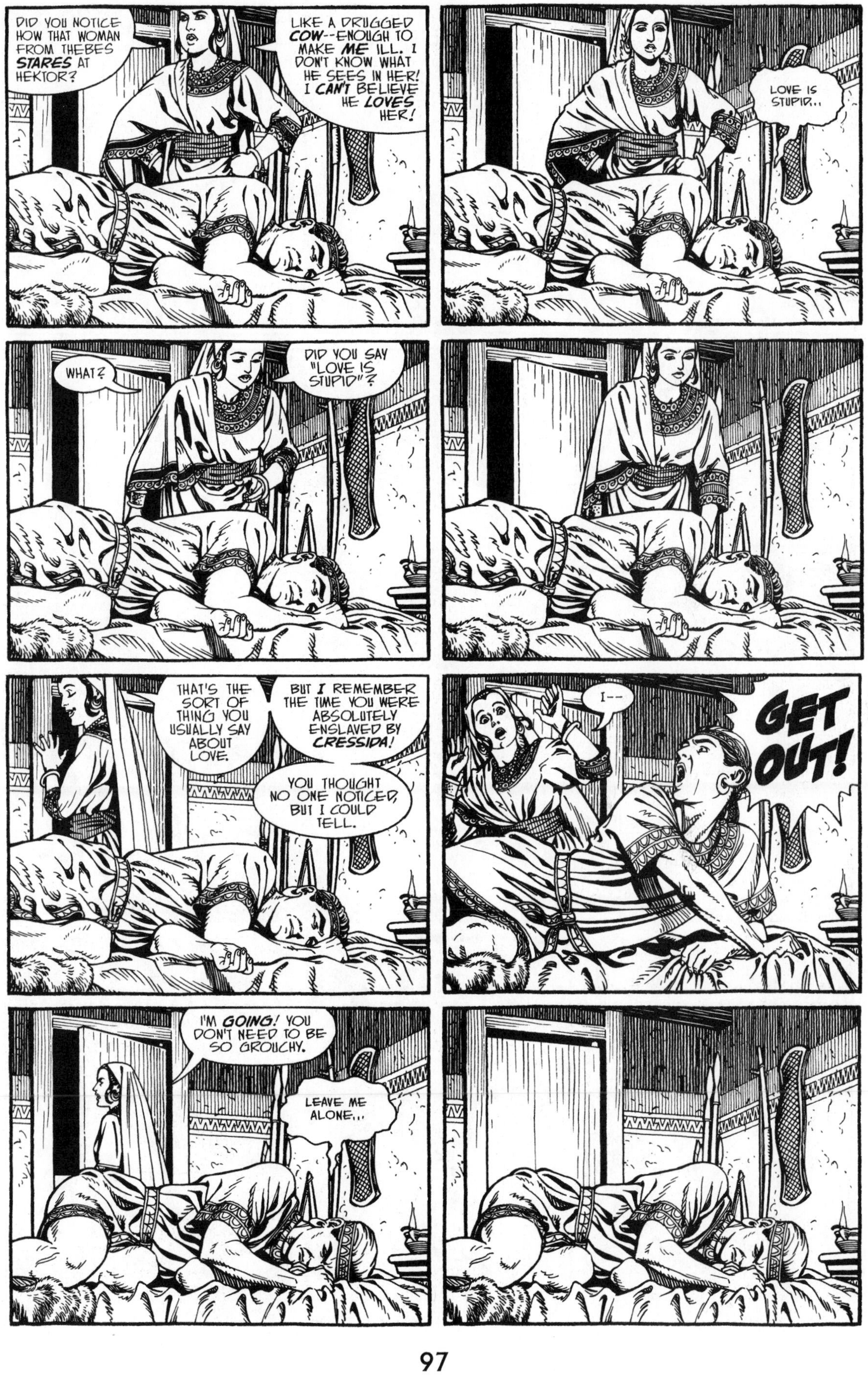
DID YOU NOTICE HOW THAT WOMAN FROM THEBES STARES AT HEKTOR?
LIKE A DRUGGED COW--ENOUGH TO MAKE ME ILL. I DON'T KNOW WHAT HE SEES IN HER! I CAN'T BELIEVE HE LOVES HER!
LOVE IS STUPID...
WHAT?
DID YOU SAY "LOVE IS STUPID"?
THAT'S THE SORT OF THING YOU USUALLY SAY ABOUT LOVE.
BUT I REMEMBER THE TIME YOU WERE ABSOLUTELY ENSLAVED BY CRESSIDA!
YOU THOUGHT NO ONE NOTICED, BUT I COULD TELL.
I--
GET OUT!
I'M GOING! YOU DON'T NEED TO BE SO GROUCHY.
LEAVE ME ALONE...

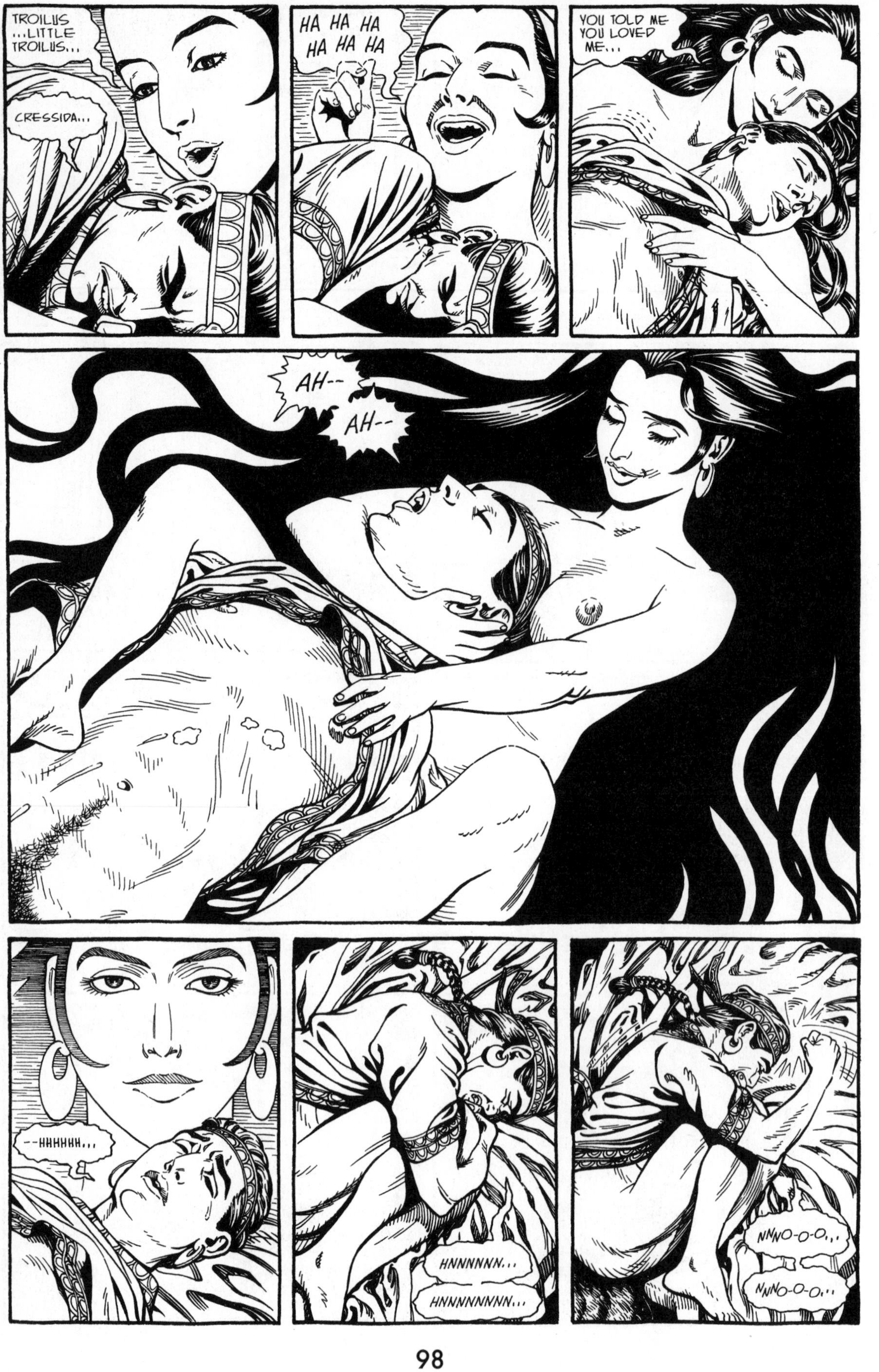
TROILUS ...LITTLE TROILUS...
CRESSIDA...
HA HA HA HA HA HA
YOU TOLD ME YOU LOVED ME...
AH--
AH--
--HHHHHH...
HNNNNNN...
HNNNNNNNN...
NNNO-O-O...
NNNO-O-O...

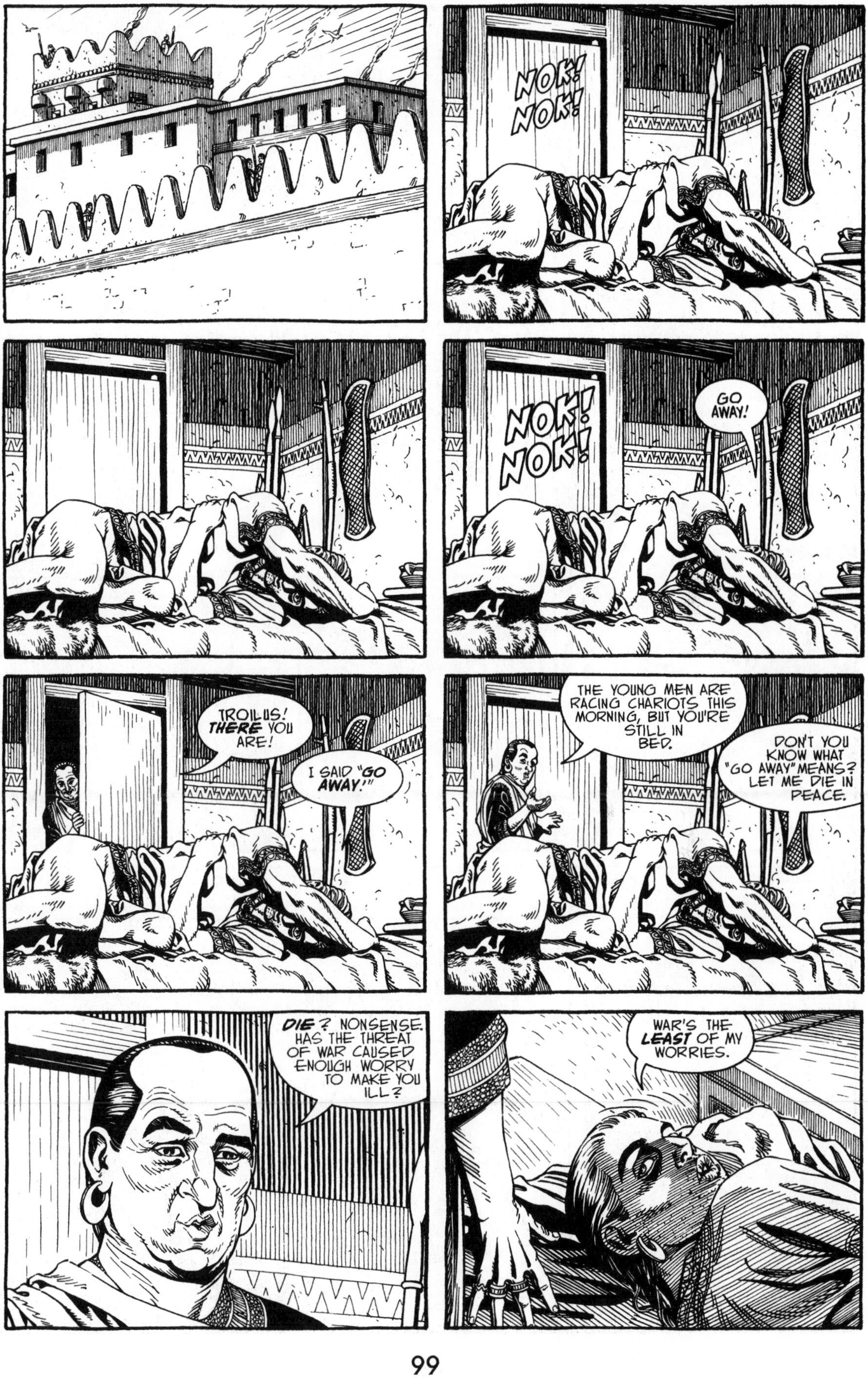
NOK! NOK!
NOK! NOK!
GO AWAY!
TROILUS! THERE YOU ARE!
I SAID "GO AWAY!"
THE YOUNG MEN ARE RACING CHARIOTS THIS MORNING, BUT YOU'RE STILL IN BED.
DON'T YOU KNOW WHAT "GO AWAY" MEANS? LET ME DIE IN PEACE.
DIE? NONSENSE. HAS THE THREAT OF WAR CAUSED ENOUGH WORRY TO MAKE YOU ILL?
WAR'S THE LEAST OF MY WORRIES.

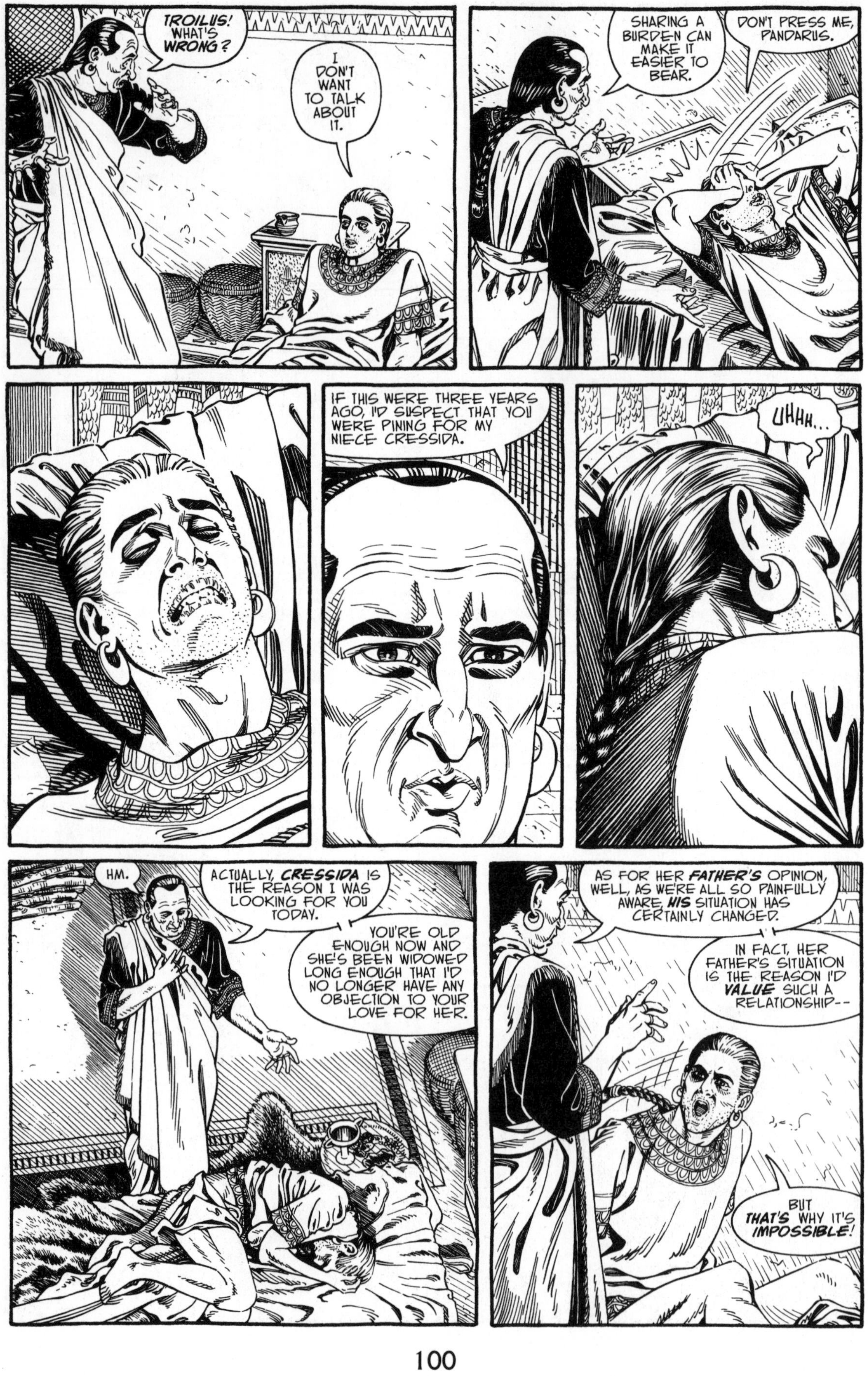
TROILUS! WHAT'S WRONG?
I DON'T WANT TO TALK ABOUT IT.
SHARING A BURDEN CAN MAKE IT EASIER TO BEAR.
DON'T PRESS ME, PANDARUS.
IF THIS WERE THREE YEARS AGO, I'D SUSPECT THAT YOU WERE PINING FOR MY NIECE CRESSIDA.
UHHH...
HM.
ACTUALLY, CRESSIDA IS THE REASON I WAS LOOKING FOR YOU TODAY.
YOU'RE OLD ENOUGH NOW AND SHE'S BEEN WIDOWED LONG ENOUGH THAT I'D NO LONGER HAVE ANY OBJECTION TO YOUR LOVE FOR HER.
AS FOR HER FATHER'S OPINION, WELL, AS WE'RE ALL SO PAINFULLY AWARE, HIS SITUATION HAS CERTAINLY CHANGED.
IN FACT, HER FATHER'S SITUATION IS THE REASON I'D VALUE SUCH A RELATIONSHIP--
BUT THAT'S WHY IT'S IMPOSSIBLE!

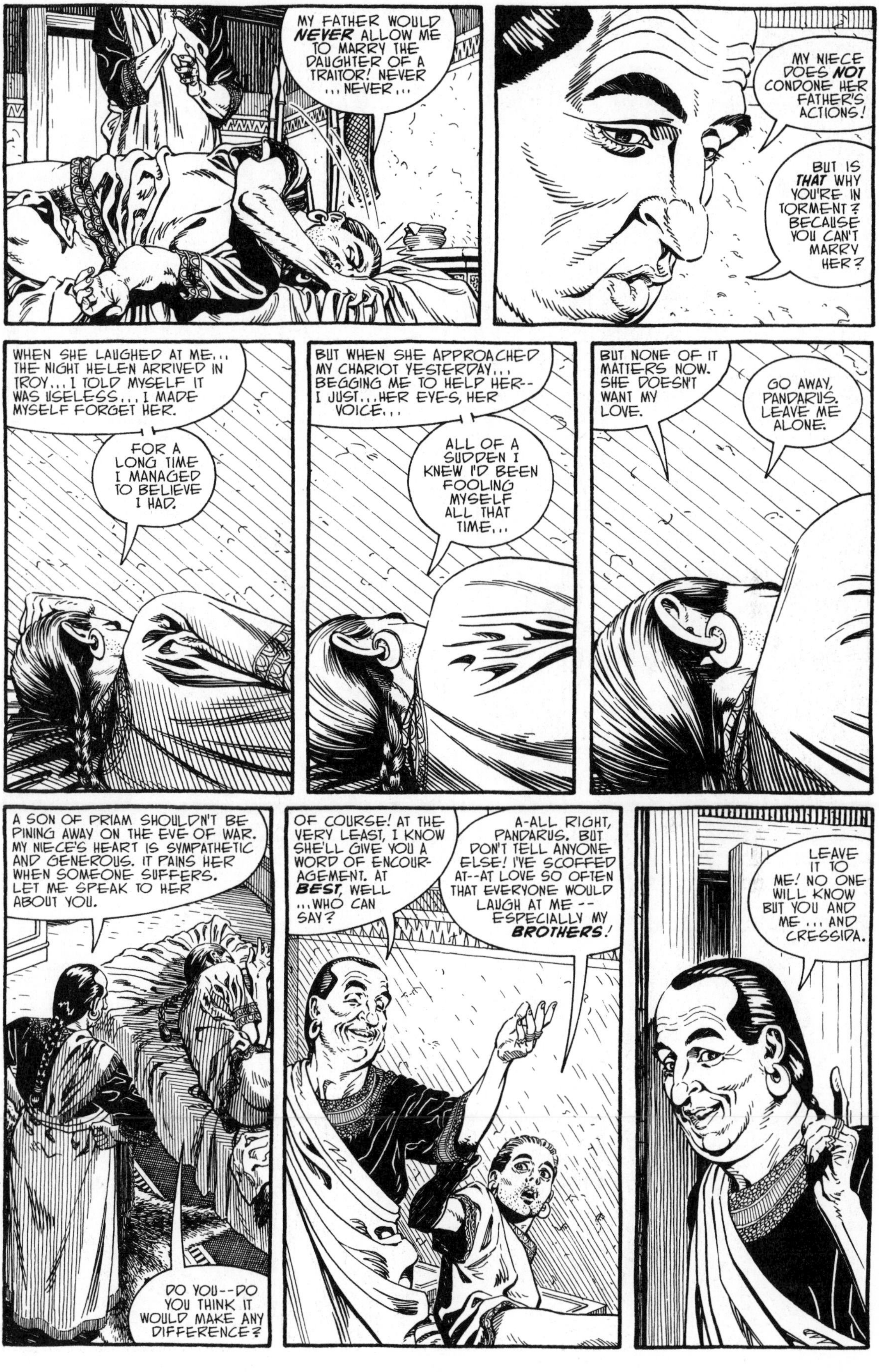
MY FATHER WOULD NEVER ALLOW ME TO MARRY THE DAUGHTER OF A TRAITOR! NEVER ... NEVER ...
MY NIECE DOES NOT CONDONE HER FATHER'S ACTIONS!
BUT IS THAT WHY YOU'RE IN TORMENT? BECAUSE YOU CAN'T MARRY HER?
WHEN SHE LAUGHED AT ME... THE NIGHT HELEN ARRIVED IN TROY... I TOLD MYSELF IT WAS USELESS... I MADE MYSELF FORGET HER.
FOR A LONG TIME I MANAGED TO BELIEVE I HAD.
BUT WHEN SHE APPROACHED MY CHARIOT YESTERDAY... BEGGING ME TO HELP HER-- I JUST... HER EYES, HER VOICE...
ALL OF A SUDDEN I KNEW I'D BEEN FOOLING MYSELF ALL THAT TIME...
BUT NONE OF IT MATTERS NOW. SHE DOESN'T WANT MY LOVE.
GO AWAY, PANDARUS. LEAVE ME ALONE.
A SON OF PRIAM SHOULDN'T BE PINING AWAY ON THE EVE OF WAR. MY NIECE'S HEART IS SYMPATHETIC AND GENEROUS. IT PAINS HER WHEN SOMEONE SUFFERS. LET ME SPEAK TO HER ABOUT YOU.
DO YOU--DO YOU THINK IT WOULD MAKE ANY DIFFERENCE?
OF COURSE! AT THE VERY LEAST, I KNOW SHE'LL GIVE YOU A WORD OF ENCOURAGEMENT. AT BEST, WELL ...WHO CAN SAY?
A-ALL RIGHT, PANDARUS. BUT DON'T TELL ANYONE ELSE! I'VE SCOFFED AT--AT LOVE SO OFTEN THAT EVERYONE WOULD LAUGH AT ME -- ESPECIALLY MY BROTHERS!
LEAVE IT TO ME! NO ONE WILL KNOW BUT YOU AND ME ... AND CRESSIDA.

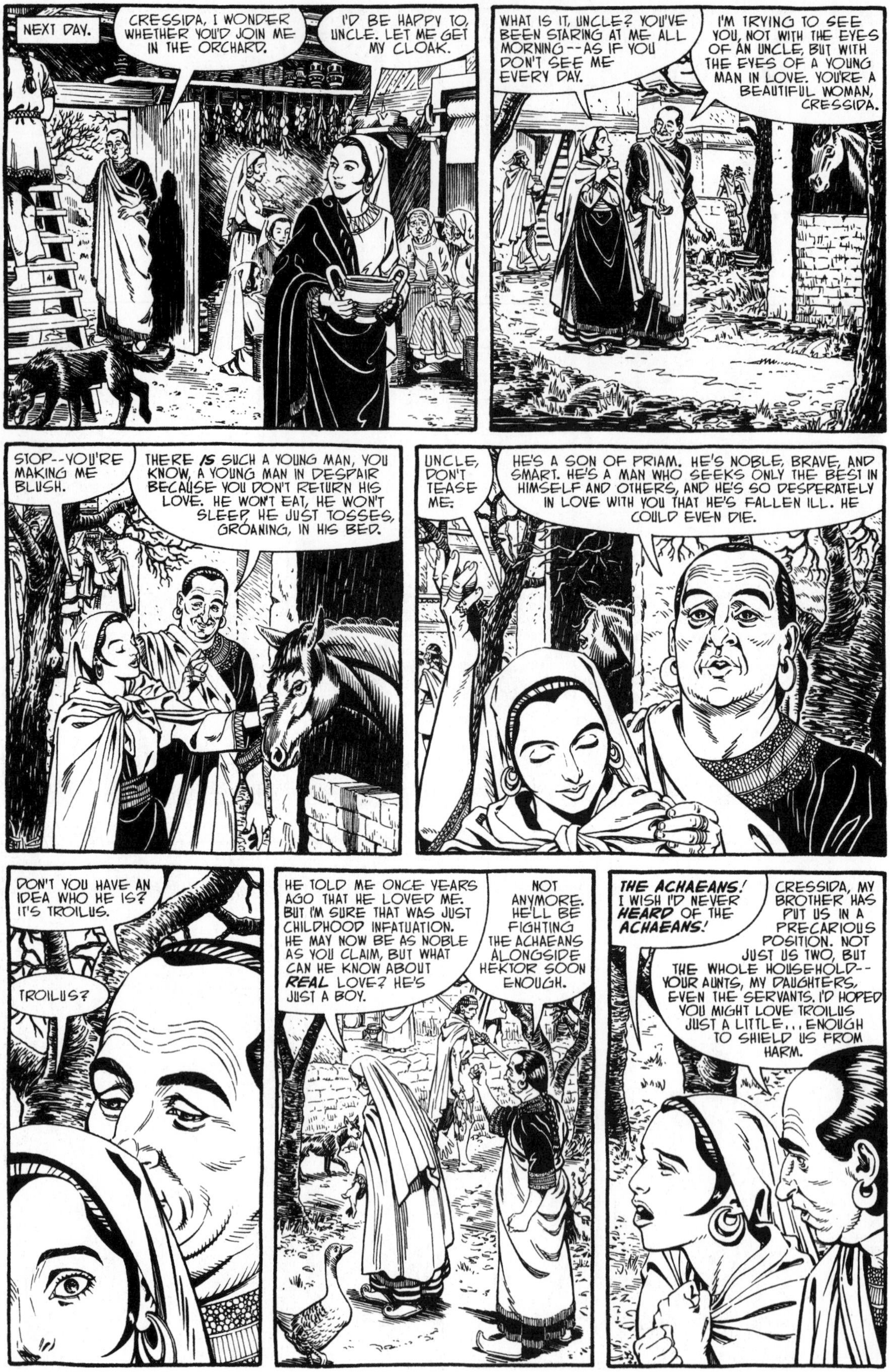

NEXT DAY.
CRESSIDA, I WONDER WHETHER YOU'D JOIN ME IN THE ORCHARD.
I'D BE HAPPY TO, UNCLE. LET ME GET MY CLOAK.
WHAT IS IT, UNCLE? YOU'VE BEEN STARING AT ME ALL MORNING--AS IF YOU DON'T SEE ME EVERY DAY.
I'M TRYING TO SEE YOU, NOT WITH THE EYES OF AN UNCLE, BUT WITH THE EYES OF A YOUNG MAN IN LOVE. YOU'RE A BEAUTIFUL WOMAN, CRESSIDA.
STOP--YOU'RE MAKING ME BLUSH.
THERE IS SUCH A YOUNG MAN, YOU KNOW, A YOUNG MAN IN DESPAIR BECAUSE YOU DON'T RETURN HIS LOVE. HE WON'T EAT, HE WON'T SLEEP, HE JUST TOSSES, GROANING, IN HIS BED.
UNCLE, DON'T TEASE ME.
HE'S A SON OF PRIAM. HE'S NOBLE, BRAVE, AND SMART. HE'S A MAN WHO SEEKS ONLY THE BEST IN HIMSELF AND OTHERS, AND HE'S SO DESPERATELY IN LOVE WITH YOU THAT HE'S FALLEN ILL. HE COULD EVEN DIE.
DON'T YOU HAVE AN IDEA WHO HE IS? IT'S TROILUS.
TROILUS?
HE TOLD ME ONCE YEARS AGO THAT HE LOVED ME. BUT I'M SURE THAT WAS JUST CHILDHOOD INFATUATION. HE MAY NOW BE AS NOBLE AS YOU CLAIM, BUT WHAT CAN HE KNOW ABOUT REAL LOVE? HE'S JUST A BOY.
NOT ANYMORE. HE'LL BE FIGHTING THE ACHAEANS ALONGSIDE HEKTOR SOON ENOUGH.
THE ACHAEANS! I WISH I'D NEVER HEARD OF THE ACHAEANS!
CRESSIDA, MY BROTHER HAS PUT US IN A PRECARIOUS POSITION. NOT JUST US TWO, BUT THE WHOLE HOUSEHOLD--YOUR AUNTS, MY DAUGHTERS, EVEN THE SERVANTS. I'D HOPED YOU MIGHT LOVE TROILUS JUST A LITTLE... ENOUGH TO SHIELD US FROM HARM.

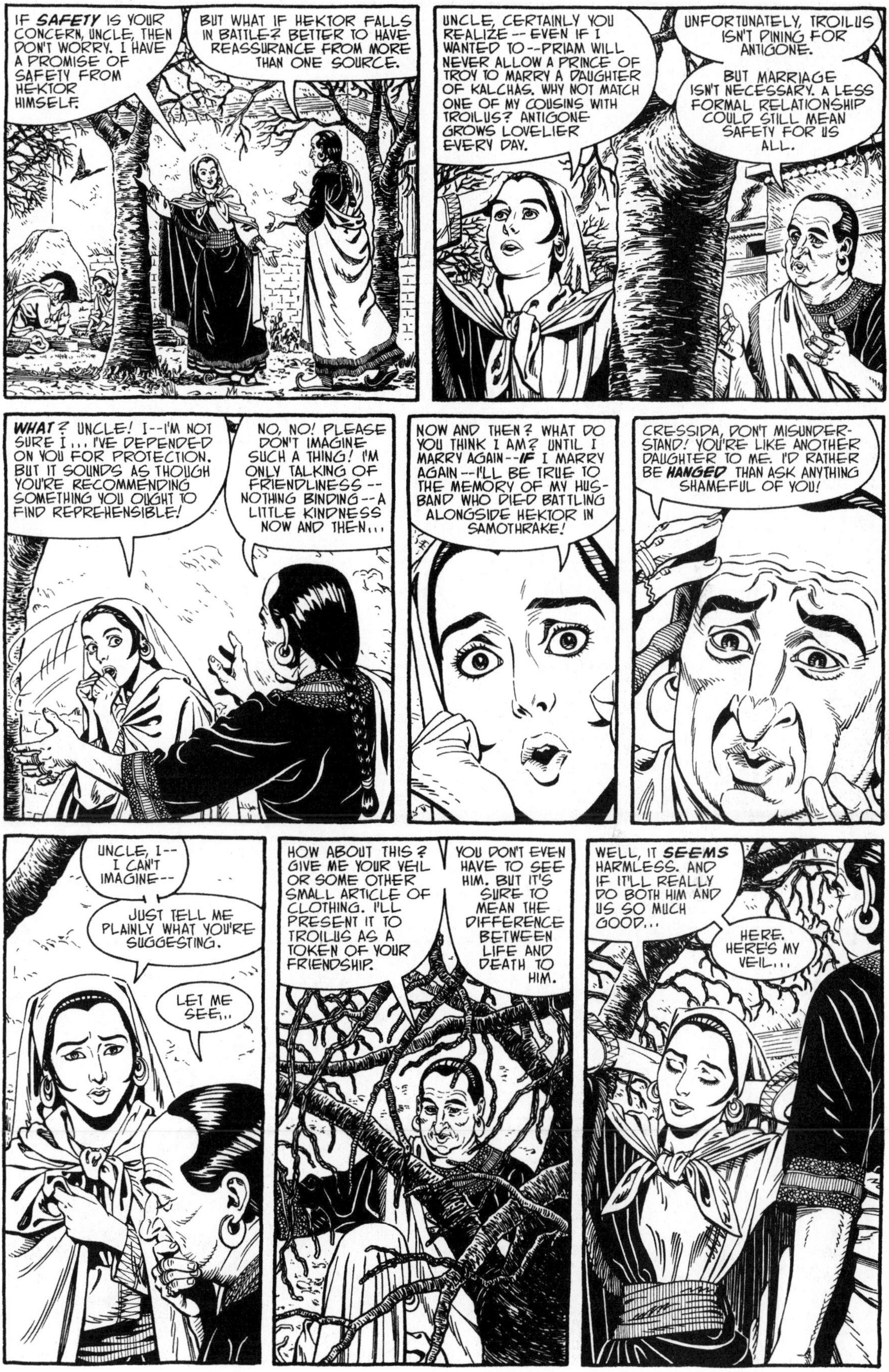
IF SAFETY IS YOUR CONCERN, UNCLE, THEN DON'T WORRY. I HAVE A PROMISE OF SAFETY FROM HEKTOR HIMSELF.
BUT WHAT IF HEKTOR FALLS IN BATTLE? BETTER TO HAVE REASSURANCE FROM MORE THAN ONE SOURCE.
UNCLE, CERTAINLY YOU REALIZE -- EVEN IF I WANTED TO -- PRIAM WILL NEVER ALLOW A PRINCE OF TROY TO MARRY A DAUGHTER OF KALCHAS. WHY NOT MATCH ONE OF MY COUSINS WITH TROILUS? ANTIGONE GROWS LOVELIER EVERY DAY.
UNFORTUNATELY, TROILUS ISN'T PINING FOR ANTIGONE.
BUT MARRIAGE ISN'T NECESSARY. A LESS FORMAL RELATIONSHIP COULD STILL MEAN SAFETY FOR US ALL.
WHAT? UNCLE! I--I'M NOT SURE I... I'VE DEPENDED ON YOU FOR PROTECTION. BUT IT SOUNDS AS THOUGH YOU'RE RECOMMENDING SOMETHING YOU OUGHT TO FIND REPREHENSIBLE!
NO, NO! PLEASE DON'T IMAGINE SUCH A THING! I'M ONLY TALKING OF FRIENDLINESS -- NOTHING BINDING -- A LITTLE KINDNESS NOW AND THEN...
NOW AND THEN? WHAT DO YOU THINK I AM? UNTIL I MARRY AGAIN -- IF I MARRY AGAIN -- I'LL BE TRUE TO THE MEMORY OF MY HUSBAND WHO DIED BATTLING ALONGSIDE HEKTOR IN SAMOTHRAKE!
CRESSIDA, DON'T MISUNDERSTAND! YOU'RE LIKE ANOTHER DAUGHTER TO ME. I'D RATHER BE HANGED THAN ASK ANYTHING SHAMEFUL OF YOU!
UNCLE, I-- I CAN'T IMAGINE--
JUST TELL ME PLAINLY WHAT YOU'RE SUGGESTING.
LET ME SEE...
HOW ABOUT THIS? GIVE ME YOUR VEIL OR SOME OTHER SMALL ARTICLE OF CLOTHING. I'LL PRESENT IT TO TROILUS AS A TOKEN OF YOUR FRIENDSHIP.
YOU DON'T EVEN HAVE TO SEE HIM. BUT IT'S SURE TO MEAN THE DIFFERENCE BETWEEN LIFE AND DEATH TO HIM.
WELL, IT SEEMS HARMLESS. AND IF IT'LL REALLY DO BOTH HIM AND US SO MUCH GOOD...
HERE. HERE'S MY VEIL...

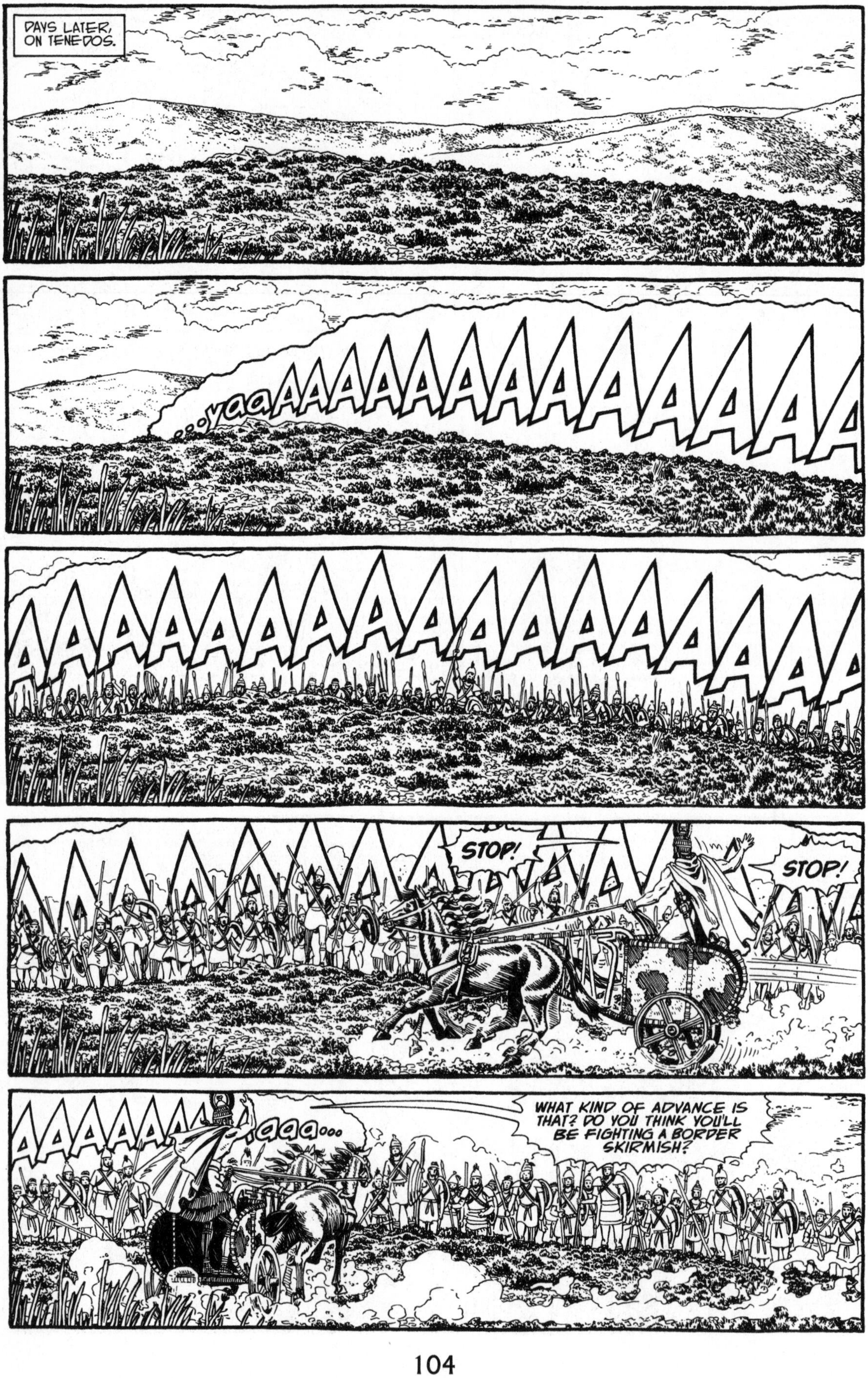
DAYS LATER, ON TENEDOS.
...yaaAAAAAAAAAAAAAAAAA
AAAAAAAAAAAAAAAAAAAAA
STOP!
STOP!
AAAAAA...aaa...
WHAT KIND OF ADVANCE IS THAT? DO YOU THINK YOU'LL BE FIGHTING A BORDER SKIRMISH?

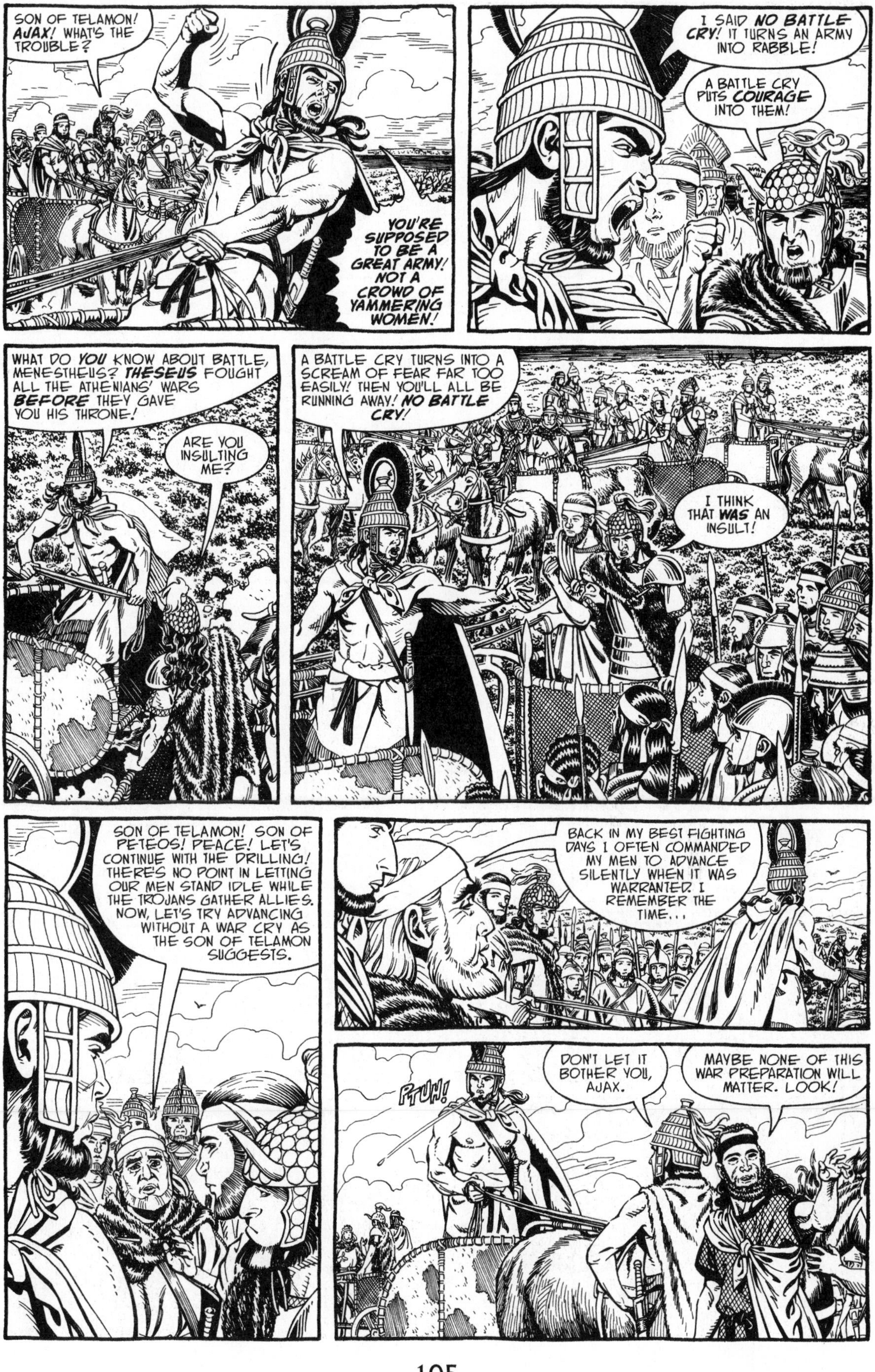
SON OF TELAMON! AJAX! WHAT'S THE TROUBLE?
YOU'RE SUPPOSED TO BE A GREAT ARMY! NOT A CROWD OF YAMMERING WOMEN!
I SAID NO BATTLE CRY! IT TURNS AN ARMY INTO RABBLE!
A BATTLE CRY PUTS COURAGE INTO THEM!
WHAT DO YOU KNOW ABOUT BATTLE, MENESTHEUS? THESEUS FOUGHT ALL THE ATHENIANS' WARS BEFORE THEY GAVE YOU HIS THRONE!
ARE YOU INSULTING ME?
A BATTLE CRY TURNS INTO A SCREAM OF FEAR FAR TOO EASILY! THEN YOU'LL ALL BE RUNNING AWAY! NO BATTLE CRY!
I THINK THAT WAS AN INSULT!
SON OF TELAMON! SON OF PETEOS! PEACE! LET'S CONTINUE WITH THE DRILLING! THERE'S NO POINT IN LETTING OUR MEN STAND IDLE WHILE THE TROJANS GATHER ALLIES. NOW, LET'S TRY ADVANCING WITHOUT A WAR CRY AS THE SON OF TELAMON SUGGESTS.
BACK IN MY BEST FIGHTING DAYS I OFTEN COMMANDED MY MEN TO ADVANCE SILENTLY WHEN IT WAS WARRANTED. I REMEMBER THE TIME...
PTUH!
DON'T LET IT BOTHER YOU, AJAX.
MAYBE NONE OF THIS WAR PREPARATION WILL MATTER. LOOK!

THE EMBASSY HAS FINISHED SACRIFICING TO THE GODS. THEY'LL BE OFF TO TROY NOW. MAYBE THEY'LL BRING HELEN BACK TOMORROW AND WE CAN ALL GO HOME.

EMBASSIES... SACRIFICES ...HUNH!

WE'RE ALREADY AT WAR. I DON'T CARE WHETHER THEY RECOVER HELEN. MY SPEAR WON'T REST WHILE EVEN ONE TROJAN WHO FAVORED HER ABDUCTION STILL LIVES.

≶HEM≶ SON OF LAERTES...

≶HEM≶

WHAT IS IT, KALCHAS? BE QUICK.

WELL, YOU SEE, I HAVE A DAUGHTER WHO'S STILL ≶HEM≶ IN TROY. I FEAR IT WON'T GO WELL WITH HER IF THE TROJANS DISCOVER THAT I ...WELL--≶HEM≶

THAT YOU'VE JOINED THE OTHER SIDE? NO, I GUESS THE TROJANS WON'T LIKE THAT ONE BIT.

YES, WELL, UM...SON OF LAERTES, I KNOW YOU'RE A CLEVER MAN...

CLEVERER THAN SOME.

AND SO I ≶HEM≶ HOPED THAT--WH-WHILE YOU'RE IN TROY--YOU COULD FIND OUT HOW MY DAUGHTER IS ≶HEM≶ DOING -- HER NAME IS CRESSIDA--AND, UH, ≶HEM≶ IF YOU'D REFRAIN FROM MENTIONING MY SITUATION TO ANYONE-- EVEN TO CRESSIDA--AND PREVENT THE OTHERS FROM MENTIONING IT, TOO.

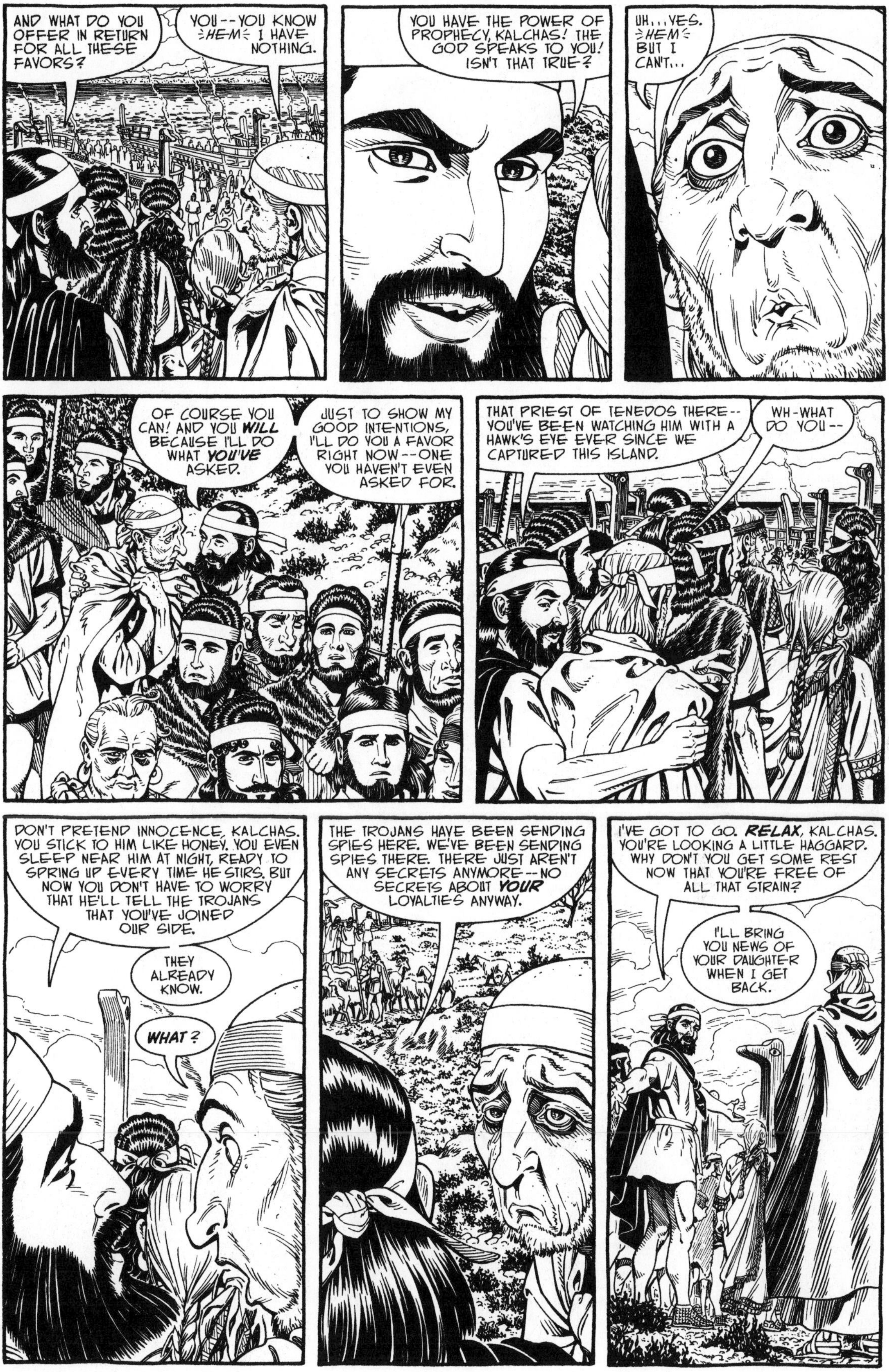
AND WHAT DO YOU OFFER IN RETURN FOR ALL THESE FAVORS?
YOU--YOU KNOW ≡HEM≡ I HAVE NOTHING.
YOU HAVE THE POWER OF PROPHECY, KALCHAS! THE GOD SPEAKS TO YOU! ISN'T THAT TRUE?
UH...YES. ≡HEM≡ BUT I CAN'T...
OF COURSE YOU CAN! AND YOU WILL BECAUSE I'LL DO WHAT YOU'VE ASKED.
JUST TO SHOW MY GOOD INTENTIONS, I'LL DO YOU A FAVOR RIGHT NOW--ONE YOU HAVEN'T EVEN ASKED FOR.
THAT PRIEST OF TENEDOS THERE--YOU'VE BEEN WATCHING HIM WITH A HAWK'S EYE EVER SINCE WE CAPTURED THIS ISLAND.
WH-WHAT DO YOU--
DON'T PRETEND INNOCENCE, KALCHAS. YOU STICK TO HIM LIKE HONEY. YOU EVEN SLEEP NEAR HIM AT NIGHT, READY TO SPRING UP EVERY TIME HE STIRS. BUT NOW YOU DON'T HAVE TO WORRY THAT HE'LL TELL THE TROJANS THAT YOU'VE JOINED OUR SIDE.
THEY ALREADY KNOW.
WHAT?
THE TROJANS HAVE BEEN SENDING SPIES HERE. WE'VE BEEN SENDING SPIES THERE. THERE JUST AREN'T ANY SECRETS ANYMORE--NO SECRETS ABOUT YOUR LOYALTIES ANYWAY.
I'VE GOT TO GO. RELAX, KALCHAS. YOU'RE LOOKING A LITTLE HAGGARD. WHY DON'T YOU GET SOME REST NOW THAT YOU'RE FREE OF ALL THAT STRAIN?
I'LL BRING YOU NEWS OF YOUR DAUGHTER WHEN I GET BACK.

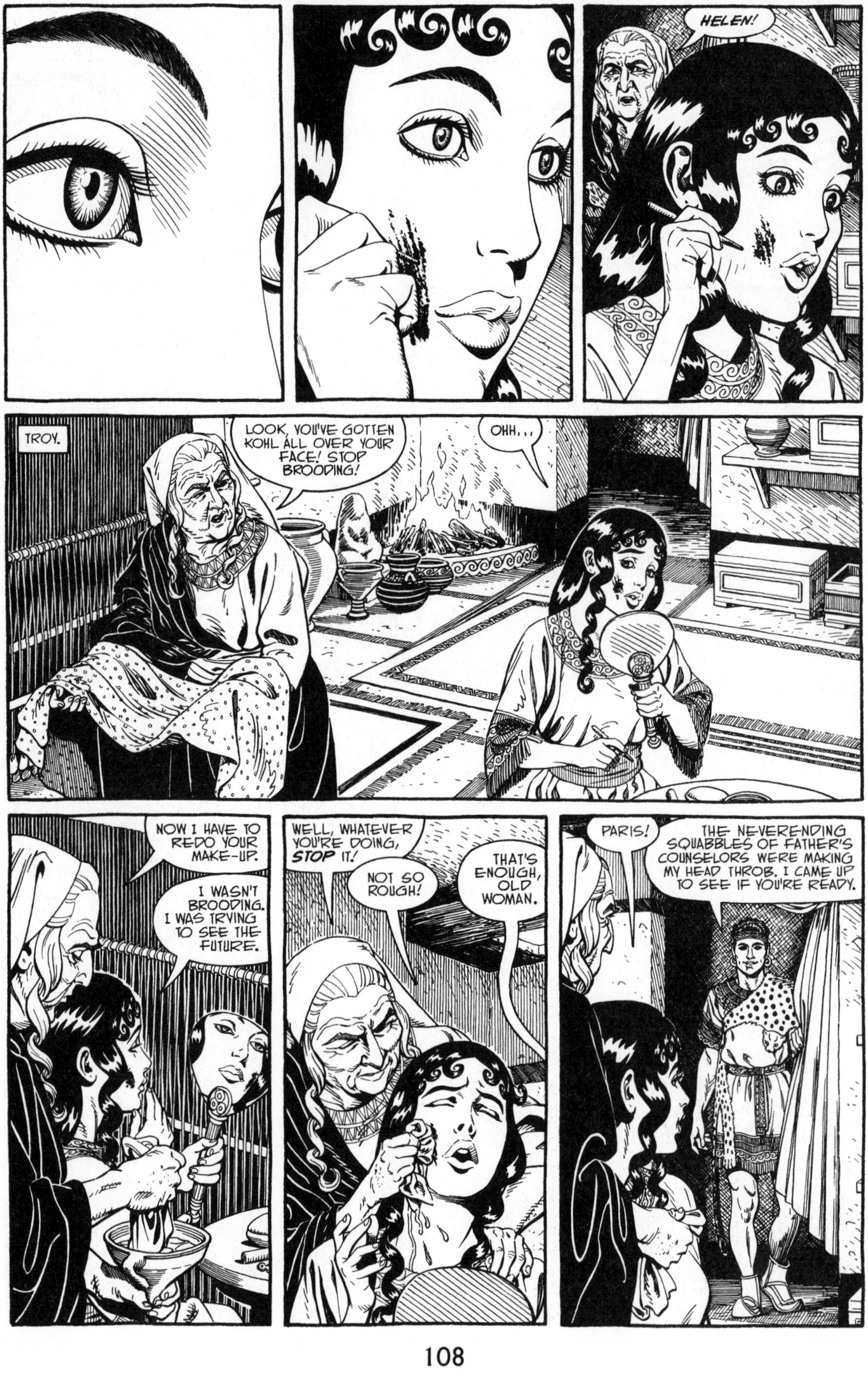
HELEN!
TROY.
LOOK, YOU'VE GOTTEN KOHL ALL OVER YOUR FACE! STOP BROODING!
OHH...
NOW I HAVE TO REDO YOUR MAKE-UP.
I WASN'T BROODING. I WAS TRYING TO SEE THE FUTURE.
WELL, WHATEVER YOU'RE DOING, STOP IT!
NOT SO ROUGH!
THAT'S ENOUGH, OLD WOMAN.
PARIS!
THE NEVERENDING SQUABBLES OF FATHER'S COUNSELORS WERE MAKING MY HEAD THROB. I CAME UP TO SEE IF YOU'RE READY.

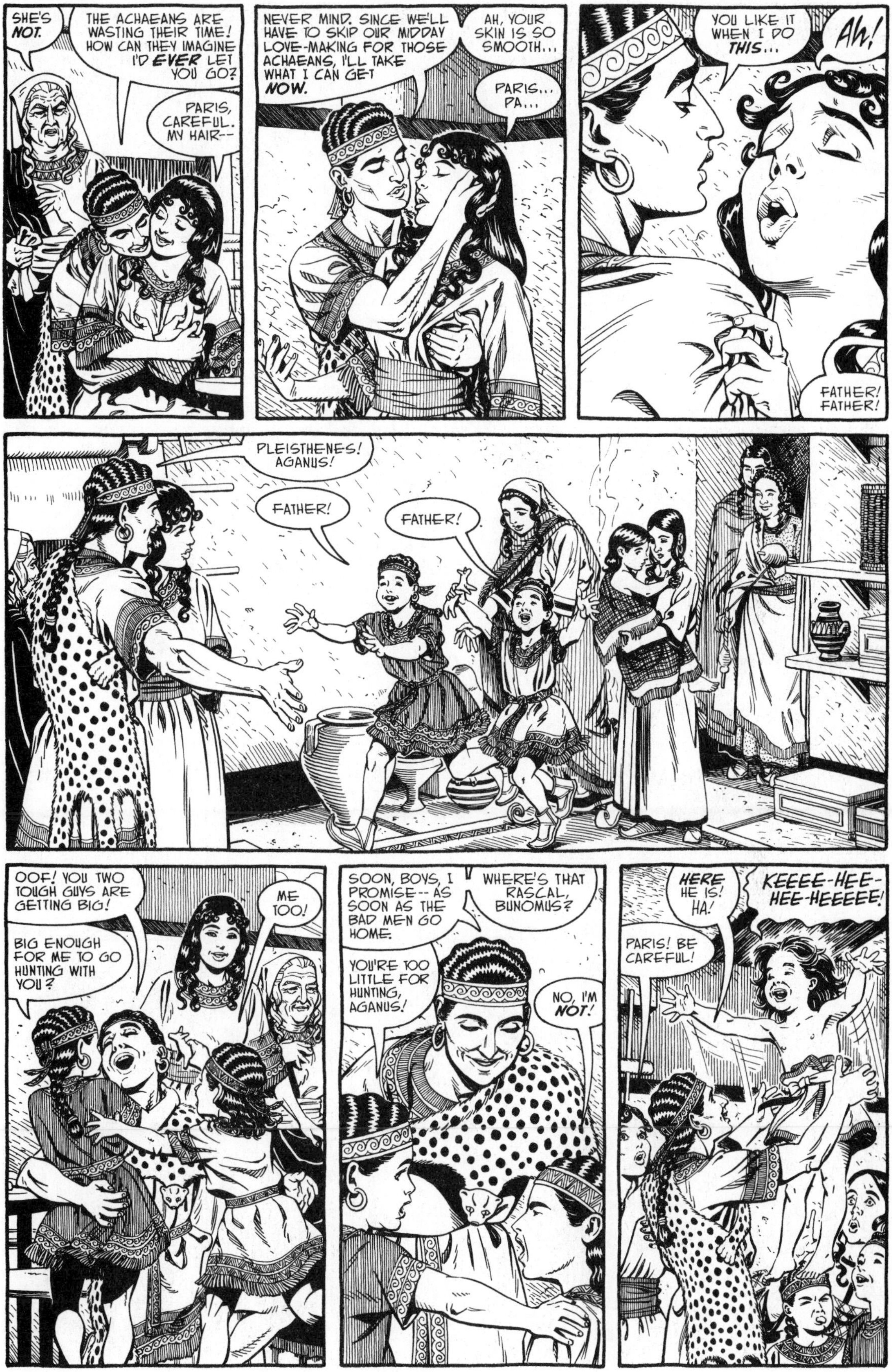
SHE'S NOT.
THE ACHAEANS ARE WASTING THEIR TIME! HOW CAN THEY IMAGINE I'D EVER LET YOU GO?
PARIS, CAREFUL. MY HAIR--
NEVER MIND. SINCE WE'LL HAVE TO SKIP OUR MIDDAY LOVE-MAKING FOR THOSE ACHAEANS, I'LL TAKE WHAT I CAN GET NOW.
AH, YOUR SKIN IS SO SMOOTH...
PARIS... PA...
YOU LIKE IT WHEN I DO THIS...
Ah!
FATHER! FATHER!
PLEISTHENES! AGANUS!
FATHER!
FATHER!
OOF! YOU TWO TOUGH GUYS ARE GETTING BIG!
ME TOO!
BIG ENOUGH FOR ME TO GO HUNTING WITH YOU?
SOON, BOYS, I PROMISE-- AS SOON AS THE BAD MEN GO HOME.
WHERE'S THAT RASCAL, BUNOMUS?
YOU'RE TOO LITTLE FOR HUNTING, AGANUS!
NO, I'M NOT!
HERE HE IS! HA!
KEEEE-HEE-HEE-HEEEEE!
PARIS! BE CAREFUL!

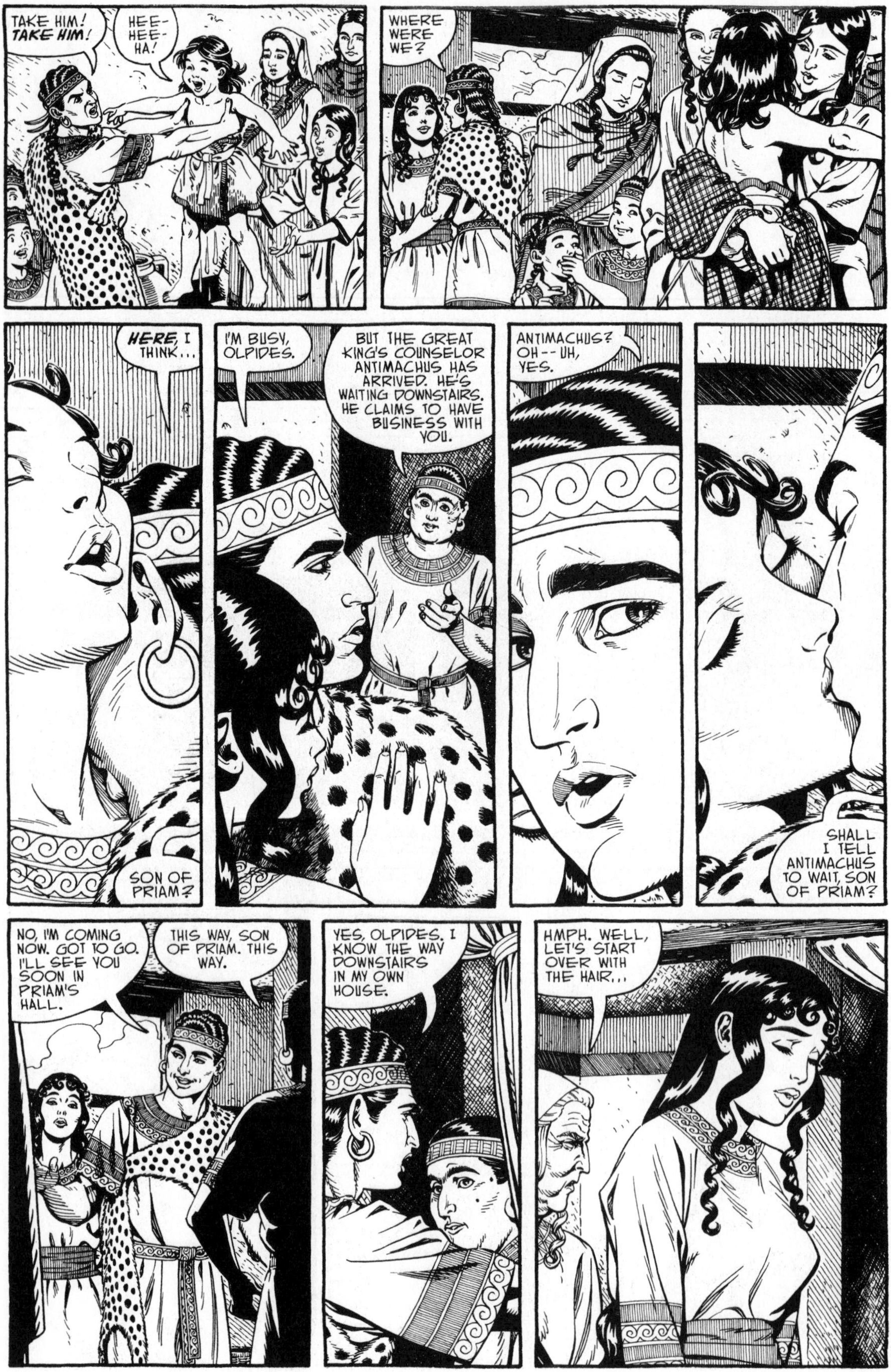
TAKE HIM! TAKE HIM!
HEE-HEE-HEE-HA!
WHERE WERE WE?
HERE, I THINK...
SON OF PRIAM?
I'M BUSY, OLPIDES.
BUT THE GREAT KING'S COUNSELOR ANTIMACHUS HAS ARRIVED. HE'S WAITING DOWNSTAIRS. HE CLAIMS TO HAVE BUSINESS WITH YOU.
ANTIMACHUS? OH -- UH, YES.
SHALL I TELL ANTIMACHUS TO WAIT, SON OF PRIAM?
NO, I'M COMING NOW. GOT TO GO. I'LL SEE YOU SOON IN PRIAM'S HALL.
THIS WAY, SON OF PRIAM. THIS WAY.
YES, OLPIDES. I KNOW THE WAY DOWNSTAIRS IN MY OWN HOUSE.
HMPH. WELL, LET'S START OVER WITH THE HAIR...

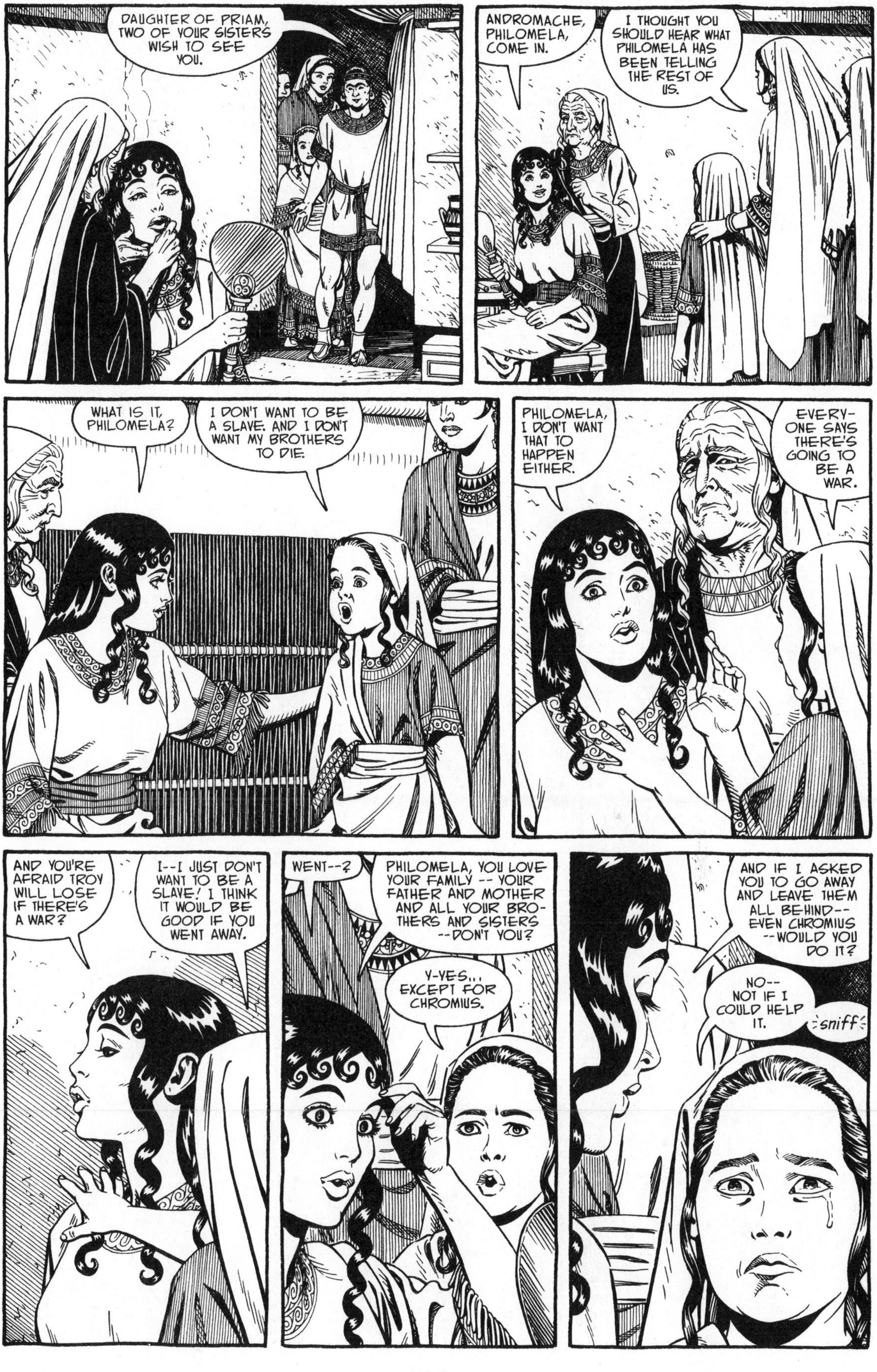
DAUGHTER OF PRIAM, TWO OF YOUR SISTERS WISH TO SEE YOU.
ANDROMACHE, PHILOMELA, COME IN.
I THOUGHT YOU SHOULD HEAR WHAT PHILOMELA HAS BEEN TELLING THE REST OF US.
WHAT IS IT, PHILOMELA?
I DON'T WANT TO BE A SLAVE. AND I DON'T WANT MY BROTHERS TO DIE.
EVERY-ONE SAYS THERE'S GOING TO BE A WAR.
PHILOMELA, I DON'T WANT THAT TO HAPPEN EITHER.
AND YOU'RE AFRAID TROY WILL LOSE IF THERE'S A WAR?
I--I JUST DON'T WANT TO BE A SLAVE! I THINK IT WOULD BE GOOD IF YOU WENT AWAY.
WENT--?
PHILOMELA, YOU LOVE YOUR FAMILY -- YOUR FATHER AND MOTHER AND ALL YOUR BRO-THERS AND SISTERS --DON'T YOU?
Y-YES... EXCEPT FOR CHROMIUS.
AND IF I ASKED YOU TO GO AWAY AND LEAVE THEM ALL BEHIND-- EVEN CHROMIUS --WOULD YOU DO IT?
NO-- NOT IF I COULD HELP IT.
sniff

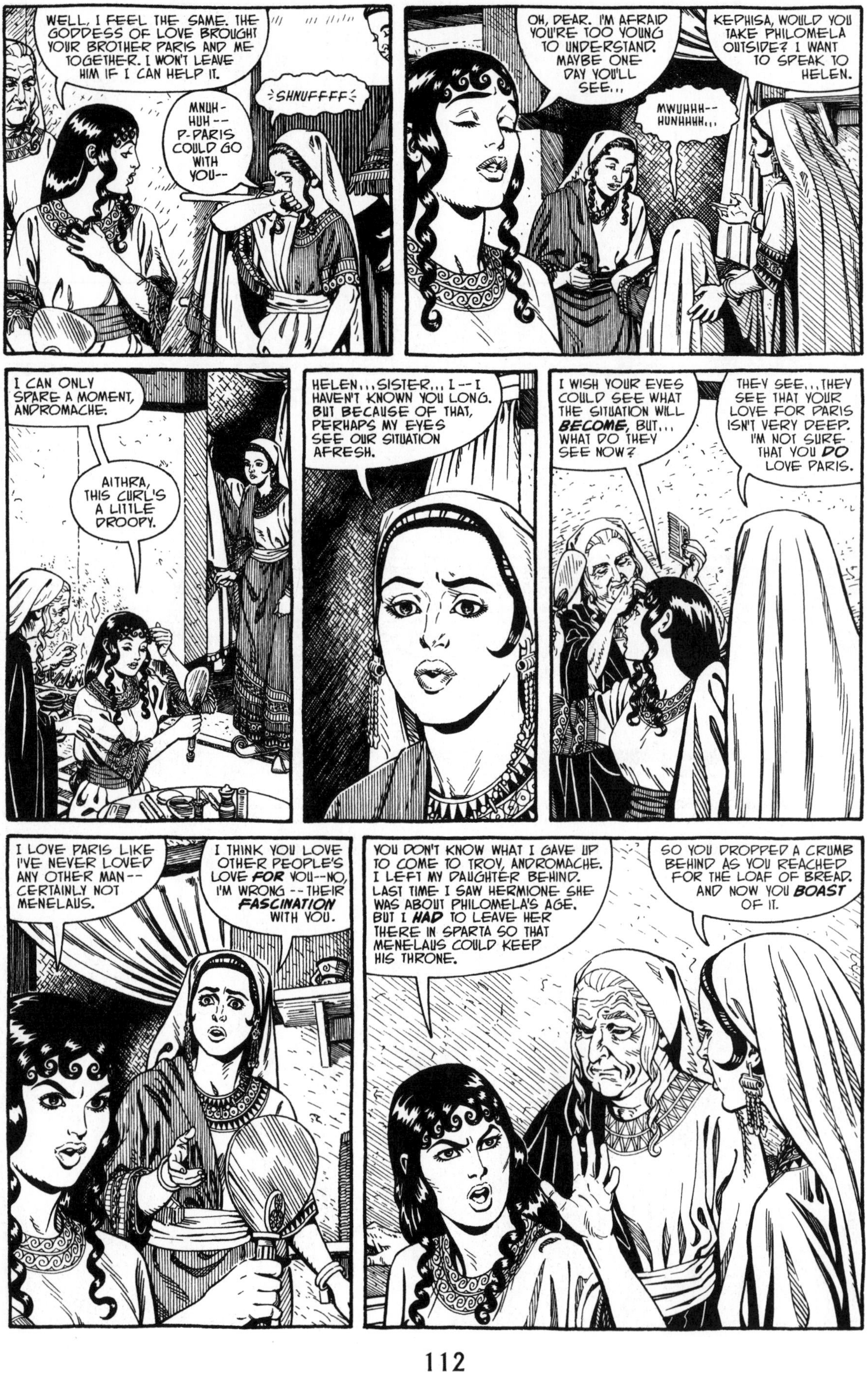
WELL, I FEEL THE SAME. THE GODDESS OF LOVE BROUGHT YOUR BROTHER PARIS AND ME TOGETHER. I WON'T LEAVE HIM IF I CAN HELP IT.
SHNUFFFF
MNUH-HUH -- P-PARIS COULD GO WITH YOU--
OH, DEAR. I'M AFRAID YOU'RE TOO YOUNG TO UNDERSTAND. MAYBE ONE DAY YOU'LL SEE...
KEPHISA, WOULD YOU TAKE PHILOMELA OUTSIDE? I WANT TO SPEAK TO HELEN.
MWUHHH-- HUNHHHH...
I CAN ONLY SPARE A MOMENT, ANDROMACHE.
AITHRA, THIS CURL'S A LITTLE DROOPY.
HELEN...SISTER... I -- I HAVEN'T KNOWN YOU LONG. BUT BECAUSE OF THAT, PERHAPS MY EYES SEE OUR SITUATION AFRESH.
I WISH YOUR EYES COULD SEE WHAT THE SITUATION WILL BECOME, BUT... WHAT DO THEY SEE NOW?
THEY SEE...THEY SEE THAT YOUR LOVE FOR PARIS ISN'T VERY DEEP. I'M NOT SURE THAT YOU DO LOVE PARIS.
I LOVE PARIS LIKE I'VE NEVER LOVED ANY OTHER MAN -- CERTAINLY NOT MENELAUS.
I THINK YOU LOVE OTHER PEOPLE'S LOVE FOR YOU--NO, I'M WRONG -- THEIR FASCINATION WITH YOU.
YOU DON'T KNOW WHAT I GAVE UP TO COME TO TROY, ANDROMACHE. I LEFT MY DAUGHTER BEHIND. LAST TIME I SAW HERMIONE SHE WAS ABOUT PHILOMELA'S AGE. BUT I HAD TO LEAVE HER THERE IN SPARTA SO THAT MENELAUS COULD KEEP HIS THRONE.
SO YOU DROPPED A CRUMB BEHIND AS YOU REACHED FOR THE LOAF OF BREAD. AND NOW YOU BOAST OF IT.

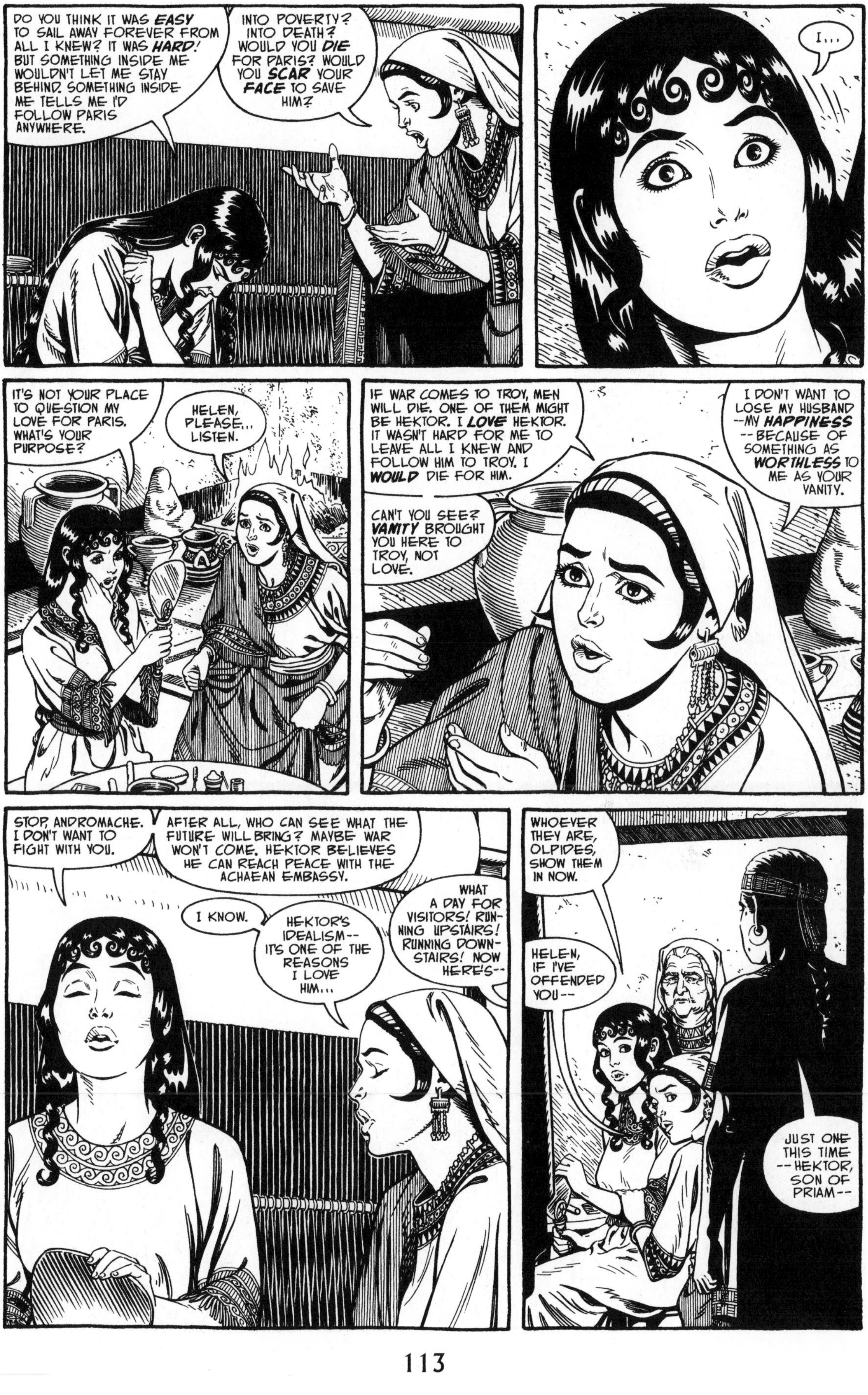
DO YOU THINK IT WAS EASY TO SAIL AWAY FOREVER FROM ALL I KNEW? IT WAS HARD! BUT SOMETHING INSIDE ME WOULDN'T LET ME STAY BEHIND. SOMETHING INSIDE ME TELLS ME I'D FOLLOW PARIS ANYWHERE.
INTO POVERTY? INTO DEATH? WOULD YOU DIE FOR PARIS? WOULD YOU SCAR YOUR FACE TO SAVE HIM?
I...
IT'S NOT YOUR PLACE TO QUESTION MY LOVE FOR PARIS. WHAT'S YOUR PURPOSE?
HELEN, PLEASE... LISTEN.
IF WAR COMES TO TROY, MEN WILL DIE. ONE OF THEM MIGHT BE HEKTOR. I LOVE HEKTOR. IT WASN'T HARD FOR ME TO LEAVE ALL I KNEW AND FOLLOW HIM TO TROY. I WOULD DIE FOR HIM.
CAN'T YOU SEE? VANITY BROUGHT YOU HERE TO TROY, NOT LOVE.
I DON'T WANT TO LOSE MY HUSBAND --MY HAPPINESS --BECAUSE OF SOMETHING AS WORTHLESS TO ME AS YOUR VANITY.
STOP, ANDROMACHE. I DON'T WANT TO FIGHT WITH YOU.
AFTER ALL, WHO CAN SEE WHAT THE FUTURE WILL BRING? MAYBE WAR WON'T COME. HEKTOR BELIEVES HE CAN REACH PEACE WITH THE ACHAEAN EMBASSY.
I KNOW.
HEKTOR'S IDEALISM-- IT'S ONE OF THE REASONS I LOVE HIM...
WHAT A DAY FOR VISITORS! RUNNING UPSTAIRS! RUNNING DOWNSTAIRS! NOW HERE'S--
WHOEVER THEY ARE, OLPIDES, SHOW THEM IN NOW.
HELEN, IF I'VE OFFENDED YOU--
JUST ONE THIS TIME --HEKTOR, SON OF PRIAM--

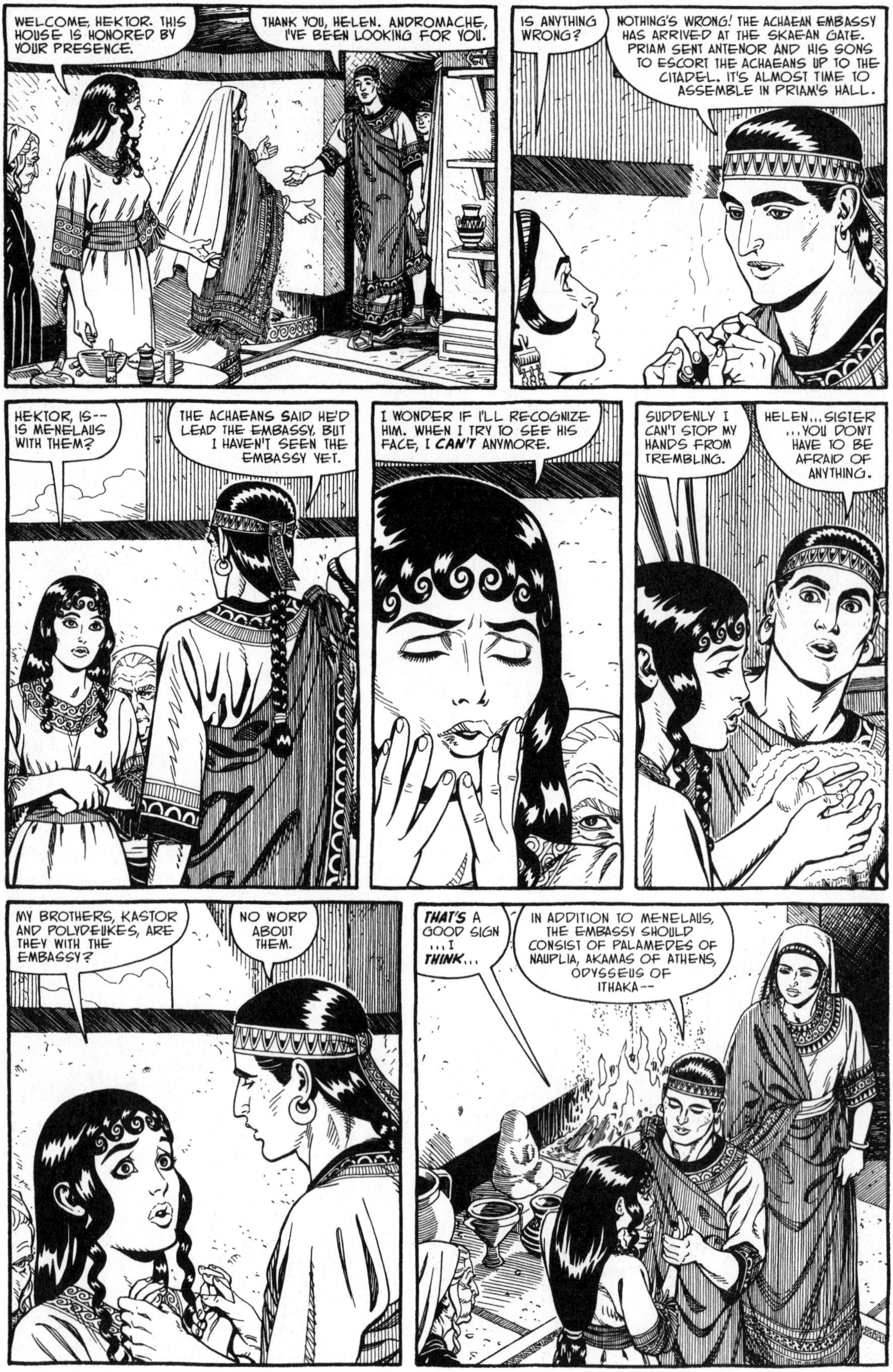
WELCOME, HEKTOR. THIS HOUSE IS HONORED BY YOUR PRESENCE.
THANK YOU, HELEN. ANDROMACHE, I'VE BEEN LOOKING FOR YOU.
IS ANYTHING WRONG?
NOTHING'S WRONG! THE ACHAEAN EMBASSY HAS ARRIVED AT THE SKAEAN GATE. PRIAM SENT ANTENOR AND HIS SONS TO ESCORT THE ACHAEANS UP TO THE CITADEL. IT'S ALMOST TIME TO ASSEMBLE IN PRIAM'S HALL.
HEKTOR, IS-- IS ME-NELAUS WITH THEM?
THE ACHAEANS SAID HE'D LEAD THE EMBASSY, BUT I HAVEN'T SEEN THE EMBASSY YET.
I WONDER IF I'LL RECOGNIZE HIM. WHEN I TRY TO SEE HIS FACE, I *CAN'T* ANYMORE.
SUDDENLY I CAN'T STOP MY HANDS FROM TREMBLING.
HELEN... SISTER ...YOU DON'T HAVE TO BE AFRAID OF ANYTHING.
MY BROTHERS, KASTOR AND POLYDEUKES, ARE THEY WITH THE EMBASSY?
NO WORD ABOUT THEM.
THAT'S A GOOD SIGN ...I *THINK*...
IN ADDITION TO ME-NELAUS, THE EMBASSY SHOULD CONSIST OF PALAMEDES OF NAUPLIA, AKAMAS OF ATHENS, ODYSSEUS OF ITHAKA--

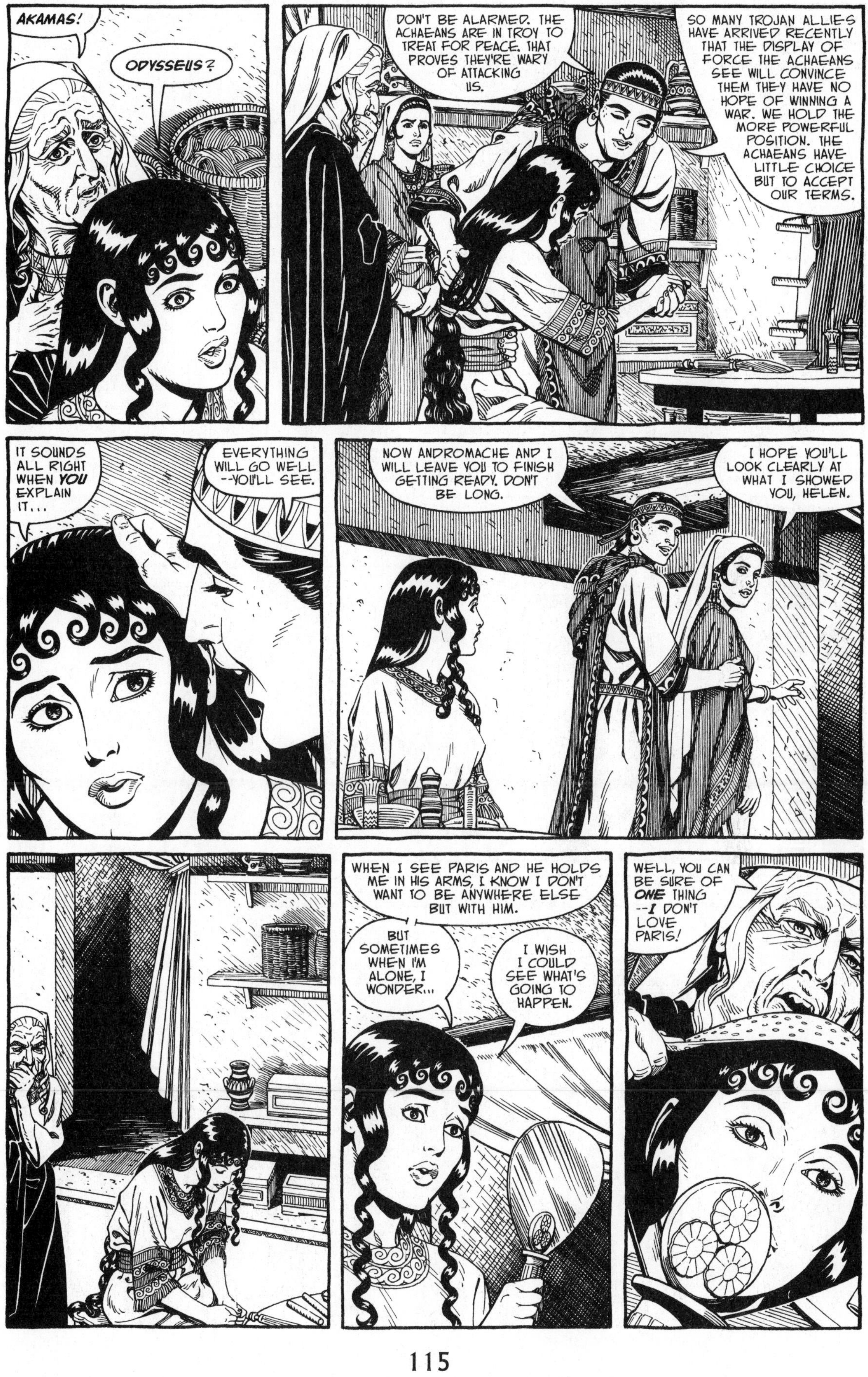
AKAMAS!
ODYSSEUS?
DON'T BE ALARMED. THE ACHAEANS ARE IN TROY TO TREAT FOR PEACE. THAT PROVES THEY'RE WARY OF ATTACKING US.
SO MANY TROJAN ALLIES HAVE ARRIVED RECENTLY THAT THE DISPLAY OF FORCE THE ACHAEANS SEE WILL CONVINCE THEM THEY HAVE NO HOPE OF WINNING A WAR. WE HOLD THE MORE POWERFUL POSITION. THE ACHAEANS HAVE LITTLE CHOICE BUT TO ACCEPT OUR TERMS.
IT SOUNDS ALL RIGHT WHEN YOU EXPLAIN IT...
EVERYTHING WILL GO WELL --YOU'LL SEE.
NOW ANDROMACHE AND I WILL LEAVE YOU TO FINISH GETTING READY. DON'T BE LONG.
I HOPE YOU'LL LOOK CLEARLY AT WHAT I SHOWED YOU, HELEN.
WHEN I SEE PARIS AND HE HOLDS ME IN HIS ARMS, I KNOW I DON'T WANT TO BE ANYWHERE ELSE BUT WITH HIM.
BUT SOMETIMES WHEN I'M ALONE, I WONDER...
I WISH I COULD SEE WHAT'S GOING TO HAPPEN.
WELL, YOU CAN BE SURE OF ONE THING --I DON'T LOVE PARIS!

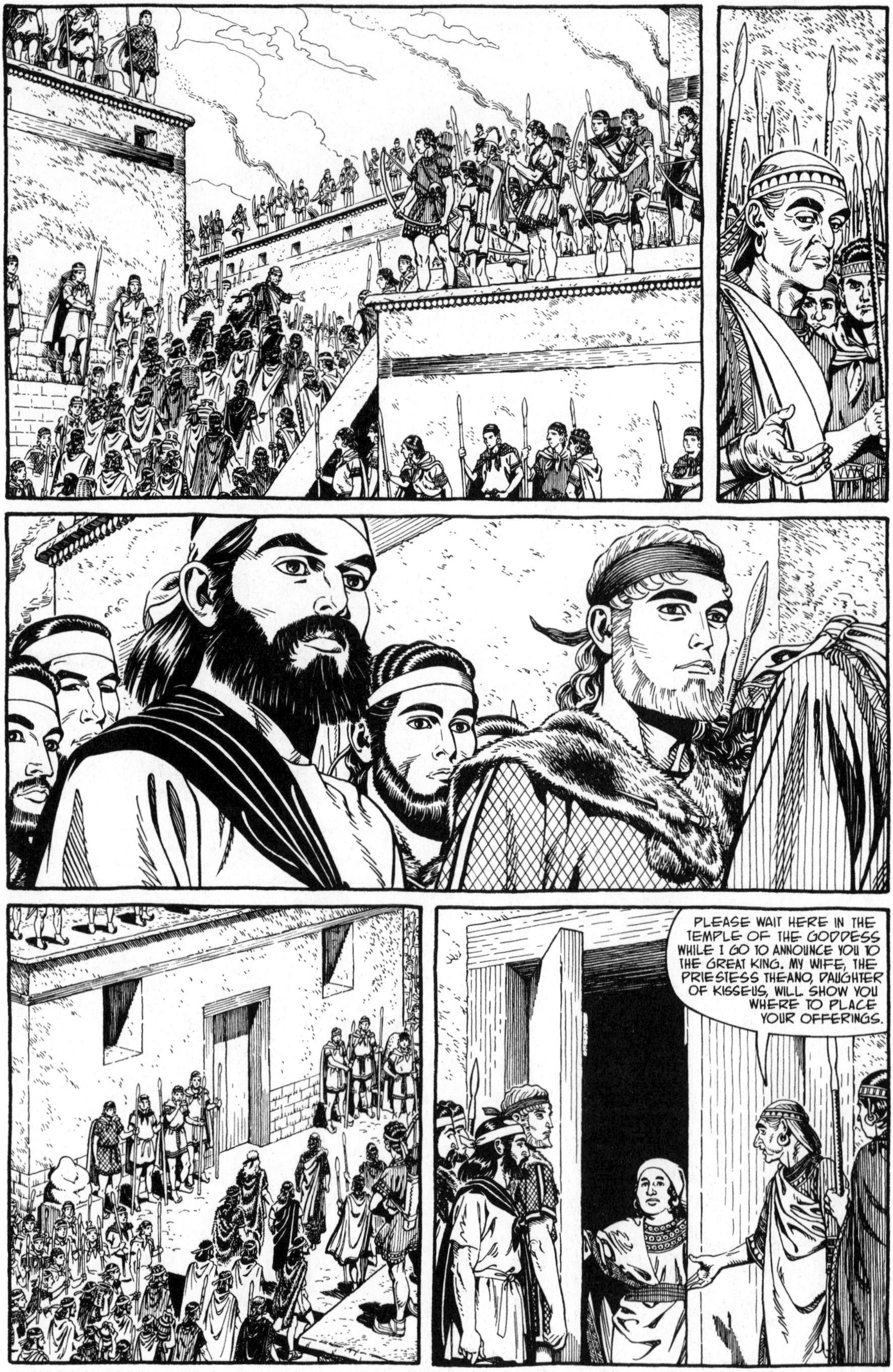
PLEASE WAIT HERE IN THE TEMPLE OF THE GODDESS WHILE I GO TO ANNOUNCE YOU TO THE GREAT KING. MY WIFE, THE PRIESTESS THEANO, DAUGHTER OF KISSEUS, WILL SHOW YOU WHERE TO PLACE YOUR OFFERINGS.

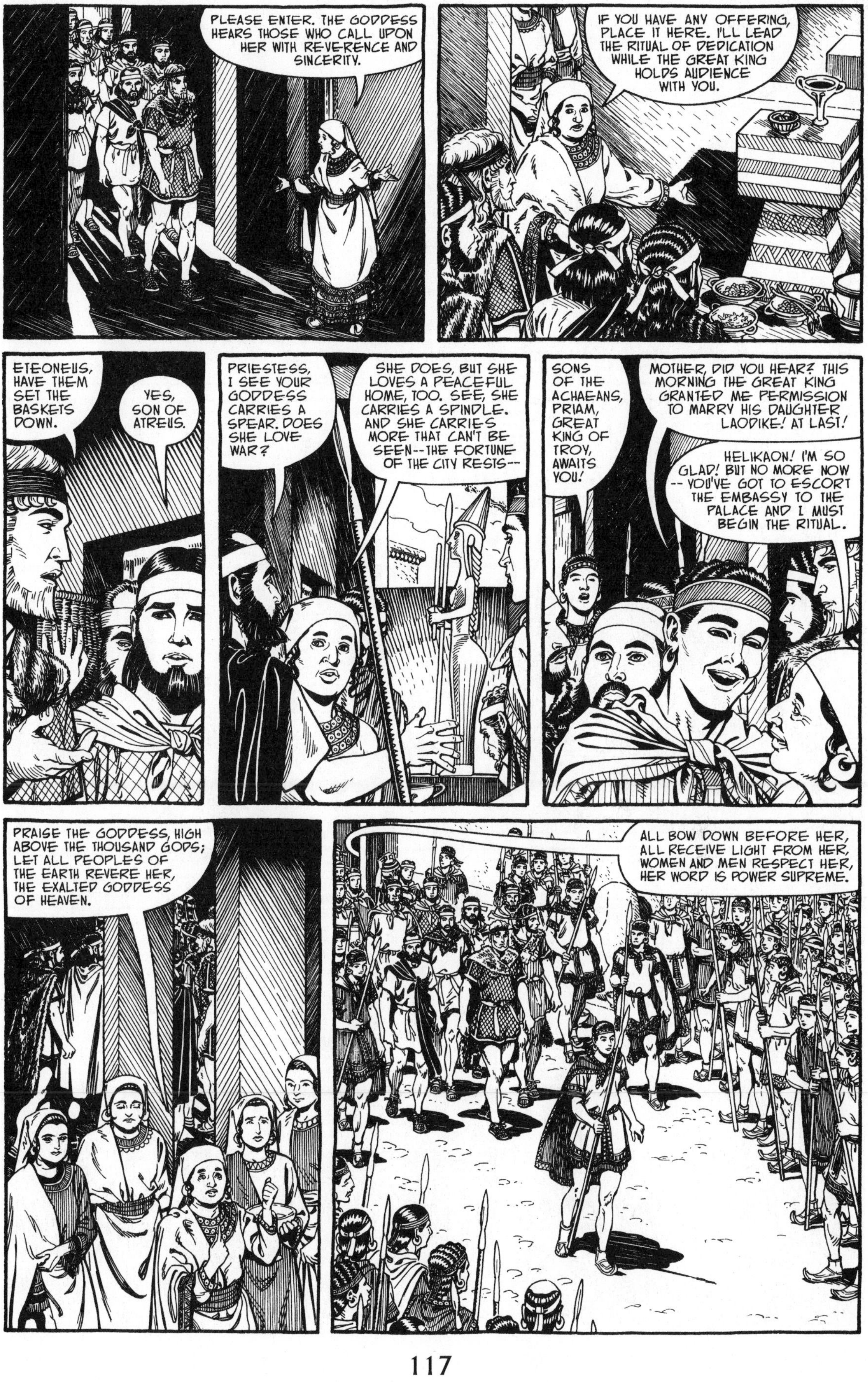
PLEASE ENTER. THE GODDESS HEARS THOSE WHO CALL UPON HER WITH REVERENCE AND SINCERITY.
IF YOU HAVE ANY OFFERING, PLACE IT HERE. I'LL LEAD THE RITUAL OF DEDICATION WHILE THE GREAT KING HOLDS AUDIENCE WITH YOU.
ETEONEUS, HAVE THEM SET THE BASKETS DOWN.
YES, SON OF ATREUS.
PRIESTESS, I SEE YOUR GODDESS CARRIES A SPEAR. DOES SHE LOVE WAR?
SHE DOES, BUT SHE LOVES A PEACEFUL HOME, TOO. SEE, SHE CARRIES A SPINDLE. AND SHE CARRIES MORE THAT CAN'T BE SEEN--THE FORTUNE OF THE CITY RESTS--
SONS OF THE ACHAEANS, PRIAM, GREAT KING OF TROY, AWAITS YOU!
MOTHER, DID YOU HEAR? THIS MORNING THE GREAT KING GRANTED ME PERMISSION TO MARRY HIS DAUGHTER LAODIKE! AT LAST!
HELIKAON! I'M SO GLAD! BUT NO MORE NOW -- YOU'VE GOT TO ESCORT THE EMBASSY TO THE PALACE AND I MUST BEGIN THE RITUAL.
PRAISE THE GODDESS, HIGH ABOVE THE THOUSAND GODS; LET ALL PEOPLES OF THE EARTH REVERE HER, THE EXALTED GODDESS OF HEAVEN.
ALL BOW DOWN BEFORE HER, ALL RECEIVE LIGHT FROM HER, WOMEN AND MEN RESPECT HER, HER WORD IS POWER SUPREME.

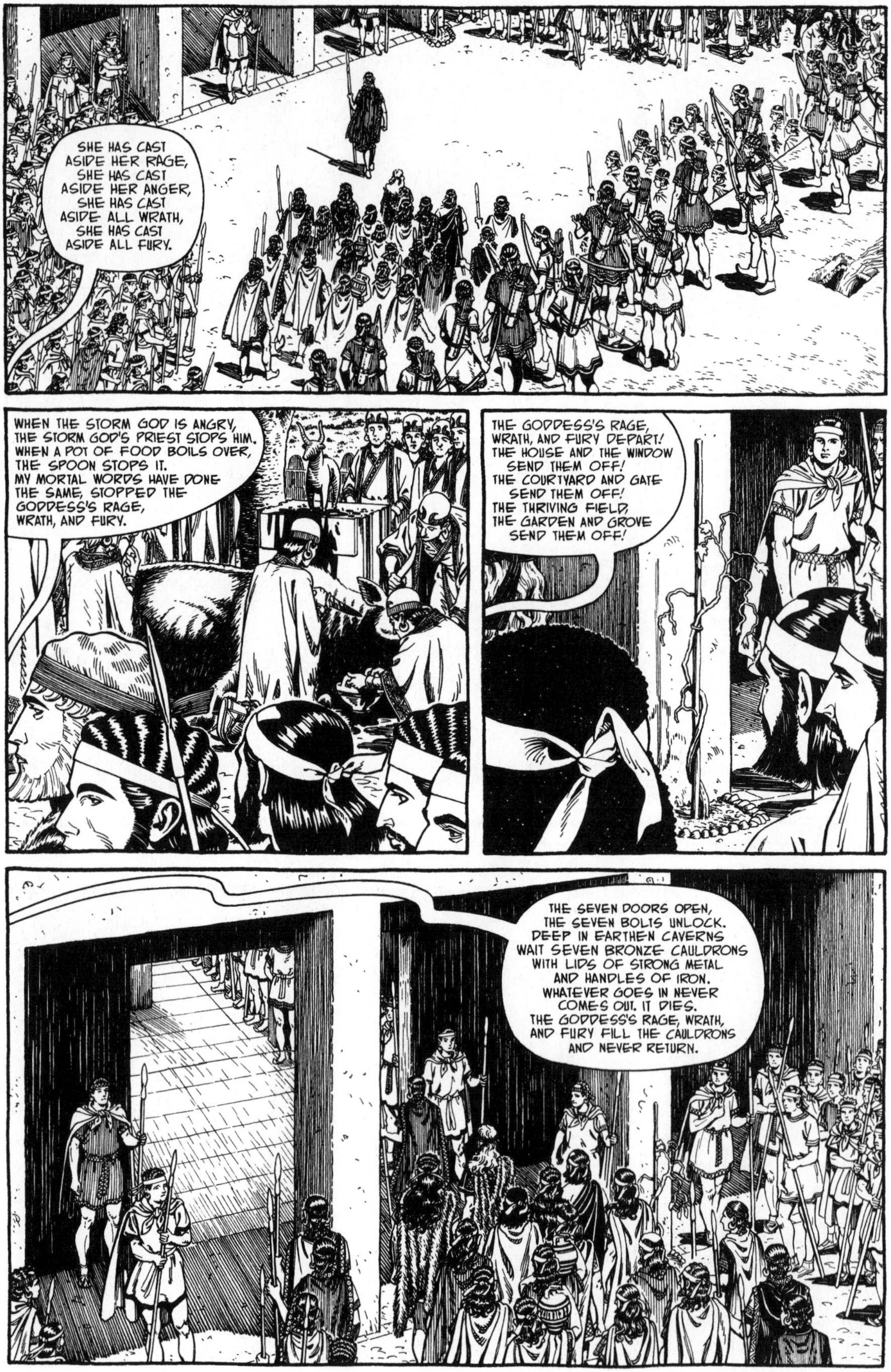
SHE HAS CAST ASIDE HER RAGE, SHE HAS CAST ASIDE HER ANGER, SHE HAS CAST ASIDE ALL WRATH, SHE HAS CAST ASIDE ALL FURY.
WHEN THE STORM GOD IS ANGRY, THE STORM GOD'S PRIEST STOPS HIM. WHEN A POT OF FOOD BOILS OVER, THE SPOON STOPS IT. MY MORTAL WORDS HAVE DONE THE SAME, STOPPED THE GODDESS'S RAGE, WRATH, AND FURY.
THE GODDESS'S RAGE, WRATH, AND FURY DEPART! THE HOUSE AND THE WINDOW SEND THEM OFF! THE COURTYARD AND GATE SEND THEM OFF! THE THRIVING FIELD, THE GARDEN AND GROVE SEND THEM OFF!
THE SEVEN DOORS OPEN, THE SEVEN BOLTS UNLOCK. DEEP IN EARTHEN CAVERNS WAIT SEVEN BRONZE CAULDRONS WITH LIDS OF STRONG METAL AND HANDLES OF IRON. WHATEVER GOES IN NEVER COMES OUT. IT DIES. THE GODDESS'S RAGE, WRATH, AND FURY FILL THE CAULDRONS AND NEVER RETURN.

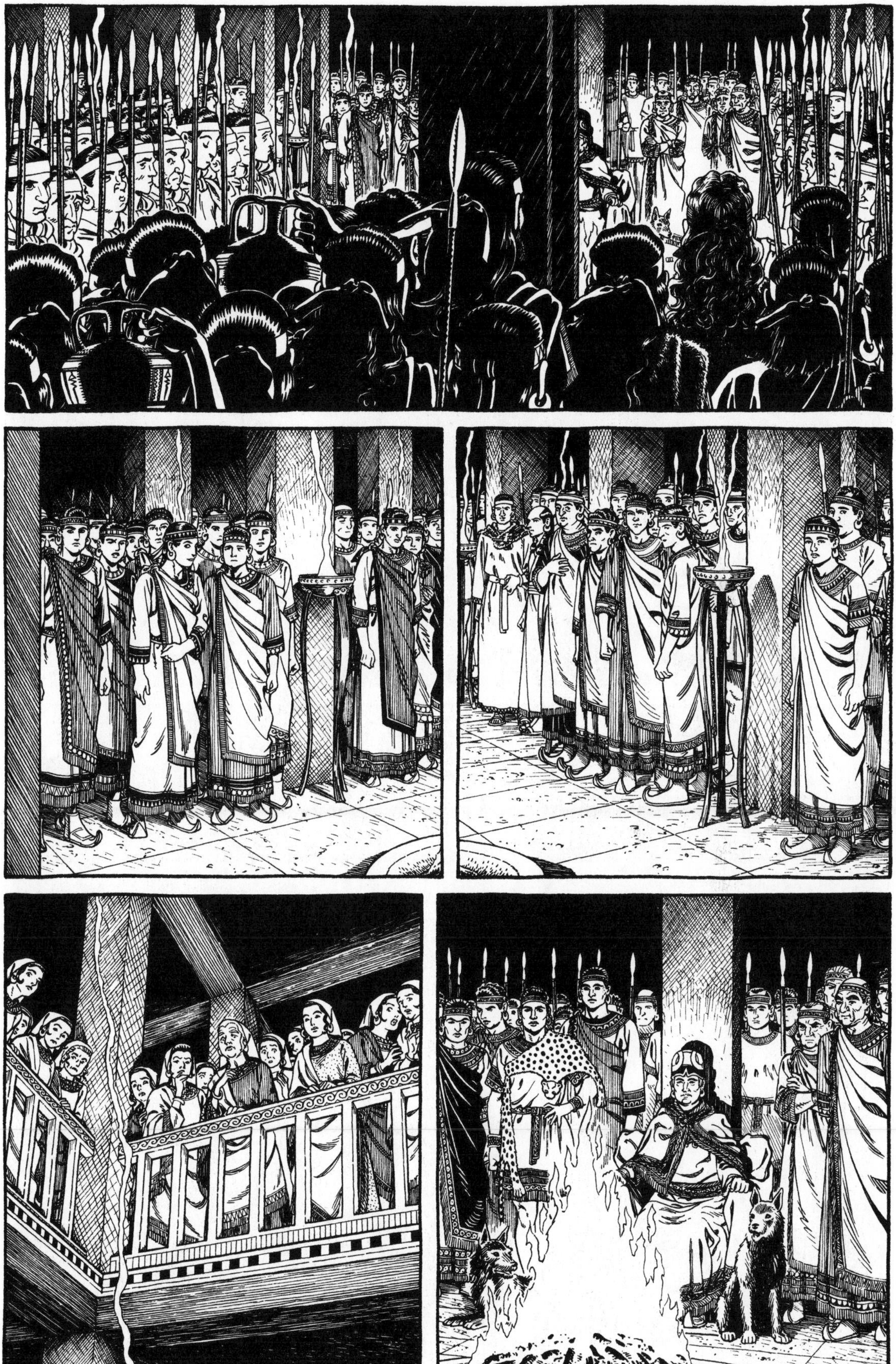

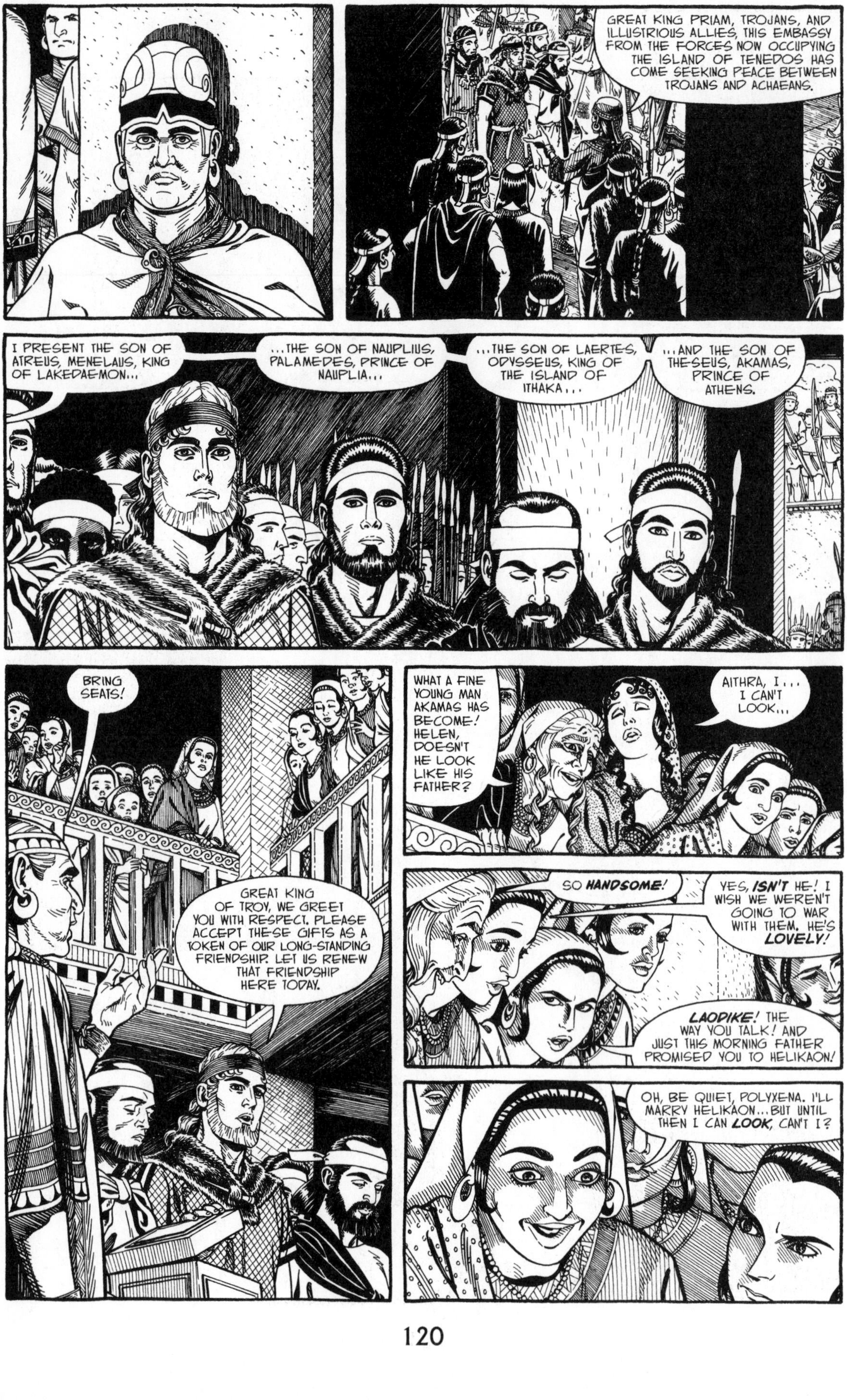

GREAT KING PRIAM, TROJANS, AND ILLUSTRIOUS ALLIES, THIS EMBASSY FROM THE FORCES NOW OCCUPYING THE ISLAND OF TENEDOS HAS COME SEEKING PEACE BETWEEN TROJANS AND ACHAEANS.
I PRESENT THE SON OF ATREUS, MENELAUS, KING OF LAKEDAEMON...
...THE SON OF NAUPLIUS, PALAMEDES, PRINCE OF NAUPLIA...
...THE SON OF LAERTES, ODYSSEUS, KING OF THE ISLAND OF ITHAKA...
...AND THE SON OF THESEUS, AKAMAS, PRINCE OF ATHENS.
BRING SEATS!
GREAT KING OF TROY, WE GREET YOU WITH RESPECT. PLEASE ACCEPT THESE GIFTS AS A TOKEN OF OUR LONG-STANDING FRIENDSHIP. LET US RENEW THAT FRIENDSHIP HERE TODAY.
WHAT A FINE YOUNG MAN AKAMAS HAS BECOME! HELEN, DOESN'T HE LOOK LIKE HIS FATHER?
AITHRA, I... I CAN'T LOOK...
SO HANDSOME!
YES, ISN'T HE! I WISH WE WEREN'T GOING TO WAR WITH THEM. HE'S LOVELY!
LAODIKE! THE WAY YOU TALK! AND JUST THIS MORNING FATHER PROMISED YOU TO HELIKAON!
OH, BE QUIET, POLYXENA. I'LL MARRY HELIKAON... BUT UNTIL THEN I CAN LOOK, CAN'T I?

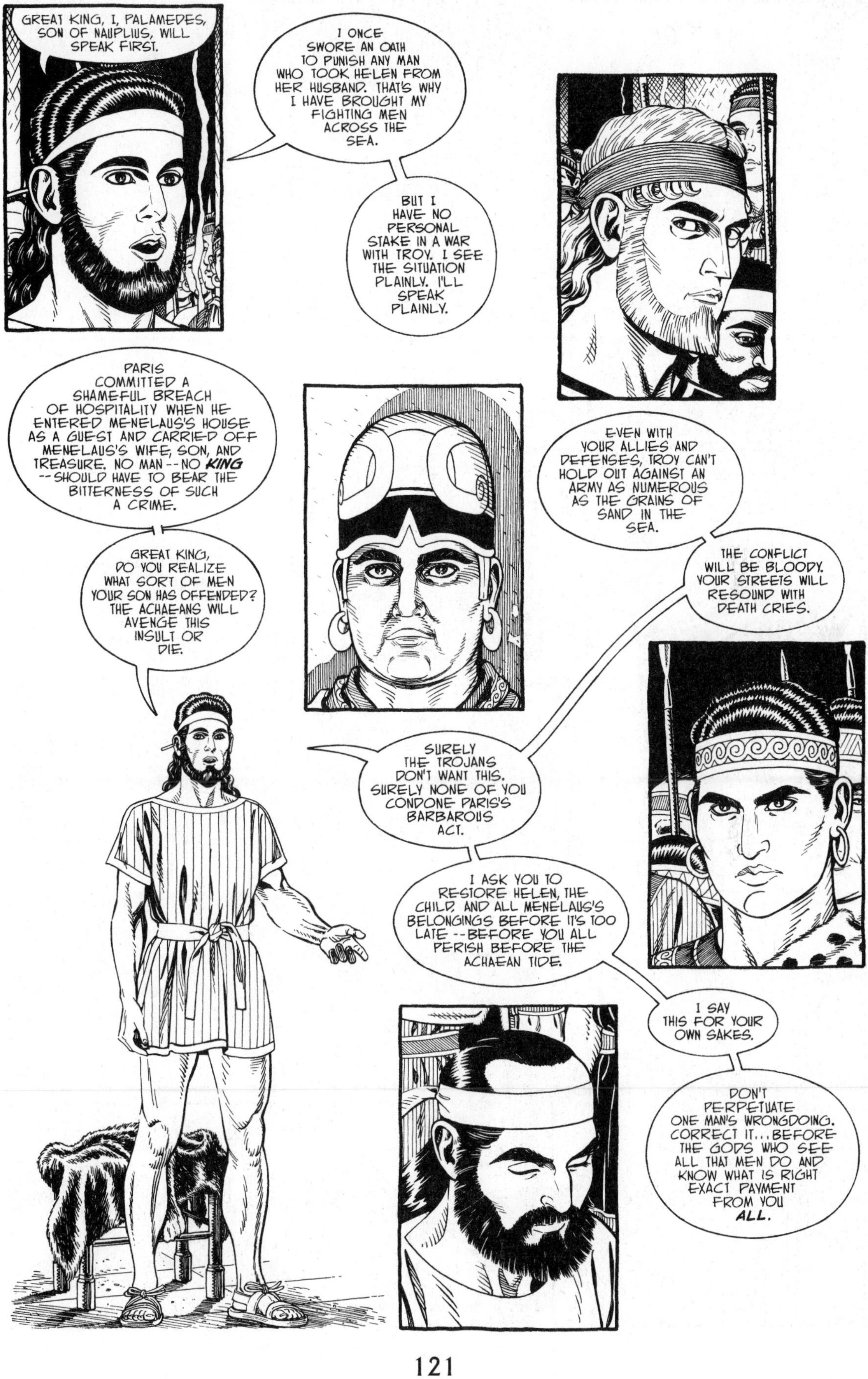
GREAT KING, I, PALAMEDES, SON OF NAUPLIUS, WILL SPEAK FIRST.
I ONCE SWORE AN OATH TO PUNISH ANY MAN WHO TOOK HELEN FROM HER HUSBAND. THAT'S WHY I HAVE BROUGHT MY FIGHTING MEN ACROSS THE SEA.
BUT I HAVE NO PERSONAL STAKE IN A WAR WITH TROY. I SEE THE SITUATION PLAINLY. I'LL SPEAK PLAINLY.
PARIS COMMITTED A SHAMEFUL BREACH OF HOSPITALITY WHEN HE ENTERED MENELAUS'S HOUSE AS A GUEST AND CARRIED OFF MENELAUS'S WIFE, SON, AND TREASURE. NO MAN--NO **KING** --SHOULD HAVE TO BEAR THE BITTERNESS OF SUCH A CRIME.
GREAT KING, DO YOU REALIZE WHAT SORT OF MEN YOUR SON HAS OFFENDED? THE ACHAEANS WILL AVENGE THIS INSULT OR DIE.
EVEN WITH YOUR ALLIES AND DEFENSES, TROY CAN'T HOLD OUT AGAINST AN ARMY AS NUMEROUS AS THE GRAINS OF SAND IN THE SEA.
THE CONFLICT WILL BE BLOODY. YOUR STREETS WILL RESOUND WITH DEATH CRIES.
SURELY THE TROJANS DON'T WANT THIS. SURELY NONE OF YOU CONDONE PARIS'S BARBAROUS ACT.
I ASK YOU TO RESTORE HELEN, THE CHILD, AND ALL MENELAUS'S BELONGINGS BEFORE IT'S TOO LATE--BEFORE YOU ALL PERISH BEFORE THE ACHAEAN TIDE.
I SAY THIS FOR YOUR OWN SAKES.
DON'T PERPETUATE ONE MAN'S WRONGDOING. CORRECT IT...BEFORE THE GODS WHO SEE ALL THAT MEN DO AND KNOW WHAT IS RIGHT EXACT PAYMENT FROM YOU **ALL**.

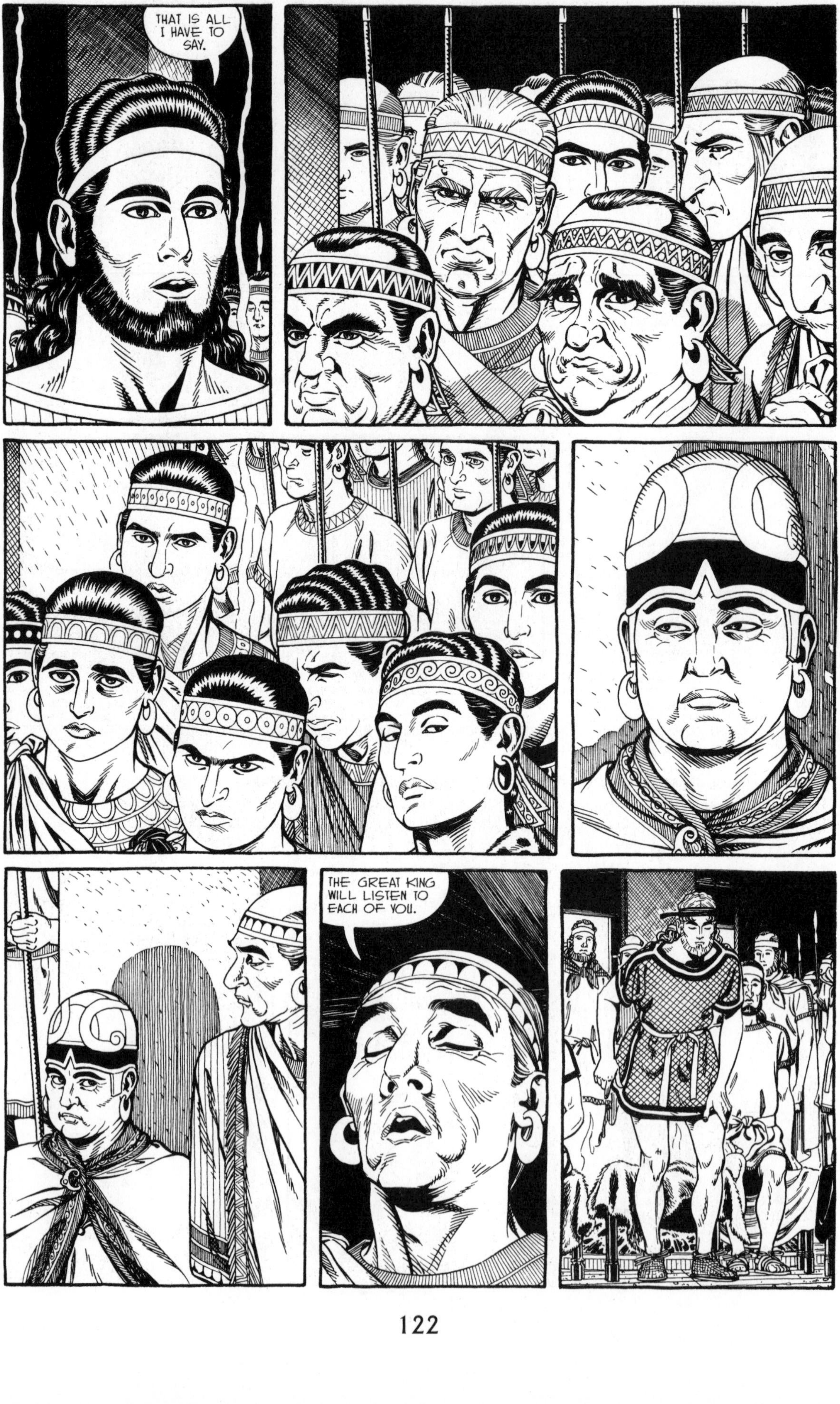
THAT IS ALL I HAVE TO SAY.
THE GREAT KING WILL LISTEN TO EACH OF YOU.

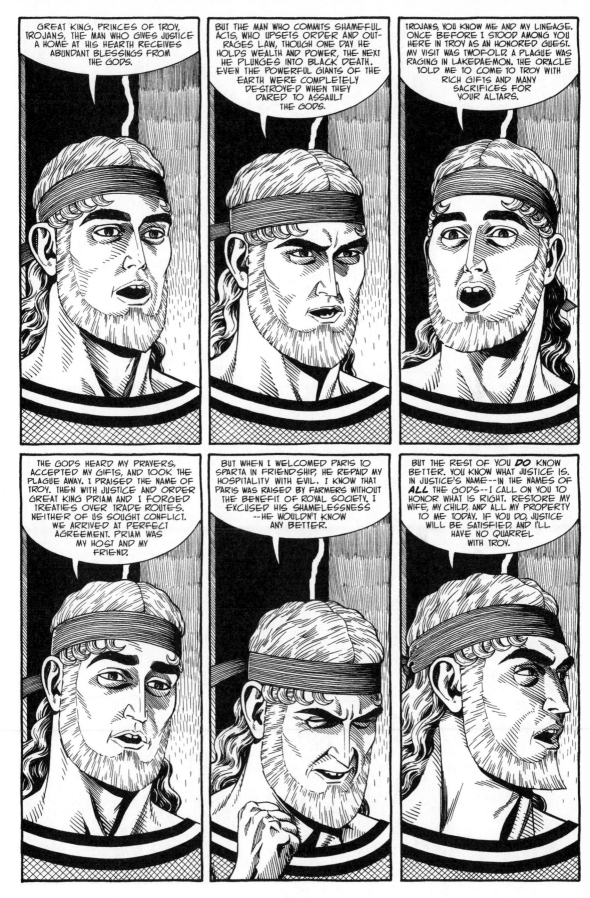

GREAT KING, PRINCES OF TROY, TROJANS, THE MAN WHO GIVES JUSTICE A HOME AT HIS HEARTH RECEIVES ABUNDANT BLESSINGS FROM THE GODS.

BUT THE MAN WHO COMMITS SHAMEFUL ACTS, WHO UPSETS ORDER AND OUTRAGES LAW, THOUGH ONE DAY HE HOLDS WEALTH AND POWER, THE NEXT HE PLUNGES INTO BLACK DEATH. EVEN THE POWERFUL GIANTS OF THE EARTH WERE COMPLETELY DESTROYED WHEN THEY DARED TO ASSAULT THE GODS.

TROJANS, YOU KNOW ME AND MY LINEAGE. ONCE BEFORE I STOOD AMONG YOU HERE IN TROY AS AN HONORED GUEST. MY VISIT WAS TWOFOLD: A PLAGUE WAS RAGING IN LAKEDAEMON. THE ORACLE TOLD ME TO COME TO TROY WITH RICH GIFTS AND MANY SACRIFICES FOR YOUR ALTARS.

THE GODS HEARD MY PRAYERS, ACCEPTED MY GIFTS, AND TOOK THE PLAGUE AWAY. I PRAISED THE NAME OF TROY. THEN WITH JUSTICE AND ORDER GREAT KING PRIAM AND I FORGED TREATIES OVER TRADE ROUTES. NEITHER OF US SOUGHT CONFLICT. WE ARRIVED AT PERFECT AGREEMENT. PRIAM WAS MY HOST AND MY FRIEND.

BUT WHEN I WELCOMED PARIS TO SPARTA IN FRIENDSHIP, HE REPAID MY HOSPITALITY WITH EVIL. I KNOW THAT PARIS WAS RAISED BY FARMERS WITHOUT THE BENEFIT OF ROYAL SOCIETY. I EXCUSED HIS SHAMELESSNESS --HE WOULDN'T KNOW ANY BETTER.

BUT THE REST OF YOU **DO** KNOW BETTER. YOU KNOW WHAT JUSTICE IS. IN JUSTICE'S NAME--IN THE NAMES OF **ALL** THE GODS--I CALL ON YOU TO HONOR WHAT IS RIGHT. RESTORE MY WIFE, MY CHILD, AND ALL MY PROPERTY TO ME TODAY. IF YOU DO, JUSTICE WILL BE SATISFIED, AND I'LL HAVE NO QUARREL WITH TROY.

123

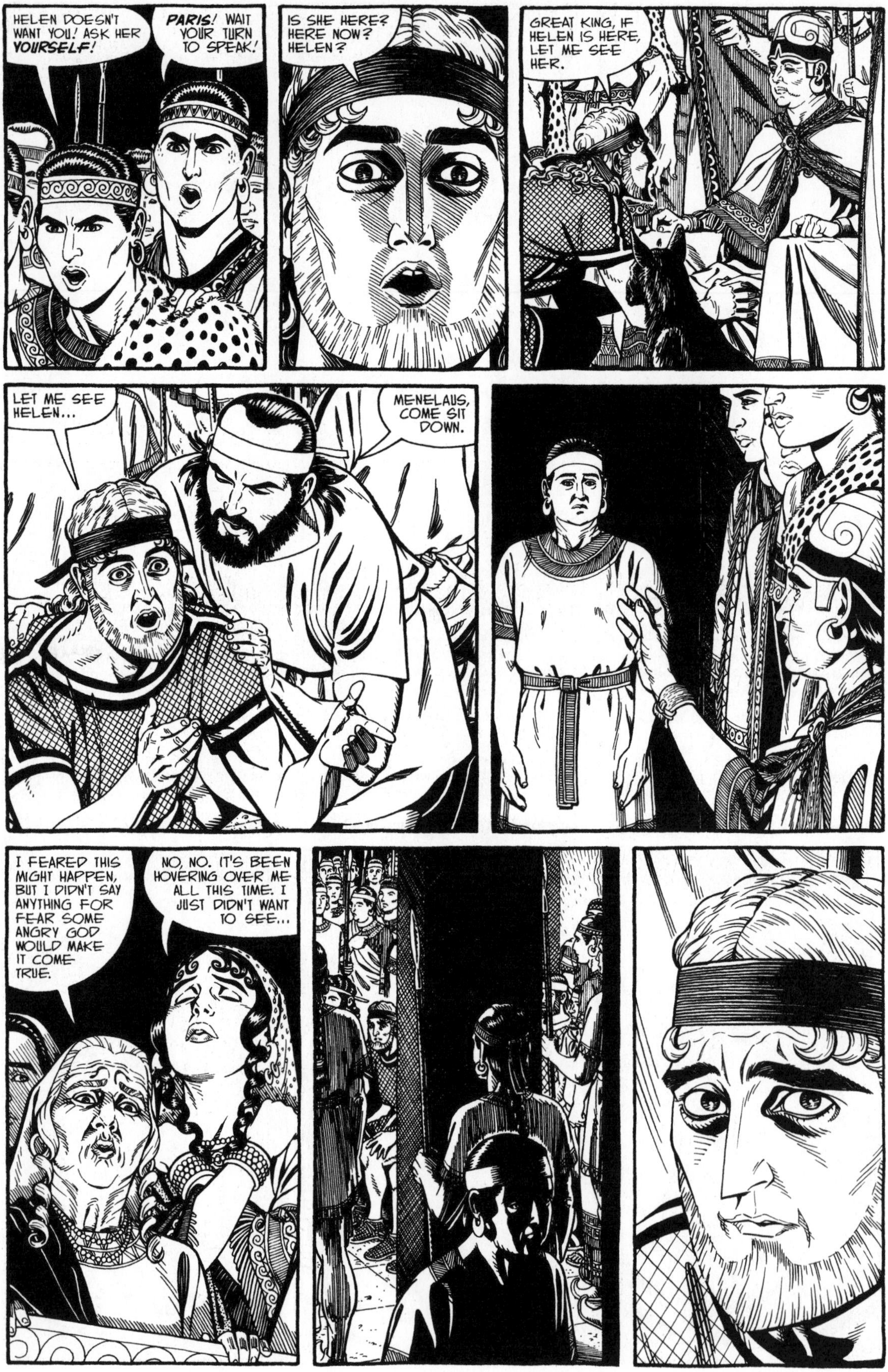
HELEN DOESN'T WANT YOU! ASK HER **YOURSELF!**
PARIS! WAIT YOUR TURN TO SPEAK!
IS SHE HERE? HERE NOW? HELEN?
GREAT KING, IF HELEN IS HERE, LET ME SEE HER.
LET ME SEE HELEN...
MENELAUS, COME SIT DOWN.
I FEARED THIS MIGHT HAPPEN, BUT I DIDN'T SAY ANYTHING FOR FEAR SOME ANGRY GOD WOULD MAKE IT COME TRUE.
NO, NO. IT'S BEEN HOVERING OVER ME ALL THIS TIME. I JUST DIDN'T WANT TO SEE...

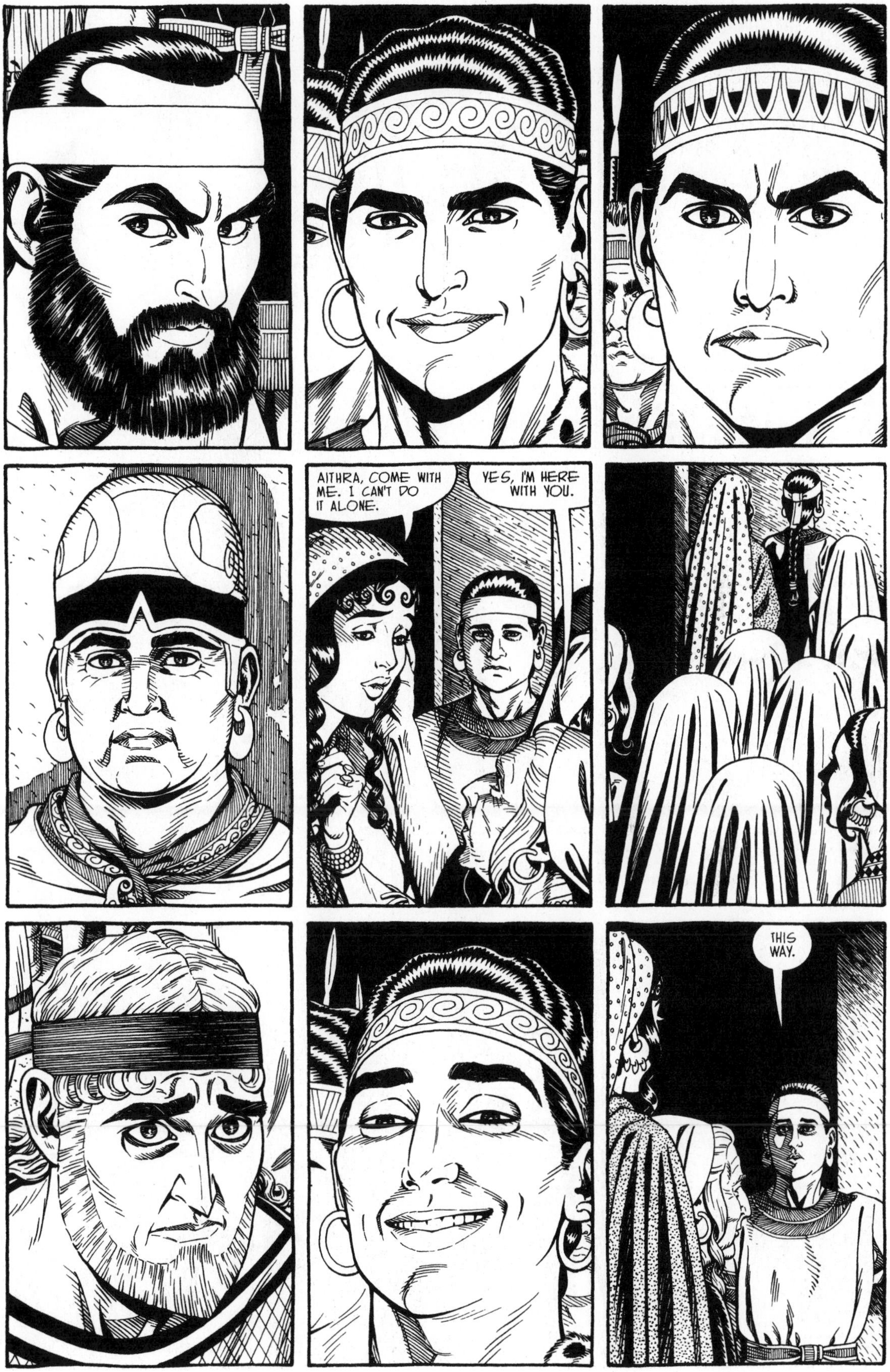
AITHRA, COME WITH ME. I CAN'T DO IT ALONE.
YES, I'M HERE WITH YOU.
THIS WAY.

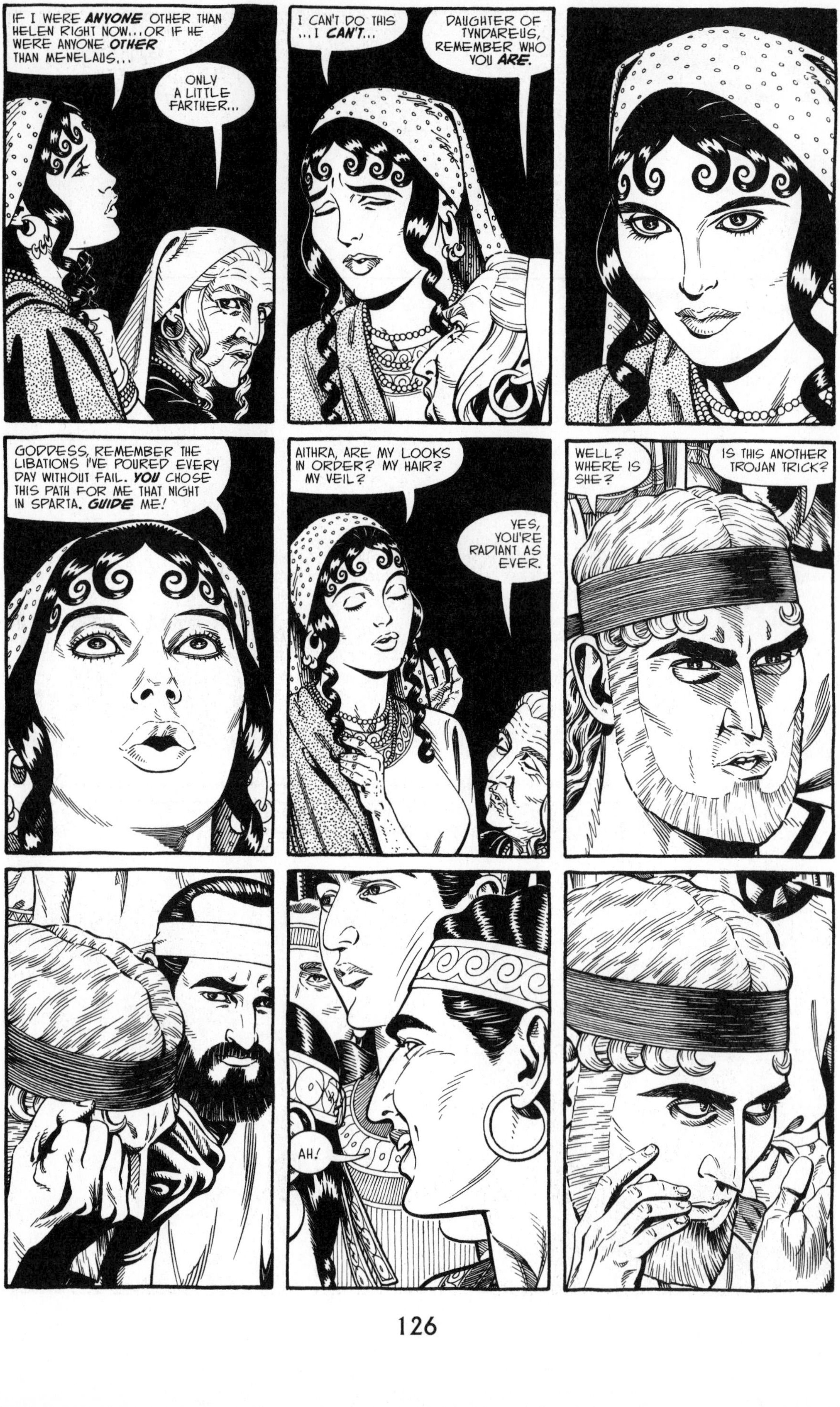
IF I WERE ANYONE OTHER THAN HELEN RIGHT NOW... OR IF HE WERE ANYONE OTHER THAN MENELAUS...
ONLY A LITTLE FARTHER...
I CAN'T DO THIS ...I CAN'T...
DAUGHTER OF TYNDAREUS, REMEMBER WHO YOU ARE.
GODDESS, REMEMBER THE LIBATIONS I'VE POURED EVERY DAY WITHOUT FAIL. YOU CHOSE THIS PATH FOR ME THAT NIGHT IN SPARTA. GUIDE ME!
AITHRA, ARE MY LOOKS IN ORDER? MY HAIR? MY VEIL?
YES, YOU'RE RADIANT AS EVER.
WELL? WHERE IS SHE?
IS THIS ANOTHER TROJAN TRICK?
AH!

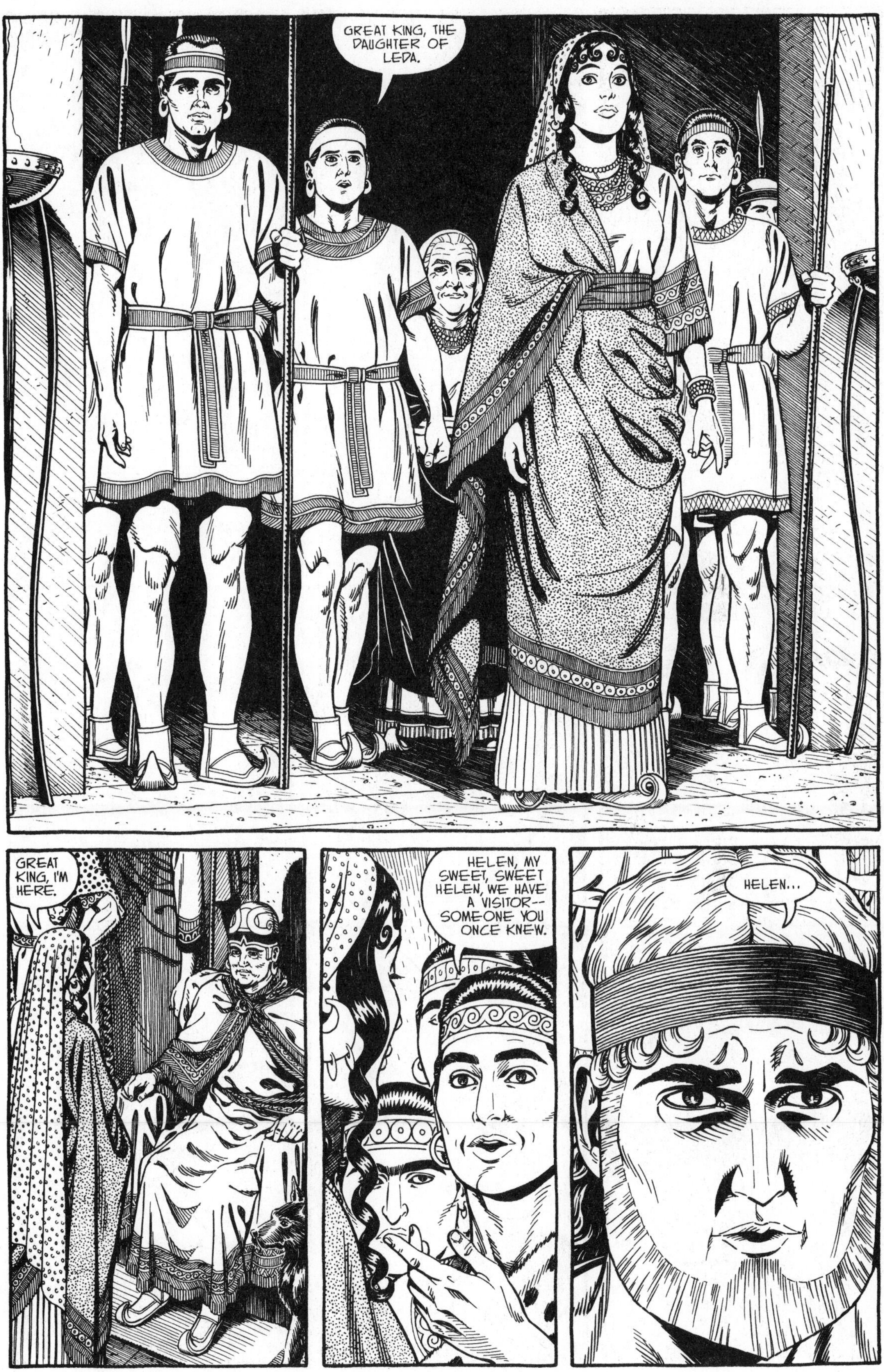
GREAT KING, THE DAUGHTER OF LEDA.
GREAT KING, I'M HERE.
HELEN, MY SWEET, SWEET HELEN, WE HAVE A VISITOR-- SOME-ONE YOU ONCE KNEW.
HELEN...

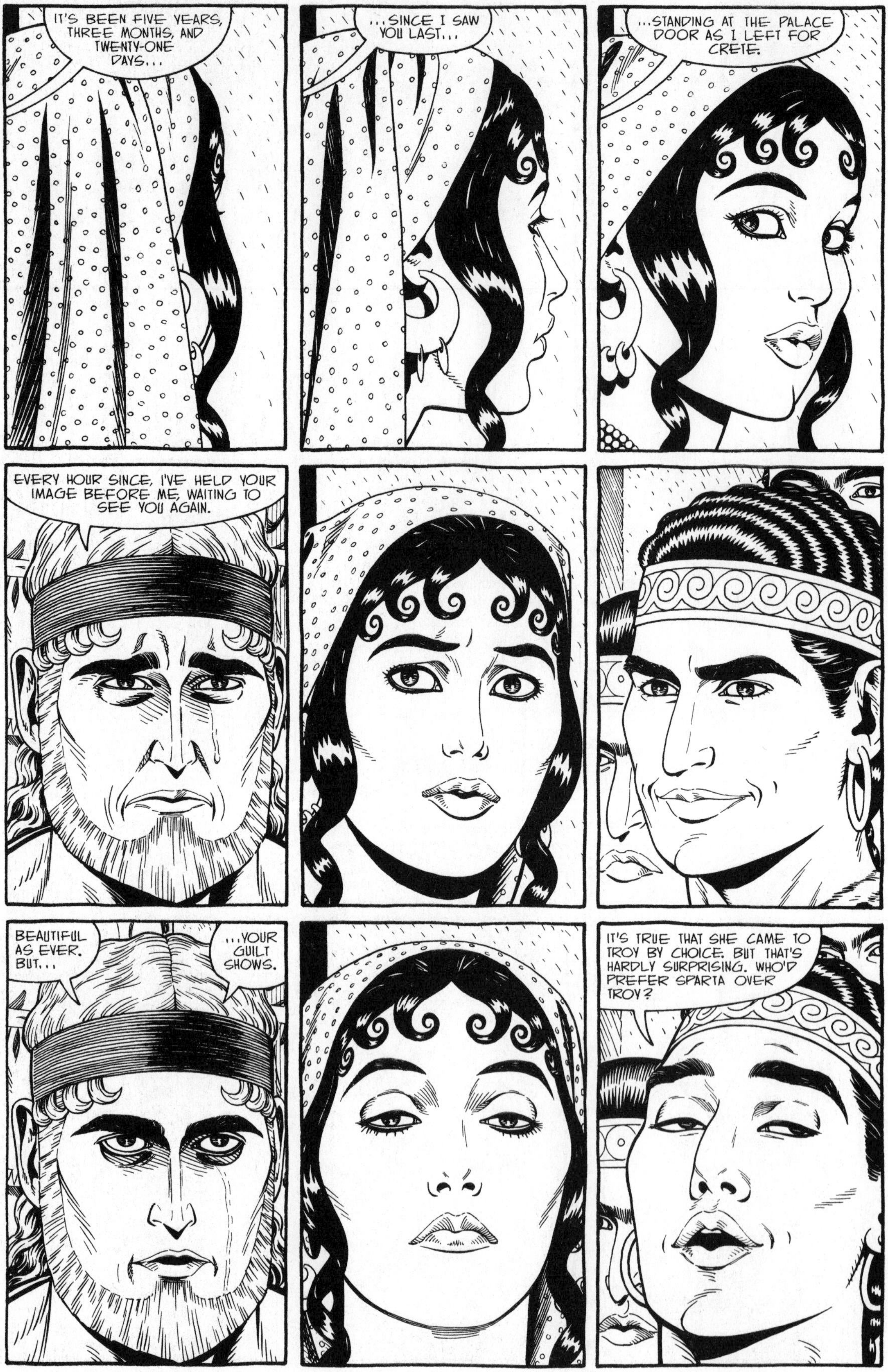
IT'S BEEN FIVE YEARS, THREE MONTHS, AND TWENTY-ONE DAYS...
...SINCE I SAW YOU LAST...
...STANDING AT THE PALACE DOOR AS I LEFT FOR CRETE.
EVERY HOUR SINCE, I'VE HELD YOUR IMAGE BEFORE ME, WAITING TO SEE YOU AGAIN.
BEAUTIFUL AS EVER. BUT...
...YOUR GUILT SHOWS.
IT'S TRUE THAT SHE CAME TO TROY BY CHOICE. BUT THAT'S HARDLY SURPRISING. WHO'D PREFER SPARTA OVER TROY?

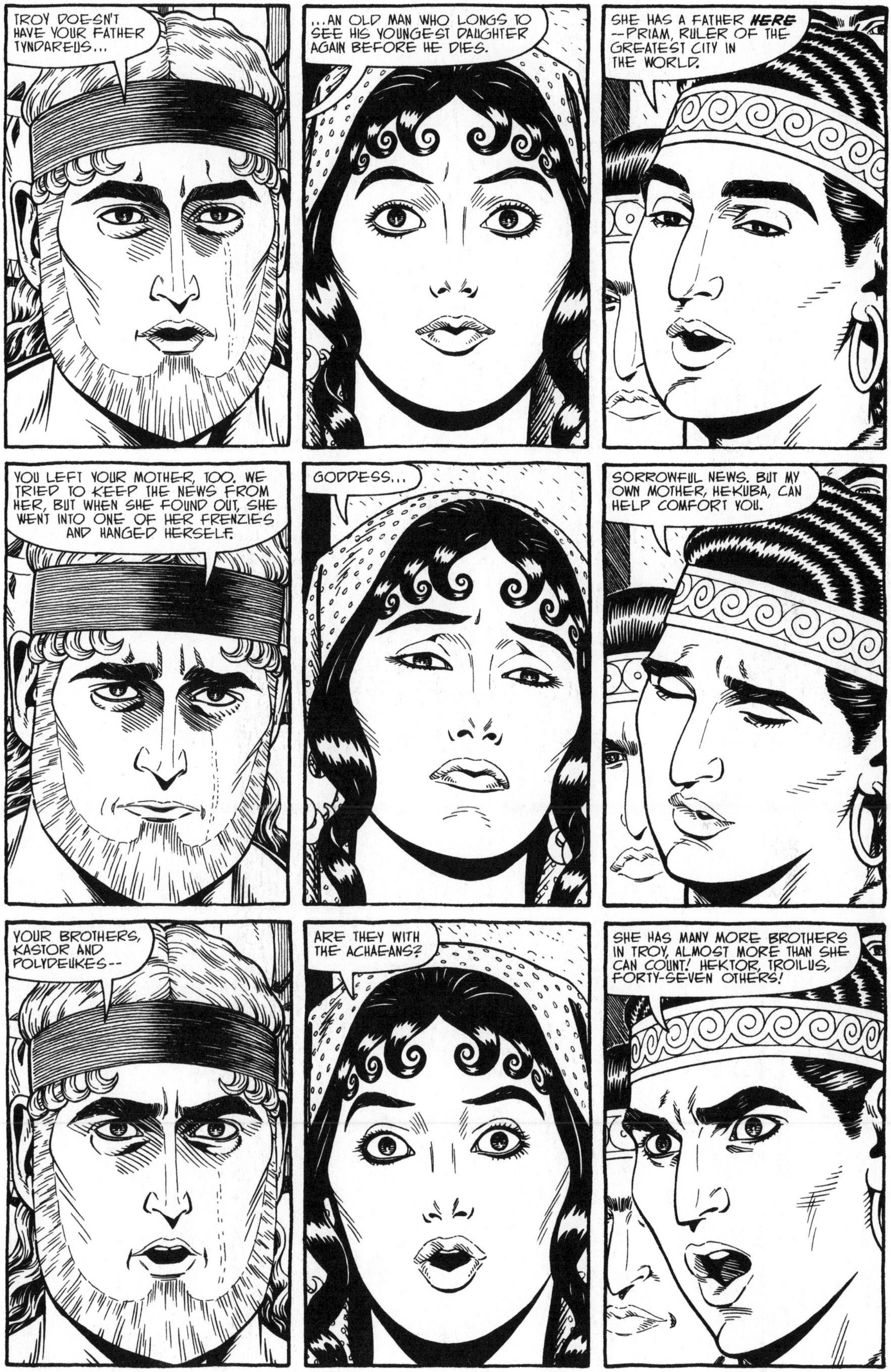
TROY DOESN'T HAVE YOUR FATHER TYNDAREUS...
...AN OLD MAN WHO LONGS TO SEE HIS YOUNGEST DAUGHTER AGAIN BEFORE HE DIES.
SHE HAS A FATHER **HERE** --PRIAM, RULER OF THE GREATEST CITY IN THE WORLD.
YOU LEFT YOUR MOTHER, TOO. WE TRIED TO KEEP THE NEWS FROM HER, BUT WHEN SHE FOUND OUT, SHE WENT INTO ONE OF HER FRENZIES AND HANGED HERSELF.
GODDESS...
SORROWFUL NEWS. BUT MY OWN MOTHER, HEKUBA, CAN HELP COMFORT YOU.
YOUR BROTHERS, KASTOR AND POLYDEUKES--
ARE THEY WITH THE ACHAEANS?
SHE HAS MANY MORE BROTHERS IN TROY, ALMOST MORE THAN SHE CAN COUNT! HEKTOR, TROILUS, FORTY-SEVEN OTHERS!

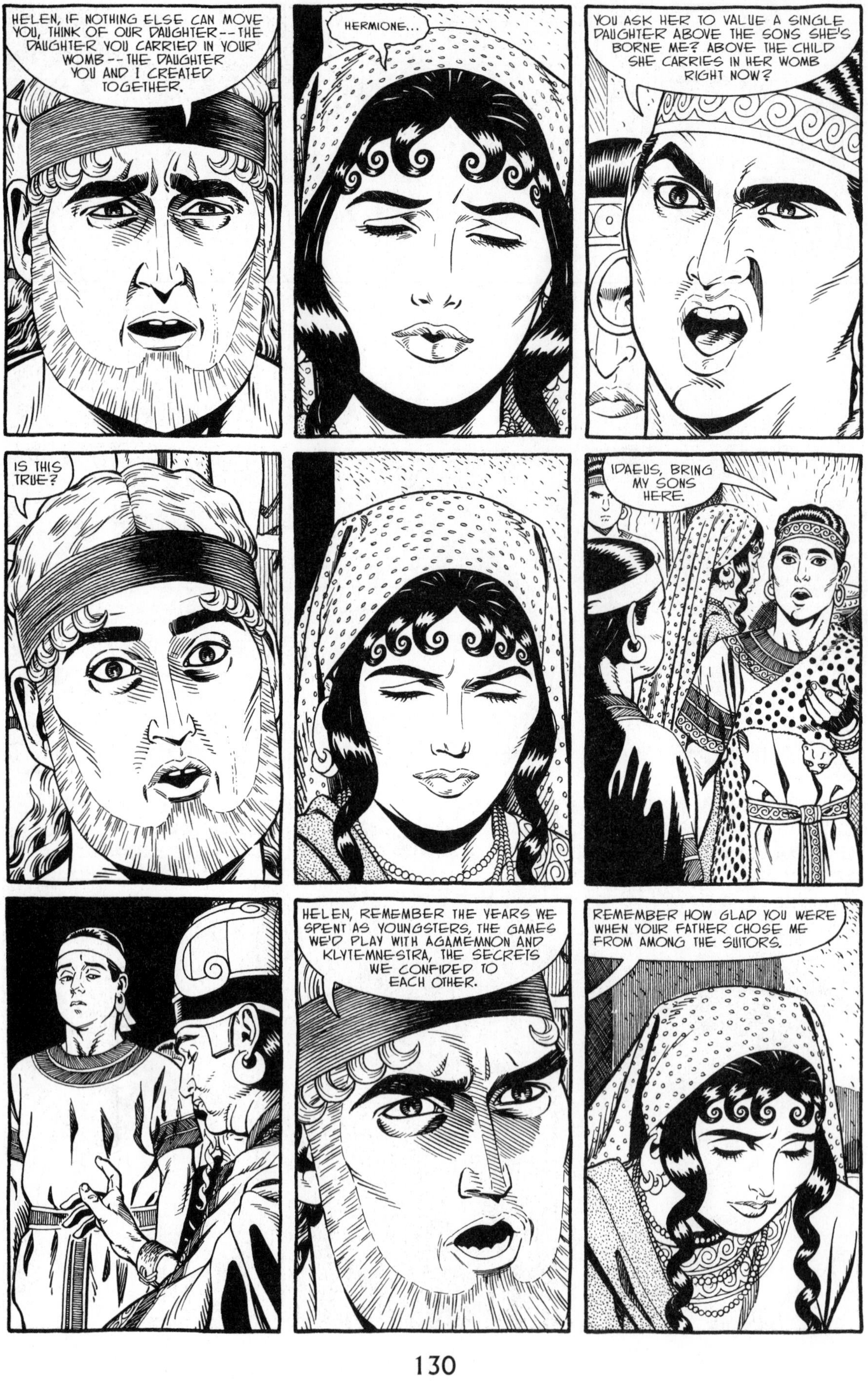
HELEN, IF NOTHING ELSE CAN MOVE YOU, THINK OF OUR DAUGHTER--THE DAUGHTER YOU CARRIED IN YOUR WOMB--THE DAUGHTER YOU AND I CREATED TOGETHER.
HERMIONE...
YOU ASK HER TO VALUE A SINGLE DAUGHTER ABOVE THE SONS SHE'S BORNE ME? ABOVE THE CHILD SHE CARRIES IN HER WOMB RIGHT NOW?
IS THIS TRUE?
IDAEUS, BRING MY SONS HERE.
HELEN, REMEMBER THE YEARS WE SPENT AS YOUNGSTERS, THE GAMES WE'D PLAY WITH AGAMEMNON AND KLYTEMNESTRA, THE SECRETS WE CONFIDED TO EACH OTHER.
REMEMBER HOW GLAD YOU WERE WHEN YOUR FATHER CHOSE ME FROM AMONG THE SUITORS.

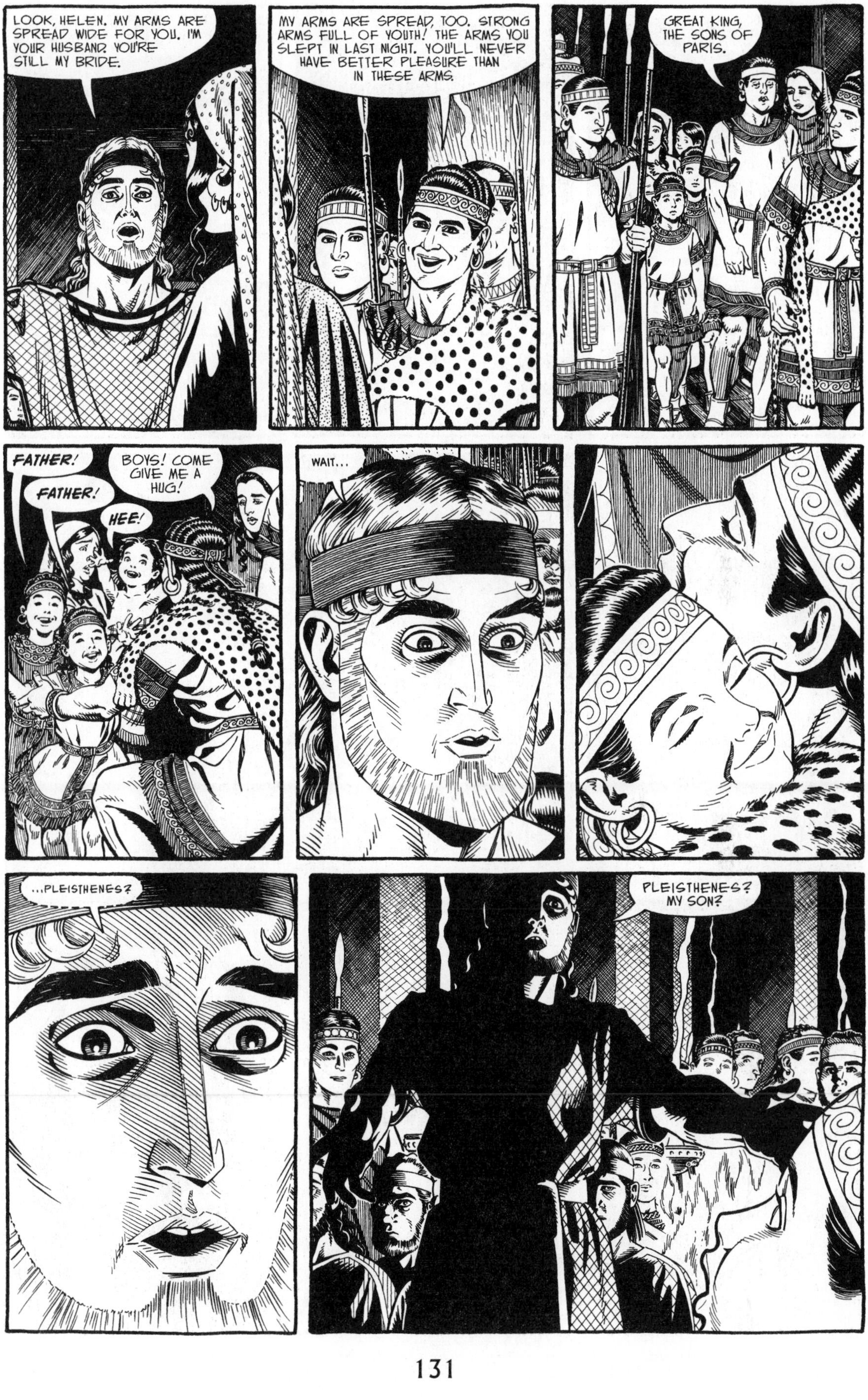
LOOK, HELEN. MY ARMS ARE SPREAD WIDE FOR YOU. I'M YOUR HUSBAND. YOU'RE STILL MY BRIDE.
MY ARMS ARE SPREAD, TOO. STRONG ARMS FULL OF YOUTH! THE ARMS YOU SLEPT IN LAST NIGHT. YOU'LL NEVER HAVE BETTER PLEASURE THAN IN THESE ARMS.
GREAT KING, THE SONS OF PARIS.
FATHER!
FATHER!
BOYS! COME GIVE ME A HUG!
HEE!
WAIT...
...PLEISTHENES?
PLEISTHENES? MY SON?

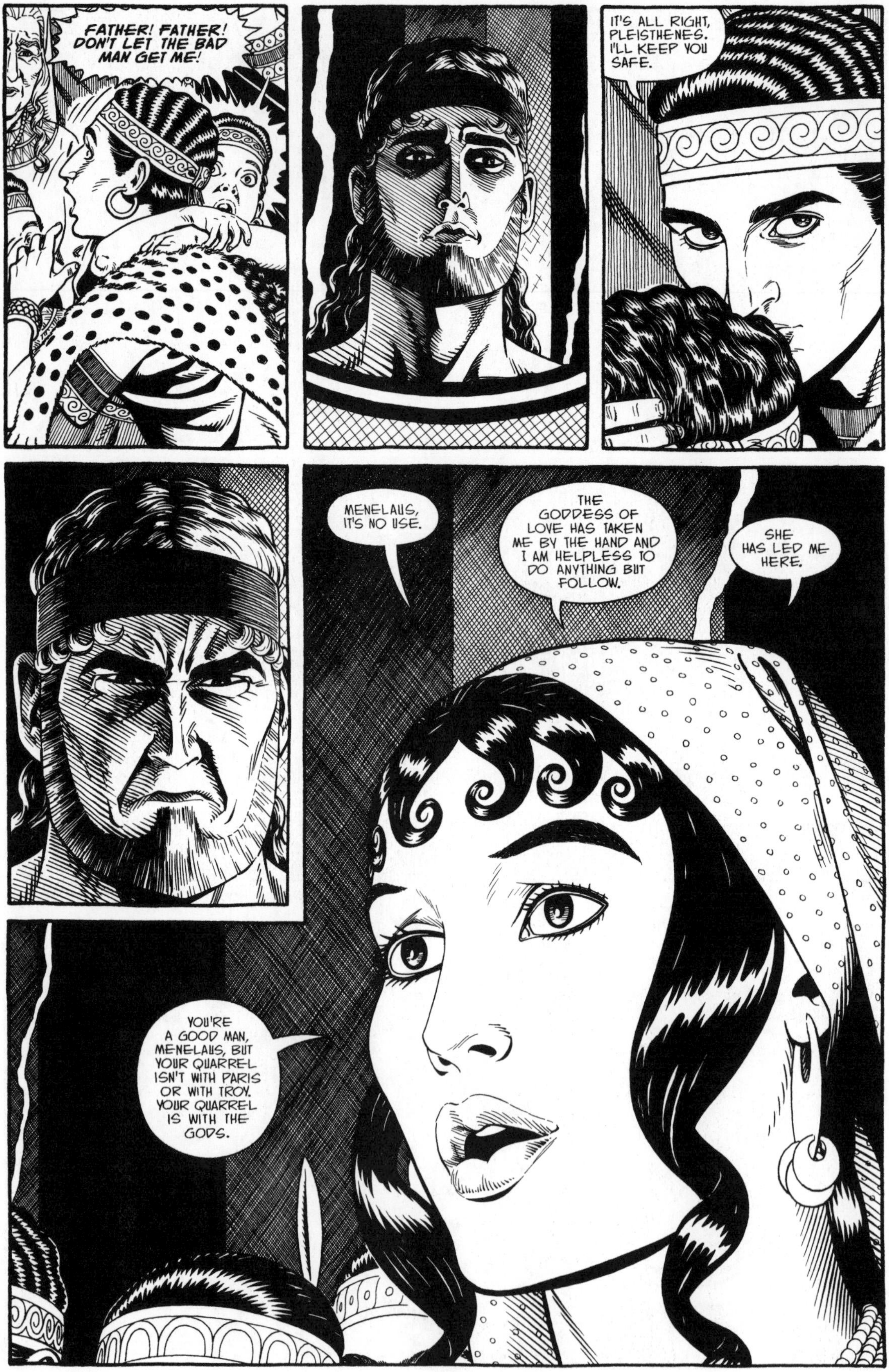
FATHER! FATHER! DON'T LET THE BAD MAN GET ME!
IT'S ALL RIGHT, PLEISTHENES. I'LL KEEP YOU SAFE.
MENELAUS, IT'S NO USE.
THE GODDESS OF LOVE HAS TAKEN ME BY THE HAND AND I AM HELPLESS TO DO ANYTHING BUT FOLLOW.
SHE HAS LED ME HERE.
YOU'RE A GOOD MAN, MENELAUS, BUT YOUR QUARREL ISN'T WITH PARIS OR WITH TROY. YOUR QUARREL IS WITH THE GODS.

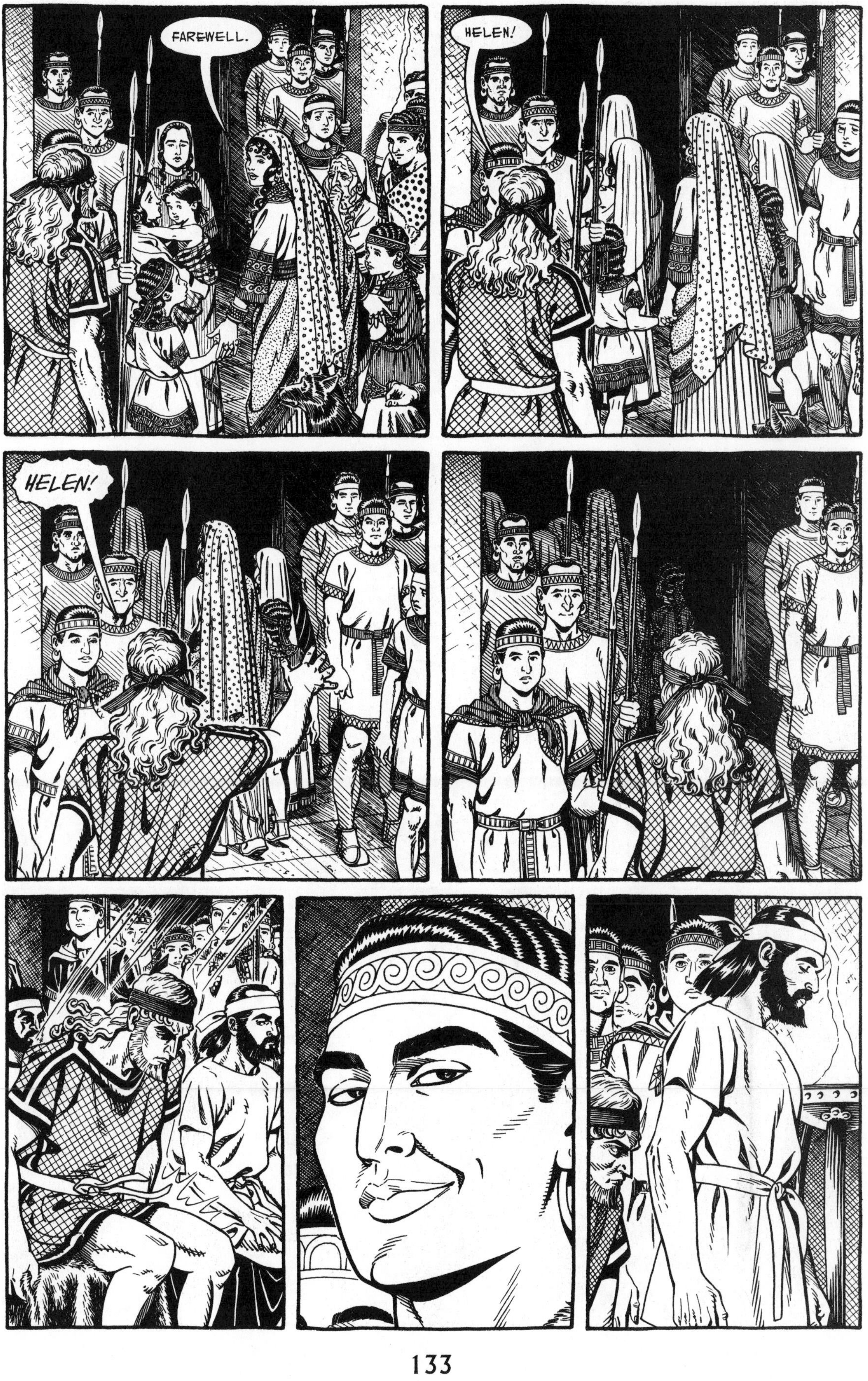
FAREWELL.
HELEN!
HELEN!

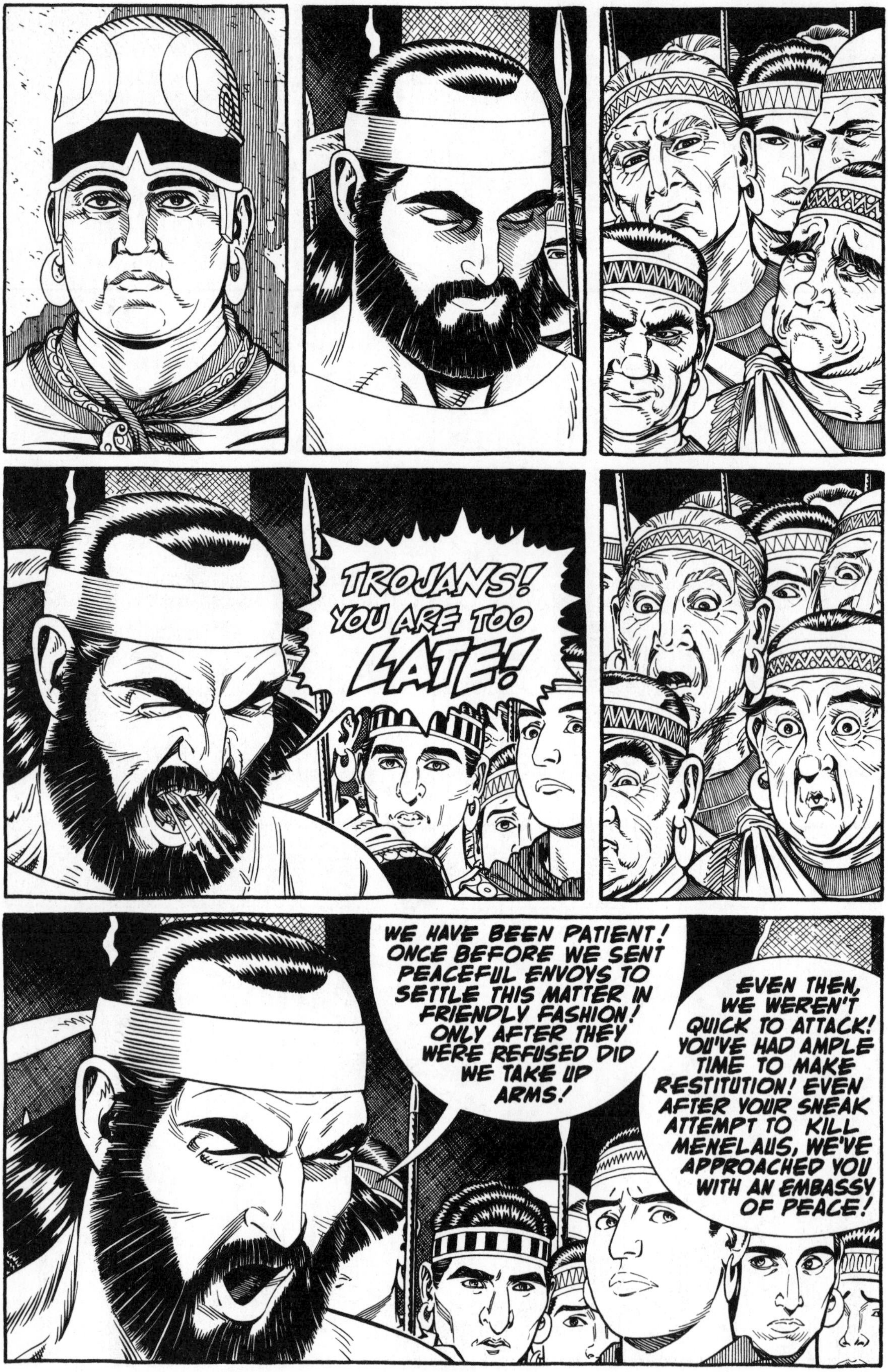
TROJANS! YOU ARE TOO LATE!
WE HAVE BEEN PATIENT! ONCE BEFORE WE SENT PEACEFUL ENVOYS TO SETTLE THIS MATTER IN FRIENDLY FASHION! ONLY AFTER THEY WERE REFUSED DID WE TAKE UP ARMS!
EVEN THEN, WE WEREN'T QUICK TO ATTACK! YOU'VE HAD AMPLE TIME TO MAKE RESTITUTION! EVEN AFTER YOUR SNEAK ATTEMPT TO KILL MENELAUS, WE'VE APPROACHED YOU WITH AN EMBASSY OF PEACE!

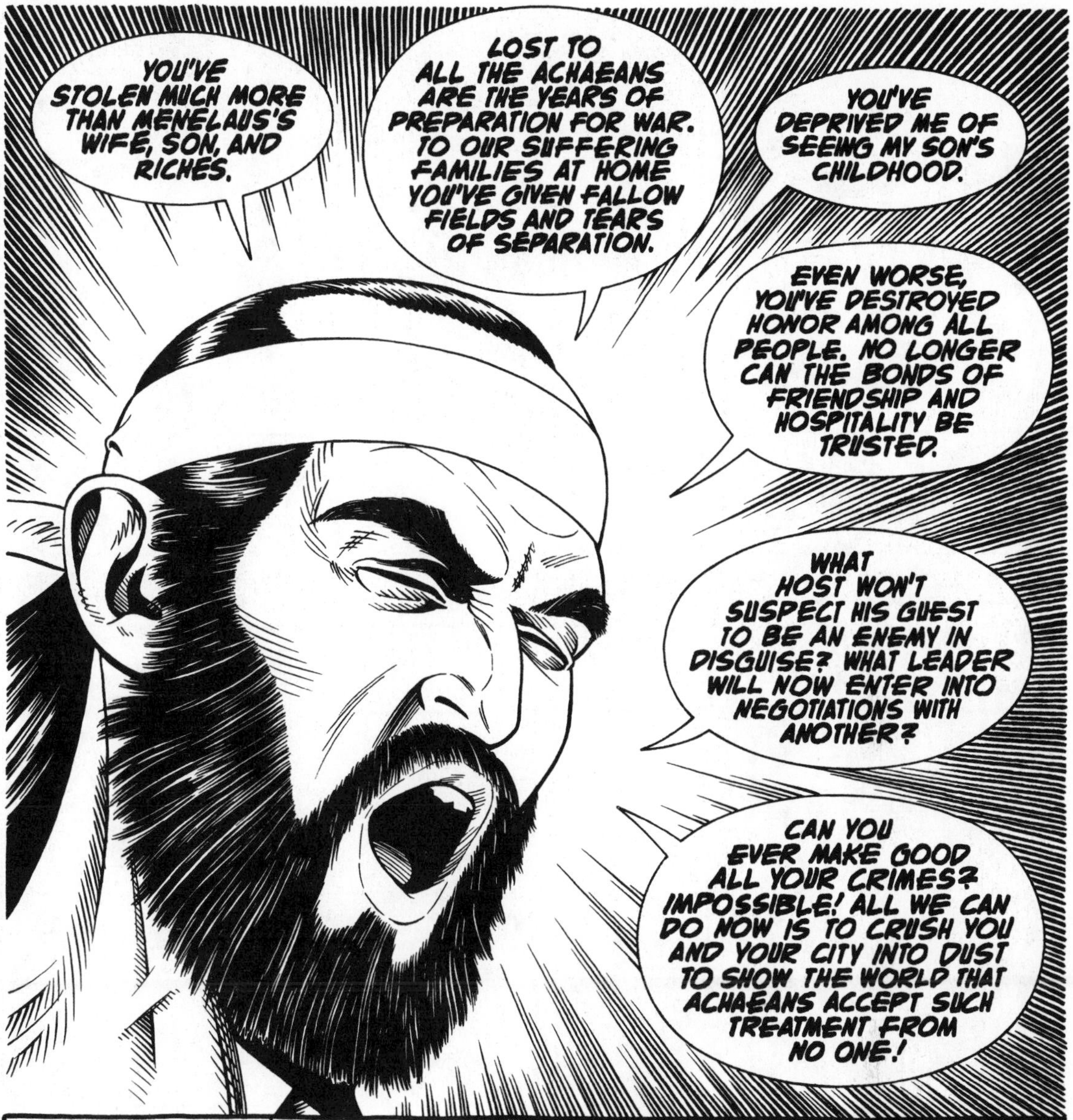
YOU'VE STOLEN MUCH MORE THAN MENELAUS'S WIFE, SON, AND RICHES.
LOST TO ALL THE ACHAEANS ARE THE YEARS OF PREPARATION FOR WAR. TO OUR SUFFERING FAMILIES AT HOME YOU'VE GIVEN FALLOW FIELDS AND TEARS OF SEPARATION.
YOU'VE DEPRIVED ME OF SEEING MY SON'S CHILDHOOD.
EVEN WORSE, YOU'VE DESTROYED HONOR AMONG ALL PEOPLE. NO LONGER CAN THE BONDS OF FRIENDSHIP AND HOSPITALITY BE TRUSTED.
WHAT HOST WON'T SUSPECT HIS GUEST TO BE AN ENEMY IN DISGUISE? WHAT LEADER WILL NOW ENTER INTO NEGOTIATIONS WITH ANOTHER?
CAN YOU EVER MAKE GOOD ALL YOUR CRIMES? IMPOSSIBLE! ALL WE CAN DO NOW IS TO CRUSH YOU AND YOUR CITY INTO DUST TO SHOW THE WORLD THAT ACHAEANS ACCEPT SUCH TREATMENT FROM NO ONE!
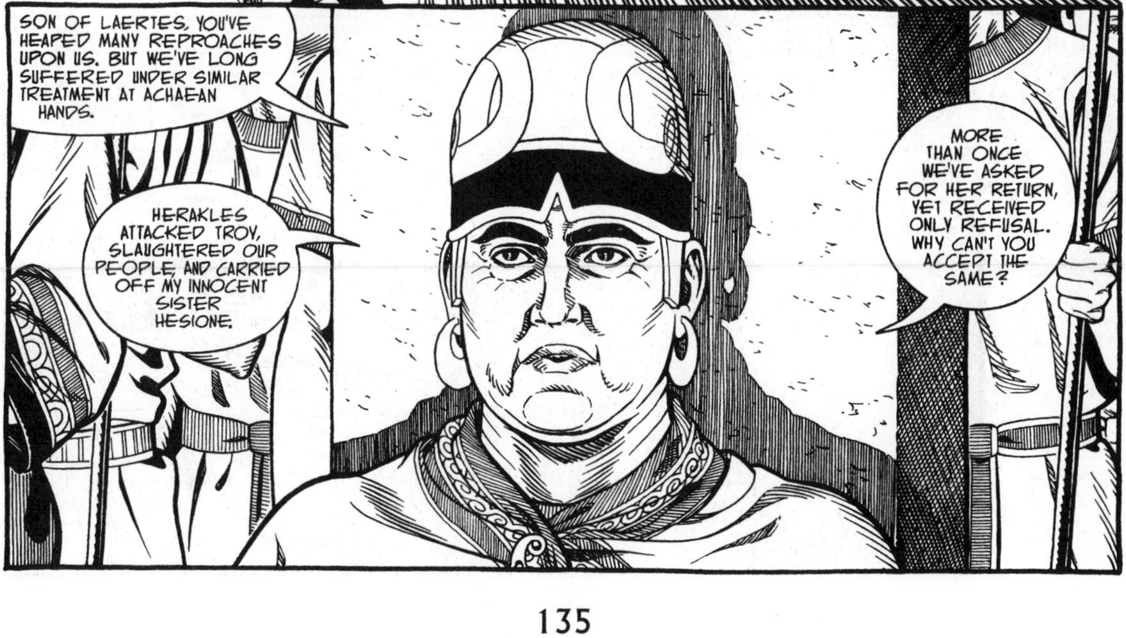
SON OF LAERTES, YOU'VE HEAPED MANY REPROACHES UPON US. BUT WE'VE LONG SUFFERED UNDER SIMILAR TREATMENT AT ACHAEAN HANDS.
HERAKLES ATTACKED TROY, SLAUGHTERED OUR PEOPLE, AND CARRIED OFF MY INNOCENT SISTER HESIONE.
MORE THAN ONCE WE'VE ASKED FOR HER RETURN, YET RECEIVED ONLY REFUSAL. WHY CAN'T YOU ACCEPT THE SAME?

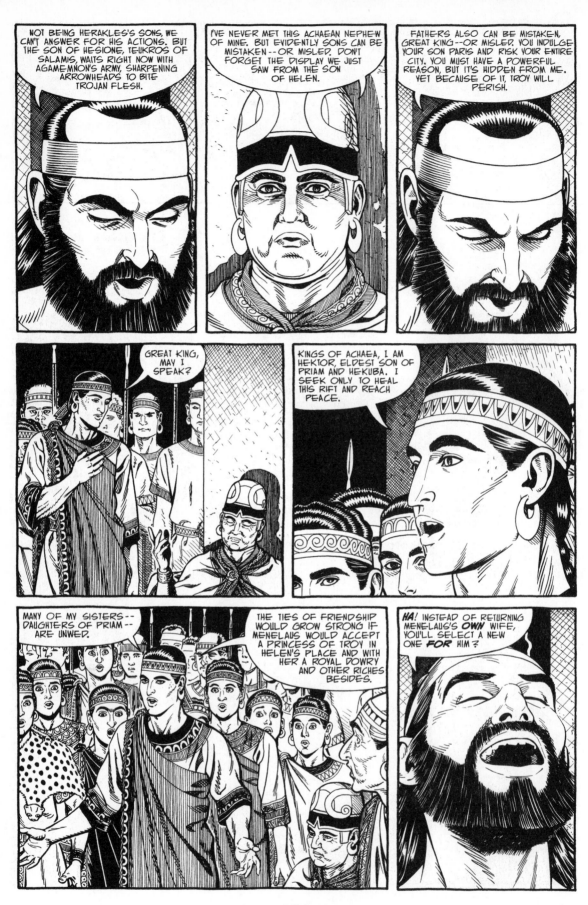

NOT BEING HERAKLES'S SONS, WE CAN'T ANSWER FOR HIS ACTIONS. BUT THE SON OF HESIONE, TEUKROS OF SALAMIS, WAITS RIGHT NOW WITH AGAMEMNON'S ARMY, SHARPENING ARROWHEADS TO BITE TROJAN FLESH.

I'VE NEVER MET THIS ACHAEAN NEPHEW OF MINE. BUT EVIDENTLY SONS CAN BE MISTAKEN--OR MISLED. DON'T FORGET THE DISPLAY WE JUST SAW FROM THE SON OF HELEN.

FATHERS ALSO CAN BE MISTAKEN, GREAT KING--OR MISLED. YOU INDULGE YOUR SON PARIS AND RISK YOUR ENTIRE CITY. YOU MUST HAVE A POWERFUL REASON, BUT IT'S HIDDEN FROM ME. YET BECAUSE OF IT, TROY WILL PERISH.

GREAT KING, MAY I SPEAK?

KINGS OF ACHAEA, I AM HEKTOR, ELDEST SON OF PRIAM AND HEKUBA. I SEEK ONLY TO HEAL THIS RIFT AND REACH PEACE.

MANY OF MY SISTERS-- DAUGHTERS OF PRIAM-- ARE UNWED.

THE TIES OF FRIENDSHIP WOULD GROW STRONG IF MENELAUS WOULD ACCEPT A PRINCESS OF TROY IN HELEN'S PLACE AND WITH HER A ROYAL DOWRY AND OTHER RICHES BESIDES.

HA! INSTEAD OF RETURNING MENELAUS'S OWN WIFE, YOU'LL SELECT A NEW ONE FOR HIM?

136

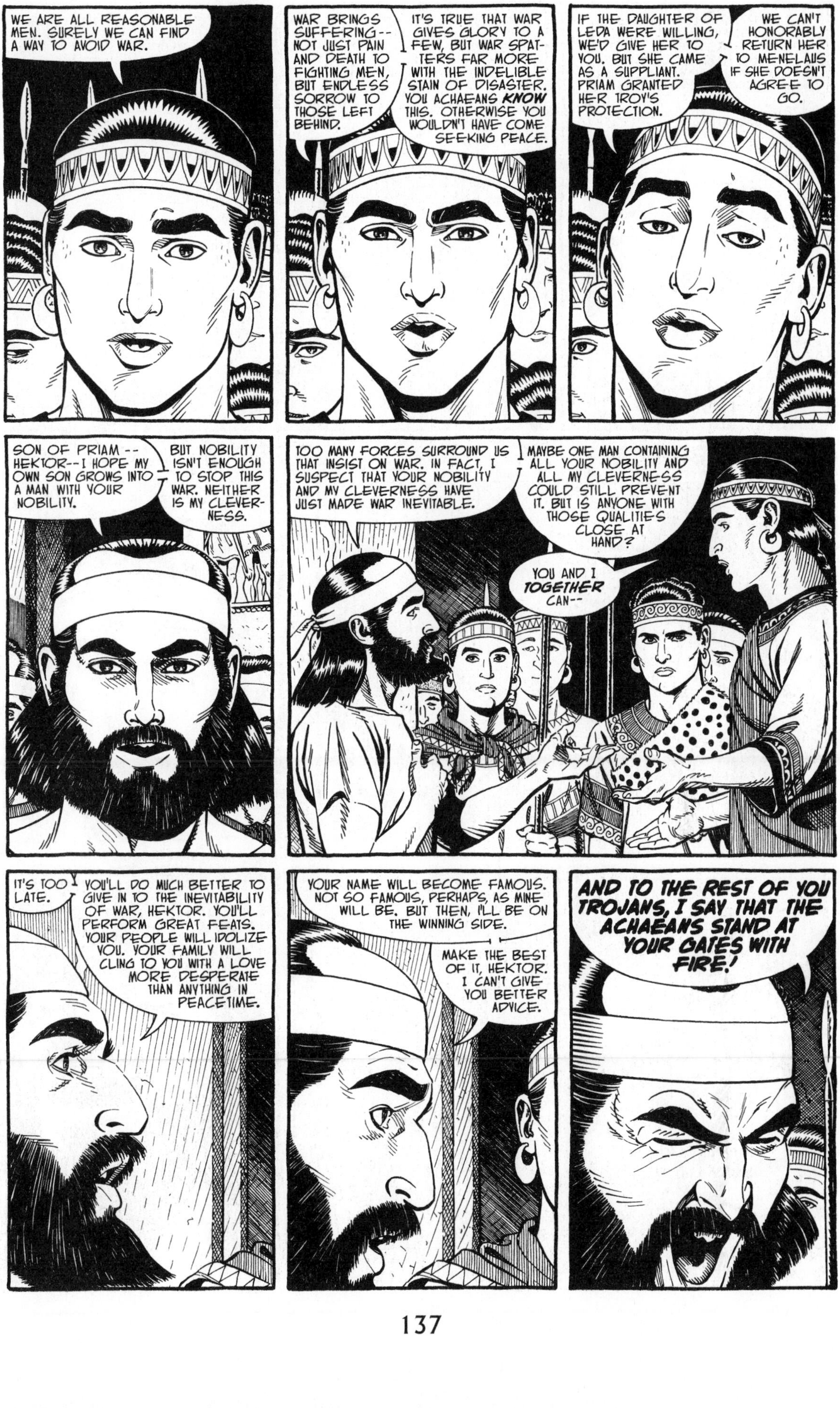

WE ARE ALL REASONABLE MEN. SURELY WE CAN FIND A WAY TO AVOID WAR.
WAR BRINGS SUFFERING-- NOT JUST PAIN AND DEATH TO FIGHTING MEN, BUT ENDLESS SORROW TO THOSE LEFT BEHIND.
IT'S TRUE THAT WAR GIVES GLORY TO A FEW, BUT WAR SPATTERS FAR MORE WITH THE INDELIBLE STAIN OF DISASTER. YOU ACHAEANS **KNOW** THIS. OTHERWISE YOU WOULDN'T HAVE COME SEEKING PEACE.
IF THE DAUGHTER OF LEDA WERE WILLING, WE'D GIVE HER TO YOU. BUT SHE CAME AS A SUPPLIANT. PRIAM GRANTED HER TROY'S PROTECTION.
WE CAN'T HONORABLY RETURN HER TO MENELAUS IF SHE DOESN'T AGREE TO GO.
SON OF PRIAM -- HEKTOR--I HOPE MY OWN SON GROWS INTO A MAN WITH YOUR NOBILITY.
BUT NOBILITY ISN'T ENOUGH TO STOP THIS WAR. NEITHER IS MY CLEVERNESS.
TOO MANY FORCES SURROUND US THAT INSIST ON WAR. IN FACT, I SUSPECT THAT YOUR NOBILITY AND MY CLEVERNESS HAVE JUST MADE WAR INEVITABLE.
MAYBE ONE MAN CONTAINING ALL YOUR NOBILITY AND ALL MY CLEVERNESS COULD STILL PREVENT IT. BUT IS ANYONE WITH THOSE QUALITIES CLOSE AT HAND?
YOU AND I ***TOGETHER*** CAN--
IT'S TOO LATE.
YOU'LL DO MUCH BETTER TO GIVE IN TO THE INEVITABILITY OF WAR, HEKTOR. YOU'LL PERFORM GREAT FEATS. YOUR PEOPLE WILL IDOLIZE YOU. YOUR FAMILY WILL CLING TO YOU WITH A LOVE MORE DESPERATE THAN ANYTHING IN PEACETIME.
YOUR NAME WILL BECOME FAMOUS. NOT SO FAMOUS, PERHAPS, AS MINE WILL BE. BUT THEN, I'LL BE ON THE WINNING SIDE.
MAKE THE BEST OF IT, HEKTOR. I CAN'T GIVE YOU BETTER ADVICE.
AND TO THE REST OF YOU TROJANS, I SAY THAT THE ACHAEANS STAND AT YOUR GATES WITH FIRE!

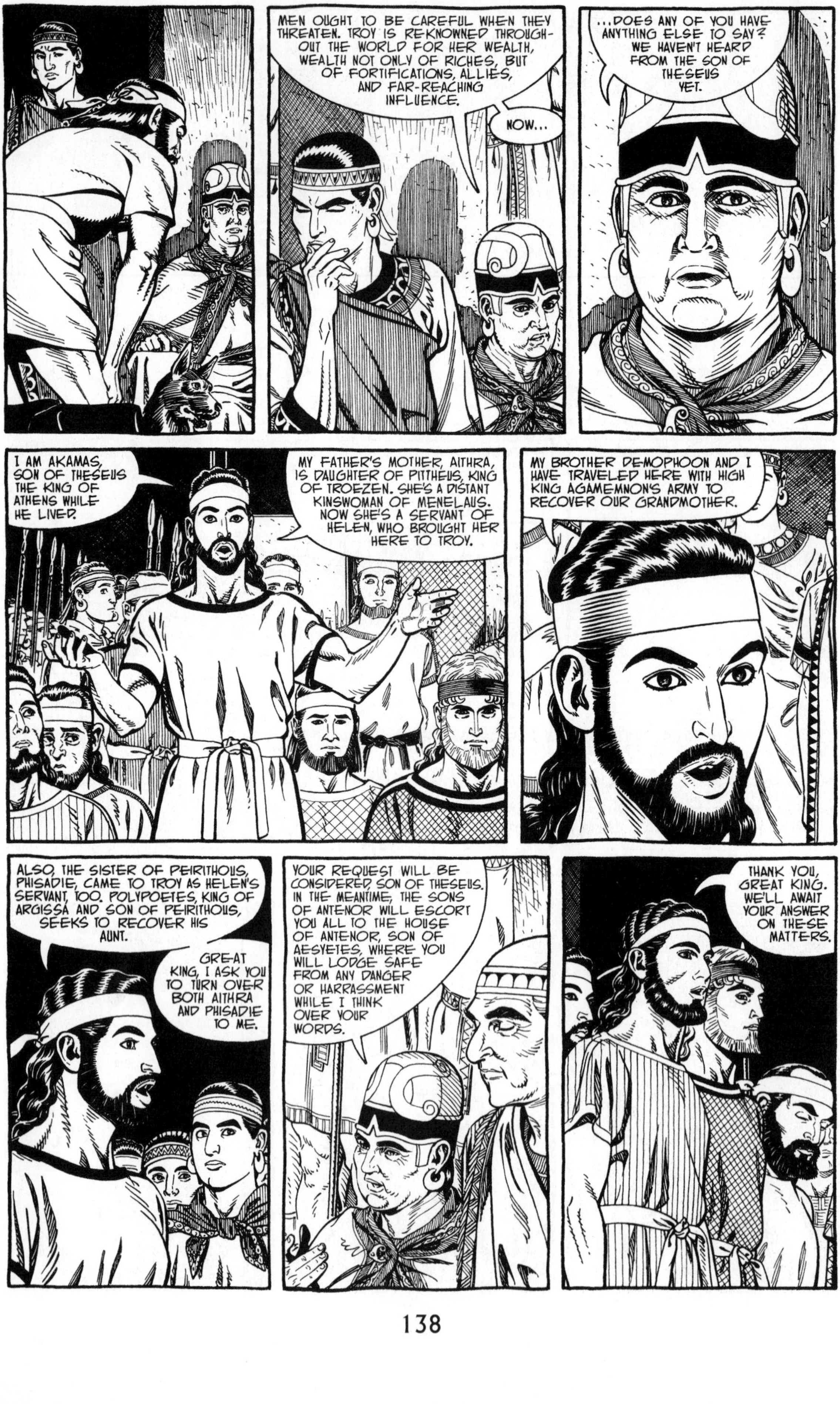
MEN OUGHT TO BE CAREFUL WHEN THEY THREATEN. TROY IS REKNOWNED THROUGHOUT THE WORLD FOR HER WEALTH, WEALTH NOT ONLY OF RICHES, BUT OF FORTIFICATIONS, ALLIES, AND FAR-REACHING INFLUENCE.
NOW...
...DOES ANY OF YOU HAVE ANYTHING ELSE TO SAY? WE HAVEN'T HEARD FROM THE SON OF THESEUS YET.
I AM AKAMAS, SON OF THESEUS THE KING OF ATHENS WHILE HE LIVED.
MY FATHER'S MOTHER, AITHRA, IS DAUGHTER OF PITTHEUS, KING OF TROEZEN. SHE'S A DISTANT KINSWOMAN OF MENELAUS. NOW SHE'S A SERVANT OF HELEN, WHO BROUGHT HER HERE TO TROY.
MY BROTHER DEMOPHOON AND I HAVE TRAVELED HERE WITH HIGH KING AGAMEMNON'S ARMY TO RECOVER OUR GRANDMOTHER.
ALSO, THE SISTER OF PEIRITHOUS, PHISADIE, CAME TO TROY AS HELEN'S SERVANT, TOO. POLYPOETES, KING OF ARGISSA AND SON OF PEIRITHOUS, SEEKS TO RECOVER HIS AUNT.
GREAT KING, I ASK YOU TO TURN OVER BOTH AITHRA AND PHISADIE TO ME.
YOUR REQUEST WILL BE CONSIDERED, SON OF THESEUS. IN THE MEANTIME, THE SONS OF ANTENOR WILL ESCORT YOU ALL TO THE HOUSE OF ANTENOR, SON OF AESYETES, WHERE YOU WILL LODGE SAFE FROM ANY DANGER OR HARRASSMENT WHILE I THINK OVER YOUR WORDS.
THANK YOU, GREAT KING. WE'LL AWAIT YOUR ANSWER ON THESE MATTERS.

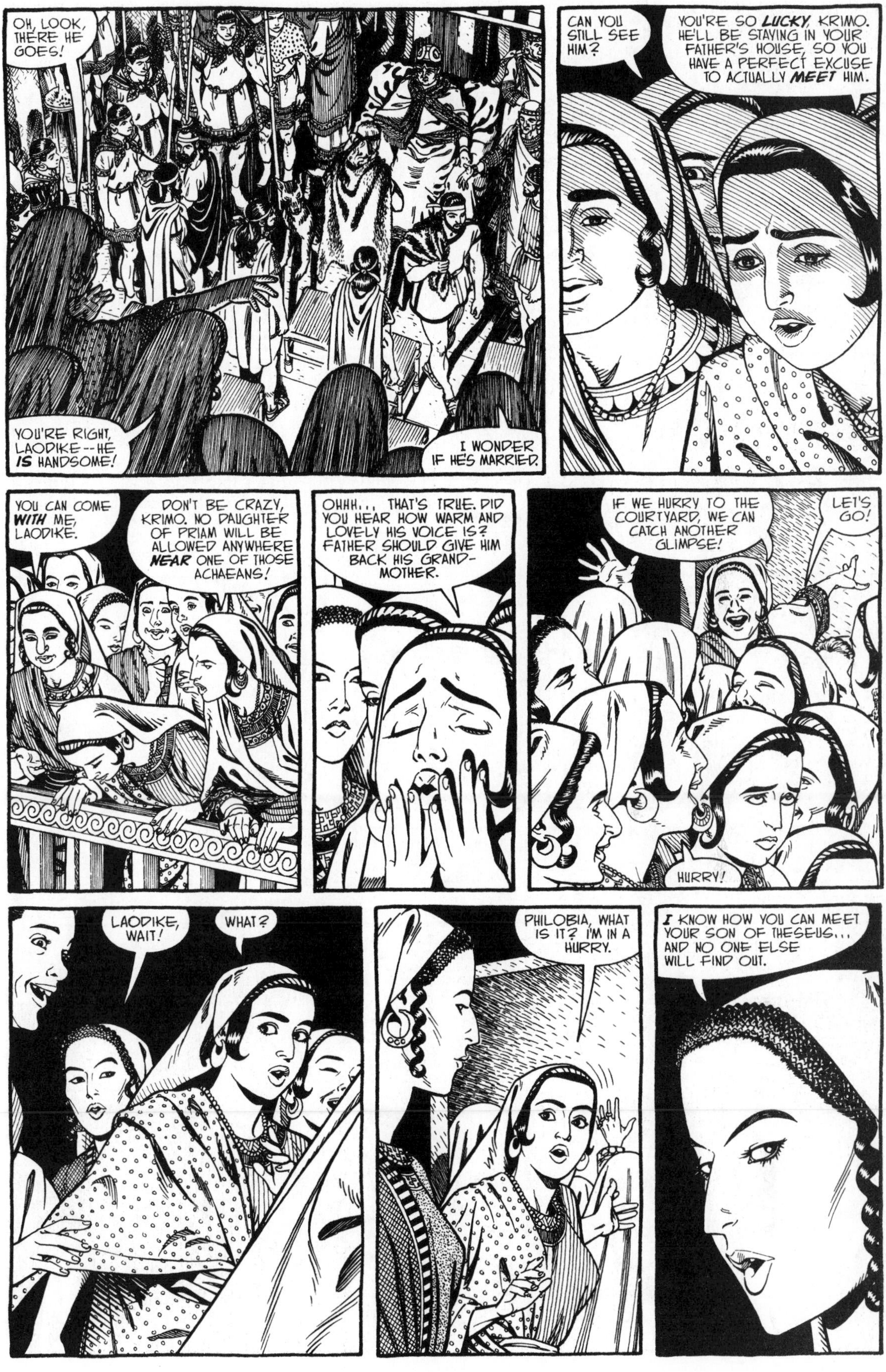
OH, LOOK, THERE HE GOES!
YOU'RE RIGHT, LAODIKE--HE IS HANDSOME!
I WONDER IF HE'S MARRIED.
CAN YOU STILL SEE HIM?
YOU'RE SO LUCKY, KRIMO. HE'LL BE STAYING IN YOUR FATHER'S HOUSE, SO YOU HAVE A PERFECT EXCUSE TO ACTUALLY MEET HIM.
YOU CAN COME WITH ME, LAODIKE.
DON'T BE CRAZY, KRIMO. NO DAUGHTER OF PRIAM WILL BE ALLOWED ANYWHERE NEAR ONE OF THOSE ACHAEANS!
OHHH... THAT'S TRUE. DID YOU HEAR HOW WARM AND LOVELY HIS VOICE IS? FATHER SHOULD GIVE HIM BACK HIS GRAND-MOTHER.
IF WE HURRY TO THE COURTYARD, WE CAN CATCH ANOTHER GLIMPSE!
LET'S GO!
HURRY!
LAODIKE, WAIT!
WHAT?
PHILOBIA, WHAT IS IT? I'M IN A HURRY.
I KNOW HOW YOU CAN MEET YOUR SON OF THESEUS... AND NO ONE ELSE WILL FIND OUT.

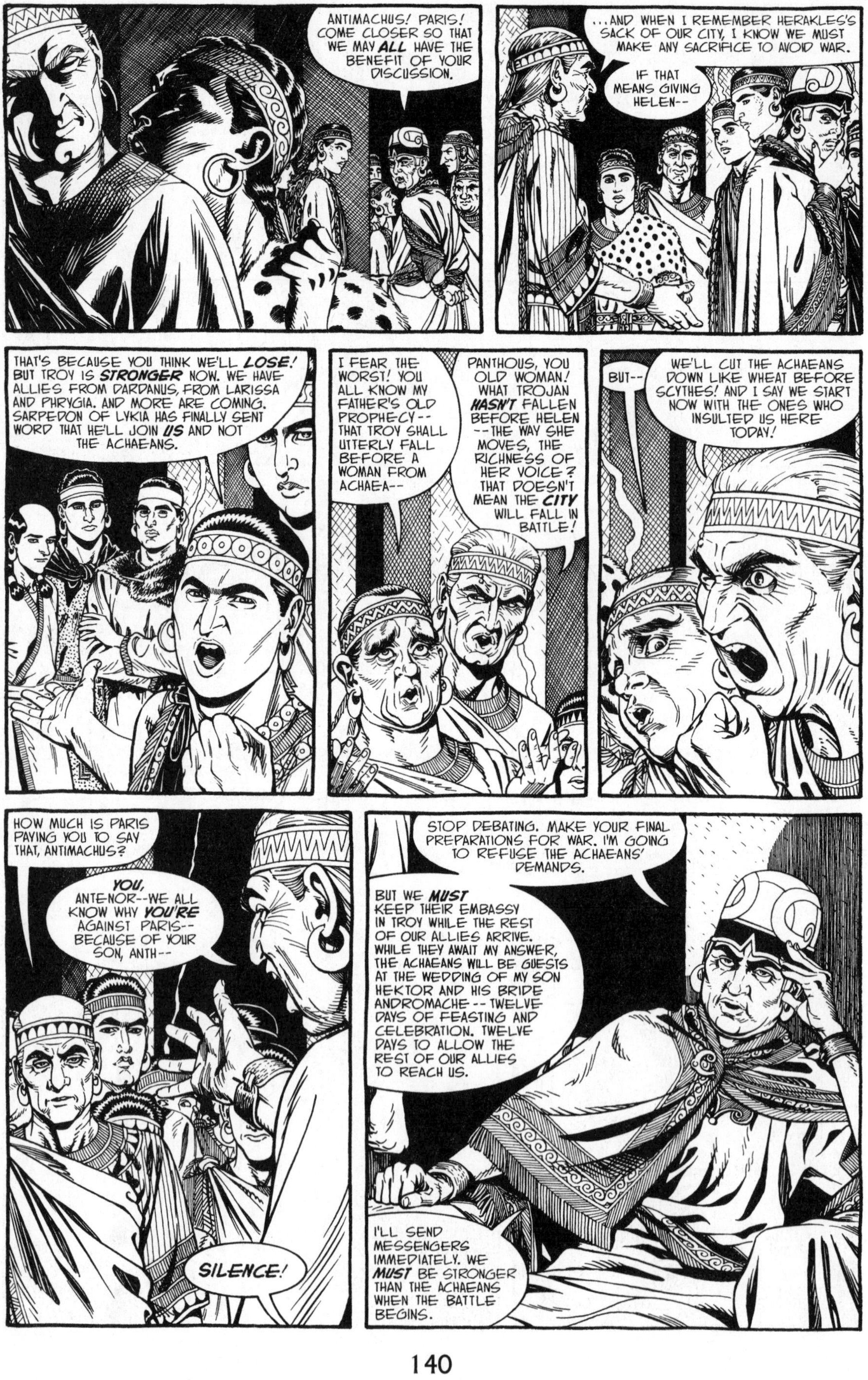
ANTIMACHUS! PARIS! COME CLOSER SO THAT WE MAY ALL HAVE THE BENEFIT OF YOUR DISCUSSION.
...AND WHEN I REMEMBER HERAKLES'S SACK OF OUR CITY, I KNOW WE MUST MAKE ANY SACRIFICE TO AVOID WAR.
IF THAT MEANS GIVING HELEN--
THAT'S BECAUSE YOU THINK WE'LL LOSE! BUT TROY IS STRONGER NOW. WE HAVE ALLIES FROM DARDANUS, FROM LARISSA AND PHRYGIA. AND MORE ARE COMING. SARPEDON OF LYKIA HAS FINALLY SENT WORD THAT HE'LL JOIN US AND NOT THE ACHAEANS.
I FEAR THE WORST! YOU ALL KNOW MY FATHER'S OLD PROPHECY--THAT TROY SHALL UTTERLY FALL BEFORE A WOMAN FROM ACHAEA--
PANTHOUS, YOU OLD WOMAN! WHAT TROJAN HASN'T FALLEN BEFORE HELEN--THE WAY SHE MOVES, THE RICHNESS OF HER VOICE? THAT DOESN'T MEAN THE CITY WILL FALL IN BATTLE!
BUT--
WE'LL CUT THE ACHAEANS DOWN LIKE WHEAT BEFORE SCYTHES! AND I SAY WE START NOW WITH THE ONES WHO INSULTED US HERE TODAY!
HOW MUCH IS PARIS PAYING YOU TO SAY THAT, ANTIMACHUS?
YOU, ANTENOR--WE ALL KNOW WHY YOU'RE AGAINST PARIS--BECAUSE OF YOUR SON, ANTH--
SILENCE!
STOP DEBATING. MAKE YOUR FINAL PREPARATIONS FOR WAR. I'M GOING TO REFUSE THE ACHAEANS' DEMANDS.
BUT WE MUST KEEP THEIR EMBASSY IN TROY WHILE THE REST OF OUR ALLIES ARRIVE. WHILE THEY AWAIT MY ANSWER, THE ACHAEANS WILL BE GUESTS AT THE WEDDING OF MY SON HEKTOR AND HIS BRIDE ANDROMACHE--TWELVE DAYS OF FEASTING AND CELEBRATION. TWELVE DAYS TO ALLOW THE REST OF OUR ALLIES TO REACH US.
I'LL SEND MESSENGERS IMMEDIATELY. WE MUST BE STRONGER THAN THE ACHAEANS WHEN THE BATTLE BEGINS.

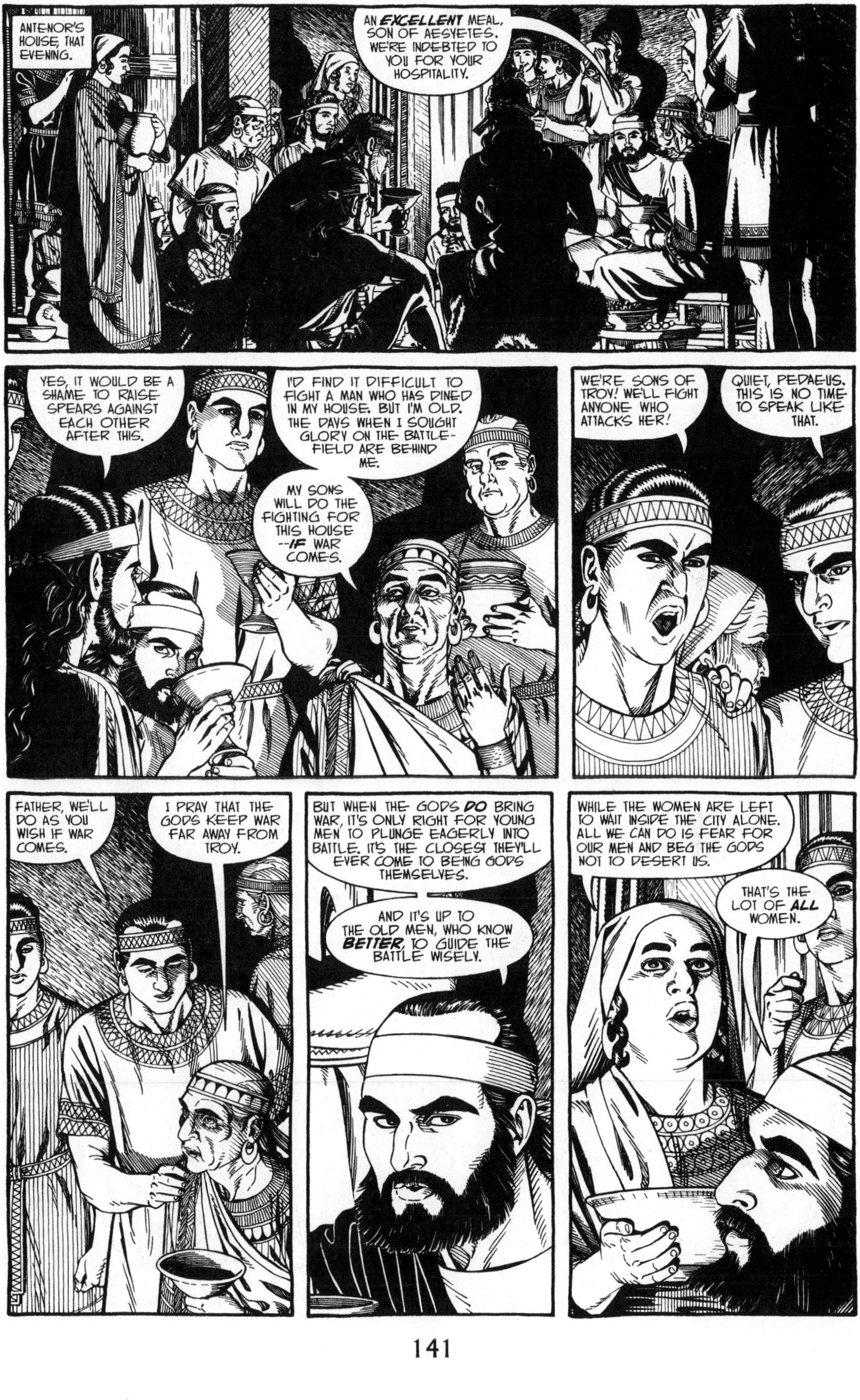
ANTENOR'S HOUSE, THAT EVENING.
AN EXCELLENT MEAL, SON OF AESYETES. WE'RE INDEBTED TO YOU FOR YOUR HOSPITALITY.
YES, IT WOULD BE A SHAME TO RAISE SPEARS AGAINST EACH OTHER AFTER THIS.
I'D FIND IT DIFFICULT TO FIGHT A MAN WHO HAS DINED IN MY HOUSE. BUT I'M OLD. THE DAYS WHEN I SOUGHT GLORY ON THE BATTLE-FIELD ARE BEHIND ME.
MY SONS WILL DO THE FIGHTING FOR THIS HOUSE --IF WAR COMES.
WE'RE SONS OF TROY! WE'LL FIGHT ANYONE WHO ATTACKS HER!
QUIET, PEDAEUS. THIS IS NO TIME TO SPEAK LIKE THAT.
FATHER, WE'LL DO AS YOU WISH IF WAR COMES.
I PRAY THAT THE GODS KEEP WAR FAR AWAY FROM TROY.
BUT WHEN THE GODS DO BRING WAR, IT'S ONLY RIGHT FOR YOUNG MEN TO PLUNGE EAGERLY INTO BATTLE. IT'S THE CLOSEST THEY'LL EVER COME TO BEING GODS THEMSELVES.
AND IT'S UP TO THE OLD MEN, WHO KNOW BETTER, TO GUIDE THE BATTLE WISELY.
WHILE THE WOMEN ARE LEFT TO WAIT INSIDE THE CITY ALONE. ALL WE CAN DO IS FEAR FOR OUR MEN AND BEG THE GODS NOT TO DESERT US.
THAT'S THE LOT OF ALL WOMEN.

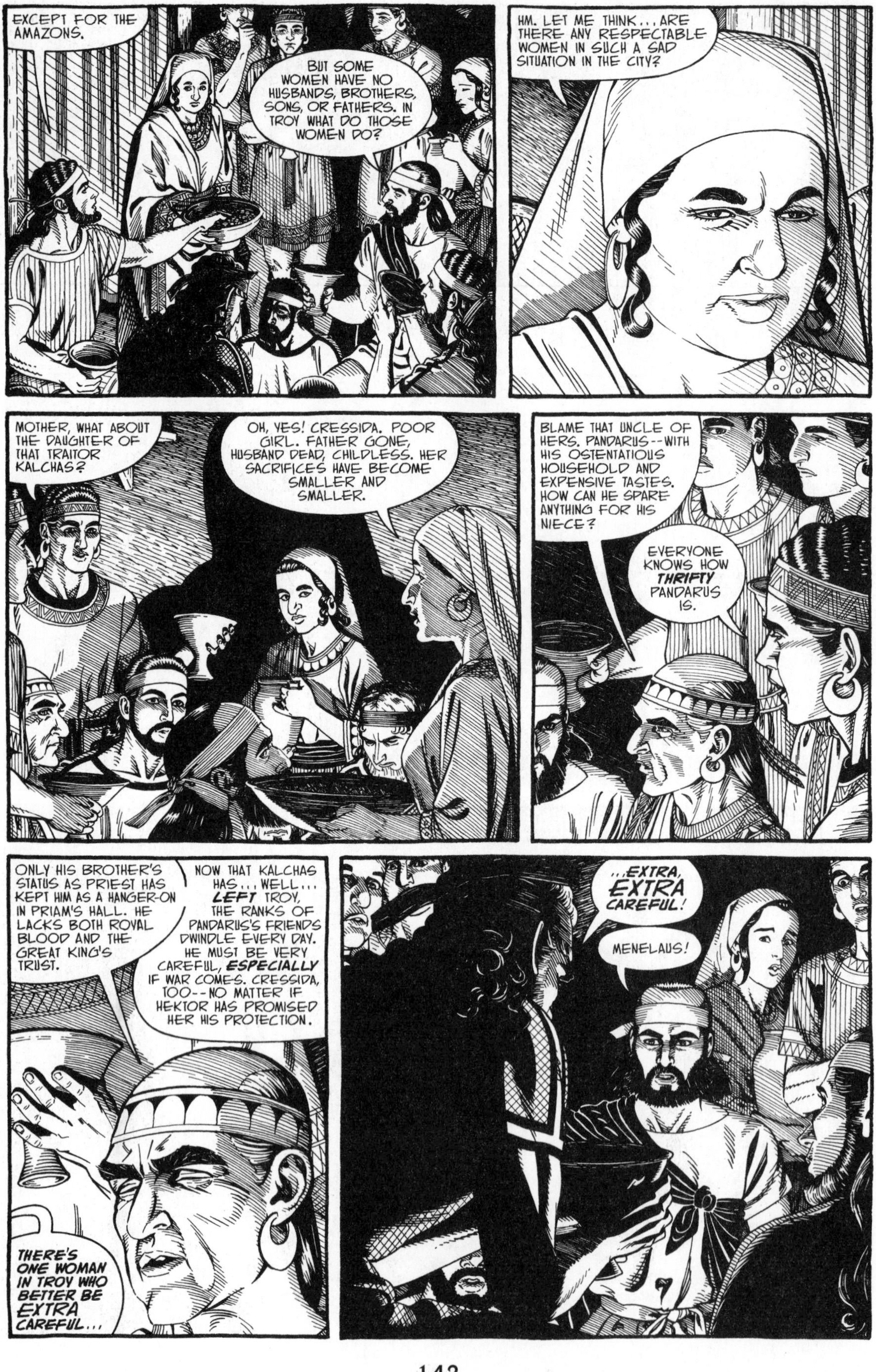
EXCEPT FOR THE AMAZONS.
BUT SOME WOMEN HAVE NO HUSBANDS, BROTHERS, SONS, OR FATHERS. IN TROY WHAT DO THOSE WOMEN DO?
HM. LET ME THINK... ARE THERE ANY RESPECTABLE WOMEN IN SUCH A SAD SITUATION IN THE CITY?
MOTHER, WHAT ABOUT THE DAUGHTER OF THAT TRAITOR KALCHAS?
OH, YES! CRESSIDA. POOR GIRL. FATHER GONE, HUSBAND DEAD, CHILDLESS. HER SACRIFICES HAVE BECOME SMALLER AND SMALLER.
BLAME THAT UNCLE OF HERS. PANDARUS--WITH HIS OSTENTATIOUS HOUSEHOLD AND EXPENSIVE TASTES. HOW CAN HE SPARE ANYTHING FOR HIS NIECE?
EVERYONE KNOWS HOW THRIFTY PANDARUS IS.
ONLY HIS BROTHER'S STATUS AS PRIEST HAS KEPT HIM AS A HANGER-ON IN PRIAM'S HALL. HE LACKS BOTH ROYAL BLOOD AND THE GREAT KING'S TRUST.
NOW THAT KALCHAS HAS... WELL... LEFT TROY, THE RANKS OF PANDARUS'S FRIENDS DWINDLE EVERY DAY. HE MUST BE VERY CAREFUL, ESPECIALLY IF WAR COMES. CRESSIDA, TOO--NO MATTER IF HEKTOR HAS PROMISED HER HIS PROTECTION.
THERE'S ONE WOMAN IN TROY WHO BETTER BE EXTRA CAREFUL...
...EXTRA, EXTRA CAREFUL!
MENELAUS!

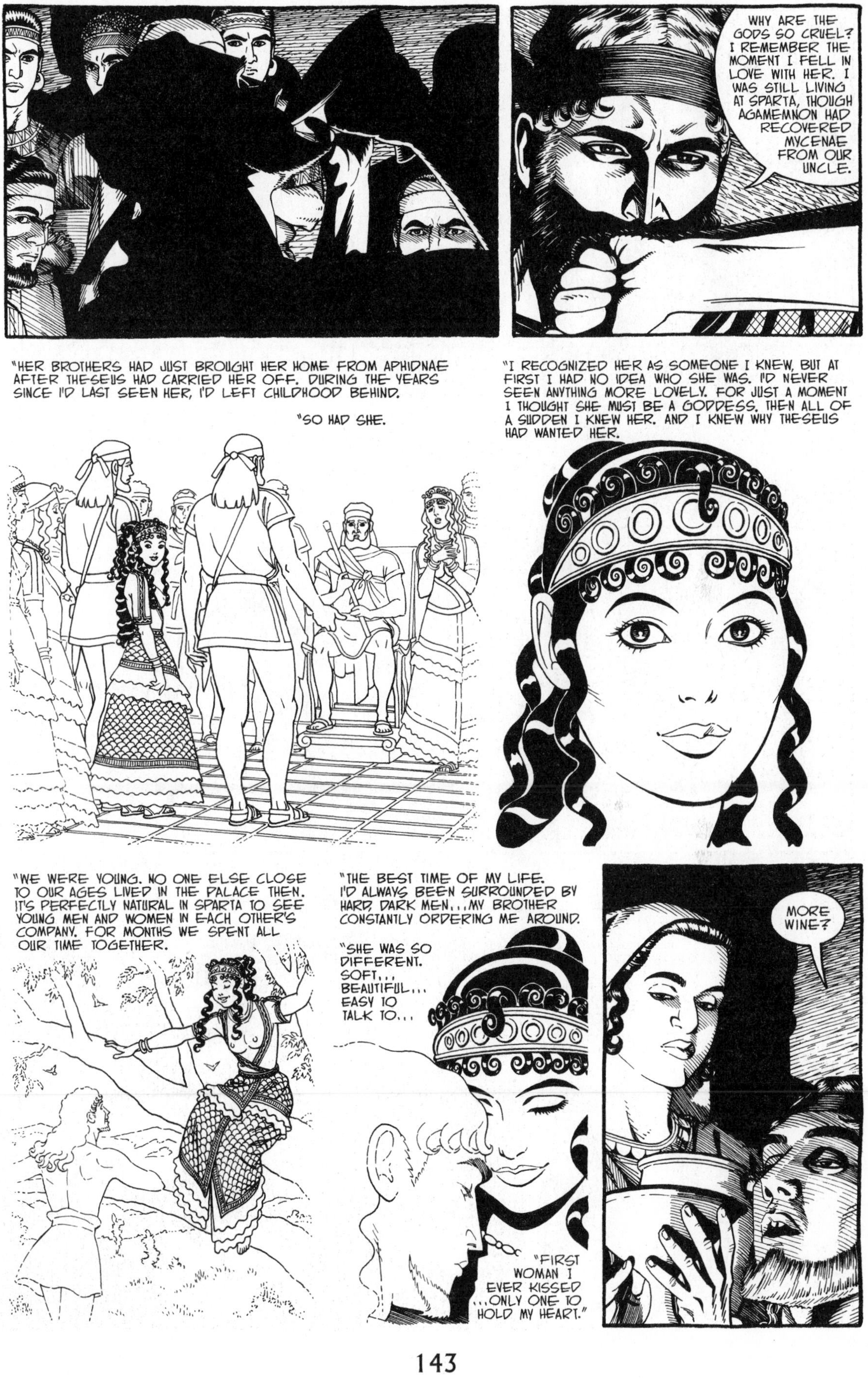
WHY ARE THE GODS SO CRUEL? I REMEMBER THE MOMENT I FELL IN LOVE WITH HER. I WAS STILL LIVING AT SPARTA, THOUGH AGAMEMNON HAD RECOVERED MYCENAE FROM OUR UNCLE.
"HER BROTHERS HAD JUST BROUGHT HER HOME FROM APHIDNAE AFTER THESEUS HAD CARRIED HER OFF. DURING THE YEARS SINCE I'D LAST SEEN HER, I'D LEFT CHILDHOOD BEHIND.
"SO HAD SHE.
"I RECOGNIZED HER AS SOMEONE I KNEW, BUT AT FIRST I HAD NO IDEA WHO SHE WAS. I'D NEVER SEEN ANYTHING MORE LOVELY. FOR JUST A MOMENT I THOUGHT SHE MUST BE A GODDESS. THEN ALL OF A SUDDEN I KNEW HER. AND I KNEW WHY THESEUS HAD WANTED HER.
"WE WERE YOUNG. NO ONE ELSE CLOSE TO OUR AGES LIVED IN THE PALACE THEN. IT'S PERFECTLY NATURAL IN SPARTA TO SEE YOUNG MEN AND WOMEN IN EACH OTHER'S COMPANY. FOR MONTHS WE SPENT ALL OUR TIME TOGETHER.
"THE BEST TIME OF MY LIFE. I'D ALWAYS BEEN SURROUNDED BY HARD, DARK MEN... MY BROTHER CONSTANTLY ORDERING ME AROUND.
"SHE WAS SO DIFFERENT. SOFT... BEAUTIFUL... EASY TO TALK TO...
"FIRST WOMAN I EVER KISSED ...ONLY ONE TO HOLD MY HEART."
MORE WINE?

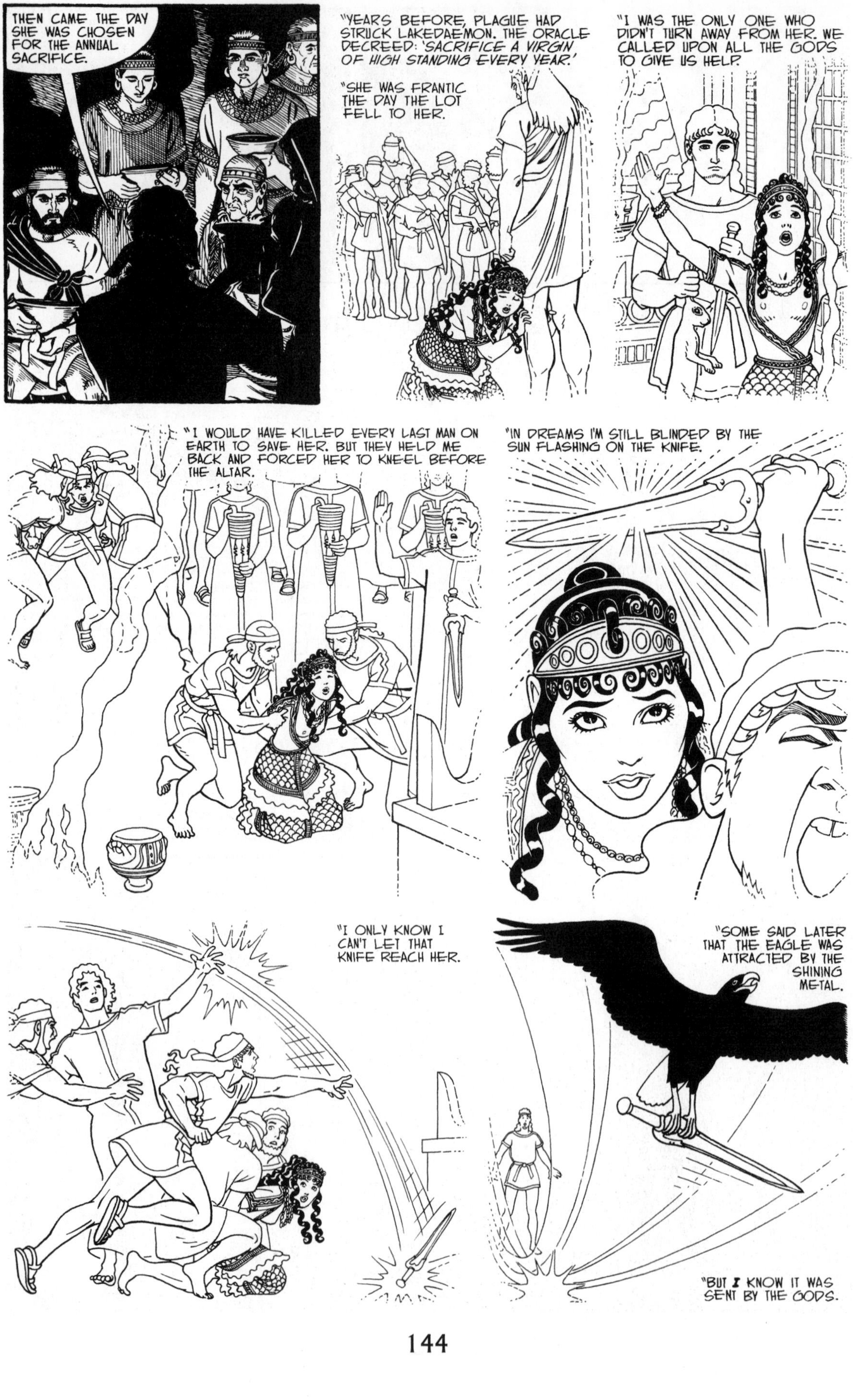
THEN CAME THE DAY SHE WAS CHOSEN FOR THE ANNUAL SACRIFICE.
"YEARS BEFORE, PLAGUE HAD STRUCK LAKEDAEMON. THE ORACLE DECREED: 'SACRIFICE A VIRGIN OF HIGH STANDING EVERY YEAR.'
"SHE WAS FRANTIC THE DAY THE LOT FELL TO HER.
"I WAS THE ONLY ONE WHO DIDN'T TURN AWAY FROM HER. WE CALLED UPON ALL THE GODS TO GIVE US HELP.
"I WOULD HAVE KILLED EVERY LAST MAN ON EARTH TO SAVE HER. BUT THEY HELD ME BACK AND FORCED HER TO KNEEL BEFORE THE ALTAR.
"IN DREAMS I'M STILL BLINDED BY THE SUN FLASHING ON THE KNIFE.
"I ONLY KNOW I CAN'T LET THAT KNIFE REACH HER.
"SOME SAID LATER THAT THE EAGLE WAS ATTRACTED BY THE SHINING METAL.
"BUT I KNOW IT WAS SENT BY THE GODS.

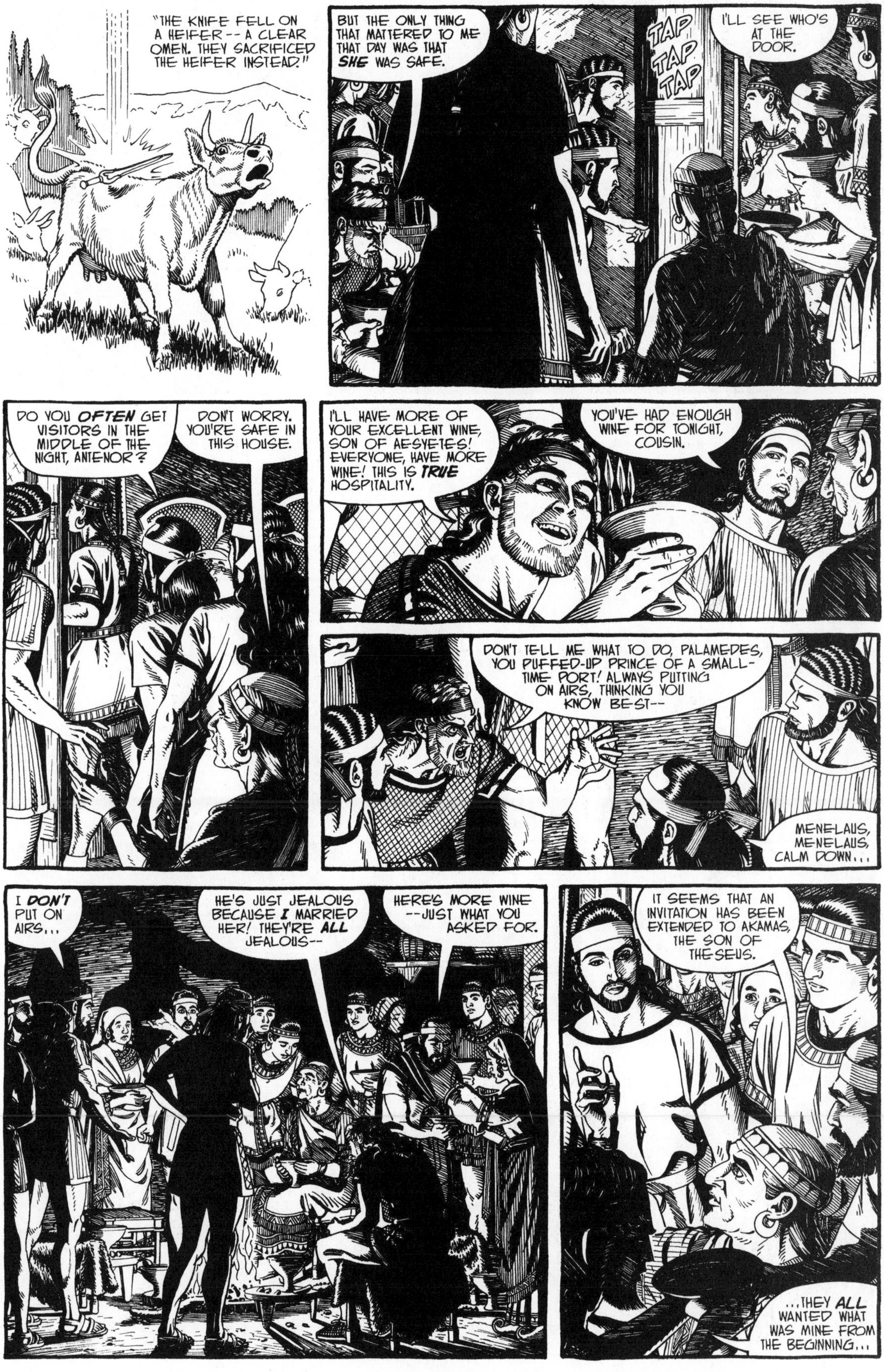
"THE KNIFE FELL ON A HEIFER -- A CLEAR OMEN. THEY SACRIFICED THE HEIFER INSTEAD."
BUT THE ONLY THING THAT MATTERED TO ME THAT DAY WAS THAT SHE WAS SAFE.
TAP TAP TAP
I'LL SEE WHO'S AT THE DOOR.
DO YOU OFTEN GET VISITORS IN THE MIDDLE OF THE NIGHT, ANTENOR?
DON'T WORRY. YOU'RE SAFE IN THIS HOUSE.
I'LL HAVE MORE OF YOUR EXCELLENT WINE, SON OF AESYETES! EVERYONE, HAVE MORE WINE! THIS IS TRUE HOSPITALITY.
YOU'VE HAD ENOUGH WINE FOR TONIGHT, COUSIN.
DON'T TELL ME WHAT TO DO, PALAMEDES, YOU PUFFED-UP PRINCE OF A SMALL-TIME PORT! ALWAYS PUTTING ON AIRS, THINKING YOU KNOW BEST--
MENELAUS, MENELAUS, CALM DOWN...
I DON'T PUT ON AIRS...
HE'S JUST JEALOUS BECAUSE I MARRIED HER! THEY'RE ALL JEALOUS--
HERE'S MORE WINE --JUST WHAT YOU ASKED FOR.
IT SEEMS THAT AN INVITATION HAS BEEN EXTENDED TO AKAMAS, THE SON OF THESEUS.
...THEY ALL WANTED WHAT WAS MINE FROM THE BEGINNING...

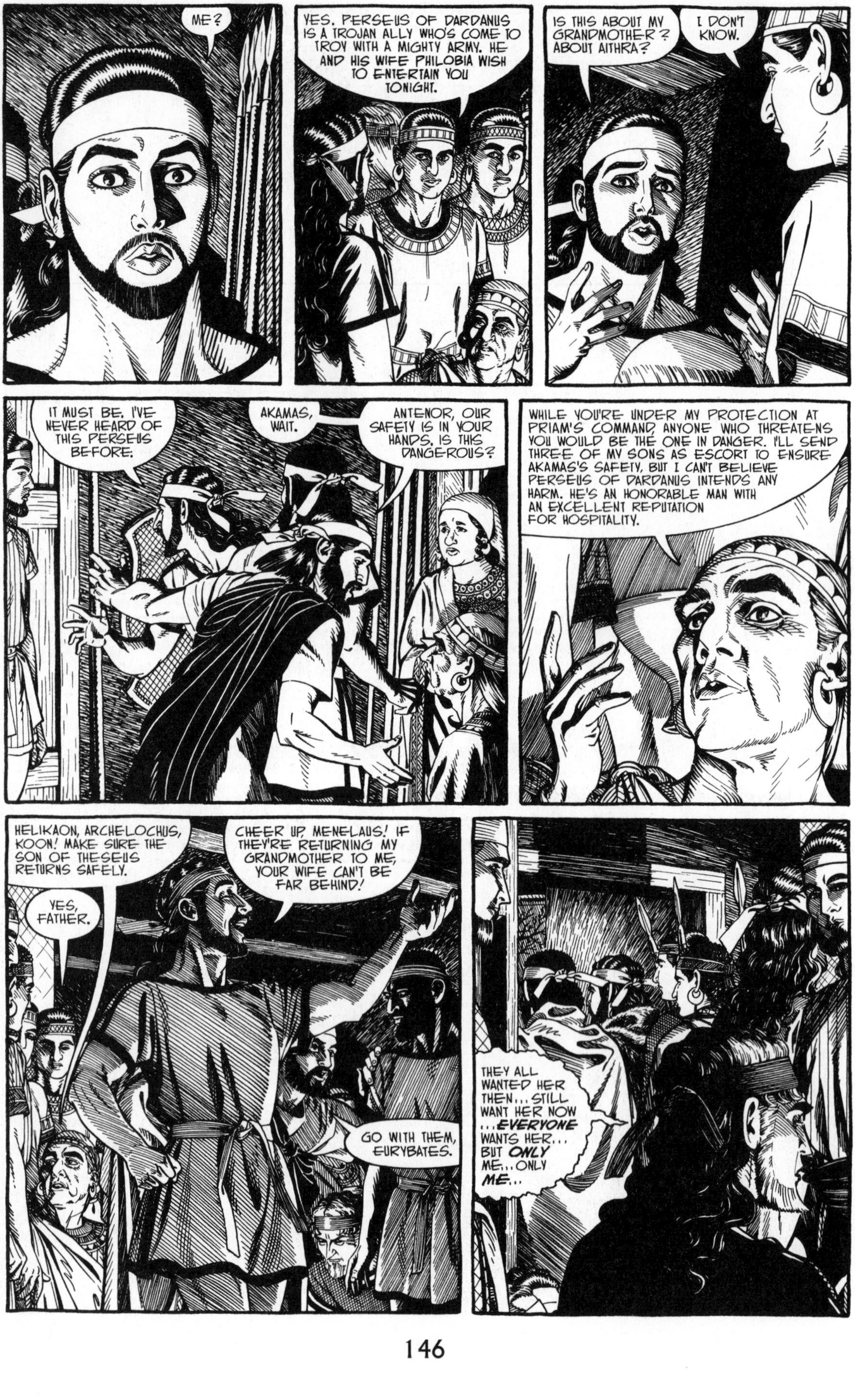
ME?
YES. PERSEUS OF DARDANUS IS A TROJAN ALLY WHO'S COME TO TROY WITH A MIGHTY ARMY. HE AND HIS WIFE PHILOBIA WISH TO ENTERTAIN YOU TONIGHT.
IS THIS ABOUT MY GRANDMOTHER? ABOUT AITHRA?
I DON'T KNOW.
IT MUST BE. I'VE NEVER HEARD OF THIS PERSEUS BEFORE.
AKAMAS, WAIT.
ANTENOR, OUR SAFETY IS IN YOUR HANDS. IS THIS DANGEROUS?
WHILE YOU'RE UNDER MY PROTECTION AT PRIAM'S COMMAND, ANYONE WHO THREATENS YOU WOULD BE THE ONE IN DANGER. I'LL SEND THREE OF MY SONS AS ESCORT TO ENSURE AKAMAS'S SAFETY, BUT I CAN'T BELIEVE PERSEUS OF DARDANUS INTENDS ANY HARM. HE'S AN HONORABLE MAN WITH AN EXCELLENT REPUTATION FOR HOSPITALITY.
HELIKAON, ARCHELOCHUS, KOON! MAKE SURE THE SON OF THESEUS RETURNS SAFELY.
YES, FATHER.
CHEER UP, MENELAUS! IF THEY'RE RETURNING MY GRANDMOTHER TO ME, YOUR WIFE CAN'T BE FAR BEHIND!
GO WITH THEM, EURYBATES.
THEY ALL WANTED HER THEN... STILL WANT HER NOW ...**EVERYONE** WANTS HER... BUT **ONLY** ME... ONLY **ME**...

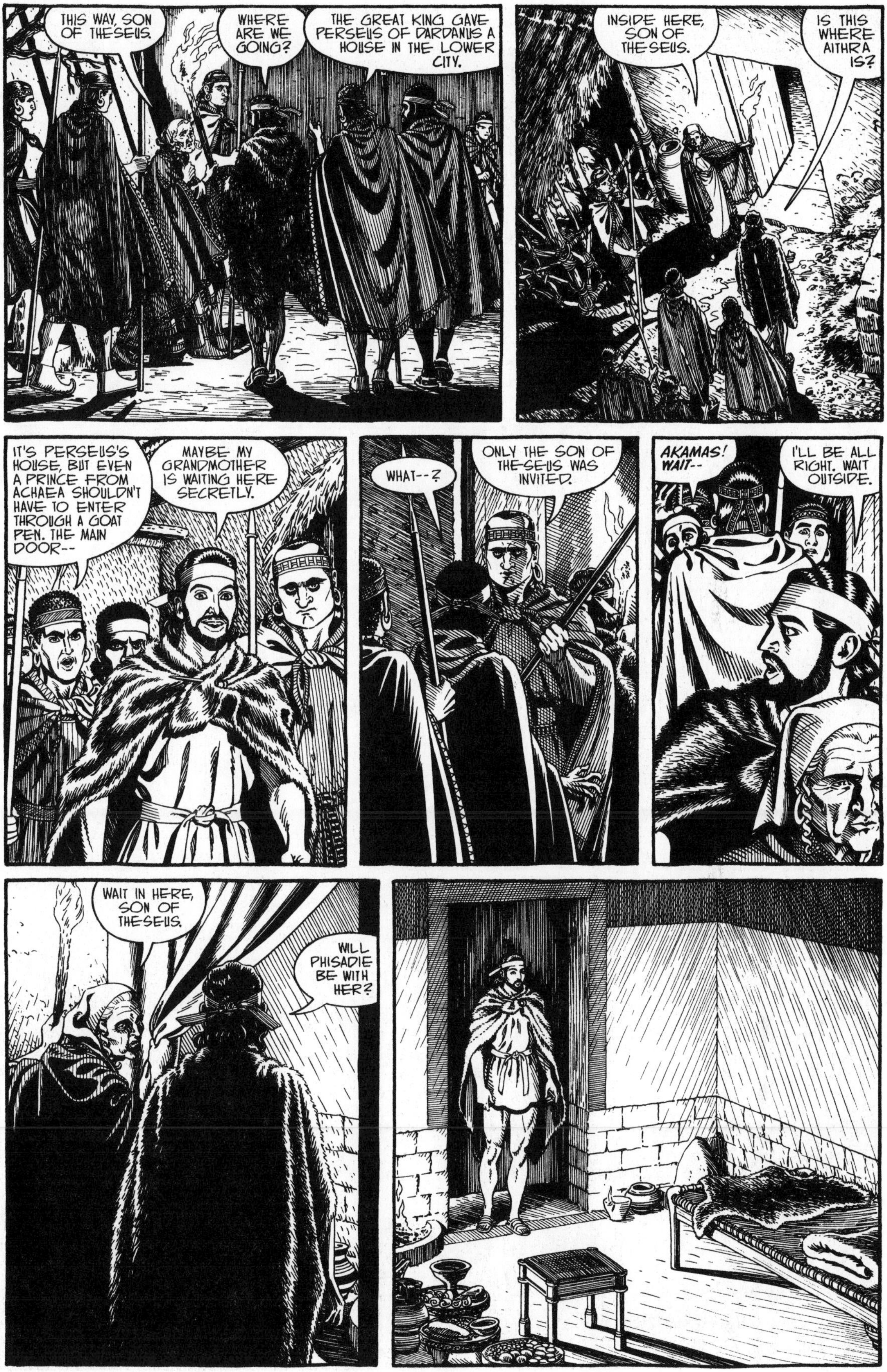
THIS WAY, SON OF THESEUS.
WHERE ARE WE GOING?
THE GREAT KING GAVE PERSEUS OF DARDANUS A HOUSE IN THE LOWER CITY.
INSIDE HERE, SON OF THESEUS.
IS THIS WHERE AITHRA IS?
IT'S PERSEUS'S HOUSE, BUT EVEN A PRINCE FROM ACHAEA SHOULDN'T HAVE TO ENTER THROUGH A GOAT PEN. THE MAIN DOOR--
MAYBE MY GRANDMOTHER IS WAITING HERE SECRETLY.
WHAT--?
ONLY THE SON OF THESEUS WAS INVITED.
AKAMAS! WAIT--
I'LL BE ALL RIGHT. WAIT OUTSIDE.
WAIT IN HERE, SON OF THESEUS.
WILL PHISADIE BE WITH HER?

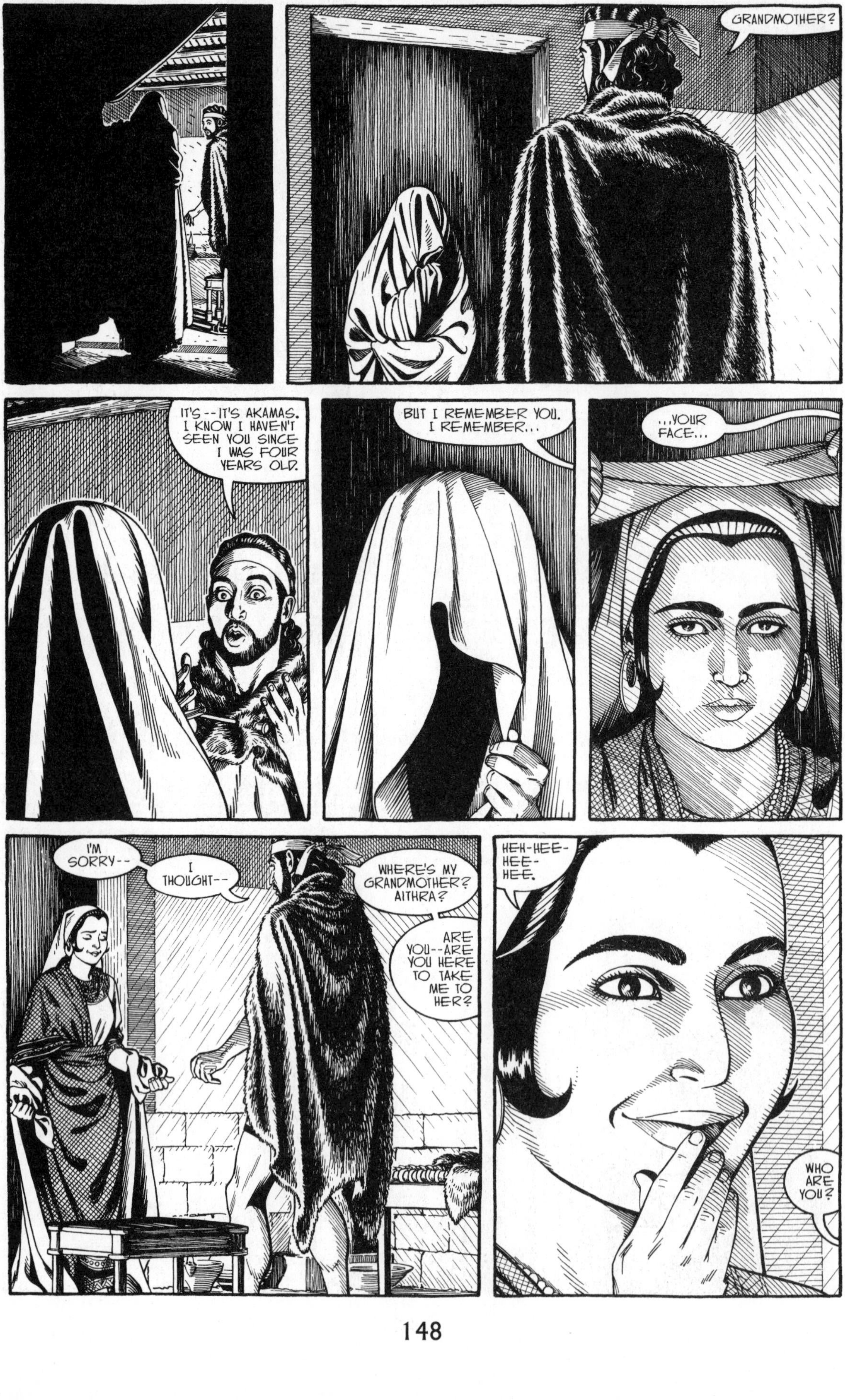
GRANDMOTHER?
IT'S --IT'S AKAMAS. I KNOW I HAVEN'T SEEN YOU SINCE I WAS FOUR YEARS OLD.
BUT I REMEMBER YOU. I REMEMBER...
...YOUR FACE...
I'M SORRY--
I THOUGHT--
WHERE'S MY GRANDMOTHER? AITHRA?
ARE YOU--ARE YOU HERE TO TAKE ME TO HER?
HEH-HEE-HEE-HEE.
WHO ARE YOU?

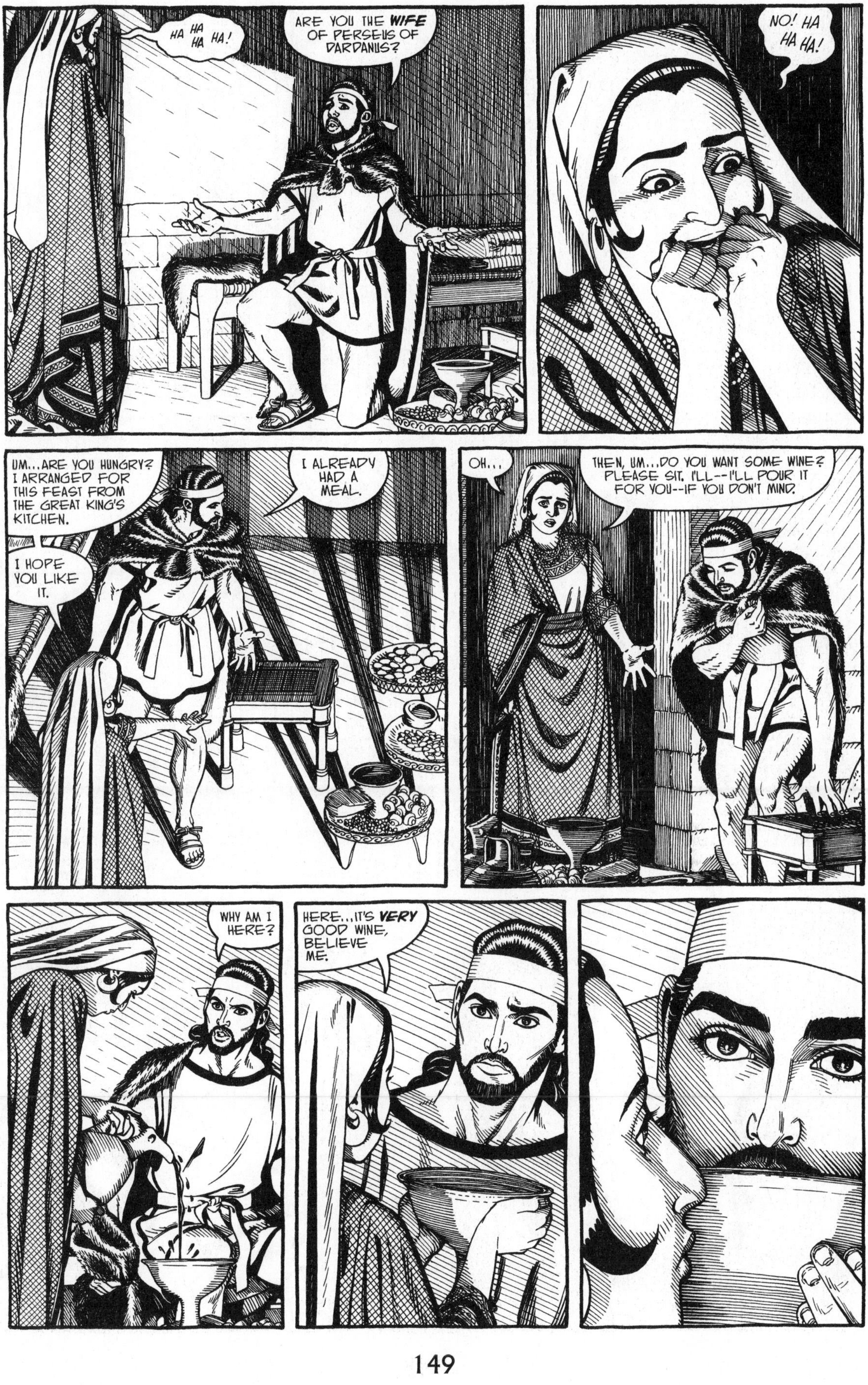
HA HA HA HA!
ARE YOU THE WIFE OF PERSEUS OF DARDANUS?
NO! HA HA HA!
UM...ARE YOU HUNGRY? I ARRANGED FOR THIS FEAST FROM THE GREAT KING'S KITCHEN.
I HOPE YOU LIKE IT.
I ALREADY HAD A MEAL.
OH...
THEN, UM...DO YOU WANT SOME WINE? PLEASE SIT. I'LL--I'LL POUR IT FOR YOU--IF YOU DON'T MIND.
WHY AM I HERE?
HERE...IT'S VERY GOOD WINE, BELIEVE ME.

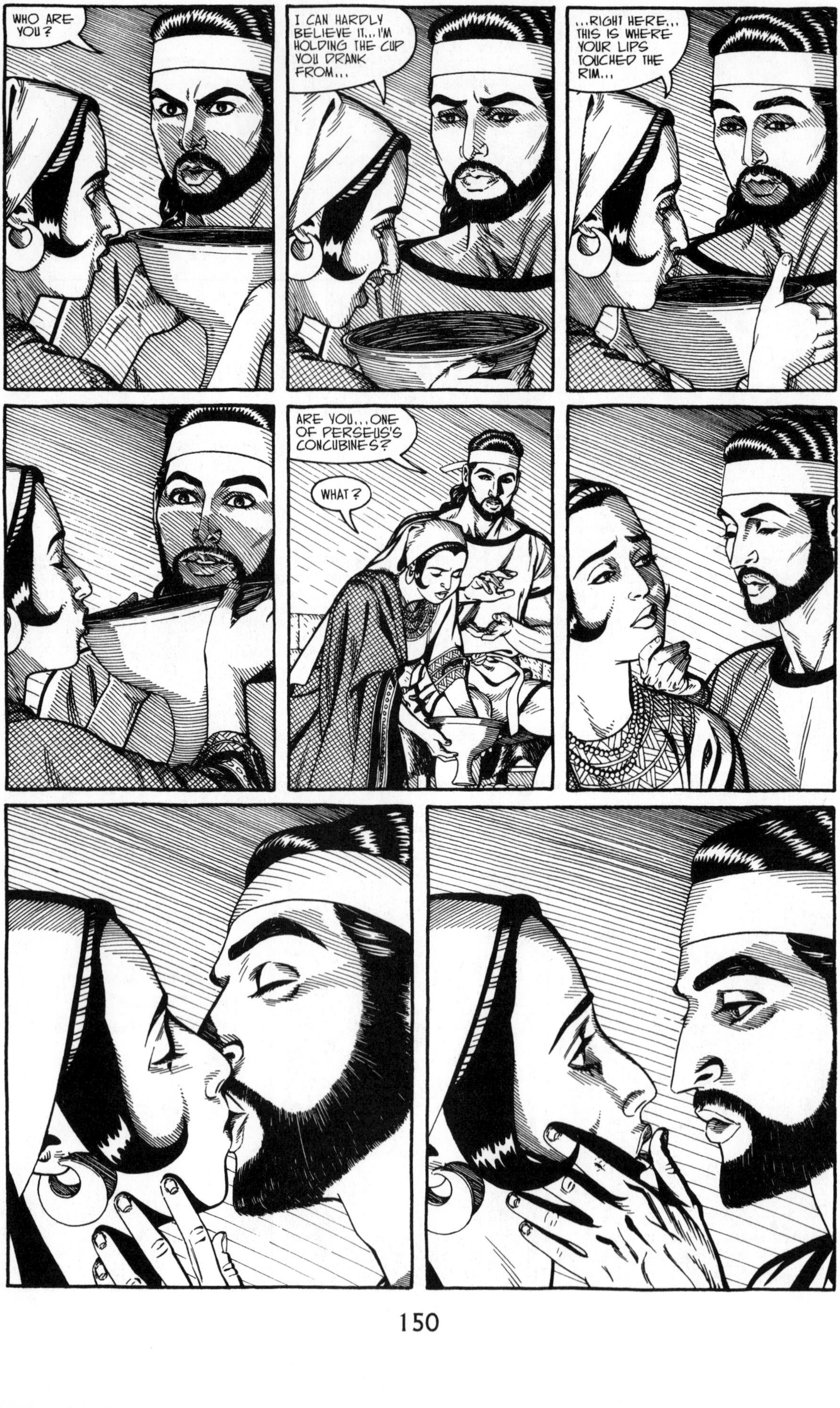
WHO ARE YOU?
I CAN HARDLY BELIEVE IT...I'M HOLDING THE CUP YOU DRANK FROM...
...RIGHT HERE... THIS IS WHERE YOUR LIPS TOUCHED THE RIM...
ARE YOU...ONE OF PERSEUS'S CONCUBINES?
WHAT?

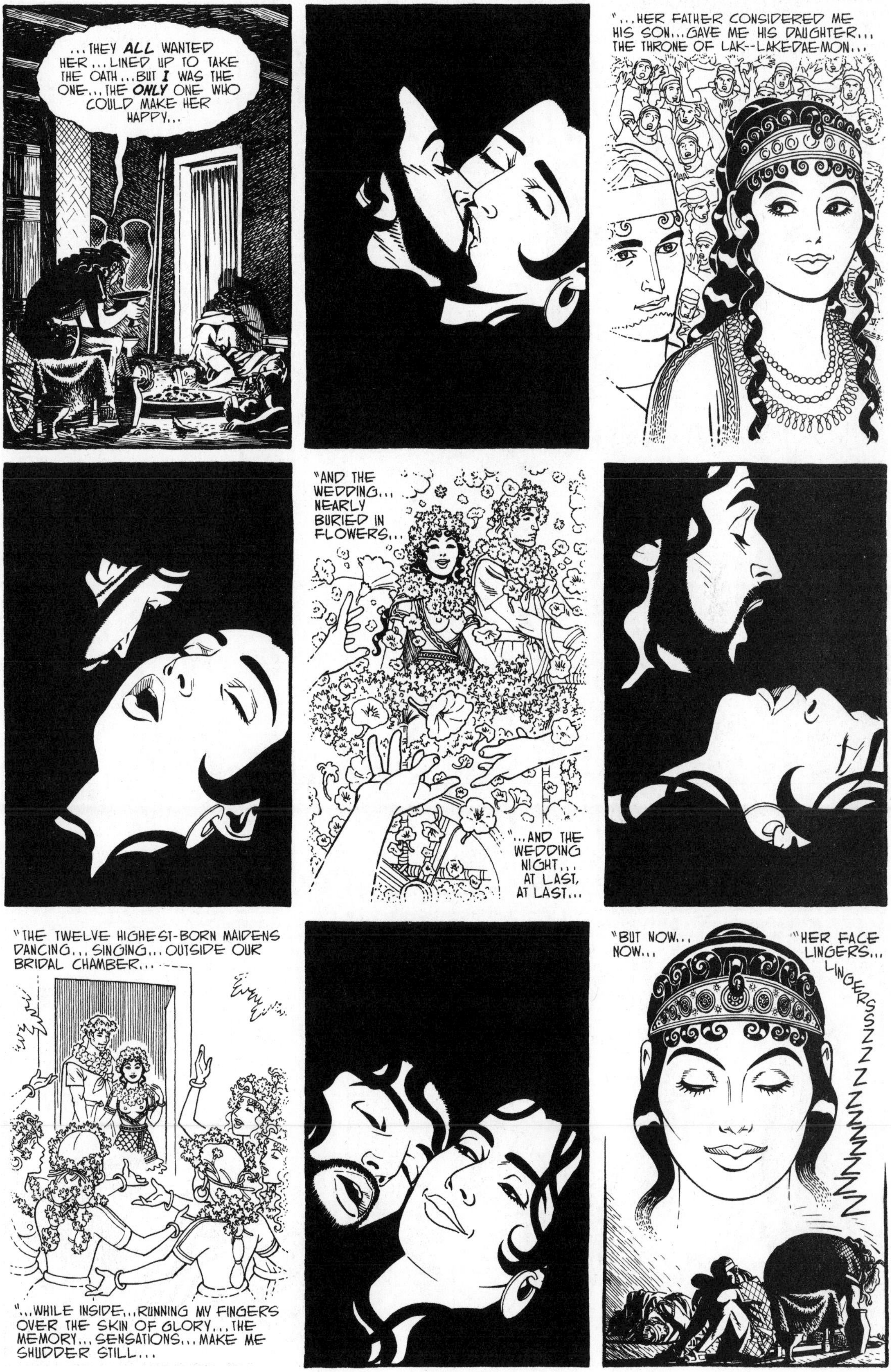
...THEY ALL WANTED HER... LINED UP TO TAKE THE OATH... BUT I WAS THE ONE... THE ONLY ONE WHO COULD MAKE HER HAPPY...
"...HER FATHER CONSIDERED ME HIS SON... GAVE ME HIS DAUGHTER... THE THRONE OF LAK--LAKEDAEMON...
"AND THE WEDDING... NEARLY BURIED IN FLOWERS...
"...AND THE WEDDING NIGHT... AT LAST, AT LAST...
"THE TWELVE HIGHEST-BORN MAIDENS DANCING... SINGING... OUTSIDE OUR BRIDAL CHAMBER...
"...WHILE INSIDE... RUNNING MY FINGERS OVER THE SKIN OF GLORY... THE MEMORY... SENSATIONS... MAKE ME SHUDDER STILL...
"BUT NOW... NOW...
"HER FACE LINGERS... LINGERSSZZZZZZZZZZZ

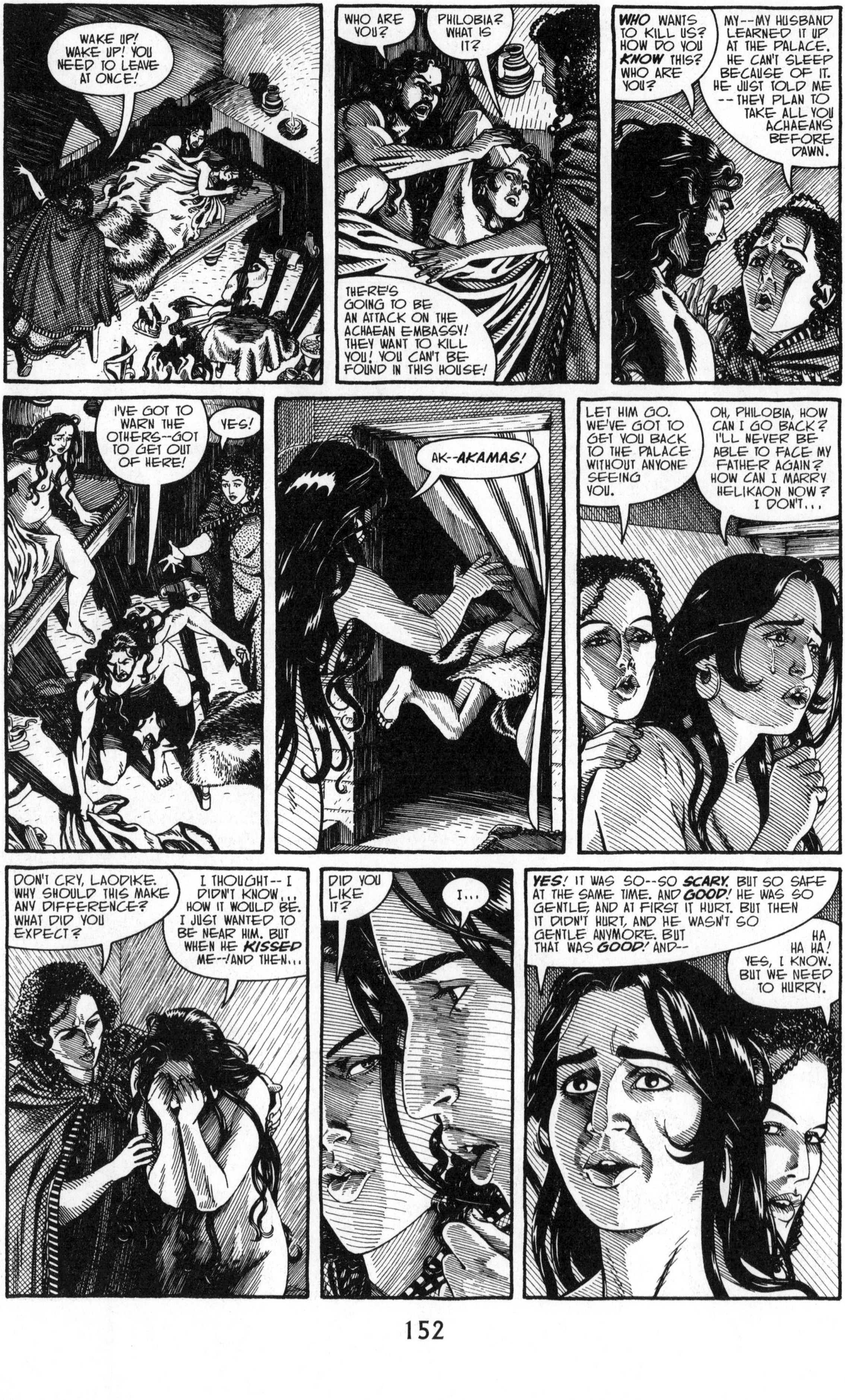
WAKE UP! WAKE UP! YOU NEED TO LEAVE AT ONCE!
WHO ARE YOU?
PHILOBIA? WHAT IS IT?
THERE'S GOING TO BE AN ATTACK ON THE ACHAEAN EMBASSY! THEY WANT TO KILL YOU! YOU CAN'T BE FOUND IN THIS HOUSE!
WHO WANTS TO KILL US? HOW DO YOU KNOW THIS? WHO ARE YOU?
MY--MY HUSBAND LEARNED IT UP AT THE PALACE. HE CAN'T SLEEP BECAUSE OF IT. HE JUST TOLD ME --THEY PLAN TO TAKE ALL YOU ACHAEANS BEFORE DAWN.
I'VE GOT TO WARN THE OTHERS--GOT TO GET OUT OF HERE!
YES!
AK--AKAMAS!
LET HIM GO. WE'VE GOT TO GET YOU BACK TO THE PALACE WITHOUT ANYONE SEEING YOU.
OH, PHILOBIA, HOW CAN I GO BACK? I'LL NEVER BE ABLE TO FACE MY FATHER AGAIN? HOW CAN I MARRY HELIKAON NOW? I DON'T...
DON'T CRY, LAODIKE. WHY SHOULD THIS MAKE ANY DIFFERENCE? WHAT DID YOU EXPECT?
I THOUGHT-- I DIDN'T KNOW... HOW IT WOULD BE. I JUST WANTED TO BE NEAR HIM. BUT WHEN HE KISSED ME--! AND THEN...
DID YOU LIKE IT?
I...
YES! IT WAS SO--SO SCARY. BUT SO SAFE AT THE SAME TIME. AND GOOD! HE WAS SO GENTLE, AND AT FIRST IT HURT. BUT THEN IT DIDN'T HURT, AND HE WASN'T SO GENTLE ANYMORE. BUT THAT WAS GOOD! AND--
HA HA HA! YES, I KNOW. BUT WE NEED TO HURRY.

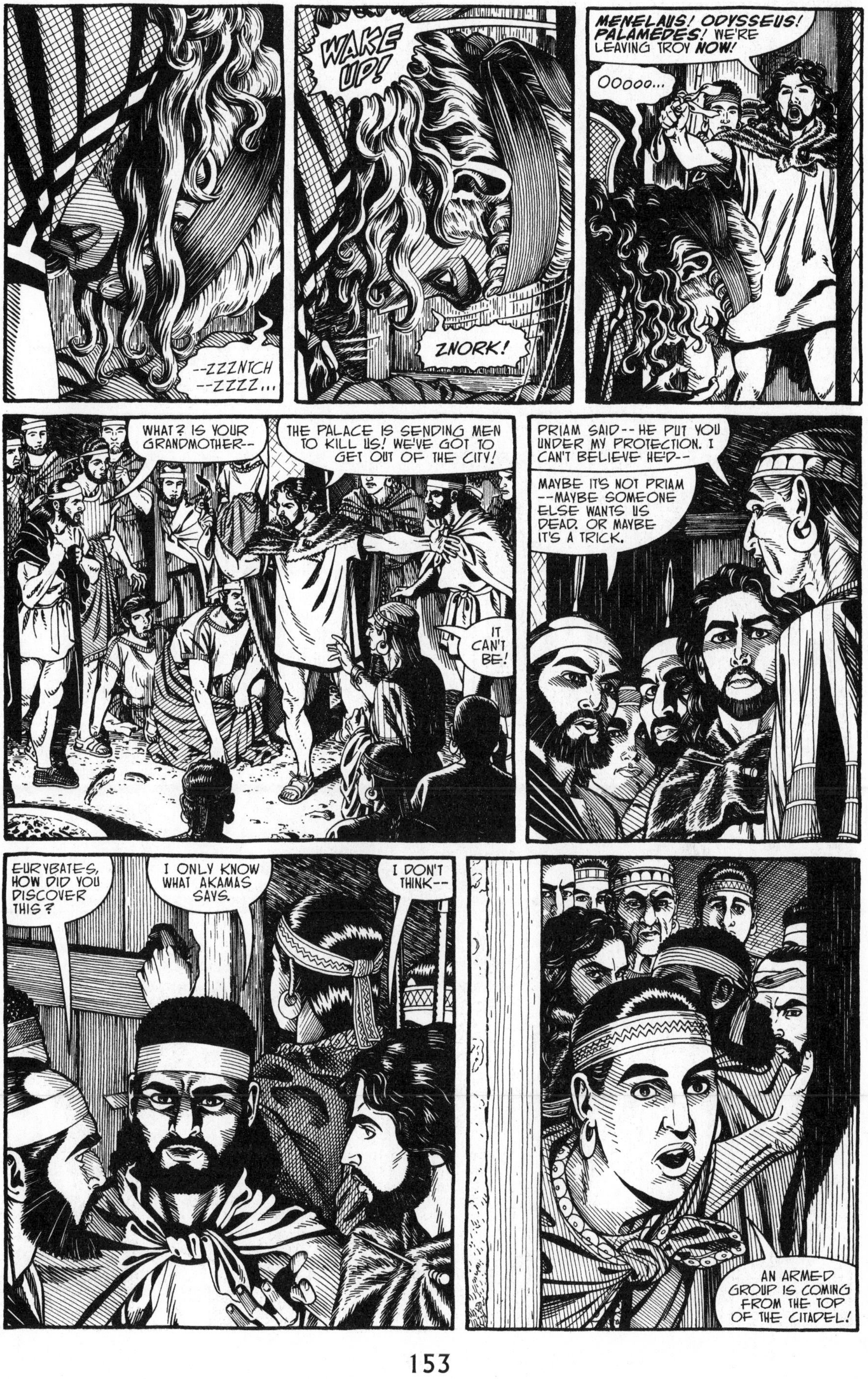
--ZZZNTCH
--ZZZZ...
WAKE UP!
ZNORK!
MENELAUS! ODYSSEUS! PALAMEDES! WE'RE LEAVING TROY NOW!
OOOOO...
WHAT? IS YOUR GRANDMOTHER--
THE PALACE IS SENDING MEN TO KILL US! WE'VE GOT TO GET OUT OF THE CITY!
IT CAN'T BE!
PRIAM SAID--HE PUT YOU UNDER MY PROTECTION. I CAN'T BELIEVE HE'D--
MAYBE IT'S NOT PRIAM --MAYBE SOMEONE ELSE WANTS US DEAD. OR MAYBE IT'S A TRICK.
EURYBATES, HOW DID YOU DISCOVER THIS?
I ONLY KNOW WHAT AKAMAS SAYS.
I DON'T THINK--
AN ARMED GROUP IS COMING FROM THE TOP OF THE CITADEL!

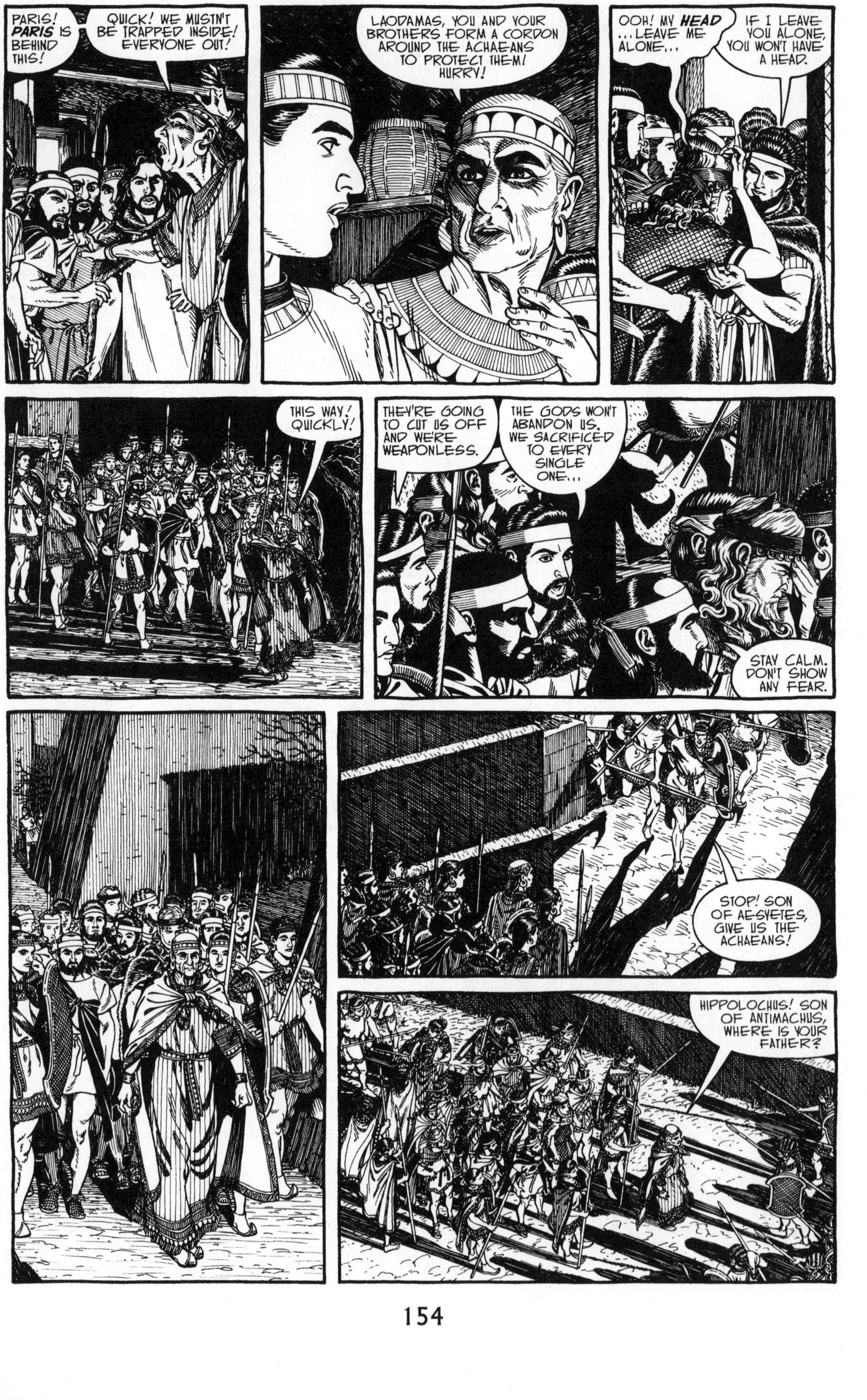
PARIS! PARIS IS BEHIND THIS!
QUICK! WE MUSTN'T BE TRAPPED INSIDE! EVERYONE OUT!
LAODAMAS, YOU AND YOUR BROTHERS FORM A CORDON AROUND THE ACHAEANS TO PROTECT THEM! HURRY!
OOH! MY HEAD ...LEAVE ME ALONE...
IF I LEAVE YOU ALONE, YOU WON'T HAVE A HEAD.
THIS WAY! QUICKLY!
THEY'RE GOING TO CUT US OFF AND WE'RE WEAPONLESS.
THE GODS WON'T ABANDON US. WE SACRIFICED TO EVERY SINGLE ONE...
STAY CALM. DON'T SHOW ANY FEAR.
STOP! SON OF AESYETES, GIVE US THE ACHAEANS!
HIPPOLOCHUS! SON OF ANTIMACHUS, WHERE IS YOUR FATHER?

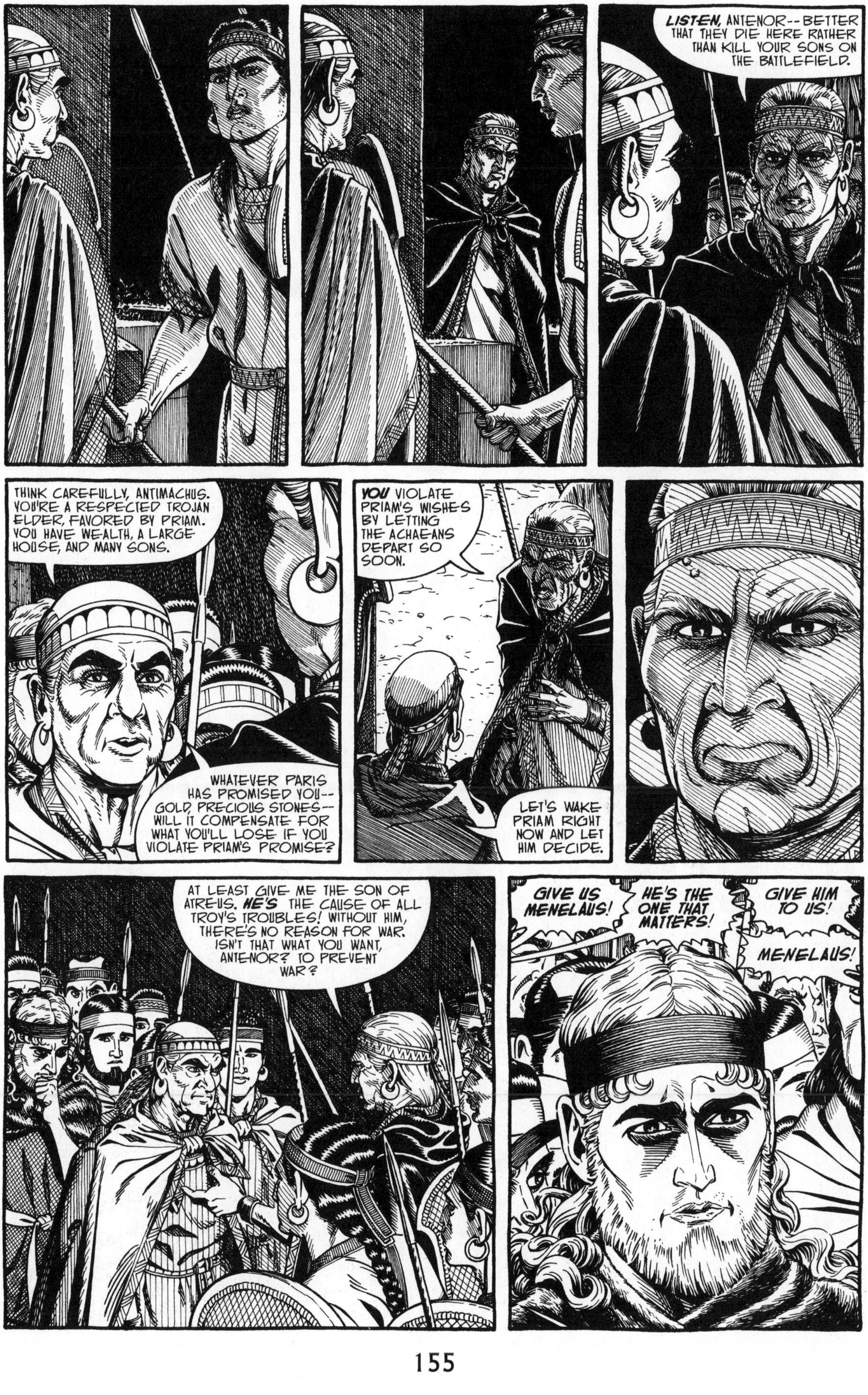
LISTEN, ANTENOR--BETTER THAT THEY DIE HERE RATHER THAN KILL YOUR SONS ON THE BATTLEFIELD.
THINK CAREFULLY, ANTIMACHUS. YOU'RE A RESPECTED TROJAN ELDER, FAVORED BY PRIAM. YOU HAVE WEALTH, A LARGE HOUSE, AND MANY SONS.
WHATEVER PARIS HAS PROMISED YOU-- GOLD, PRECIOUS STONES-- WILL IT COMPENSATE FOR WHAT YOU'LL LOSE IF YOU VIOLATE PRIAM'S PROMISE?
YOU VIOLATE PRIAM'S WISHES BY LETTING THE ACHAEANS DEPART SO SOON.
LET'S WAKE PRIAM RIGHT NOW AND LET HIM DECIDE.
AT LEAST GIVE ME THE SON OF ATREUS. HE'S THE CAUSE OF ALL TROY'S TROUBLES! WITHOUT HIM, THERE'S NO REASON FOR WAR. ISN'T THAT WHAT YOU WANT, ANTENOR? TO PREVENT WAR?
GIVE US MENELAUS!
HE'S THE ONE THAT MATTERS!
GIVE HIM TO US!
MENELAUS!

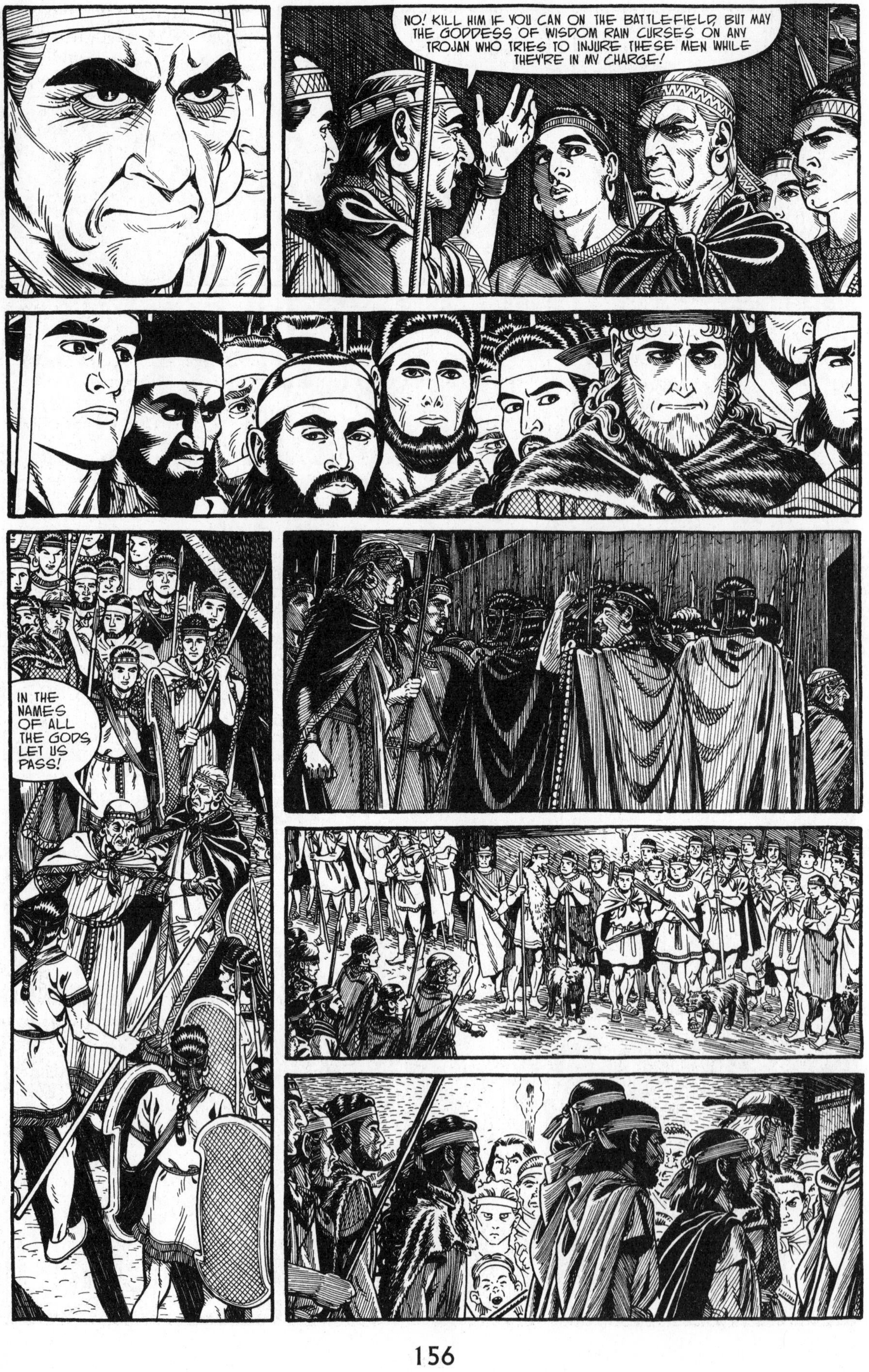
NO! KILL HIM IF YOU CAN ON THE BATTLEFIELD, BUT MAY THE GODDESS OF WISDOM RAIN CURSES ON ANY TROJAN WHO TRIES TO INJURE THESE MEN WHILE THEY'RE IN MY CHARGE!
IN THE NAMES OF ALL THE GODS, LET US PASS!

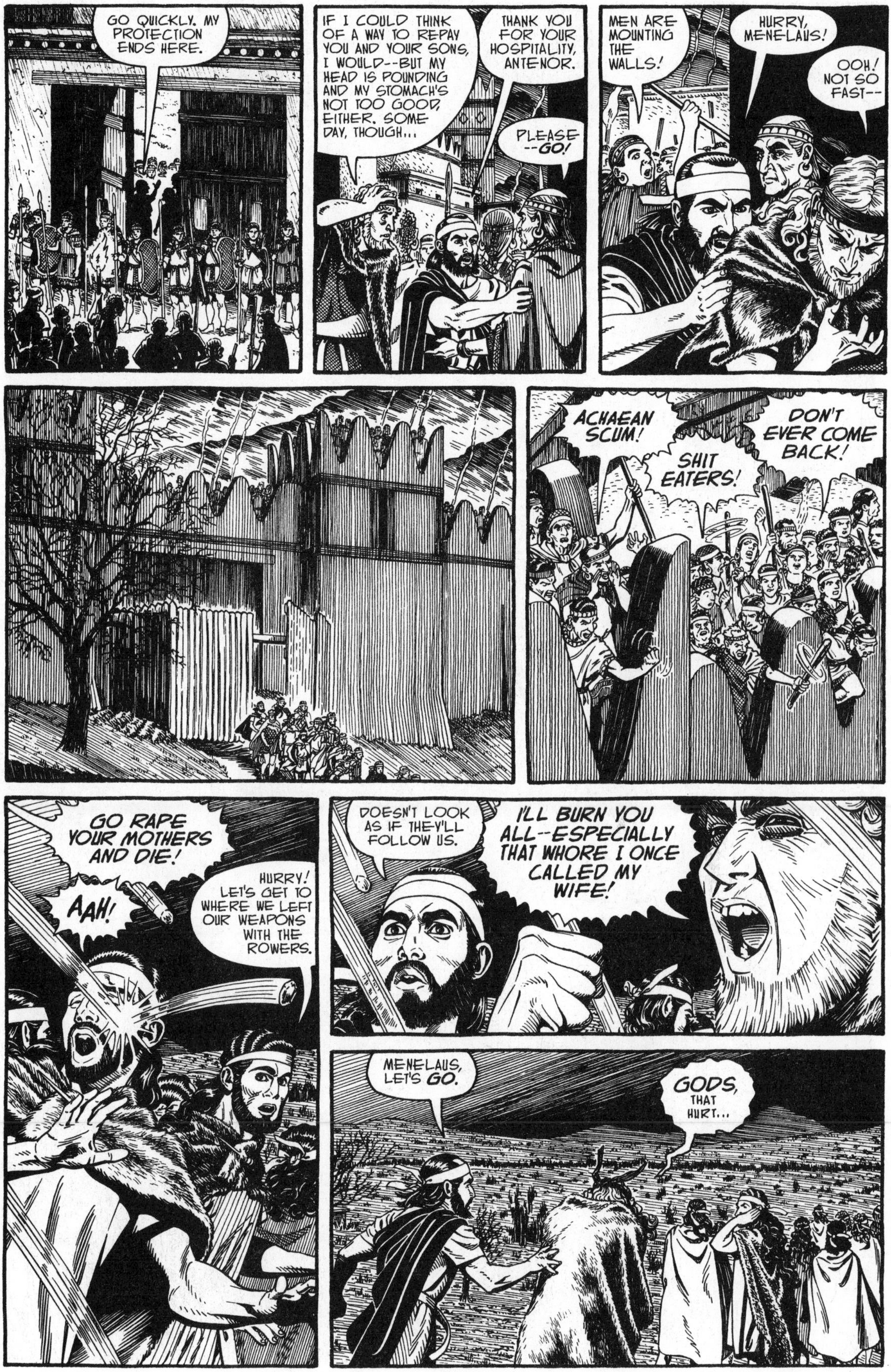
GO QUICKLY. MY PROTECTION ENDS HERE.
IF I COULD THINK OF A WAY TO REPAY YOU AND YOUR SONS, I WOULD--BUT MY HEAD IS POUNDING AND MY STOMACH'S NOT TOO GOOD, EITHER. SOME DAY, THOUGH...
THANK YOU FOR YOUR HOSPITALITY, ANTENOR.
PLEASE --GO!
MEN ARE MOUNTING THE WALLS!
HURRY, MENELAUS!
OOH! NOT SO FAST--
ACHAEAN SCUM!
SHIT EATERS!
DON'T EVER COME BACK!
GO RAPE YOUR MOTHERS AND DIE!
AAH!
HURRY! LET'S GET TO WHERE WE LEFT OUR WEAPONS WITH THE ROWERS.
DOESN'T LOOK AS IF THEY'LL FOLLOW US.
I'LL BURN YOU ALL--ESPECIALLY THAT WHORE I ONCE CALLED MY WIFE!
MENELAUS, LET'S GO.
GODS, THAT HURT...

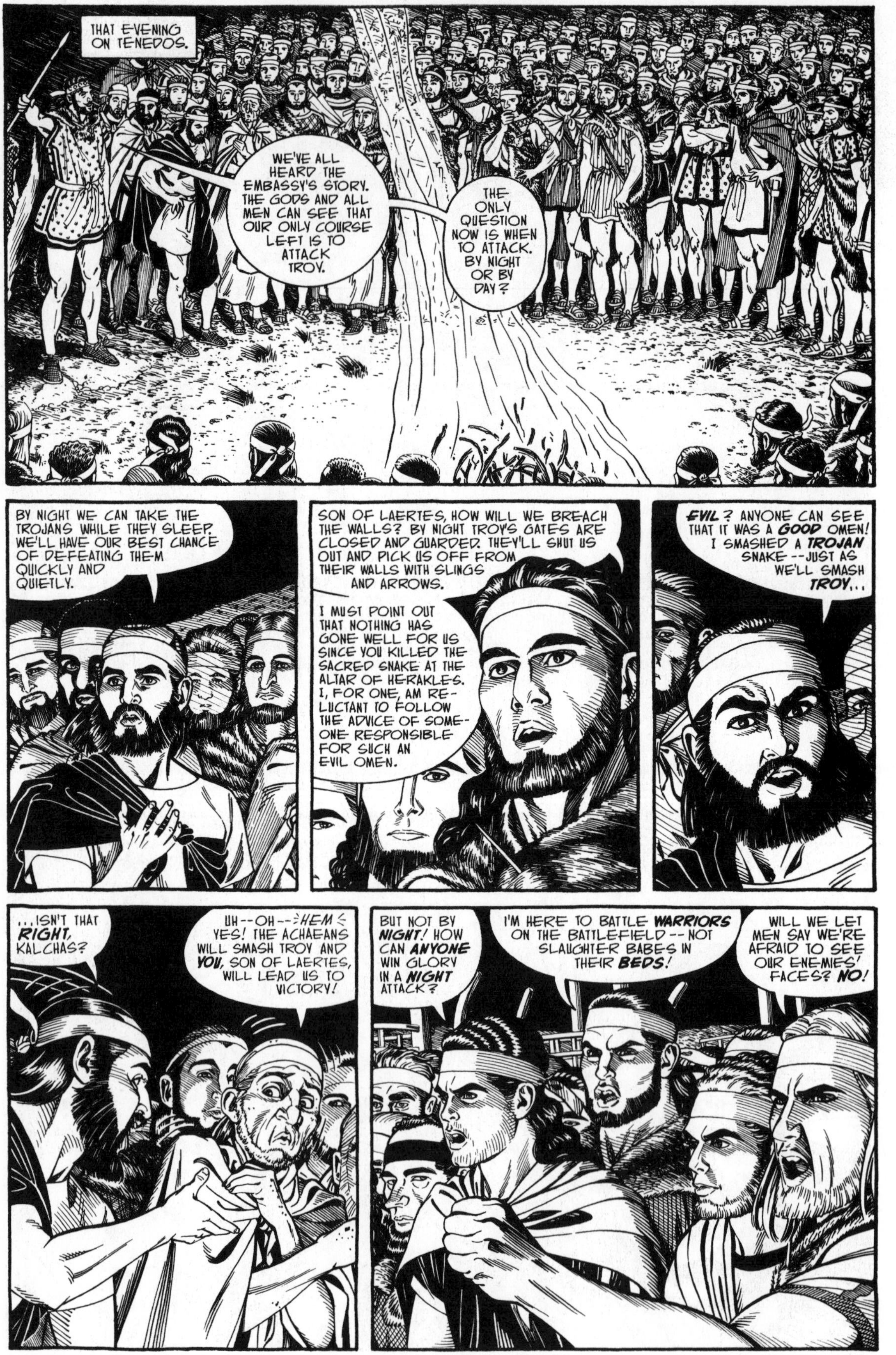
THAT EVENING ON TENEDOS.
WE'VE ALL HEARD THE EMBASSY'S STORY. THE GODS AND ALL MEN CAN SEE THAT OUR ONLY COURSE LEFT IS TO ATTACK TROY.
THE ONLY QUESTION NOW IS WHEN TO ATTACK. BY NIGHT OR BY DAY?
BY NIGHT WE CAN TAKE THE TROJANS WHILE THEY SLEEP. WE'LL HAVE OUR BEST CHANCE OF DEFEATING THEM QUICKLY AND QUIETLY.
SON OF LAERTES, HOW WILL WE BREACH THE WALLS? BY NIGHT TROY'S GATES ARE CLOSED AND GUARDED. THEY'LL SHUT US OUT AND PICK US OFF FROM THEIR WALLS WITH SLINGS AND ARROWS.
I MUST POINT OUT THAT NOTHING HAS GONE WELL FOR US SINCE YOU KILLED THE SACRED SNAKE AT THE ALTAR OF HERAKLES. I, FOR ONE, AM RELUCTANT TO FOLLOW THE ADVICE OF SOMEONE RESPONSIBLE FOR SUCH AN EVIL OMEN.
EVIL? ANYONE CAN SEE THAT IT WAS A GOOD OMEN! I SMASHED A TROJAN SNAKE --JUST AS WE'LL SMASH TROY...
...ISN'T THAT RIGHT, KALCHAS?
UH--OH--HEM YES! THE ACHAEANS WILL SMASH TROY AND YOU, SON OF LAERTES, WILL LEAD US TO VICTORY!
BUT NOT BY NIGHT! HOW CAN ANYONE WIN GLORY IN A NIGHT ATTACK?
I'M HERE TO BATTLE WARRIORS ON THE BATTLEFIELD--NOT SLAUGHTER BABES IN THEIR BEDS!
WILL WE LET MEN SAY WE'RE AFRAID TO SEE OUR ENEMIES' FACES? NO!

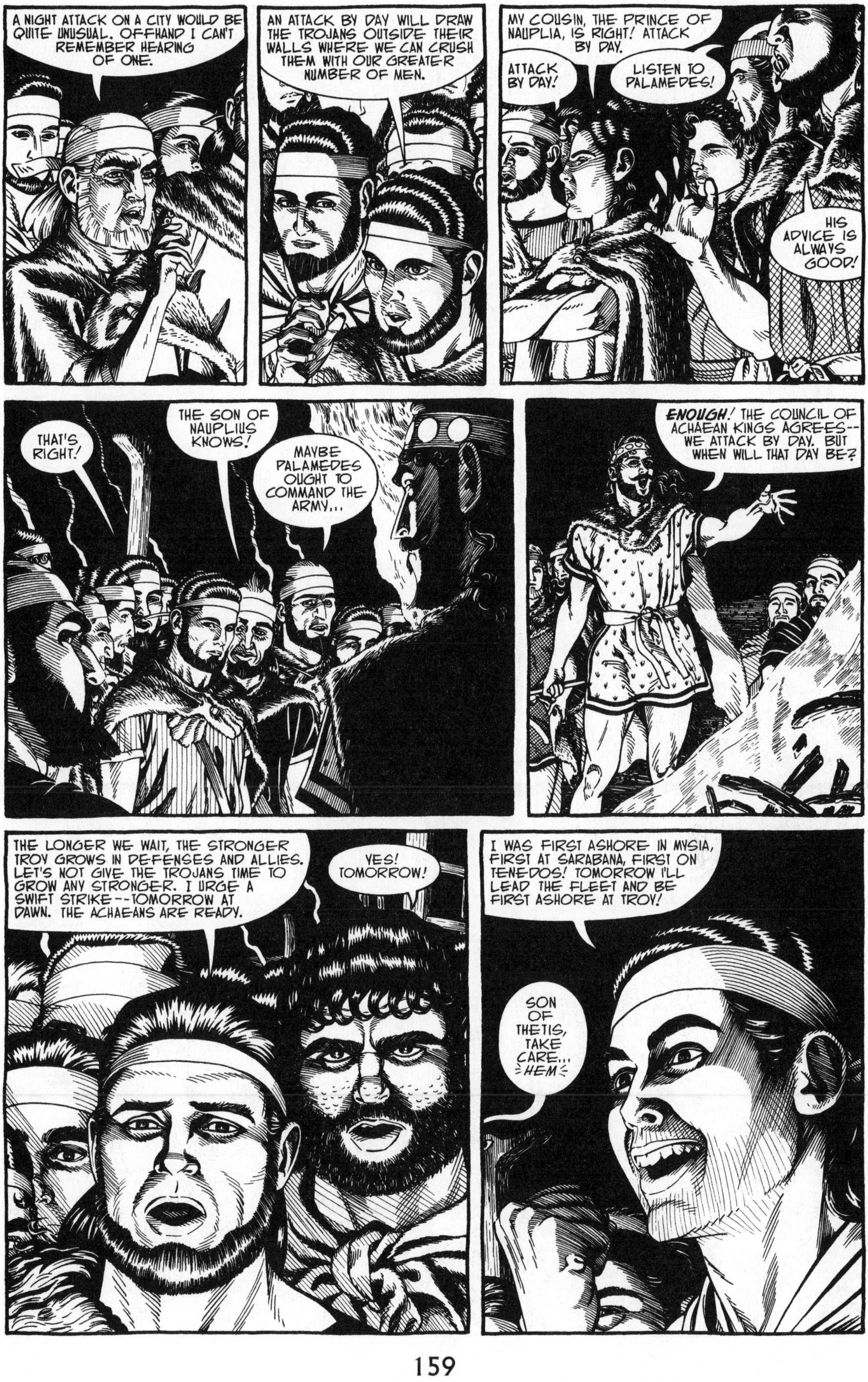
A NIGHT ATTACK ON A CITY WOULD BE QUITE UNUSUAL. OFFHAND I CAN'T REMEMBER HEARING OF ONE.
AN ATTACK BY DAY WILL DRAW THE TROJANS OUTSIDE THEIR WALLS WHERE WE CAN CRUSH THEM WITH OUR GREATER NUMBER OF MEN.
MY COUSIN, THE PRINCE OF NAUPLIA, IS RIGHT! ATTACK BY DAY.
ATTACK BY DAY!
LISTEN TO PALAMEDES!
HIS ADVICE IS ALWAYS GOOD!
THAT'S RIGHT!
THE SON OF NAUPLIUS KNOWS!
MAYBE PALAMEDES OUGHT TO COMMAND THE ARMY...
ENOUGH! THE COUNCIL OF ACHAEAN KINGS AGREES-- WE ATTACK BY DAY. BUT WHEN WILL THAT DAY BE?
THE LONGER WE WAIT, THE STRONGER TROY GROWS IN DEFENSES AND ALLIES. LET'S NOT GIVE THE TROJANS TIME TO GROW ANY STRONGER. I URGE A SWIFT STRIKE--TOMORROW AT DAWN. THE ACHAEANS ARE READY.
YES! TOMORROW!
I WAS FIRST ASHORE IN MYSIA, FIRST AT SARABANA, FIRST ON TENEDOS! TOMORROW I'LL LEAD THE FLEET AND BE FIRST ASHORE AT TROY!
SON OF THETIS, TAKE CARE... HEM

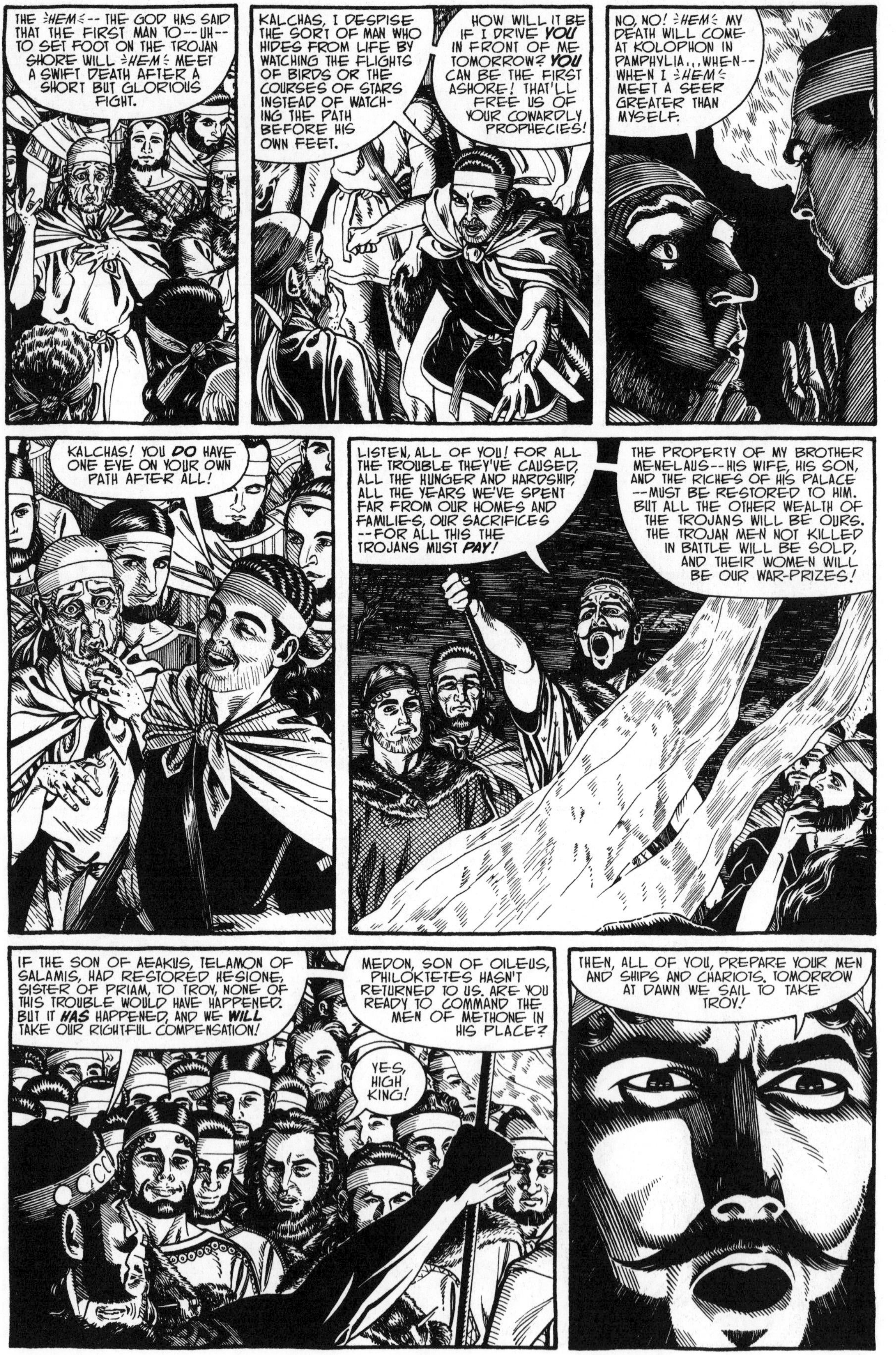
THE ≷HEM≶-- THE GOD HAS SAID THAT THE FIRST MAN TO--UH-- TO SET FOOT ON THE TROJAN SHORE WILL ≷HEM≶ MEET A SWIFT DEATH AFTER A SHORT BUT GLORIOUS FIGHT.
KALCHAS, I DESPISE THE SORT OF MAN WHO HIDES FROM LIFE BY WATCHING THE FLIGHTS OF BIRDS OR THE COURSES OF STARS INSTEAD OF WATCHING THE PATH BEFORE HIS OWN FEET.
HOW WILL IT BE IF I DRIVE **YOU** IN FRONT OF ME TOMORROW? **YOU** CAN BE THE FIRST ASHORE! THAT'LL FREE US OF YOUR COWARDLY PROPHECIES!
NO, NO! ≷HEM≶ MY DEATH WILL COME AT KOLOPHON IN PAMPHYLIA...WHEN-- WHEN I ≷HEM≶ MEET A SEER GREATER THAN MYSELF.
KALCHAS! YOU **DO** HAVE ONE EYE ON YOUR OWN PATH AFTER ALL!
LISTEN, ALL OF YOU! FOR ALL THE TROUBLE THEY'VE CAUSED, ALL THE HUNGER AND HARDSHIP, ALL THE YEARS WE'VE SPENT FAR FROM OUR HOMES AND FAMILIES, OUR SACRIFICES --FOR ALL THIS THE TROJANS MUST **PAY**!
THE PROPERTY OF MY BROTHER MENELAUS--HIS WIFE, HIS SON, AND THE RICHES OF HIS PALACE --MUST BE RESTORED TO HIM. BUT ALL THE OTHER WEALTH OF THE TROJANS WILL BE OURS. THE TROJAN MEN NOT KILLED IN BATTLE WILL BE SOLD, AND THEIR WOMEN WILL BE OUR WAR-PRIZES!
IF THE SON OF AEAKUS, TELAMON OF SALAMIS, HAD RESTORED HESIONE, SISTER OF PRIAM, TO TROY, NONE OF THIS TROUBLE WOULD HAVE HAPPENED. BUT IT **HAS** HAPPENED, AND WE **WILL** TAKE OUR RIGHTFUL COMPENSATION!
MEDON, SON OF OILEUS, PHILOKTETES HASN'T RETURNED TO US. ARE YOU READY TO COMMAND THE MEN OF METHONE IN HIS PLACE?
YES, HIGH KING!
THEN, ALL OF YOU, PREPARE YOUR MEN AND SHIPS AND CHARIOTS. TOMORROW AT DAWN WE SAIL TO TAKE TROY!

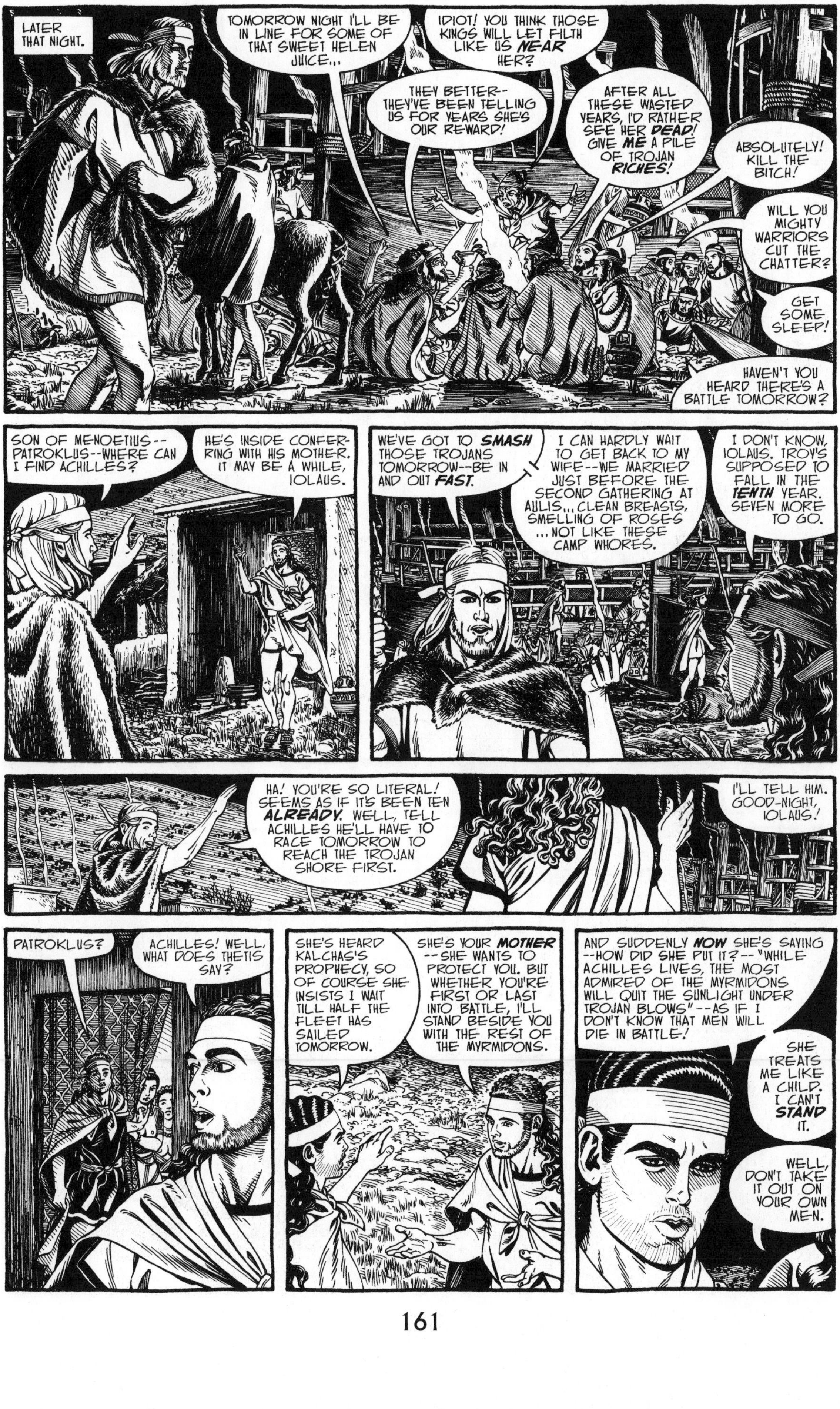
LATER THAT NIGHT.
TOMORROW NIGHT I'LL BE IN LINE FOR SOME OF THAT SWEET HELEN JUICE...
IDIOT! YOU THINK THOSE KINGS WILL LET FILTH LIKE US NEAR HER?
THEY BETTER-- THEY'VE BEEN TELLING US FOR YEARS SHE'S OUR REWARD!
AFTER ALL THESE WASTED YEARS, I'D RATHER SEE HER DEAD! GIVE ME A PILE OF TROJAN RICHES!
ABSOLUTELY! KILL THE BITCH!
WILL YOU MIGHTY WARRIORS CUT THE CHATTER?
GET SOME SLEEP!
HAVEN'T YOU HEARD THERE'S A BATTLE TOMORROW?
SON OF MENOETIUS-- PATROKLUS--WHERE CAN I FIND ACHILLES?
HE'S INSIDE CONFERRING WITH HIS MOTHER. IT MAY BE A WHILE, IOLAUS.
WE'VE GOT TO SMASH THOSE TROJANS TOMORROW--BE IN AND OUT FAST.
I CAN HARDLY WAIT TO GET BACK TO MY WIFE--WE MARRIED JUST BEFORE THE SECOND GATHERING AT AULIS... CLEAN BREASTS, SMELLING OF ROSES ...NOT LIKE THESE CAMP WHORES.
I DON'T KNOW, IOLAUS. TROY'S SUPPOSED TO FALL IN THE TENTH YEAR. SEVEN MORE TO GO.
HA! YOU'RE SO LITERAL! SEEMS AS IF IT'S BEEN TEN ALREADY. WELL, TELL ACHILLES HE'LL HAVE TO RACE TOMORROW TO REACH THE TROJAN SHORE FIRST.
I'LL TELL HIM. GOOD-NIGHT, IOLAUS!
PATROKLUS?
ACHILLES! WELL, WHAT DOES THETIS SAY?
SHE'S HEARD KALCHAS'S PROPHECY, SO OF COURSE SHE INSISTS I WAIT TILL HALF THE FLEET HAS SAILED TOMORROW.
SHE'S YOUR MOTHER --SHE WANTS TO PROTECT YOU. BUT WHETHER YOU'RE FIRST OR LAST INTO BATTLE, I'LL STAND BESIDE YOU WITH THE REST OF THE MYRMIDONS.
AND SUDDENLY NOW SHE'S SAYING --HOW DID SHE PUT IT?-- "WHILE ACHILLES LIVES, THE MOST ADMIRED OF THE MYRMIDONS WILL QUIT THE SUNLIGHT UNDER TROJAN BLOWS" --AS IF I DON'T KNOW THAT MEN WILL DIE IN BATTLE!
SHE TREATS ME LIKE A CHILD. I CAN'T STAND IT.
WELL, DON'T TAKE IT OUT ON YOUR OWN MEN.

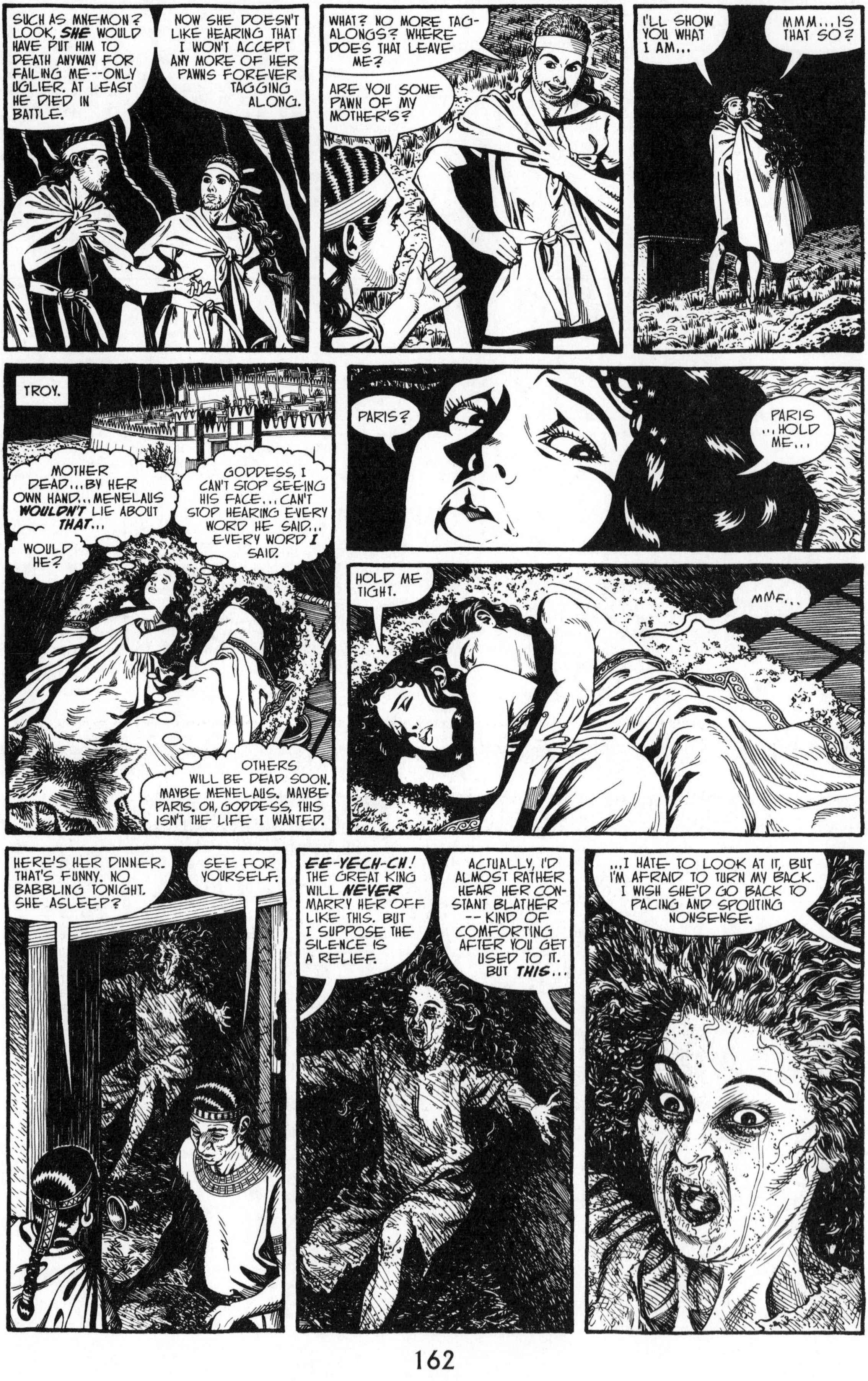
SUCH AS MNEMON? LOOK, SHE WOULD HAVE PUT HIM TO DEATH ANYWAY FOR FAILING ME--ONLY UGLIER. AT LEAST HE DIED IN BATTLE.
NOW SHE DOESN'T LIKE HEARING THAT I WON'T ACCEPT ANY MORE OF HER PAWNS FOREVER TAGGING ALONG.
WHAT? NO MORE TAG-ALONGS? WHERE DOES THAT LEAVE ME?
ARE YOU SOME PAWN OF MY MOTHER'S?
I'LL SHOW YOU WHAT I AM...
MMM... IS THAT SO?
TROY.
MOTHER DEAD... BY HER OWN HAND... MENELAUS WOULDN'T LIE ABOUT THAT...
WOULD HE?
GODDESS, I CAN'T STOP SEEING HIS FACE... CAN'T STOP HEARING EVERY WORD HE SAID... EVERY WORD I SAID.
OTHERS WILL BE DEAD SOON. MAYBE MENELAUS. MAYBE PARIS. OH, GODDESS, THIS ISN'T THE LIFE I WANTED.
PARIS?
PARIS ...HOLD ME...
HOLD ME TIGHT.
MMF...
HERE'S HER DINNER. THAT'S FUNNY. NO BABBLING TONIGHT. SHE ASLEEP?
SEE FOR YOURSELF.
EE-YECH-CH! THE GREAT KING WILL NEVER MARRY HER OFF LIKE THIS. BUT I SUPPOSE THE SILENCE IS A RELIEF.
ACTUALLY, I'D ALMOST RATHER HEAR HER CONSTANT BLATHER -- KIND OF COMFORTING AFTER YOU GET USED TO IT. BUT THIS...
...I HATE TO LOOK AT IT, BUT I'M AFRAID TO TURN MY BACK. I WISH SHE'D GO BACK TO PACING AND SPOUTING NONSENSE.

Glossary of Names

Pronunciation of names can vary widely. What I present here is merely a guide and needn't be considered definitive.

Anyone seeking consistency among the forms of character and place names should look elsewhere. In general, I've used the more familiar Roman forms for the better-known characters—for instance, Achilles instead of Akhilleos, Helen instead of Helena. Lesser-known and minor characters use a more Greek form—for instance, Teukros instead of Teucer, Polydeukes instead of Pollux.

a as in lap	ee as in see	i as in sit	oo as in wool	u as in us
ay as in say	eye as in hike	o as in not	s as in less	uh as in duh
e as in bed	g as in get	oh as in note	th as in thick	

Listed alphabetically   Stress italicized syllable

Achaean a-*kee*-an, of roughly the area of modern Greece, a person who resides there
Aeakus *ee*-a-kus, grandfather of Achilles, father of Peleus and Telamon
Aeneas ee-*nee*-as, prince of Dardania, cousin of Trojan royal family
Aesakus *ee*-sa-kus, seer son of Priam and Arisbe
Aesyetes ee-seye-*ee*-teez, father of Antenor
Agamemnon a-ga-*mem*-non, king of Mycenae, High King of the Achaeans, brother of Menelaus
Aganus a-*gay*-nus, son of Paris and Helen
Agarista a-ga-*ris*-ta, Philoktetes's daughter
Aithra *ay*-thra, Helen's servant, mother of Theseus, grandmother of Akamas and Demophoon
Ajax (Great) *ay*-jax, son of Telamon, prince of Salamis
Ajax (Little) *ay*-jax, king of Lokris
Akamas *a*-ka-mas, prince of Athens, son of Theseus, grandson of Aithra, brother of Demophoon
Anchises an-*keye*-seez, father of Aeneas, leader of the Dardanians
Andromache an-*dro*-ma-kee, daughter of Eetion of Thebes, wife of Hektor
Antenor an-*tee*-nor, Trojan elder, councilor to Priam
Antigone an-*ti*-goh-nee, cousin of Cressida
Antimachus an-*ti*-ma-kus, Trojan elder
Antiphos *an*-ti-fus, companion of Odysseus
Aphidnae a-*fid*-nee, town near Athens that once hid Helen
Archelochus ar-ke-*loh*-kus, son of Antenor
Argissa ar-*jis*-a, city ruled by Polypoetes
Askalaphus as-*ka*-la-fus, king of Orchomenus
Askania as-*kayn*-ya, a city in Phrygia
Athenians a-*theen*-yanz, inhabitants of Athens
Athens *a*-thenz, city in Attika, ruled by Menestheus
Atreus *ay*-tryoos, father of Agamemnon and Menelaus
Aulis *aw*-lis, bay where the Achaean army assembled before sailing to Troy
Bunomus byoo-*noh*-mus, second son of Paris and Helen
Cheiron *keye*-ron, kentaur teacher of royal youths including Achilles
Chromius *kro*-mee-us, son of Priam and Hekuba
Chryse *kry*-see, goddess worshipped on Tenedos
Cressida *kres*-i-da, daughter of Kalchas, niece of Pandarus
Crete kreet, island ruled by Idomeneus
Dardanians dar-*day*-nee-uhnz, people of the kingdom of Anchises

164

Dardanus *dar*-da-nus, area just southeast of Troy

Dares *da*-reez, Trojan priest

Deiphobus de-*if*-o-bus, prince of Troy

Demophoon dee-mo-*foh*-on, prince of Athens, son of Theseus, brother of Akamas, grandson of Aithra

Diomedes deye-o-*mee*-deez, king of Tiryns

Eetion ee-*et*-ee-on, king of Hypoplakian Thebes, father of Andromache

Ekhinos e-*kee*-nos, companion of Odysseus

Eteoneus et-ee-*ohn*-yoos, herald of Menelaus

Eurybates yoo-*rib*-a-teez, herald and comrade of Odysseus

Evadne e-*vad*-nee, handmaid of Cressida

Ganymedes ga-ni-*mee*-deez, Priam's great-uncle taken by the thunder god

Halizonians ha-li-*zoh*-nee-anz, a people northeast of Troy

Hatti *ha*-tee, internationally influential area east of Troy

Hekamede hek-a-*mee*-dee, Tenedan captive awarded to Nestor

Hektor *hek*-tor, eldest son of Priam and Hekuba, prince of Troy

Hekuba *he*-kyoo-ba, chief wife of Priam

Helen *he*-len, wife first of Menelaus and then of Paris

Helenus *he*-le-nus, seer son of Priam and Hekuba, Trojan prince, twin brother of Kassandra

Helikaon he-li-*kay*-on, son of Antenor, engaged to Laodike

Hemithea he-mi-*thee*-uh, sister of Tennes

Hephaistos hee-*fays*-tos, Achaean god of fire

Herakles *her*-a-kleez, greatest of Achaean heroes, father of Tlepolemus and Telephus

Hermione hur-*meye*-o-nee, daughter of Menelaus and Helen

Hesione he-*seye*-o-nee, sister of Priam captured by Herakles and awarded to Telemon by whom she bore Teukros

Hippolochus hi-*po*-loh-kus, son of Antimachus

Idaeus eye-*dee*-us, herald of Priam

Idas *eye*-das, Achaean hero, an Argonaut

Iolaus ee-oh-*lay*-us, king of Phylake

Ithaka *i*-tha-ka, island ruled by Odysseus

Jason *jay*-son, king of Iolchos who led the Argonauts on the quest for the Golden Fleece

Kalchas *kal*-kas, former Trojan priest, father of Cressida, brother of Pandarus

Kassandra ka-*san*-dra, seer daughter of Priam and Hekuba, twin sister of Helenus

Kastor *kas*-tor, brother of Helen, twin brother of Polydeukes

Kephisa ke-*fee*-sa, servant of Andromache

Kikones ki-*koh*-neez, a people of Thrace north of Troy

Kisseus *kis*-yoos, father of Theano

Klytemnestra kleye-tem-*nes*-tra, wife of Agamemnon and sister of Helen

Kolchis *kol*-kis, city on the eastern edge of the Black Sea

Kolophon *ko*-lo-phon, city in Pamphylia south of Troy

Koon *koh*-on, son of Antenor

Kreusa kree-*oo*-sa, eldest daughter of Priam and Hekuba, wife of Aeneas

Krimo *kreye*-mo, daughter of Antenor

Laertes lay-*er*-teez, father of Odysseus

Lakedaemon la-ke-*dee*-mon, area ruled by Menelaus

Laodamas lay-*o*-da-mas, son of Antenor

Laodike lay-*o*-di-kee, daughter of Priam and Hekuba, engaged to Helikaon

Larissa la-*ris*-a, city of the Pelasgians, allied to Troy

Leda *lee*-da, mother of Helen
Lemnos *lem*-nos, island northwest of Troy
Lesbos *lez*-bos, island southwest of Troy
Leukophrys lyoo-*koh*-fris, former name of the island of Tenedos
Lykia *li*-kee-a, area south of Troy ruled by Sarpedon
Lykians *lik*-yans, a people south of Troy ruled by Sarpedon
Machaon ma-*kay*-on, healer, king in Trikka, son of Asklepius, brother of Podalirius
Maeonians mee-*oh*-nee-anz, a people near Lake Gyge east of Troy
Medesikaste mee-des-i-*kas*-tee, daughter of Priam, wife of Imbrius
Medon *mee*-don, bastard son of Oileus, half brother of Little Ajax
Menelaus me-ne-*lay*-us, king of Lakedaemon, former husband of Helen, brother of
    Agamemnon
Menestheus me-*nes*-thyoos, king of Athens
Menoetius men-ee-shus, father of Patroklus
Mestor *mes*-tor, prince of Troy
Methone mee-*thoh*-nee, city ruled by Philoktetes
Mnemon *nee*-mon, guide assigned to Achilles by Thetis
Mycenae meye-*see*-nee, city ruled by Agamemnon
Mygdon *mig*-don, leader of the Phrygians
Myria *meye*-ree-a, alternate name for the area around Troy
Myrmidons *mur*-mi-donz, followers of Achilles, men ruled by Peleus of Phthia
Mysia *mi*-sha, area south of Troy ruled by Telephus
Nauplia *naw*-plee-uh, area ruled by Nauplius on coast of Argolid
Nauplius *naw*-plee-us, king of Nauplia, father of Palamedes and Oeax
Nea Chryse *nee*-a *kreye*-see, tiny island off the coast of Lemnos
Neleus *neel*-yoos, father of Nestor
Nereus *nee*-ree-us, Achaean god of ocean, father of Thetis
Nestor *nes*-tor, king of Pylos, father of Thrasymedes
Odysseus o-*dis*-yoos, king of Ithaka
Oeax *ee*-ax, prince of Nauplia, brother of Palamedes
Oeta *ee*-ta, mountain where Herakles burned upon a funeral pyre and where his
    apotheosis took place
Oileus oh-*eel*-yoos, father of Little Ajax and Medon
Olpides ol-*peye*-deez, servant of Paris
Paeonians pee-*oh*-nee-anz, a people northwest of Troy, beyond Thrace
Palamedes pa-la-*mee*-deez, prince of Nauplia; cousin of Agamemnon, Menelaus, and
    Idomeneus; brother of Oeax
Pamphylia pam-*fi*-lee-a, area on the coast south of Troy
Pandarus *pan*-da-rus, brother of Kalchas, uncle of Cressida
Paphlagonians pa-fla-*goh*-nee-anz, a people northeast of Troy
Paris *pa*-ris, prince of Troy, husband and lover of Helen
Patroklus pa-*trok*-lus, Achilles's closest companion
Pedaeus pe-*dee*-us, son of Antenor
Peirithous peye-*rith*-oh-us, Achaean hero, brother of Phisadie, father of Polypoetes
Peleus *peel*-yoos, father of Achilles, king of Phthia, former husband of Thetis
Perseus *per*-syoos, king of Dardanus
Peteos *pet*-ee-os, father of Menestheus
Philobia fi-loh-*bee*-a, wife of Perseus of Dardanus
Philoktetes fil-ok-*tee*-teez, king of Methone
Philomela fi-loh-*mee*-luh, daughter of Priam and Hekuba

Philomeleides fi-lo-me-*lee*-i-deez, a king on the island of Lesbos

Phineus *fin*-yoos, relative of Hekuba

Phisadie fi-sa-*deye*-ee, Helen's servant, aunt of Polypoetes, sister of Peirithous

Phrygia *fri*-ja, area northeast of Troy

Phrygians *fri*-jans, a people northeast of Troy

Phthia *ftheye*-a, area ruled by Peleus, home of Achilles

Pittheus *pit*-thyoos, former king of Troezen, father of Aithra, uncle of Agamemnon and Menelaus

Pleisthenes plee-*is*-the-neez, son of Helen and Menelaus

Podalirius po-da-*leye*-ree-us, healer, king in Trikka, son of Asklepius, brother of Machaon

Poias *poy*-as, father of Philoktetes, companion of Herakles

Polites po-*leye*-teez, prince of Troy

Polydeukes po-li-*dyoo*-keez, brother of Helen, twin brother of Kastor

Polypoetes po-li-*pee*-teez, son of Peirithous, nephew of Phisadie, king of the Lapiths of Argissa

Polyxena poh-*liks*-ee-na, daughter of Priam and Hekuba

Priam *preye*-am, king of Troy

Prokleia pro-*klee*-uh, mother of Tennes and Hemithea, half sister of Priam

Pylaemenes pi-*lee*-me-neez, leader of the Paphlagonians

Salamis *sa*-la-mis, island ruled by Telamon

Samothrake *sam*-oh-thray-kee, island west of Troy

Sarabana sa-ra-*bah*-na, a city west of Troy

Sarpedon sar-*pee*-don, king of Lykia

Sidon *seye*-don, city on the Levantine coast

Sisyphus *sis*-i-fus, Corinthian hero who outwitted the gods and was sentenced to forever push a stone up a hill only to have it roll to the bottom when he neared the summit; sometimes called the father of Odysseus

Skaean Gate *skee*-an, a gate of Troy

Skyros *skeye*-ros, island ruled by Lykomedes

Sparta *spar*-tuh, city ruled by Menelaus

Talthybius tal-*thi*-bee-us, herald of Agamemnon

Telamon *tel*-a-mon, king of Salamis, father of Great Ajax and Teukros

Telephus *te*-le-fus, king of Mysia, son of Herakles

Tenedan *ten*-e-den, of Tenedos

Tenedos *ten*-e-dos, island just off the coast southwest of Troy

Tennes *ten*-eez, king of Tenedos, brother of Hemithea

Teukros *tyoo*-kros, son of Telamon and Hesione, half brother of Great Ajax

Teuthrania tyooth-*rayn*-ya, city in Mysia where Telephus rules

Theano thee-*ay*-no, Trojan priestess, wife of Antenor

Thebes theebz, city ruled by Eetion

Thersites ther-*seye*-teez, cousin of Diomedes, ugliest Achaean

Theseus *thees*-yoos, an Achaean hero, former king of Athens, son of Aithra, father of Akamas and Demophoon

Thetis *thee*-tis, influential Achaean priestess, mother of Achilles, former wife of Peleus

Thrasymedes thra-si-*mee*-deez, son of Nestor

Troezen *tree*-zen, city once ruled by Pittheus

Troilus *troy*-lus, prince of Troy

Tyndareus tin-*dar*-yoos, father of Helen

Zeus zyoos, Achaean god of thunder

GENEALOGICAL CHART: THE ACHAEANS

Characters in bold appear and are named in *Betrayal Part One.*

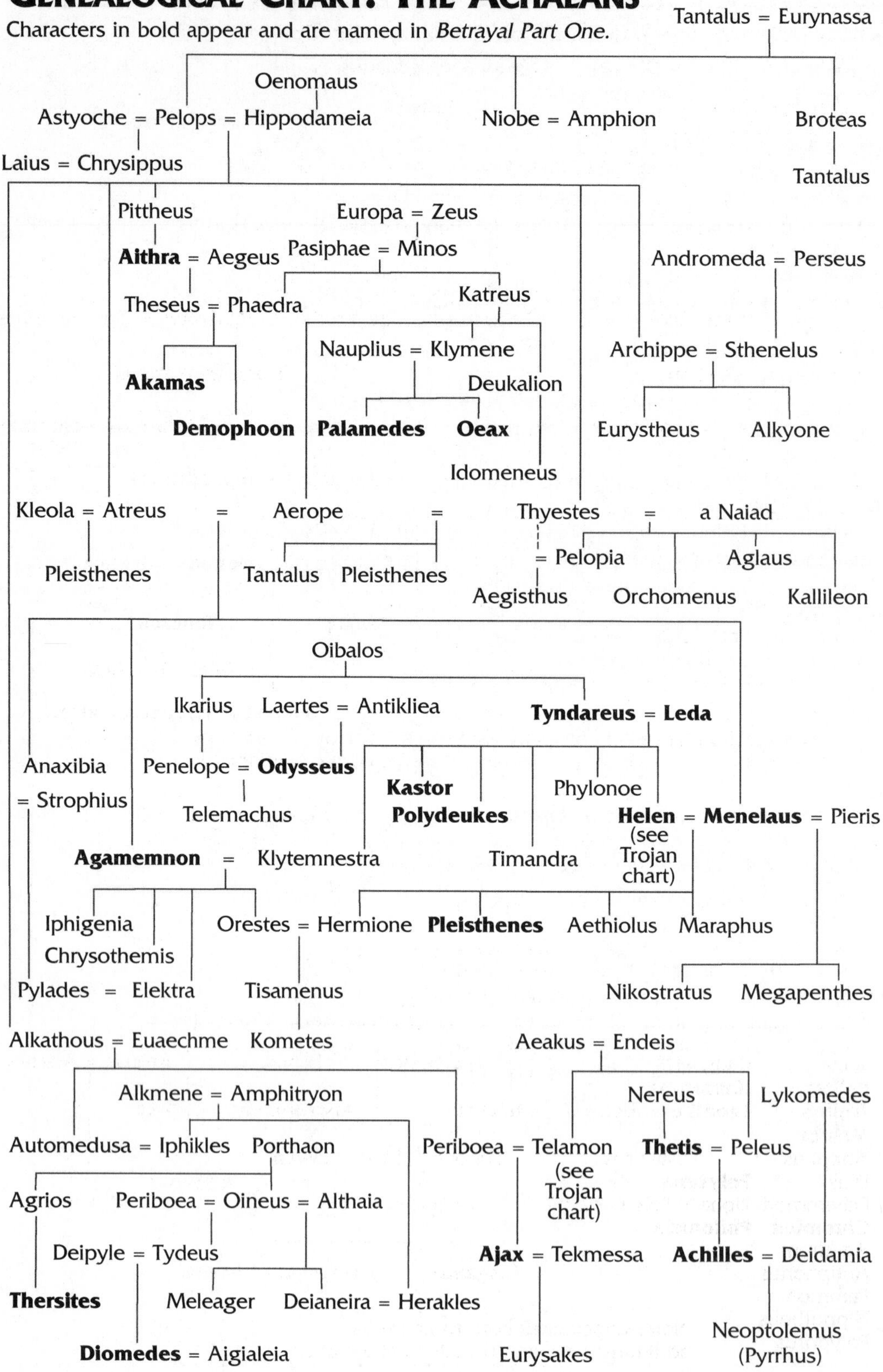
Tantalus = Eurynassa
Oenomaus
Astyoche = Pelops = Hippodameia
Niobe = Amphion
Broteas
Laius = Chrysippus
Tantalus
Pittheus
Europa = Zeus
Aithra = Aegeus
Pasiphae = Minos
Andromeda = Perseus
Theseus = Phaedra
Katreus
Nauplius = Klymene
Archippe = Sthenelus
Akamas
Deukalion
Demophoon
Palamedes
Oeax
Eurystheus
Alkyone
Idomeneus
Kleola = Atreus
=
Aerope
=
Thyestes
=
a Naiad
Pleisthenes
Tantalus
Pleisthenes
= Pelopia
Aglaus
Aegisthus
Orchomenus
Kallileon
Oibalos
Ikarius
Laertes = Antikliea
Tyndareus = Leda
Anaxibia
Penelope = Odysseus
Kastor
Phylonoe
= Strophius
Telemachus
Polydeukes
Helen = Menelaus = Pieris
(see Trojan chart)
Agamemnon
=
Klytemnestra
Timandra
Iphigenia
Orestes = Hermione
Pleisthenes
Aethiolus
Maraphus
Chrysothemis
Pylades = Elektra
Tisamenus
Nikostratus
Megapenthes
Alkathous = Euaechme
Kometes
Aeakus = Endeis
Alkmene = Amphitryon
Nereus
Lykomedes
Automedusa = Iphikles
Porthaon
Periboea = Telamon
Thetis = Peleus
(see Trojan chart)
Agrios
Periboea = Oineus = Althaia
Deipyle = Tydeus
Ajax = Tekmessa
Achilles = Deidamia
Thersites
Meleager
Deianeira = Herakles
Neoptolemus (Pyrrhus)
Diomedes = Aigialeia
Eurysakes

Genealogical Chart: The Trojan Royal Family

Characters in bold appear and are named in *Betrayal Part One.*

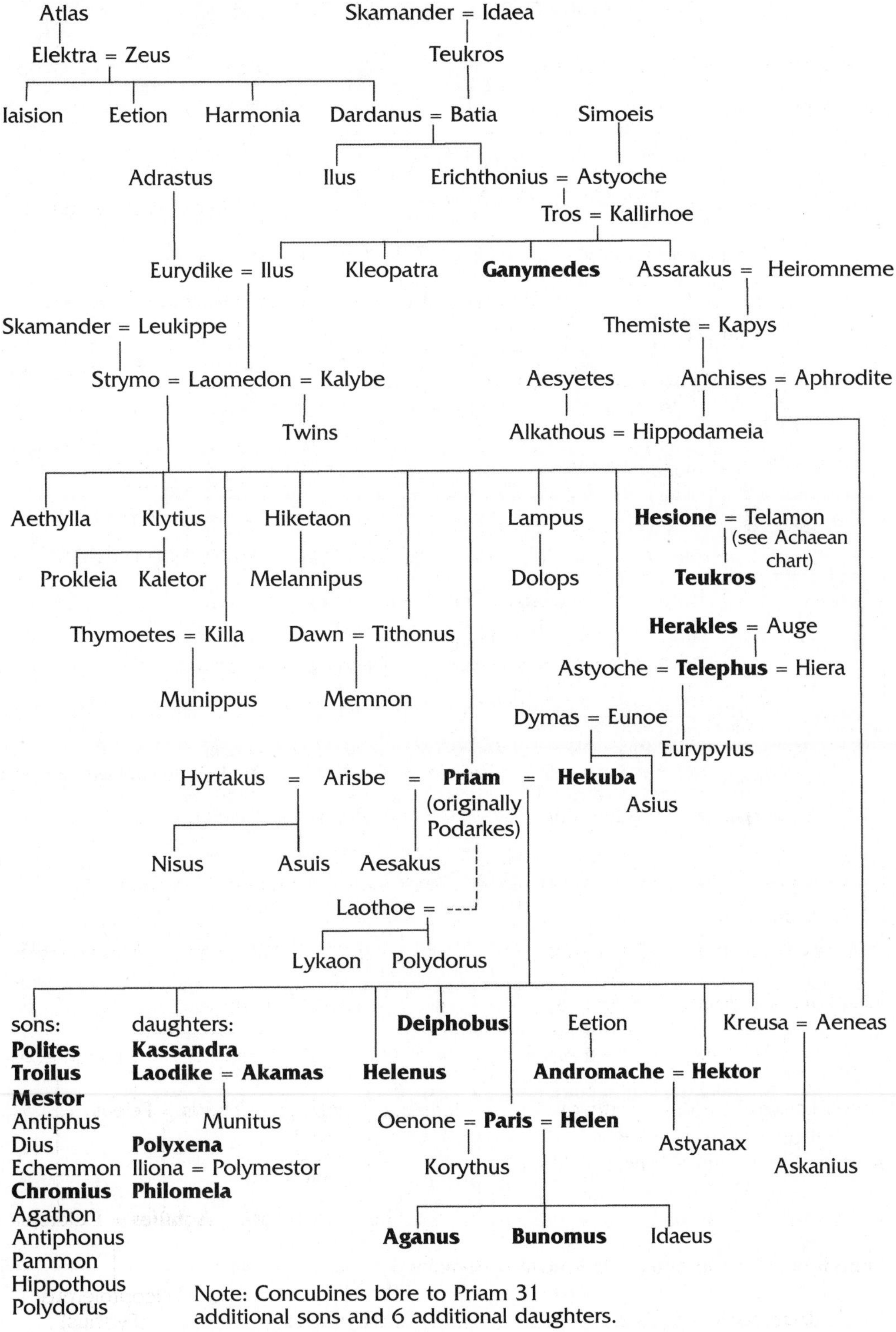

Atlas
Skamander = Idaea
Elektra = Zeus
Teukros
Iaision
Eetion
Harmonia
Dardanus = Batia
Simoeis
Adrastus
Ilus
Erichthonius = Astyoche
Tros = Kallirhoe
Eurydike = Ilus
Kleopatra
Ganymedes
Assarakus = Heiromneme
Skamander = Leukippe
Themiste = Kapys
Strymo = Laomedon = Kalybe
Aesyetes
Anchises = Aphrodite
Twins
Alkathous = Hippodameia
Aethylla
Klytius
Hiketaon
Lampus
Hesione = Telamon
(see Achaean chart)
Prokleia
Kaletor
Melannipus
Dolops
Teukros
Herakles = Auge
Thymoetes = Killa
Dawn = Tithonus
Astyoche = **Telephus** = Hiera
Munippus
Memnon
Dymas = Eunoe
Eurypylus
Hyrtakus = Arisbe = **Priam** = **Hekuba**
(originally Podarkes)
Asius
Nisus
Asuis
Aesakus
Laothoe =
Lykaon
Polydorus
sons:
Polites
Troilus
Mestor
Antiphus
Dius
Echemmon
Chromius
Agathon
Antiphonus
Pammon
Hippothous
Polydorus
daughters:
Kassandra
Laodike = **Akamas**
Munitus
Polyxena
Iliona = Polymestor
Philomela
Deiphobus
Helenus
Eetion
Andromache = **Hektor**
Kreusa = Aeneas
Oenone = **Paris** = **Helen**
Korythus
Astyanax
Askanius
Aganus
Bunomus
Idaeus

Note: Concubines bore to Priam 31 additional sons and 6 additional daughters.

BIBLIOGRAPHY

The following list of sources is an addendum to the lists in previous volumes.

THE STORY

ABBA. "Cassandra." *The Visitors.* Cd. Polar Music Production. 314 549 965-2, 2001.

Aelian. *Historical Miscellany.* Loeb Classical Library 486. Trans. N.G. Wilson. Cambridge and London: Harvard University Press, 1997.

Agamemnon. By Euripides. Grass Roots Greeks, San Diego. 14 Feb 2005.

Ajax. By Sophocles. Dir. Forrest Aylsworth. Trans. Marianne McDonald. 21 Jan 2006.

Alfred, William. *Agamemnon.* New York: Alfred A. Knopf, 1954.

Allan, Tony, and Piers Vitebsky. *Triumph of the Hero: Greek and Roman Myth.* Amsterdam: Time-Life Books BV, 1998.

Ariosto, Ludovico. "Canto 20" in *Orlando Furioso.* 9 Feb 2002. Project Gutenberg. 1999. <http://www.gutenberg.org/dirs/etext96/orfur10.txt>

Benjamin, S.G.W. *Troy, its Legends, History and Literature.* Epochs of Ancient History. New York: Charles Scribner's Sons, 1880.

Bennett, Florence Mary. "Chapter 1: The Amazons in Greek Legend" in *Religious Cults Associated With the Amazons.* Ed. John Bruno Hare. 6 Jan 2004. The Sacred Texts Archive. Jan 2007. <http://www.sacred-texts.com/wmn/rca/rca02.htm>

Bespaloff, Rachel. "On the Iliad" in *War and The Iliad.* New York: New York Review of Books, 2005, 39-100.

Bion. "Myrson and Lycidas" in *The Greek Bucolic Poets.* Loeb Classical Library 28. Trans. J.M. Edmonds. Cambridge and London: Harvard University Press, 1928.

Boitani, Piero. *The European Tragedy of Troilus.* Oxford: Clarendon Press, 1989.

Brown, Joseph M. *Astyanax, an Epic Romance of Ilion, Atlantis, and Amaraca.* New York: Broadway Publishing Co., 1907.

Brown, Malcolm Kenneth. Commentary. *The Narratives of Konon.* Munchen and Leipzig: K.G. Saur, 2002.

Buchthal, Hugo. *Historia Troiana.* London: The Warburg Institute, University of London; Leiden: E.J. Brill, 1971.

Cavafy, C.P. "The Horses of Achilles," "The Funeral of Sarpedon," "Interruption," "Unfaithfulness," and "Trojans" in *Collected Poems.* Trans. Edmund Keeley and Philip Sherrard. Princeton: Princeton University Press, 1975, 5, 7-8, 13, 16, 21.

Chaucer, Geoffrey. "The Hous of Fame" in *The Complete Works of Geoffrey Chaucer 3.* 1899. Oxford: Clarendon Press, 1972.

Cheney, David. *Son of Minos.* New York: Robert M. McBride and Company, 1930.

Christodorus of Thebes in Egypt. *Greek Anthology 1.* Loeb Classical Library 67. Trans. W.R. Paton. Cambridge: Harvard University Press, 1916.

The Conspiracy of Aeneas and Antenor Against the State of Troy. London: Printed for John Spicer, 1682.

Delle Colonne, Guido. *Historia Destructionis Troiae.* Trans. Mary Elizabeth Meek. Bloomington, IN, and London: Indiana University Press, 1974.

Diane-Myrick, Leslie. *From the De Excidio Troiae Historia to the Togail Troi.* Heidelberg: Universitatsverlag C. Winter, 1993.

Diodorus of Sicily. *The Library of History 3.* Loeb Classical Library 340. Trans. C.H. Oldfather. Cambridge and London: Harvard University Press, 1993.

Dionysius of Halicarnassus: Roman Antiquities. *LacusCurtius.* Ed. Bill Thayer. 15 March 2006. University of Chicago. 24 August 2007. <http://penelope.uchicago.edu/Thayer/E/Roman/Texts/Dionysius_of_Halicarnassus/home.html>

Donald, Lea. *A Daughter of the Gods.* New York: The Grafton Press, 1906.

Drinkwater, John. "X=O: a Night of the Trojan War" in *A Book of One-Act Plays.* By Drinkwater. London: Allenson and Co. Ltd., 1936, 11-23.

Dryden, John. *Dryden: The Dramatic Works 5.* Ed. Montague Summers. London: The Nonesuch Press, 1932.

The Eumenides. By Aeschylus. Trans. Robert Fagles. Grass Roots Greeks, San Diego, 15 Sept 2002.

Euripides. "Rhesus," "Orestes," and "Iphigenia in Aulis" in *Euripides 4.* The Complete Greek Tragedies. Trans. Richmond Lattimore, et. al. Chicago and London: The University of Chicago Press, 1958.

—. *The Nineteen Tragedies and Fragments of Euripides.* Trans. Michael Wodhull. London: John Walker; T. Payne; Vernor, Hood, & Sharpe; et. al., 1809.

Fraker, Charles F. *The Libro de Alexandre: Medieval Epic and Silver Latin.* Chapel Hill: North Carolina Studies in The Romance Languages and Literatures, 1993.

Giraudoux, Jean. *Tiger at the Gates.* Trans. Christopher Fry. New York: Samuel French, Inc., n.d.

Gluck, Christophe Willibald. *Paride ed Elena.* Cd. Libretto by Raniero de' Calzabigi. With Magdalena Kozena and Susan Gritton. Cond. Paul McCreesh. Archiv Produktion. 00289 477 5415, 2005.

Good Breeding. Writer and Dir. Robert O'Hara. University of California, San Diego Theatre and Dance. Mandell Weiss Theatre, La Jolla. 23 Feb 2007.

Gower, John. *Confessio Amantis.* Trans. Terence Tiller. Baltimore: Penguin Books, 1963.

Green, R.P.H. Commentary and Notes. *The Works of Ausonius.* Decimus Magnus Ausonius. Oxford: Clarendon Press, 1991.

Hecuba. By Euripides. Dir. Esther Emery. Trans. Marianne McDonald. 6th@Penn Theatre, San Diego. 10 Dec 2004.

—. By Euripides. Dir. Linda Castro. Trans. William Arrowsmith. Grass Roots Greeks, San Diego. 10 Jan 2005.

Helen. By Euripides. Dir. Linda Castro. Grass Roots Greeks, San Diego. 14 March 2005.

Herodotus. *The Histories.* Trans. Robin Waterfield. Oxford and New York: Oxford University Press, 1998.

Howard, Donald R., and James Dean, eds. *Scene Outline of Chaucer's Troilus.* 2 August 2001. Jan 2006. <http://www174.pair.com/mja/tranal.html>

Hyginus. *Fabulae.* Trans. Jennifer Stewart. Unpublished work.

Iphigenia at Aulis. By Euripides. Dir. Douglas Lay. Trans. Marianne McDonald. 6th@Penn Theater. 14 July 2006.

—. By Euripides. Dir. Rosina Reynolds. Trans. Marianne McDonald. University of San Diego, San Diego. 30 June 2004.

Isocrates. "Encomium of Helen" in *Isocrates 1.* Trans. David Mirhady. Austin: University of Texas Press, 2000, 31-48.

James, Heather. *Shakespeare's Troy.* Cambridge: Cambridge University Press, 1997.

Kastan, David Scott, and Tom Dale Keever. " 'To End a Tale at Length': Pandarus' Epilogue, Act V Scene II." *Troilus and Cressida.* 19 Oct 2004. Theatre for a New Audience. Jan 2006. <http://www.tfana.org/2001/troilus/troilus09.htm>

Kellogg, Laura D. *Boccaccio's and Chaucer's Cressida.* New York: Peter Lang, 1995.

Lafferty, Maura K. *Walter of Chatillon's Alexandreis: Epic and the Problem of Historical Understanding.* N.p.: The Medieval Latin Association of North America, 1998.

Landor, Walter Savage. "Corythos" and Notes in *The Poetical Works 1.* Ed. Stephen Wheeler. Oxford: The Clarendon Press, 1937,103-119, 500-511.

—. "The Shades of Agamemnon and Iphigenia," "Menelaus and Helen at Troy," "Achilles and Helena on Ida," "The Altar of Modesty," "The Espousals of Polyxena," "The Marriage of Helena and Menelaos," and Notes in *The Poetical Works 2.* Ed. Stephen Wheeler. Oxford: The Clarendon Press, 1937, 79-85, 91-94, 97-101, 203-210, 214-219, 234-238, 502-507, 529-540.

Lang, Andrew. *Helen of Troy.* McLean, VA: IndyPublish.com, n.d.

Lewis, C. S. *The Allegory of Love.* New York: Oxford University Press, 1936.

The Libation Bearers. By Aeschylus. Trans. Robert Fagles. Grass Roots Greeks, San Diego. 9 June 2002.

Louden, Bruce. *The Iliad: Structure, Myth, and Meaning.* Baltimore: The Johns Hopkins University Press, 2006.

McCarty, Nick. *Troy, the Myth and Reality Behind this Epic Legend.* New York: Barnes and Noble Books, 2004.

Meen, Rev. H. *Remarks on the Cassandra of Lycophron, a Monody.* London: Bunney & Gold, 1800.

Moncrieff, A.R. Hope. *A Treasury of Classical Mythology.* New York: Barnes and Noble Books, 1992.

Monro, Thomas. *Philoctetes in Lemnos. A Drama, in Three Acts.* London: Printed for William Bingley, 1795.

Mourning Becomes Electra. 1978. Dir. Nick Havinga. By Eugene O'Neill. Image Entertainment, 2001.

Offenbach, Jacques. *La Belle Helene.* Trans. unidentified. Boston: Oliver Ditson Company, n.d.

Orestes. By Euripides. Dir. Linda Castro. Trans. William Arrowsmith. Grass Roots Greeks. 6th@Penn Theatre, San Diego. 7 June 2004.

Ovid. *Metamorphoses.* Trans. Charles Martin. New York and London: W.W. Norton and Co., 2004.

Papp, Joseph. "Directing *Troilus and Cressida*" in *Troilus and Cressida.* By William Shakespeare. New York: The Macmillan Company; London: Collier-Macmillan Limited, 1967, 23-72.

Parada, Carlos. Map: Achaeans and Trojans. *Greek Mythology Link.* 18 Sept 1997. 1998. <http://www.maicar.com/GML/MapAchaeansTrojans.html>

Paris. Cd. English, Jon, and David Mackay. With John Parr. Paris Music Ltd. PML001/2, 1990.

Pausanius. *Description of Greece 4.* Loeb Classical Library 297. Trans. W.H.S. Jones. Cambridge: Harvard University Press, 1918.

The Perseus Digital Library. Ed. Gregory Crane. 24 August 2007. Department of the Classics, Tufts University. 1999. <http://www.perseus.tufts.edu/>

Pinsent, John. *Greek Mythology.* New York: Peter Bedrick Books, 1982.

Plato. *The Collected Dialogues of Plato.* Eds. Edith Hamilton and Huntington Cairns. Princeton: Princeton University Press, 1961.

Rossetti, Gabriel Charles Dante. "Sonnet 87: Death's Songsters," "Cassandra," and "Troy Town" in *The Works.* Ed. William. M. Rossetti. Hildesheim and New York: George Olms Verlag, 1972, 103, 213, 214-216.

Sackville, Thomas, Lord Buckhurst and Earl of Dorset. "Induction" in *The Poetical Works.* London: C. Chapple, 1820, 133-134.

Section 2: The Scythian Amazons. Jan 2007. <http://www.lisasmedman.topcities.com/Amazon02.pdf>

Shepard, Alan, and Stephen D. Powell, eds. *Fantasies of Troy.* Toronto: Centre for Reformation and Renaissance Studies, 2004.

Smith, J.C., ed. "When stout Achilles . . ." (Commendatory verse by W.L.) in *Spenser's Faerie Queene 2.* Oxford: The Clarendon Press, 1909, 490-491.

Smith, Ole L. Introduction and Commentary. *The Byzantine Achilleid: The Naples Version.* Wiener Byzantinistische Studien Band XXI. Eds. Panagiotis A. Agapitos and Karin Hult. Wien: Verlag der Osterreichishen Akademie der Wissenschaften, 1999.

Spenser, Edmund. "Virgil's Gnat" in *Shorter Poems of Edmund Spenser.* New Haven and London: Yale University Press, 1989, 316-323.

Stephen A. Barney, ed. *Troilus and Criseyde with Facing-page Il Filostrato.* A Norton Critical Edition. New York and London: W.W. Norton and Company, 2006.

Theocritus. "Idyll 18" in *Theocritus, Bion and Moschus Rendered into English Prose with an Introductory Essay by Andrew Lang.* Trans. Lang. 16 March 2002. Project Gutenberg. Feb 2007. <http://www.gutenberg.org/dirs/etext03/thbm10.txt>

—. "Idyll XVIII" in *Greek Bucolic Poets.* Loeb Classical Library 28. Trans. J.M. Edmonds. Cambridge and London: Harvard University Press, 1928.

—. *The Idylls of Theocritus with the Fragments of Bion and Moschus.* Trans. J.H. Hallard. London: George Routledge & Sons, Ltd.; New York: E.P. Dutton & Co., n.d.

Thomas, Carol G., and Craig Conant. *The Trojan War.* Westport, CT, and London: Greenwood Press, 2005.

Thompson, Diane P. *The Trojan War.* Jefferson, NC, and London: McFarland & Company, Inc., 2004.

Townsend, David, trans. *The Alexandreis of Walter of Chatillon: A Twelfth Century Epic.* Philadelphia: University of Pennsylvania Press, 1996.

The Trojan Horse. 1962. Dir. Giorgio Ferroni. With Steve Reeves. Trimark Home Video, 2000.

The Trojan Women. By Euripides. Dir. Linda Castro. Trans. Marianne McDonald. Grass Roots Greeks, San Diego. 13 Dec 2004.

Troy. Dir. Wolfgang Petersen. With Brad Pitt, Eric Bana, Peter O'Toole. Warner Bros., 2004.

Valasca, Merina. *The Amazons.* Hod Hasharon, Israel: Astrolog Publishing House, 2005.

Valerius Flaccus. *Argonautica.* Loeb Classical Library 286. Trans. J.H. Mozley. Cambridge: Harvard University Press; London: William Heinemann Ltd., 1972.

Vegio, Maffeo. *Short Epics.* The I Tatti Renaissance Library. Ed. and trans. Michael C.J. Putnam with James Hankins. Cambridge and London: Harvard University Press, 2004

Ward, Anne G. *The Quest for Theseus.* New York, Washington, and London: Praeger Publishers, 1970.

Windeatt, Barry. *Troilus and Criseyde.* Oxford Guides to Chaucer. Oxford: Clarendon Press, 1992.

The Settings in General

Archaologisches Landesmuseum Baden-Wurttemberg, et. al. *Troia, Traum und Wirklichkeit.* Stuttgart: Konrad Theiss Verlag GmbH, 2001.

Balfour, Henry. "The Archer's Bow in the Homeric Poems" in *The Journal of the Royal Anthropological Institute of Great Britain and Ireland 51* (July-Dec 1921): 289-309.

Barber, R.L.N. *The Cyclades in the Bronze Age.* Iowa City: University of Iowa Press, 1987.

Bozcaada—Tenedos. 11 August 2007. Ada Cafe—AdaTurizm. Feb 2005. <http://www.bozcaada.info/main.html>

Bronze Age Shipwreck Excavation at Cape Gelidonya. Project Dir. George F. Bass. 28 Feb 2003. Texas A&M University. 2006. <http://ina.tamu.edu/capegelidonya.htm>

Bronze Age Shipwreck Excavation at Uluburun. Project Dirs. Cemal Pulak and George F. Bass. 11 Sept 2006. Texas A&M University. 2006. <http://ina.tamu.edu/ub_main.htm>

Carter, Jane B., and Sarah P. Morris, eds. *The Ages of Homer.* Austin: University of Texas Press, 1995.

Casson, Lionel. *The Greek Conquerors.* Treasures of the World. Chicago: Stonehenge Press, 1981.

Cistern on Crete. 31 Oct 1998. 2006. <http://www.uk.digiserve.com/mentor/minoan/pyrgos4b.jpg>

Davis, Jack L. "Minos and Dexithea: Crete and the Cyclades in the Late Bronze Age" in *Papers in Cycladic Prehistory.* Eds. Jack L. Davis and John R. Cherry. Los Angeles: Institute of Archaeology, University of California, Los Angeles, n.d., 148-179.

Easton, D.F. "Hittite History and the Trojan War" in *The Trojan War: Its Historicity and Context.* Eds. Lin Foxhall and John K. Davies. Bristol: Bristol Classics Press, 1984, 23-37.

—. Discussion. *The Trojan War: Its Historicity and Context.* Eds. Lin Foxhall and John K. Davies. Bristol: Bristol Classics Press, 1984, 57-61.

Fields, Nic. *Bronze Age War Chariots.* Oxford: Osprey Publishing, 2006.

Fleischman, John. "Homer's Bones" in *Discover* (July 2002): 58-65.

In Search of the Trojan War. 1985. Writer and presenter Michael Wood. Warner Bros. and BBC, 2004.

Jones, Bernice. "The Minoan 'Snake Goddess.' New Interpretations of her Costume and Identity" in *Potnia: Deities and Religion in the Aegean Bronze Age. Aegaeum 22.* Liege: Universite de Liege, 2001, 259-65.

—. "Veils and Mantles: An Investigation of the Construction and Function of the Costumes of the Veiled Dancer from Thera and the Camp Stool Banqueter from Knossos" in *Metron; Measuring the Aegean Bronze Age. Aegaeum 24.* Eds. Foster and Laffineur. Liege and Austin: University de Liege, University of Texas at Austin, 2003, 441-449, plates LXXXIV-XC.

"Lesson 23: Troy VI" in *Prehistoric Archaeology of the Aegean.* 18 March 2000. Foundation of the Hellenic World and Dartmouth College. 2000. <http://projectsx.dartmouth.edu/history/bronze_age/lessons/les/23.html>

Mark, Samuel. *Homeric Seafaring.* College Station: Texas A&M University Press, 2005.

McLeod, Wallace E. "Egyptian Composite Bows in New York" in *American Journal of Archaeology 66.1* (Jan 1962): 13-19.

Mee, C.B. "The Mycenaeans and Troy" in *The Trojan War: Its Historicity and Context.* Eds. Lin Foxhall and John K. Davies. Bristol: Bristol Classics Press, 1984, 45-56.

Melchert, H. Craig. *Mycenaean and Hittite Diplomatic Correspondence: Fact and Fiction.* 2 Aug 2007. University of North Carolina at Chapel Hill. 2006. <http://www.unc.edu/~melchert/montreal-text.pdf>

Mountjoy, Penelope. *Regional Mycenaean Decorated Pottery.* Rahden/Weste: Verlag Marie Leidorf GmbH, 1999.

Mylonas, Georgios E. *O Taphikos Kyklos B Ton Mykenon.* (Vol. B.) Athens: Athens Archaeological Society, 1972.

Nestor: Bibliography of Aegean Prehistory and Related Areas. 27 Feb 2004. Department of Classics, University of Cincinnati. 15 Nov 2005. <http://classics.uc.edu/nestor/>

Robbins, Manuel. *Collapse of the Bronze Age.* San Jose, New York, Lincoln, Shanghai: Authors Choice Press, 2001.

Sahin, Haluk. *The Bozcaada Book.* Trans. Ayse A. Sahin. Mugla, Turkey: Troya Publishing, 2005.

Sahlas, Demetrios J., MD, MSc. "Functional Neuroanatomy in the Pre-Hippocratic Era: Observations from the *Iliad* of Homer" in *Neurosurgery 48.6* (June 2001): 1352-1357.

Salimbeti, Andrea. *The Greek Age of Bronze.* 14 Jan 2007. 6 May 2007. <http://www.salimbeti.com/micenei/index.htm>

Steel, Louise. *Arediou-Vouppes, Cyprus.* 20 August 2007. Department of Archaeology and Anthropology, University of Wales, Lampeter. Jan 2007. <http://www.lamp.ac.uk/archanth/staff/louise/arediou-vouppes.htm>

Stillman, Nigel. *Chariot Wars.* N.p.: Warhammer, 1999.

Terzioglu, Nihat. *Bozcaada (Tenedos).* 6 April 2007. 2006. <http://www.bozcaadatenedos.com/Tenedos_Eng/aboutus.htm>

Troy: Ancient Myths and Unsolved Mysteries. Dir. Tim Baney. National Geographic, 2004.

Troy: Myth or Reality? Eagle Media, 2004.

Troy: The True Story of Love, Power, Honor and the Pursuit of Glory. Delta Entertainment, 2004.

Troy: Unearthing the Legend. The History Channel, 2004.

Wachsmann, Shelley. "Some Notes on Drawing the Bow" in *Eretz Israel.* Ephraim Stern volume. In press.

Winkler, Martin M., ed. *Troy from Homer's Iliad to Hollywood Epic.* Malden, MA, Oxford, and Carlton, VIC: Blackwell Publishing, 2007.

Yasur-Landau, Assaf. "Old Wine in New Vessels: Intercultural Contact, Innovation and Aegean, Canaanite and Philistine Foodways" in *Tel Aviv 32.2*, 2005, 168-191.

Troy and the Trojans

Askin, Mustafa. *Troy with Legends, Facts, and New Developments.* Rev. ed. Istanbul: Keskin Color Kartpostalcilik Ltd. Sti. Matbaasi, 2006.

Aslan, Rustem, and Christoph Haussner. *Troia: Neue Spuren Zwischen Alten Mauern.* Remshalden, Germany: Verlag Ernhard Albert Greiner, 2004.

Brandau, Birgit, Hartmut Schickert, and Peter Jablonka. *Resimlerle Troya.* Ankara: Arkadas, 2004.

Bryce, Trevor. *The Trojans and Their Neighbors.* London and New York: Routledge, 2006.

Chandler, Graham. "In Search of the Real Troy" in *Saudi Aramco World 56.1* (Jan/Feb 2005): 2-11.

Cook, J.M. *The Troad: an Archaeological and Topographical Study.* Oxford: The Clarendon Press, 1973.

Fields, Nic. *Troy c. 1700-1250 BC.* Fortress 17. Oxford: Osprey Publishing, 2004.

Jablonka, Peter, and Steffen Kirchner. Reconstructions. Troy VI. *Troy VR.* 19 June 2004. Universitat Tubingen. Jan 2006. <http://www.uni-tuebingen.de/troia/vr/vr0207_en.html>

Jablonka, Peter. *Friends of Troy Newsletter.* Oct 2005. Privately printed.

Korfmann, Manfred O. *Friends of Troy Newsletter.* Oct 2004. Privately printed.

—. "Troia, an Ancient Anatolian Palatial and Trading Center: Archaeological Evidence for the Period of Troia VI/VII" in *The World of Troy: Homer, Schliemann, and the Treasures of Priam.* Washington, DC: Society for the Preservation of the Greek Heritage, 1997.

—. *Troia in Light of New Research.* Redenan der Universitat. Trans. Joan Clough and William Aylward. Trier, Germany: Universitat Trier, 2004.

—. *Troia/Wilusa.* Canakkale, Turkey, and Tubingen, Germany: Canakkale-Tubingen Troia Vakfi, 2005.

—, and Brian Rose. *Friends of Troy Newsletter.* Autumn 2002. Privately printed.

—, and Brian Rose. "How Big Was Troy" in *Current World Archaeology 1.1* (Sept 2003): 52-60.

Latacz, Joachim. *Troy and Homer: Towards a Solution of an Old Mystery.* Trans. Kevin Wandle and Rosh Ireland. Oxford: Oxford University Press, 2004.

—. *Wilusa (Wilios/Troia). Centre of a Hittite Confederate in North-West Asia Minor.* Trans. Joan Clough-Laube. 21 Nov 2001. Universitat Tubingen. March 2006. <http://www.uni-tuebingen.de/troia/eng/lataczwilusaeng.pdf>

Pernicka, Ernst, and Peter Jablonka. *Friends of Troy Newsletter.* Fall 2006. Privately printed.

Projekt Troia. Eds. Hans G. Jansen and John Wallrodt. 27 April 2007. Institut fur Ur- und Fruhgeschichte und Archaologie des Mittelalters, Universitat Tubingen; Department of Classics, University of Cincinnati. April 1998. <http://www.uni-tuebingen.de/troia/eng/index.html>

Rose, Brian. "Built to Last" in *Dig: Homer's World.* Peru, IL: Cobblestone Publishing Company, 2004, 10-12.

Schliemann, Heinrich. *Troy and Its Remains.* 1875. New York: Arno Press, 1976.

Studia Troica. Band 12. Mainz am Rhein: Verlag Philipp Von Zabern, 2002.

—. Band 13. Mainz am Rhein: Verlag Philipp Von Zabern, 2003.

—. Band 14. Mainz am Rhein: Verlag Philipp Von Zabern, 2004.

—. Band 15. Mainz am Rhein: Verlag Philipp Von Zabern, 2005.

—. Band 16. Mainz am Rhein: Verlag Philipp Von Zabern, 2006.

Troy. *Metis.* Ed. Bruce Hartzler. 24 August 2007. Stoa.org. 12 May 2007. <http://www.stoa.org/metis/cgi-bin/qtvr?site=troy;node=6>

Troy VI: A Trading Center and Commercial City? Online discussion forum. 25 April 2005. American Journal of Archaeology. 2006. <http://www.ajaonline.org/forum/viewforum.php?f=1&sid=0b0d77ae02df231026ef9f6e466adbde>

Wagner, Gunther A., Ernst Pernicka, and Hans-Peter Uerpmann. *Troia and the Troad: Scientific Approaches.* Berlin: Springer, 2003.

Yayinlari, Ege. *A Guide to Troia.* Istanbul: Arslanyatagi Sok, 2001.

Zoller, Wolfgang, and Rosemarie Ackermann. *Troia: 3000 Jahre Geschichte im Modell.* Cd-rom. Theiss, n.d.

The Mycenaeans

Blegen, Carl. W., and Marion Rawson. *A Guide to the Palace of Nestor.* Revised by Jack L. Davis and Cynthia W. Shelmerdine. Princeton: American School of Classical Studies at Athens, 2001.

Blegen, Carl. W., Marion Rawson, Lord William Taylour, and William P. Donovan. *The Palace of Nestor at Pylos in Western Messenia 3.* Princeton: Princeton University Press, 1973.

Castleden, Rodney. *Mycenaeans.* London and New York: Routledge, 2005.

Davis, Jack L., ed. *Sandy Pylos: An Archaeological History from Nestor to Navarino.* Austin: The University of Texas Press, 1998.

Davis, Jack, and Sharon Stocker. "Bony Clues" in *Dig: Homer's World*. Peru, IL: Cobblestone Publishing Company, 2004, 24-26.

Fields, Nic. *Mycenaean Citadels c.1350-1200 BC*. Oxford: Osprey Publishing, 2004.

Gallery. *The Thera Foundation*. 24 August 2007. The Thera Foundation and Idryma Theras. August 2007. <http://www.therafoundation.org/gallery/>

Grguric, Nicolas. *The Mycenaeans c. 1650-1100 BC*. Oxford: Osprey Publishing, 2005.

Hitchcock, Louise A. "The Minoan Hall System: Writing the Present out of the Past" in *Meaningful Architecture: Social Interpretations of Buildings*. Ed. Martin Locock. Aldershot, Brookfield, Hong Kong, Singapore, Sydney: Avebury, 1994, 16-44.

—. "Understanding the Minoan Palaces" in *Athena Review 3.3:* 27-35.

Hood, Sinclair. *The Arts in Prehistoric Greece*. New Haven and London: Yale University Press, 1978.

Maggidis, Christofilis. "The 'Telltale' Vase" in *Dig: Homer's World*. Peru, IL: Cobblestone Publishing Company, 2004, 22-23.

Marakas, Gemma. "Sanctuaries and their surroundings: The role of 'space' in the religion of the LBA to EIA of Greece" in *Rosetta 2*. Spring 2007. University of Birmingham. 24 August 2007. <http://www.rosetta.bham.ac.uk/Issue_02/Marakas.htm>

Nilsson, Martin P. *Homer and Mycenae*. 1933. New York: Cooper Square Publishers, Inc., 1968.

The Pylos Project. *Minnesota Archaeological Researches in the Western Peloponessus*. Ed. Michael Nelson. 1991. University of Minnesota. June 2004. <http://clvl.cla.umn.edu/marwp/index.html>

The Pylos Regional Archaeological Project. Ed. Sebastian Heath. 2005. Department of Classics, University of Cincinnati. 15 Nov 2005. <http://classics.uc.edu/prap/>

Renfrew, Colin. *The Archaeology of Cult: The Sanctuary at Phylakopi*. London: The British School of Archaeology at Athens, Thames and Hudson, 1985.

Urso, Carmelo. *Philoctetes' Disease*. 17 July 2005. October 2005. <http://xoomer.alice.it/cylagu/ML pag03eng.html>

—. *The Achaean Disease*. 17 July 2005. October 2005. <http://xoomer.alice.it/cylagu/MLpag02eng.html>

Wright, James C., ed. *The Mycenaean Feast. Hesperia: The Journal of the American School of Classical Studies at Athens 73.2* (2004). Princeton: American School of Classical Studies at Athens, 2004.

The Characters

Commager, Steele, ed. *Virgil, a Collection of Critical Essays*. Englewood Cliffs, NJ: Prentice-Hall, Inc., 1966.

Cotroneo, Christian. *Pandarus, the Broker*. 16 Sept 2001. Luminarium. Jan 2006. <http://www.luminarium.org/medlit/pandarus.htm>

Hughes, Bettany. *Helen of Troy, Goddess, Princess, Whore*. New York: Alfred A. Knopf, 2005.

Pugh, Tison. "Queer Pandarus? Silence and sexual ambiguity in Chaucer's *Troilus and Criseyde*" in *Philological Quarterly 80.1* (Winter 2001): 17-36. 30 Nov 2005. Jan 2006. <http://www.geocities.com/salferrat/chaucpugh2.htm>

Redfield, James M. *Nature and Culture in the Iliad*. Durham and London: Duke University Press, 1994.

Shoaf, R.A. "Chapter 8: Pandarus" in *Dante, Chaucer, and the Currency of the Word: Money, Images, and Reference in Late Medieval Poetry*. Pilgrim Books, 1983. 29 April 1999. Jan 2006. <http://www.clas.ufl.edu/users/rashoaf/currency/eight.html>

Slatkin, Laura M. *The Power of Thetis: Allusion and Interpretation in The Iliad*. Berkeley: University of California Press, 1991.

Suzuki, Mihoko. *Metamorphoses of Helen*. Ithaca and London: Cornell University Press, 1989.

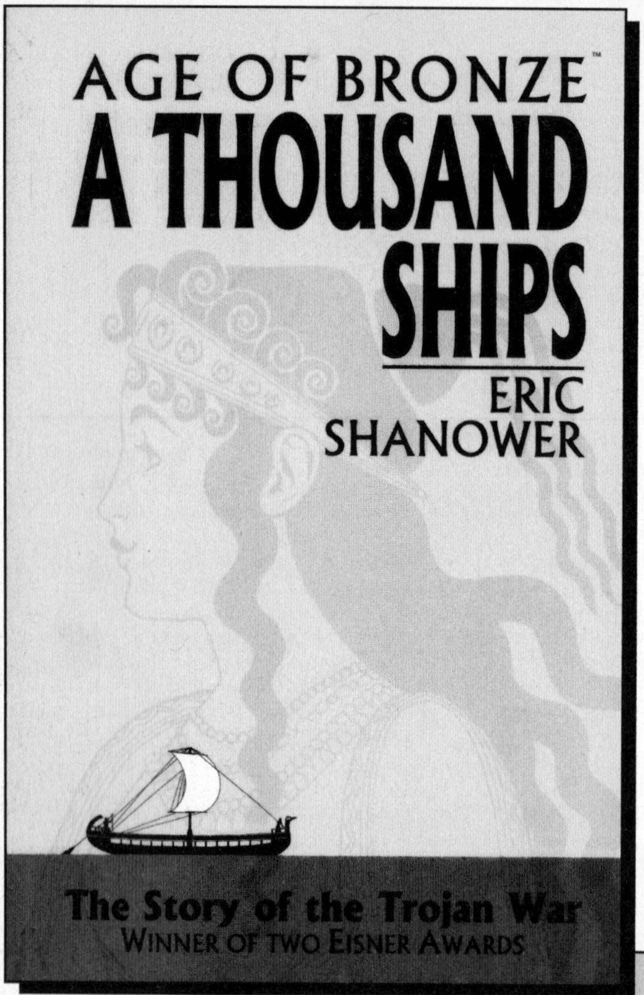
AGE OF BRONZE™
A THOUSAND SHIPS
ERIC SHANOWER
The Story of the Trojan War
WINNER OF TWO EISNER AWARDS

ALSO AVAILABLE FROM ERIC SHANOWER AND IMAGE COMICS

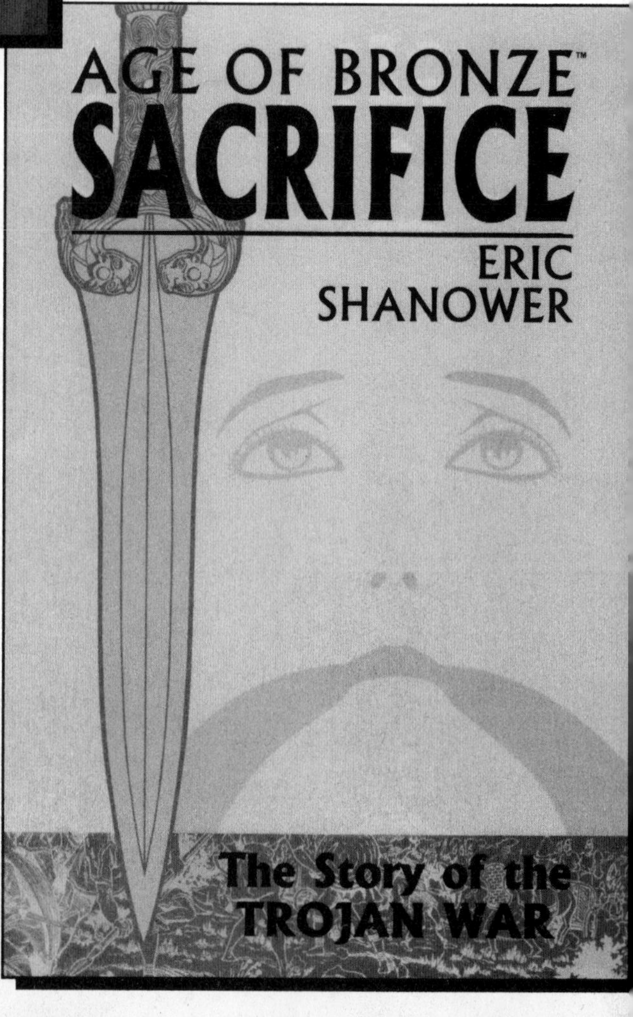
AGE OF BRONZE™
SACRIFICE
ERIC SHANOWER
The Story of the TROJAN WAR

AGE OF BRONZE VOLUME ONE: A THOUSAND SHIPS (PAPERBACK)
ISBN: 978-1582402000

AGE OF BRONZE VOLUME TWO: SACRIFICE (PAPERBACK)
ISBN: 978-1582403991